Scribe Publications
ASBESTOS HOUSE

Gideon Haigh has been a journalist for more than twenty years. His books range from *One of a Kind: the story of Bankers Trust Australia 1969–1999*, *Bad Company: the cult of the CEO*, to *The Vincibles: a suburban cricket season*. He lives in Melbourne.

for Philippa

Contents

Prologue
'I really thought he would want to know ...'

ON THE AFTERNOON OF 15 MAY 2001, three men met briefly in a small office in a Sydney commercial building. The trio knew one another well. Their greetings were cordial and the tone of their conversation friendly — the only hint of an underlying tension was a single gesture, which would haunt all of them. Peter Macdonald, the chief executive of James Hardie Industries, would be hounded from office. Sir Llew Edwards, a former Hardie director, and Dennis Cooper, a past Hardie executive, would be plunged into four enervating years of public controversy. Diseases borne quietly by numberless thousands of suffering people would be revealed as the public health crisis they constitute.

No tables were thumped and no voices raised that day, and none in the affair really were until very near its end, even if few business stories in Australian history have ramified quite so widely and deeply. The devil, instead, was in the detail. The location itself was richly resonant. Seventy-five years had elapsed since Macdonald's employer had acquired the site at the corner of York and Barrack Streets, paying £95,000 for land occupied by a derelict warehouse. The tower that the company erected symbolised its aspirations rather than reflecting its stature. Moving staff in took just a day, personnel simply carrying their desks and documents across the street from temporary quarters in the Alcocks Building diagonally opposite. The building's christening, however, involved a confident statement about its owner's future: what became James Hardie Asbestos took up residence at Asbestos House.

Fifty years to the month had passed since Hardie had given a mortgage over the building to the AMP to see it through a period of financial turbulence—one that led on to one of the great post-war business success stories, as Hardie's asbestos cement, known popularly as 'fibro', spread across the Australian landscape. And with none of the eerie ring its name would later take, Asbestos House seemed an expression of its builder's blue-chip solidity. It featured prominently in the company's advertising; stockists knew its telephone number, B7721, by heart; by the mid-1950s, Hardie occupied all twelve floors, with the ground level remodelled as a showroom by Gordon Andrews, later the designer of Australia's decimal currency. Visitors flocked to events like its 'Sydney of Tomorrow' exhibition, whose centrepiece was a giant scale model of the Sydney Opera House in its original design. As recently as the mid-1970s, Asbestos House was the workplace of as many as 300 employees.

Twenty-five years on, the building had a different symbolic significance. It was showing its age. After decentralisation and downsizing, Hardie occupied only two and a half floors, and none too happily. Despite renovations in the mid-1980s, employees now found the place heavy, dark and airless, its small windows impossible to open. 'It was like a prison,' recalls one Hardie executive, who found he needed glasses after about a year working there. The building was no longer even Hardie's, having been sold and leased back in the late 1980s; the lease was coming up, in fact, and Hardie wasn't planning to renew.

Most particularly, it was no longer called Asbestos House. With the material's latter-day connotations of death and disease, the building had, like the company, shed its old moniker in 1979. James Hardie House remained the house that asbestos built, and James Hardies Industries the company that asbestos had made, but the meeting that day concerned a sealing off of that past now almost complete. Macdonald himself no longer even maintained an office in the building, his usual workspace being an unostentatious corner of Hardie's Californian headquarters at Mission Viejo, between Los Angeles and San Diego. When he came to Sydney for group management team meetings, as he had on this occasion, he simply flipped open his laptop in one of the company's lookalike nooks on the eighth floor. Such was his nature. Macdonald scorned the normal trappings of seniority. He had no personal assistant, shared a secretary and did his own typing. He flew economy class everywhere, booking flights for himself. His reserves of smalltalk were negligible, his personal austerity a byword among his executive circle. Even his smile seemed economical: a reflex rictus rather than a hint of unguarded warmth.

For all this, Sir Llew Edwards was an admirer, even thinking of Macdonald as a friend. The former deputy premier of Queensland set great store by ceremony, and found Macdonald unfailingly 'gentlemanly and courteous'. And Cooper, while he found Macdonald personally remote, admired his acute and unflagging attention to detail. It was this, in fact, that had made the events bringing their meeting about so surprising. Three months earlier, Edwards as chairman and Cooper as managing director had joined the board of a trust called the Medical Research and Compensation Foundation composed chiefly of two entities that had formerly been subsidiaries of James Hardie Industries: Amaca Pty Ltd, previously James Hardie & Coy Pty Ltd, and Amaba Pty Ltd, previously Jsekarb Pty Ltd. In days gone by, both had manufactured products containing asbestos; in the last twenty years or so, accordingly, they had been named as defendants in a host of compensation claims by sufferers of asbestos-related diseases. Their consignment to the foundation with net assets of $293 million had been sold to the stockmarket as Hardie's last parting from its fibrous past. The foundation, essentially Cooper and his secretary, had set up shop, as an interim arrangement, in suite number 602 on the sixth floor of Hardie House. Claims themselves were processed by essentially the same team that had done the job at Hardie, which had turned itself into a consultancy a block away in York Street called Litigation Management Group under the direction of its old boss Wayne Attrill.

On Wednesday 11 April, however, Cooper had received from LMG a financial accounting of the foundation's operations which puzzled him. The report revealed net litigation costs before insurance recoveries of $32 million for the year ended 31 March, and projected similar costs for the year just underway. This stood at odds with the cost expectations of the actuaries Trowbridge, on whose figurings the foundation had been established, of nearer $22 million: the result was a budget based on the LMG numbers featuring an unsightly 'black hole', and a future alarmingly curtailed. Still more disturbing was the explanation at which Cooper arrived for the discrepant numbers. Trowbridge's calculations seemed to have excluded nine months of claims data to the end of calendar 2000. Cooper's apprehensions were not eased when he rang Attrill, who had been part of the Hardie team that had devised the MRCF. 'I thought you knew,' Attrill insisted. 'I thought you knew the latest data wasn't used.' Cooper was perplexed: 'No, I did not. I'd have thought that an up-to-date actuarial forecast would have used the most recent information.'

Cooper, a fastidious man, soft-spoken sometimes to the point of inaudibility, kept his cool. Casting his mind back to discussions before the trust's launch, he recalled Macdonald's soothing sentiments. 'The foundation,' he had heard Macdonald say, 'will have no better friend than James Hardie.' And with the foundation still bunking at James Hardie's headquarters, their separation seemed more a legal nicety than a practical reality: the MRCF was even still receiving help from Hardie's accounting and public affairs personnel. In an informal twenty-minute catch-up with Macdonald eight days later, everything seemed in accord. Cooper had confined himself largely to operational issues; Macdonald had seemed solicitous of the foundation's welfare. Cooper mentioned the apparent risk of underprovision as a 'sensitive issue'. But as he thought it something of which the chairman should have carriage, he left it at that. After a phone discussion with Edwards, Cooper agreed to prepare a short briefing document outlining the foundation's budget and its pressures.

Edwards and Cooper had only two floors to ascend on the afternoon of 15 May 2001, and Macdonald received them with the usual pleasantries. The foundation directors concerned themselves initially with anodyne detail: meetings with government, discussion of research initiatives into lung disease which the foundation was planning to endow. Macdonald listened intently. When the discussion turned to financial details, it was Edwards who led it. Claims and settlements, he said, had both been higher than expected, and indications were that the trends were robust. 'If this continues,' he added, 'we are going to be out of business in a very short time.' Both men studied Macdonald for a reaction, but he was impassive. Edwards then formally introduced Cooper: 'I would now like to ask Dennis to take you through the detail of these figures to give you the full story. As you know he is always across the figures and he can best explain them to you. We also have some information we would like to leave with you.'

'Peter, I'm very concerned about the level of claims, and the expenditures,' Cooper began. 'But what I'm really concerned about is that the information we were given really didn't update the position for December. I've done my own projections based on my budgeting and experience, and I'd just like to show you what I've come up with.' He was leaning forward to pass the briefing paper across the desk when Macdonald finally reacted, and in a quite unanticipated way: he held up his hand. Cooper, confused, made to present it again: this time, Macdonald held up both hands. 'No no,' Macdonald said. 'I don't want to receive that. It's not appropriate that I accept that from you.'

Cooper was taken aback: 'I really thought he would want to know —that, if an error had been made, he would want to be informed.' Then he told himself: 'Maybe he *does* want to know. Maybe he's just concerned about the formality of the exchange of information'.' Cooper sat there, feeling momentarily foolish. 'You're a student of statistics, Dennis,' said Macdonald finally. 'You're a mathematician. I think you'll find that there are peaks and troughs in this data. We're talking long-term experience and trends and actuarial calculations. You'll need more experience and more data before you can be confident of the things you are saying.' With this, the exchange became stilted, and the meeting faltered to a conclusion after forty-five minutes.

Edwards was somewhat disquieted. Four years later, he was still puzzling over the gesture: 'To this day I've never been able to understand why he would not accept what we'd put together. It was very strange. I would have thought that any company which had set up a subsidiary that six months later faced liquidation within a few years would have wanted to be informed. I can only assume that he had legal advice that he could listen to us, but should not accept anything from us.' He instructed Cooper to post the paper to Macdonald anyway—whether it was ever read is unknown. His confidence in Macdonald at the time, however, was unshaken. Within hours they would meet again in a social setting, at a Sydney club in Macquarie Street across the road from Parliament. It was long-planned farewell dinner for Edwards from the Hardie board, on which he'd served almost twelve years, attended by directors and senior managers. In a warm speech, Hardie's chairman Alan MacGregor proposed Edwards' health, to which his former colleagues drank. The concerns of the day slipped to the back of Edwards' mind. They'd sort it all out, wouldn't they?

Cooper wasn't so sure. He returned to his office that afternoon with a 'kind of sick feeling'. It wasn't even simply the document; there'd not even been acknowledgement of the foundation's position. 'One minute we're all one family,' he thought. 'Next minute, that's it.' Driving home that night to Beecroft, the thought nagged at him: 'He doesn't want to know. He's saying this is an aberration. We're going to have to capture their attention somehow. But he's saying we're on our own.' He shook his head. 'Bugger it.'

And the former Asbestos House? Within a year, after a restructuring that involved moving the company's official domicile to Amsterdam and consolidating its headquarters in Mission Viejo, Hardie had relocated its Australian senior management to a single floor of a nondescript office building at the end of Pitt Street called, not inappropriately, Export House. Even the James Hardie logo was removed from the top of James Hardie House, leaving only a vestigial outline visible. But while buildings and domiciles and headquarters can always be left behind, the past is another matter. And Hardie's past, like its old home, was heavy, dark and airless.

-1-

'Let's give them to Hardies'

'When one comes to inquire into the qualities of this truly wonderful mineral—one of nature's marvels—and its multitudinous uses of today, how surprising it appears that thousands of years have been allowed by civilisation to elapse between the present time and the period when the ancients first made use of it, before finally giving serious attention to its immense possibilities.'

—Leonard Summers, *Asbestos and the Asbestos Industry*, 1920

THROUGH MOST OF HIS LIFE, Bernie Banton was an inexhaustibly active man for whom there were never enough hours in a day. When he worked for the insulation manufacturer Hardie-BI at Camellia between 1968 and 1974, he preferred night shifts, so he could ply his trade as a painter and decorator by day. But, since being tethered to a respirator by the asbestosis with which he was diagnosed in 1999, he has had to compress his ebullience into his story-telling, which is by turns furious, mischievous, harrowing and hilarious. Sitting in his living room in West Pennant Hills recounting his first meeting with Hardie representatives in October 2004, it is the fury that flashes.

When Hardie's chairman Meredith Hellicar began proceedings, Banton says, he sized her up. He heard her say she was 'truly, truly sorry' for the suffering of those with asbestos-related diseases. But what did she really know, or even care? 'Well, Meredith, actions will speak louder than any of these words,' Banton recalls saying. 'Let's see you come up with the money.' But it was Hardie's lead negotiator, Peter Hunt of the blue-chip advisory firm Caliburn Partnership, who chiefly aroused Banton's ire:

Greg [ACTU secretary Greg Combet] spoke, I spoke, then this guy Hunt. And—would you believe it?—he starts telling us what a great company Hardie's was. Two minutes into it, I said: 'Let's just cut the crap. I'm not going to sit here and listen to this. This is absolutely unadulterated crap. The only reason Hardie's is a successful company is the thousands of lives they put at risk when they knew it was a dangerous product. They knew what was going on and did nothing about it. So don't you tell me what a great company Hardie's is. You're a lot of grubs. I don't know how you can look at yourselves in the mirror. How dare you! This is a despicable company with no morals whatsoever.'

As he spits the story out, Banton's voice rises an octave. He almost runs out of puff. But he'll harangue Hardie's, he assures you, for as long as there's breath in his body.

Sitting across a long conference table at Export House, Meredith Hellicar cuts an altogether cooler figure, immaculate in a powder-pink power suit. She, too, has always worked hard, and ever upward, through public service then private sector executive ranks; today she turns in the standard seventy-hour week of the fully employed public company director. But as she enlarges on her own understanding of Hardie's history, you can hear the keen edge of frustration through her usual serenity:

No, I didn't feel a great sense of shame that we'd made asbestos. I felt a great sadness about the people suffering as a result. But it had been the great wonder material. There are all these discussions about when we knew. But if you talk to John Reid [Hardie's former chairman], he'll tell you that we tried our absolute hardest, as soon as we got the information, to treat it as a health risk. And we asked the workers to wear masks, and they didn't like that because the masks stopped them from smoking. John Reid will tell you that the workers hated him for forcing them to wear masks. They'd say: 'How dare you try to stop us smoking!'

Then we realised it wasn't just a health and safety issue. And I've just had a letter from a 93-year-old woman whose two husbands worked for James Hardie, and she said: 'My husband loved asbestos so

8

much that he lined our driveway with it.' And of course governments specified that you used it. My sense was: 'My God, this product turned out to be deadly.' It would be like sitting on the board of Nokia in fifty years' time when they discover that some early medical reports now were right and that mobile phones turned out to be deadly.

While Hardie has been criticised, with some force, for its dedication to corporate 'spin', Hellicar does not sound like somebody reading from an autocue. The frustration is authentic. She sighs and assumes a 'what-can-you-do?' expression.

Decades of medical research have been devoted to the effects of prolonged exposure to asbestos; the effects of prolonged exposure to the James Hardie story would probably also repay study. In most public controversies, there is at least some common ground, some agreed set of facts or principles. Where Hardie is concerned, virtually nothing is shared. People cleave instinctively to extremes. Hardie's detractors will swear that the toxicity of asbestos was common knowledge as far back as the 1920s; Hardie's defenders will point out that asbestos was in widespread use all over the world throughout the period of the company's involvement, and in many countries still is. Hardie will be described to you as a charnel house that murdered its workers with malice aforethought, and as a victim of misplaced emotion, tabloid sensationalism and a compensation system gone mad. Those I approached to discuss the Hardie story routinely prefaced their response with the question, 'What's your angle?'; it was as though a vested interest was a prerequisite of involvement. When they spoke, it was often with extreme vehemence. The word 'asbestos' is derived from the Greek for 'inextinguishable': this could easily refer to the animosities it engenders.

Some of this pent-up fury arises from the rudeness of the awakening: for most of the last century, asbestos was a substance identified with safety, disarmingly familiar and ubiquitous. Some of it is a function of the insidious aetiology of the diseases that asbestos causes: with mesothelioma, the most carnivorous of cancers, as long as forty-five years can elapse between exposure and emergence. The result is that misfortune falls with cruelly disproportionate weight on people just about to enjoy the fruits of a lifetime's labour, dashing their dreams as it wrings out their lungs. Yet by the time they have been diagnosed, not merely is remission a faint hope, but responsibility is a hazy concept. James Hardie dominated the Australian market for asbestos products: its conspicuousness as a defendant of compensation claims in New South Wales' Dust Diseases Tribunal is a perverse tribute to the acumen of previous management. But a corporation has no face to smite or soul to damn. And — let an obvious point be made at the earliest possible opportunity — none of the directors of James Hardie who deliberated on the constitution of the Medical Research and Compensation Foundation in February 2001 had the remotest connection with the company's asbestos past.

At least some of the anger, too, springs from popular ambivalence about modern industrial capitalism, reputedly red in tooth and claw, and the forces of globalisation, apparently inescapable and ineluctable. A story widely told of Enron's Jeffrey Skilling, a most notorious recent archetype of the chief executive, concerns a class at Harvard Business School where he was asked what he would do if he learned that a product his company was making had harmful side effects. 'I'd keep making and selling the product,' Skilling answered. 'My job as a businessman is to be a profit centre and maximise return to shareholders.' Hardie seems the ultimate profit-before-people story. The profits here entailed the forfeiture of the peoples' lives. In fact, this view can be at least partly dismissed immediately. The decisions for which this generation of victims are paying were taken not five years ago, but rather decades ago — at a time when, we are commonly led to believe, a kinder, gentler form of capitalism operated, the forces of globalisation were faint and far-off, and Australia was at its most 'relaxed and comfortable'. And the origins of the industry of which Hardie was a pathfinder lie long before any of the *dramatis personae* in recent events were born.

A COUPLE OF DAYS before Christmas in 1968, James Hardie & Coy's chief engineer Frank Page sent a wry note to the boss of the company's Camellia works quoting Rudyard Kipling's 'Tomlinson' —

'a scurrilous satire in verse on the academic way of thinking'. He had been reading a number of recent medical papers and press reports about asbestos whose authors had airily cited the Greek geographer Strabo and the Roman naturalist Pliny the Elder, both of whom had mentioned in passing a sickness of the lungs in slaves whose occupation was to weave asbestos into cloth. They had reminded him, he said, of the lines where Tomlinson gives an account of his life, which proves to have been lived exclusively through his library: 'This, I have felt, this, I have guessed, and this, was noised abroad/This, I read in a Belgian book on the word of a dead French lord.'*Page was still griping about it the following April in a letter to his friend Geoffrey Sutcliffe of the British asbestos giant Turner & Newall: 'Like the rest of the asbestos-using industry, I am heartily sick of articles in the popular press and learned papers — so called which allege that Pliny and Strabo noted the occupational hazards of working in asbestos and then proceed to quote the housewife whose claim to fame was that she lived in a "pre-fab" for six months and had an "asbestos body" in a specimen of her lung tissue on death.'

If he made it rather brutally, Page had a point. Strabo and Pliny did note that asbestos weavers were prone to sickness of the lungs, and favoured protective masks from animal bladders, but their observations are mostly of unabashed wonder. Asbestos is a freak of nature. In its varying states it could be mineral, animal or even vegetable in origin: the earliest written references were in the fourth century BC by the 'Father of Botany', Theophrastus, part of Aristotle's circle. As late as the 1960s, it is reported, a major shareholder in an English asbestos firm visiting its raw-material supplier in South Africa asked where the plantations were.

Asbestos is, in fact, a fibrous silicate. Microscopic study reveals that each fibre consists of thousands of strands, stronger than steel per unit cross-section, subdividing into diameters that artificial fibres cannot. A single strand weighing less than 50 grams can be strung out for more than 300 metres; and a square metre of woven

---

* This is an elision of three couplets from 'Tomlinson', comprising remarks the speaker makes to both St Peter and the Devil.

cloth will weigh about 220 grams. Not all asbestos, as we shall see, is equal: of the three varieties used commercially, curly fibred chrysotile (white) is known as a serpentine; straighter crocidolite (blue) and amosite (brown) are called amphiboles. But all have been prized for their tensile strength and their imperviousness to electricity, vibration, abrasion, vermin, acids and bases, salt, dust, frost and, of course, fire.

Asbestos has been mined since prehistoric times — it has been detected in Finnish pots dating from as early at 2500BC — and its original uses in perpetual wicks in sacred lamps and funeral raiments for dead kings evoke its almost supernatural reputation. Despite its properties, however, asbestos has been a novelty for much of human history. Charlemagne amazed guests by casting his asbestos table cloth into the fire for cleaning; Marco Polo described encountering asbestos textile on his traverse of Siberia; Benjamin Franklin affected an asbestos purse when he first visited England. But it seldom threatened to support an industry. The first factory, established in Russia in 1720 during the reign of Peter the Great after the discovery of substantial deposits of the mineral in the Ural Mountains, closed because of a lack of demand for its handbags, socks, gloves and textiles. It was also difficult to mine, especially in remote areas: in Italy, where it was found in the Susa Valley, it had to be delivered from the alpine heights by toboggan, and work was occasionally disrupted by avalanches.

Asbestos was not truly rediscovered until the industrial revolution, when the advent of the power of steam in pipes, turbines, ovens and kilns placed a premium on substances that were heat resistant. The origins of the global asbestos industry lie in the second half of the nineteenth century, when virtually all the major players were established. American Henry Ward Johns first experimented with asbestos in 1858, inspired by an entry in an encyclopedia, and founded the H. W. Johns Manufacturing Co in West Stockbridge, Massachussetts, taking out patents to manufacture roofing materials from asbestos, pitch, jute and burlap; in 1879, the company diversified into asbestos paints. That same year, Turner Brothers, a textile firm in Yorkshire, first wove asbestos on its looms.

H. W. Johns Manufacturing would merge with Milwaukee's Manville Covering Company to form Johns-Manville; Turner Brothers would come together with Washington Chemicals, J. W. Roberts, Newall Insulation and the brake manufacturer Ferodo (an anagram of its founder's name, Herbert Frood) to form Turner & Newall. A third giant company, British Belting and Asbestos, originally W. Willson Cobbett Ltd and later BBA Group, emerged from a similar process of mergers. The emergence of manufacturers stimulated demand for raw material. Two huge chrysotile mines in Quebec, the Kingsville and the Jeffrey, begat their own towns, Thetford Mines and Asbestos respectively. In December 1893, merchant venturers also founded Cape Asbestos, listed on London's stock exchange, to exploit a huge crocidolite deposit at Prieska, 800km north of Cape Town.

Paints and textiles were the material's original industrial applications. The former were used at the British Museum, Crystal Palace, the National Gallery, the Houses of Parliament and Hampton Court Palace; Edward VII became a public enthusiast. And when appalling theatre fires in Moscow, Vienna, Nice and Kronstadt in 1881 cost 1300 lives, impresarios hastened to entice patrons with asbestos curtains. In Australia, asbestos products first achieved notice when they were exhibited at the Sydney International Exhibition in September 1879, a year after making a considerable impact at the Paris Universal Exposition, and were first popularised by importers, the largest of which was Melbourne's Australasian Asbestos Company, formed to act as agents for H. W. Johns Manufacturing Co. Strangely, some of the best publicity the company enjoyed was when, in July 1884, a huge fire swept through Little Collins Street and burned out its store. *The Age* reported:

> One incident in connection with the fire in Little Collins Street which is worth noting was that the Australasian Asbestos Company, who occupy a portion of the building, were enabled to save their books through having taken the precaution to paint their walls with the fireproof paint, and although the fire ravaged quite close to the wooden partition which divided the company's office from the store, the inside

of the office was found to be uninjured, the paint not being so much as blistered.

Mining did not flourish. Asbestos mines operated in Australia at Jones Creek, near Gundagai, from 1880, and at Robertstown, north of the Barossa Valley, from 1894. They achieved little. And where fire had failed to stop Australasian Asbestos Company, finance did. A mine it developed at Anderson's Creek, near the Tasmanian town of Beaconsfield, became instead a money pit: the company steadily 'expended its capital and died a natural death'. It was a breakthrough far away that would, in time, turn Australia into the world's biggest *per capita* consumer of asbestos.

From Russia in 1896 came the first samples of a tough but lightweight building material under the trade name Uralite, in honour of the mountains from which the mineral had been hewn. Within three years, the process had been considerably improved by an Austrian engineer, Ludwig Hatschek, operating from a factory in Vöcklabruck using a second-hand strawboard-making machine that he had bought out of a newspaper. He called his material Eternit to evoke its durability, and the corporate descendant of his experiments remains one of Europe's top building-products companies. Uralite and Eternit were prototypes of the product that Australians know colloquially as 'fibro': fibre-cement. Technology for its manufacture would change hugely over the next seventy years, but the principles did not alter much: a slurry of asbestos fibre, cement, and water was circulated through an agitator into tubs, dried at high temperature, then deposited in laminations for rolling to the required thickness. The result—more durable than wood, far cheaper than masonry, and as adaptable as either—would be the foundation on which fortunes were built. The biggest was to be James Hardie's.

The man James Hardie was born on 27 July 1851 in the Scottish city of Linlithgow. The second child of a leather-trading family, he was rising thirty-six when he booked a passage to Melbourne on the *Oroya*, opening an eponymous supplier to tanners and curriers in January 1888 at 523 Little Flinders Street West. Just as Tom Spencer of Marks & Spencer retains an equal share of its letterhead despite only eleven long-ago years with the retailer, Hardie's connection with the company he founded is less significant than its abiding use of his name suggests. Its driving force was his younger partner, Andrew Reid. Seventh of ten children to another Linlithgow family, he was twenty-four when he traced Hardie's steps to Melbourne in November 1891, enthused by a letter from the older man about business prospects. Where Hardie was self-described as 'rather a nervous man', Reid was a busy, bustling fortune-hunter. During the journey on the barque *Loch Sheil*, he practised bookkeeping and arithmetic, practised his shorthand by eavesdropping on other passengers, and read Kipling, Haggard and Jerome, as well as a history of Victoria and an account of the exploits of the indefatigable American immigrants, the Chaffey brothers, and their Mildura Irrigation Colony.

The prior relations between Hardie and Reid are unknown. Genealogical research undertaken by John Balmforth, an indefatigable researcher of the company, suggests that they may have been distantly related by marriage; otherwise they were merely friendly. Hardie did not offer Reid a job on receipt of his letter, and actually sounded a cautionary note: 'Anyone coming out from the old country has almost to begin life again, by taking a situation at whatever he can get it.' But he encouraged in Reid, who had worked as a shipping clerk in Glasgow, the thought he would find a similar station, and offered his help in securing same; the young man's first position, at £2 a month, appears to have been with the Melbourne Shipping Company. Reid seems, though, to have been a born salesman, not least of himself. Beginning as Hardie's outdoor representative, he become his partner on 1 January 1896, then proposed leading the firm's thrust into Sydney. Reid opened an office at 51 Pitt Street, coincidentally barely 100 metres from Hardie's headquarters today, in March 1900.

Australian Leather Journal, in whose founding Reid was a prime mover, returned the compliment by describing him 'one of those very much alive and up-to-date businessmen who are always on the go'. Hardie advertisements that the journal carried now read like an exhibit list for a museum of industrial Victoriana, from 'Messrs

Slack & Co's Celebrated Evaporated Sod & Cod Oils' to 'Messrs Bunten & Co's Valonia, Myrabs, Sumac, Terra-Japonica & c'. James Hardie's range of lines, in fact, was its hallmark; the *Cyclopedia of Victoria* of 1903 reported: '... the firm have a high reputation for keeping the best goods obtainable and also making arrangements to get all the materials at bedrock prices so as to give its customers the immediate benefit of whatever is best and most up-to-date in all parts of the world.' It was around June that year when Hardie himself first encountered fibre-cement at the premises of his firm's London agents, W. A. Sparrow & Co, and company lore has it that the old man was tricked into the initial £100 order. Finding samples sent by the French Fibro-Cement Company dusty with neglect, a young shipping manager is alleged to have said: 'Let's get rid of those. Let's give them to Hardie's.'[†]

The first imported fibre-cement was used to roof railway workers' huts, and it was initially marketed as a substitute for roofing slate. But it was, at first, a slow-moving line, being notorious for its brittleness and breakages. George Sutton, the bookkeeper Reid hired in September 1900, saw it lose money year after year. Finally, in 1908, Reid turned over responsibility for the product to Stewart D'Arrietta, who had joined the company as an office boy: the turnaround was prompt and complete. He found a new supplier, Eternit. He landed some prestigious jobs, Sydney's Bondi Surf Shed and Melbourne's Spencer Street Railway Station. He found an under-exploited corner of the market—churches, always impecunious but undeniably respectable—and roofed scores of them, from St Philip's in South Brisbane to the Wagga Wagga Monastery. Fibre-cement sheet was even used in the first permanent buildings in Canberra, at the new Duntroon Military Training College. D'Arrietta couldn't take all the credit. One vital suggestion was made by his female stenographer who, reading all the complaints that fibro split when struck with a pointed nail, suggested that

---

† The young shipping manager was W. C. Bolton, later a director of the shipping company. His son George, later knighted, was the inaugural executive director of the International Monetary Fund.

builders be instructed to use blunt-point or sheer-point variants. But, as became characteristic, D'Arrietta took what credit was going.

The company moved to newer, bigger premises in the Naval Stores at Circular Quay, and when James Hardie's involvement in the company he founded ended with his retirement in May 1912, Reid confidently agreed to buy him out for £17,000 in a decade's worth of installments following a £5000 deposit. With by now three young sons, he could perhaps already see a commercial dynasty in the making.

ON ITS CENTENARY IN 1988, James Hardie Industries saw to the publication of a very thorough company history, *A Very Good Business*, by the Melbourne-based freelance journalist Brian Carroll; *Asbestos House* is, in a sense, its uncommissioned sequel. While *A Very Good Business* usefully chronicles key dates in Hardie's evolution, it is largely devoid of context. It is worth pointing out at an early stage here, for example, how strongly Hardie has been influenced by its distance from the rest of the commercial world, with two principal effects: limited competition and a hankering for self-sufficiency.

In the beginning, Hardie's only rival of significance in the importation of fibre-cement was provided by three exotic brothers: Ernest, Alfred and Otto Wunderlich, sons of a indigo merchant, who had been schooled at Vevey and Laussane in Switzerland. Unlike the Hardie enterprise, Wunderlich always specialised in building materials, beginning with the zinc ornamental roofings that they manufactured at a plant in Redfern's Baptist Street, and which they introduced to such prestigious buildings as the Colonial Secretary's Office, Sydney Hospital and Sydney Town Hall. And unlike their rival Andrew Reid, who settled with age into the role of gruff patriarch, the brothers adopted the motto: 'To laugh and never be downhearted.' Ernest founded Sydney's Century Club with J. F. Archibald to foment 'rebellion against the leaden dullness of conventional clubs', and built the Port Hacking Observatory which he later donated to the people of New South Wales. Alfred was a member of the Philaharmonic Society, and a Francophile of such ardency that he became a Chevalier de la Legion d'Honneur. Otto translated *Chanson de Roland* into English as well as publishing texts on accounting and bookkeeping. 'They are not mere money spinners,' wrote *The Bulletin*. 'They are an unusual combination who apply art and idealism to a business basis.'

Both Andrew Reid and the Wunderlich brothers responded similarly, however, when the outbreak of World War I exacerbated their geographic isolation by seeking to replace their imports with onshore manufacturing. The Wunderlichs moved first, opening fibre-cement works in the Sydney suburb of Cabarita in July 1915 to manufacture what they called 'Durasbestos'. Hardie was not far behind. Reid licensed manufacturing technology from Manchester's Felber Jucker & Co in November 1915, then commissioned works on a four-hectare site in Camellia on the Parramatta River to operate initially as the Asbestos Slate and Sheet Manufacturing Company.[‡]

There was nothing fancy about the enterprise. The prospectus was typed out by a seventeen-year-old girl typist at Hardie's office in the Naval Stores at Circular Quay; the works were laid out not after a design but by the directors, Reid, Sutton and D'Arrietta, who simply wandered round the site deciding where everything should go and leaving everything else to their first works manager, Cyprian Truman. But it worked. Flat sheets of their rival to 'Durasbestos', which they called 'Fibrolite', began rolling off the production line in May 1917, and demand was soon such that an adjacent four hectares had to be bought to accommodate the works' expansion. A new head office building was acquired, the first Asbestos House, at the corner of York and Wynyard Streets, in September 1917. Reid even lured to Australia a Swiss expert on fibre-cement, 23-year-old Ernest Witzig, who became its production guru, and talked James Hardie 'breakfast, dinner and tea'. When Sutton visited England in November 1921 and negotiated a commutation of the licensing deal with Felber Jucker for £30,000, Hardie was a fully fledged building-products manufacturer.

---

‡ The ship on which the machinery travelled to Australia, *SS Clan McCorquodale*, was torpedoed and sunk en route home.

The duopoly's dilemmas weren't over. They were still vulnerable to disruption of supplies of imported fibre. Both companies had abiding dreams of mining their own — dreams nourished by government, which saw asbestos as a strategic resource. Again, Wunderlich was first, reviving the mine at Tasmania's Anderson's Creek in 1916; Hardie, through an entity called Asbestos Mining Company of Australia, then sought to develop a chrysotile deposit at Woodsreef, east of Ironbark Creek near Barraba in the New England Ranges of north-east New South Wales. The lockstep in which the companies moved tightened when Wunderlich immediately acquired adjacent leases at Woodsreef, and built its own mill just 670 metres north of Hardie's. Both companies also had identical experiences, finding the dust of the mine distinctly inhospitable to workers. A visitor to Anderson's Creek in December 1917 was staggered by the 'impalpable dust which covers everything in its range', bleaching not merely the ground and trees but the mill, 'which in its glaring brightness recalls the "white cities"'; the mine closed little more than a year later. A little more progress was made at Woodsreef, but industrial problems closed both operations in July 1920, and both companies had given up by January 1922.

By this stage, nonetheless, fibre-cement was established as Hardie's core business, and advancing as a cheap but tasteful alternative to brick. Hardie used Sydney's 1917 Royal Agricultural Show to unveil a fibre-cement home — a custom it would maintain until 1965. It opened works at Rivervale in Perth in September 1921 and at Brooklyn in Melbourne in June 1927, Truman and Witzig supervising the building of both. The product range was broadened to cover customers from above, taking in corrugated roof sheets called Super Six, and below, in the form of Fibrolite pipes. The former roofed buildings as diverse as the Roxy Cinema in Parramatta and the new grandstand at the Melbourne Cricket Ground; the latter became integral to the opening of new housing estates. Hardie also bought its Brisbane agent, Charles Sadgrove Pty Ltd. The acquisition would form a bridgehead to the commissioning of another fibre-cement works at Newstead.

The issue most troublesome to Reid was the friction between his satraps. For no reasons, it would seem, other than intercity rivalry and an accumulation of petty grievances, D'Arrietta in Sydney and George Gregson in Melbourne were seldom on speaking terms. The Sydney and Melbourne operations were separately incorporated in April 1918 — the Sydney business as James Hardie & Coy, the Melbourne business as James Hardie & Co — but this proved only an interim arrangement. In September 1926, Asbestos Slate & Sheet acquired the building-materials operations in all states, and somewhat cheekily adopted the name of its parent, James Hardie & Coy. The general merchandise operations in each state, meanwhile, were reconstituted as free-standing entities, and eventually became the basis of Hardie Trading, which cradled the old businesses in tanning, dyes, chemicals, laundry and engineering supplies alongside newer agencies for products like Spartan Paints and United Alkali. James Hardie & Coy and Hardie Trading shared Reid-family control and directors, but generally operated quite independently, sometimes antagonistically. Otherwise, the steady ascent of newly commissioned Asbestos House throughout the second half of the decade was an index of the company's fortunes.

In retrospect, the 1920s were a crucial period in Hardie's development. Wunderlich also expanded interstate, opening a Melbourne works at Sunshine in 1926 to manufacture fibre-cement and terracotta tiles. But the brothers were not nearly so aggressive: Ernest believed that one had to 'smooth out the harshness of business, realizing that Trade is virtually warfare, only that no blood is seen to flow'. Hardie secured a market leadership it would never lose. A third competitor emerged in 1928 when the Goliath Portland Cement Company was formed to take over a cement works at Railton, sixteen kilometres south of Devonport in Tasmania, but its fibre-cement brand, Tasbestos, was seldom seen on the mainland. More crucially in history's eyes, however, is that it was in the same period that asbestos was first identified as dangerous.

2

'The workers that breathe death'

'Looking back in the light of present knowledge, it is impossible not to feel that opportunities for discovery and prevention [of asbestos-related disease] were badly missed.'
—Sir Thomas Legge, *Industrial Maladies*, 1934

THE MEDICO-LEGAL CASES for and against James Hardie can be seen as arguments about the distinction between 'dangerous' and 'lethal'. Asbestos has long been known to be dangerous. But in Hardie's defence, no substance has ever been declared unexploitable simply because it is dangerous; no one, for example, has advocated outlawing petroleum, even though its combustion is known to produce a deadly gas, carbon monoxide. Industry harnesses a great many substances known to be deleterious to health—indeed, few useful substances are not. And because substances do not declare themselves all at once, cognisance of risk is often a slow-dawning phenomenon.

The knowledge that respirable dust in an industrial setting can cause pneumoconioses—the generic term for dust-induced diseases of the lung—stretches into antiquity. The first pathological description of silicosis dates from 1672, and the guises under which it went before it was christened clinically two hundred years later demonstrate how intimately it has been associated with work: potters' rot, stonecutter's asthma, grinders' rot, miners' phthisis. It was to 'dust phthisis pneumonitis' that Johns-Manville founder Henry Johns succumbed in 1898—even if many sources, with a sense of divine justice, suggest that this was probably a euphemism for asbestosis.

It was in this same year that asbestos first began to attract attention in a health context, in the mills of England's industrial north. 'Of all the injurious, dusty processes of which I have ... received complaints,' noted one factory inspector, 'none, I believe, surpass in injuriousness to the workers ... asbestos manufacture.' Another, looking askance at 'the sharp, glass-like, jagged nature of the particles' under microscopic examination, commented that 'where they are allowed to rise and to remain suspended in the air of a room, in any quantity, the effects have been found to be injurious, as might have been expected.' Within a year, the first autopsy in which asbestos could be fingered as a killer had been held. H. Montague Murray, a physician at Charing Cross Hospital, found advanced pulmonary fibrosis in the lungs of a 33-year-old man at autopsy—the last of ten who had worked in the carding room of a factory. Seven years later, an inspector named Auribault in the French Department of Labour published the first study of asbestos deaths in a workplace in *Bulletin de l'Inspection du Travail et l'Hygiene Industrielle*: a case study built up from fifty mortalities at an asbestos-weaving mill in Conde-Sur-Noireau in Calvados.

Incuriosity and ignorance got the better of early researchers. Murray, when he testified about his autopsy before a parliamentary commission, said meekly: 'One hears, generally speaking, that considerable trouble is taken now to prevent the inhalation of dust, so the disease is not so likely to occur as heretofore.' Auribault thought the malady he was studying was chalicosis, a form of silicosis common among stonecutters, and made only ineffectual suggestions for reform. There was tacit acknowledgement of the premature mortality of asbestos workers. In 1918, the US Bureau of Labour even published a report by the consulting statistician for the Prudential Insurance Company of America, Frederick Hoffman, stating not merely that asbestos mining and manufacture 'unquestionably involve a considerable hazard', but revealing that some American and Canadian insurers would not offer life policies to workers in it because of its 'assumed health-injurious conditions'. Yet not until July 1924 was asbestosis finally cornered and revealed.

Nellie Kershaw had begun working for Turner & Newall in

Rochdale at the age of thirteen; after another thirteen years, stricken by shortness of breath and lassitude, she could work no longer. When her physician diagnosed 'asbestos poisoning' in December 1922, the Newbold Friendly Society of which she was a member sought compensation from her employer, only to be rebuked: 'We repudiate the term "asbestos poisoning". Asbestos is not poisonous and no definition or knowledge of such disease exists. Such a description is not to be found among the list of industrial diseases in the schedule published with the Workmen's Compensation Act.' Nellie Kershaw's fame would be anonymous and posthumous as the subject of a brief article in the *British Medical Journal* of July 1924 by W. E. Cooke, pathologist at Wigan Infirmary. Cooke found Kershaw's lungs extensively scarred, and 'curious bodies' amid the dense strands of abnormal fibrous tissue connecting the lungs and the pleural membranes: 'We have never seen anything parallel to this in pneumoconiosis due to other dusts, nor have we been able to find such occurrence in literature … We cannot think there is any reasonable doubt that the particles in the lung are the heavy, brittle, iron-containing fragments of asbestos fibre.'

In 1928, after a number of other journal articles discussing asbestosis and the third report of an asbestos worker's death, the Factories Department of Britain's Home Office commissioned medical inspector Edward Merewether and ventilation engineer Charles Price to survey the conditions and health of workers. The domestic asbestos industry was as yet relatively small, with only 160 factories and 2200 workers, of whom Merewether was able to examine 363: fully 15 per cent of the total. The findings of the 'Report on the Effects of Asbestos Dust on the Lungs and Dust Suppression in the Asbestos Industry' were stark: more than one in four workers were suffering pulmonary fibrosis; among those with twenty years or more in the industry, that proportion rose to four in five. And, if anything, the survey underestimated the numbers, confining itself to current workers, so those who had left the industry through ill-health went uncounted; and not x-raying every subject, as this was still an expensive process. But Merewether was in no doubt of the pernicious effects of asbestos; thus his oft-quoted reply to a question about whether two years' exposure was enough to kill a young girl: 'Yes. If she lives long enough.' British understatement was temporarily abandoned in headlines such as one in *John Bull*: 'The Workers Who Breathe Death'.

Merewether and Price pushed asbestos to the front rank of industrial dusts, judging it more dangerous than traditional bogeys such as coal and silica, and threw down the challenge: 'The asbestos manufacturers are clearly confronted with the necessity of attaining conditions in their industry which will ensure much less dust in the atmosphere than can safely be tolerated in many comparable trades not using asbestos.' It was partly taken up: Britain shortly became the first country to bring asbestosis within its Workmen's Compensation Act. But when the big British manufacturers, including Turner & Newall and Cape Asbestos, were summoned to the Home Office in July 1930 to respond to the report's recommendations for dust control, exhaust systems, process modifications, vacuum cleaning and exclusion of the young, they adeptly mitigated the effects, successfully confining the legislative framework to the dry areas of factories, like crushing, carding, spinning and weaving.

When the asbestos regulations were proclaimed the next year, only about a quarter of the workforce was covered — those involved in cleaning and lagging, for instance, remained exposed. And while there were genuine improvements in ventilation, the respirators and masks that Merewether and Price foresaw in other areas were uncomfortable when they weren't ineffective. In their history of the Scottish asbestos industry, *Lethal Work*, authors Johnston and McIvor cite an interviewee who saw a framed copy of the regulations on his factory floor at Turner & Newall at Dalmuir on Clydebank: 'When you went in the door of Turner's Asbestos, there was a Factory Act with all the stuff. The only problem was that you couldnae see through to it with the layer of asbestos cement on the glass, you know.'

In the United States, asbestosis took a somewhat different route, albeit to a similar destination. In 1929, representatives of Johns-Manville and Raybestos-Manhattan approached Metropolitan Life Insurance to perform a hygienic study of their industry, being 'desirous of ascertaining if asbestos dust was an occupational hazard in their establishments'. The research was led by Dr Anthony Lanza, a brahmin of American industrial hygiene, who had joined the insurer from the US Public Health Service three years earlier. Between October 1929 and January 1931, Lanza and his colleagues performed chest X-rays of 126 workers with three or more years in the trade. Again, the results were shocking: more than half had asbestosis; another quarter had signs of it. But then, in one of the dark deals for which the American industry would go down in infamy, Johns-Manville's general counsel Vandivar Brown lent on Lanza:

> I am sure that you understand fully that no one in our organisation is suggesting for a moment that you alter by one jot or tittle any scientific facts or inevitable conclusions revealed or justified by your preliminary survey. All we ask is that all the favourable aspects of the survey be included and that none of the unfavourable be unintentionally pictured in darker tones than the circumstances justify. I feel confident we can depend upon you … to give us this 'break'.

So it was that by the time it was published by the US Public Health Service in January 1935, the report had been modified along lines suggested by Johns-Manville's attorneys, and Lanza had become a craven apologist for the industry, claiming that 'asbestos plants are being cleaned up and the dust is being controlled'. His text book, *Silicosis and Asbestosis*, contains the optimistic prediction: 'As soon as the hazard was realised, industrial firms fabricating asbestos took energetic steps to control the dust so that it is probable that cases of asbestosis will become uncommon.' The author's sunny self-regard is evoked in the long list of offices he enumerates on his title page — including 'Adviser on Industrial Hygiene to the Commonwealth of Australia'.

BECAUSE AUSTRALIA'S CONSTITUTION limited the federal government's power over public health and medical care to matters of quarantine, it was not until 1916 that a Department of Health was even mooted; a further five years then elapsed until its creation. And given the record of public health authorities in Australia on asbestos, it is somehow fitting that the new department's consultant, when it instigated its Industrial Hygiene Division, was destined to be a cat's paw of the industry. Lanza was then at the US Public Health Service, one of the world's leading experts on pneumoconiosis, and his two years in Australia were thanks to the beneficence of the Rockefeller Foundation. He made the first contribution to the *Medical Journal of Australia* on the subject of industrial hygiene in August 1922, then was the special guest the following month at the First Commonwealth Industrial Hygiene Conference, called by prime minister Billy Hughes of delegates from state health and labour departments to 'arrive at a concerted basis of action and a uniform basis for standards and records'. At the conference, in fact, he was largely scornful of the states' efforts: 'There is an entire lack of anything like skilled technical assistance in inspection, there is no medical inspection of any sort whatsoever, and many of the hygienic standards upon which the inspector's rules and regulations are founded are obsolete.'

Asbestos at the time did not loom nearly so large in public health as silica. As early as 1896, the New South Wales Health Act had included a section noting that 'in a factory where grinding, glazing or polishing on a wheel or any other process is carried out whereby dust is generated which is inhaled by the employees to an injurious extent, such inhalation could be to a great extent prevented by the use of a fan or by other mechanical means of ventilation'.

Australia had also been at the forefront of research into pneumoconiosis among miners since Walter Summons' acclaimed textbook, *Miners' Phthisis*, in 1907. The industrial hygiene division's first director, Dr D. G. Robertson, listed 'asbestos worker' as a risky occupation in his *An Index to Health Hazards in Industry*. Dust inhalation in general, Robertson warned, could 'greatly impair the general health, owing to pulmonary irritation, purulent bronchial secretion, and defective oxidation, so that the victim becomes anaemic and emaciated'. But asbestos poisoning was not listed among notifiable diseases agreed at the Second Commonwealth

Industrial Hygiene Conference in August 1924, nor was it subject of any of the studies the division initiated. Mines were the chief concern when the New South Wales government initiated its own Industrial Hygiene Department in 1923, and miners the chief beneficiary when it four years later inaugurated the Silicosis Board — the workers' compensation body that was forerunner to the Dust Diseases Board.

Word, nonetheless, was spreading. J. V. Sparks, a London radiologist, visited Los Angeles in 1930 to present a paper at a meeting of the Radiological Society of North America. Sparks and colleagues at the City of London Chest Hospital had seen fifty cases of asbestosis and examined half-a-dozen post-mortem records. Hitherto, their advice to sufferers had usually been to leave the industry; this, they now realised, was too optimistic: 'The fact that they cease to be exposed to the dust does not ... prevent the disease, when once established, from progressing ... Prophylaxis is all-important and the only hope for the asbestos worker lies in the adoption of proper means of protection against the risk attendant on the inhalation of the fibers.' The paper was published in the society's journal, *Radiology*, the following year, and in March 1932 had the distinction, albeit in abstracted form, of mentioning asbestosis for the first time in the *Medical Journal of Australia:*

> Clinically, the condition resembles silicosis, and radiologically a diffuse fibrosis is seen, of a rather finer type than that which occurs in silicosis. The small asbestos fibres can be recognised microscopically in the sputum. The prognosis is grave, and once the asbestos bodies appear in the sputum, the course of the disease would appear to be progressively downwards. Cessation of exposure to the dust is of no avail in checking the spread of the disease process.

By the early 1930s, the signs, symptoms, radiological appearance and pathology of asbestosis was well understood. It was known to be fatal, and to continue to develop after exposure to dust was discontinued. Diagnosis wasn't always easy: X-ray reading was unreliable, lung function tests were not widely available, and the disease was often misread either as bronchitis or tuberculosis. But as asbestos's foremost medico-legal historian Barry Castleman observes: 'Virtually everywhere asbestosis was looked for, it was found.' It had even been identified in animals. The *Journal of Industrial Hygiene* for July 1933 featured six cases of asbestosis studied by pulmonary physician Philip Ellman of London's Tuberculosis and Chest Clinic, including one in a male rat terrier, 'lethalled in its own interests due to the distress of dyspnea', and whose lungs were riddled with scar tissue. Victims were as young as the eighteen-year-old van boy reported in *The Lancet* in 1934, who had mixed powdered asbestos in an open yard.

Filaments from this research had also reached Australia, especially the report of Merewether and Price, which provided the impetus for the initial inspections of James Hardie facilities by public health authorities. Western Australia's chief inspector of factories homed in on Rivervale, a disproportionately dusty site, set on two hectares adjacent to Swan Portland Cement. The plant had been laid out by Hardie's Swiss fibro guru, Ernest Witzig, whose fascination with engineering and indifference to everything else was apparent to visitors as soon as they arrived. A Hardie executive later described his first sight:

> My initial impressions were: 'For heaven's sake. Why did I take this post? I think I'll go back home!' It was an absolute shocker ... I don't think I've ever seen a more dilapidated run-down building in all my life that served as, well, our office, in Western Australia ... It was built as an asbestos-cement factory but the office was just a small 10-12 square building constructed of asbestos-cement ... The grass was knee-high. In fact, I remember our septic tank went on the blink on one occasion as it took us two days to find out where it was.

On 5 April 1935, Western Australia's chief inspector of factories forwarded the commissioner of public health a comprehensive analysis of the Britons' report, and mentioned that it may have implications for the Hardie works:

So far as I am aware we have only one factory in this State, that of James Hardie and Co. Ltd., Rivervale, in which any of the processes which were subject to the investigations are carried on. In this factory 62 men are employed and comparatively only a few have been employed for a lengthy period in what might be regarded as the dangerous processes.

I attach hereto for your information a copy of a report recently submitted by Mr. Inspector Mooney of this Department on the factory referred to and from which it will be noted that two employees ... employed for 6 years, and ... for 10 years, appear to the Inspector to be suffering in a marked degree from the effects of asbestos dust.

It may be possible if the disclosures warrant it, to arrange for these workers to be transferred to some less dangerous of the processes carried on in the factory. This Department is already taking action to secure the installation in the factory of effective means for the collection and disposal of dust generated in the factory.

The report was far-seeing. It was also, already, a squib. Even in 1935, the literature on asbestosis indicated that the disease was progressive; to use Sparks' words, 'cessation of exposure to the dust is of no avail in checking the spread of the disease process'. From the very first, manufacturers and medical authorities were geared to a mutual accommodation that they would find harder and harder to break. Their common cause had one very notable result. Hankering for an answer to the vexed question of when 'dangerous' phased into 'lethal', they seized with alacrity on what looked like an answer in a survey of workforces in three American asbestos textile plants led by Waldermar Dreessen and published in August 1938 by the US Public Health Service. Dreessen and four colleagues found asbestosis in seventy of 339 persons exposed to dust concentrations of greater that five million particles per cubic foot of air, but in only three of 108 persons exposed to less; they concluded, therefore, that this should be 'regarded as the threshhold value for asbestos-dust exposure until better data are available'. The recommendation was taken up by the American Conference of Industrial Hygienists.

The Dreessen Standard, as it became known, would have been

inexact even had the mills surveyed not covertly laid off the oldest quarter of the workforce before the tests were done. Dust measurement by impinging was still cumbersome and imprecise, and made no allowances for individual susceptibility. As a Johns-Manville safety executive said in a confidential memo: 'There is so much variation in the reaction of individuals to a particular type of material that no guarantee of full protection can be assumed at any level of exposure'. But, although even Dreessen himself had intended no more than it be a 'tentative' study, the standard became the locus of unwarranted confidence, because it was an answer to so many quiet prayers: those of industrialists, trying to establish boundaries within which they could continue to make money; and scientists, avid always for an unambiguous number and established rule. It was reinforced by the fact that at around 5mppcf — as it is usually abbreviated — asbestos clouds become visible. What you couldn't see, was the implicit message, couldn't hurt you.

At the time, hazards in Australia were still a long way from invisibility. Visits by an inspector from the New South Wales Public Health Department in July and December 1938 to an unidentified fibre-cement factory — almost certainly Camellia — found it far from compliant. The process of hand mixing occasioned dust levels ten times the standard, and the air in the general premises wasn't much cleaner. Not surprisingly, it was a mixer from Camellia whose last dying breath was the first attempt to extract compensation from Hardie.

The spectre of litigation had hovered over the American industry already. In April 1933, Johns-Manville had quietly settled eleven cases brought against the company for asbestosis for $35,000, also extracting a promise from the attorney concerned that he would never cause another suit to be brought against the company. The industry worked hard to contain claims within the realms of worker's compensation, where they were covered by insurance; as a speaker at an industrial disease conference in January 1935 put it: 'The strongest bulwark against future disaster for industry is the enactment of properly drawn industrial disease legislation'. The case of 'the widow Jones' in the New South Wales Compensation

Commission ended with suitable ignominy.

In January 1939, a Macquarie Street physician, Dr Walter Fisher, was called to a cottage in Granville's Irongate Street to attend one Samuel Jones. Fifty-four-year-old Jones had mined anthracite coal in Wales before emigrating to Australia and working at Camellia for eighteen years from 1919. He had developed a hacking cough in September 1935, accompanied by sputum that was 'scanty, white and frothy, and on one occasion … blood-stained', and steadily lost breath and weight. Fisher found him 'a dark elderly man, exceedingly wasted, sitting upright in bed with synosis, clubbing of the fingers and marked breathlessness … With regard to his chest, it was deformed, gross wasting above and below both collar bones and the whole of the right lower chest, front and side, was restricted and almost motionless'. He diagnosed pulmonary fibrosis and concluded that 'the outlook was extremely grave' — as it proved, for Jones died the following month, leaving his widow Sarah to pursue a claim.

The complication was not here corporate intransigence or legal chicanery, but Jones' own occupational history. Three doctors testified that Jones' illness might evidence pre-existing silicosis, and Fisher could not preclude the possibility:

> I think that one has to admit the possibility that some degree of pneumoconiosis may have been present as a result of his mining experience in Wales before he ever came to this country — that is a possibility I would not deny. If on the other hand my information as to the nature of his dust exposure in Australia is correct, I think it is equally possible that the whole of his terminal clinical picture as I saw it could be accounted for by exposure to asbestos dust.

Justice Lamond went with the medical majority, concluding that Sarah Jones' case was 'entirely conjectural', and that Jones had perished of silicosis 'complicated by a super-added infection'. There would be many more widows like the widow Jones before asbestos was cornered in the dock.

3

'We'll shoot the bastard!'

'The wisest man is he who has the sense to say nothing at the right time.'

—*Trimmings*, journal of James Hardie's Brooklyn factory, August 1946

ASBESTOS, IN ITS PHYSICAL CHARACTERISTICS and chemical properties, is frankly extraordinary; the company that harnessed it was not. At Asbestos House in the 1920s and 1930s, even the tea breaks were hierarchical: directors received a cup of tea with two biscuits; managers, a cup with one biscuit; seniors, a cup of tea; juniors, a drink of water. The environment of staid attitudes and rigid conventions would persist for decades yet.

Business, of course, had stabler, simpler mores in those days; there was also the sense of stability and continuity afforded by the Reids' unchanging presence as commanding shareholder. For much of the company's history, in fact, the family have provided the sense of a warm, beating heart at the sense of the enterprise, originating in the persona of the family patriarch. Andrew Reid was a notable philanthropist: his favoured causes were the Burnside Homes orphanage in Parramatta, which he not only sponsored but from which he employed many young men; and the Fairbridge Movement, which brought underprivileged child migrants from Britain. He was an apostle of self-improvement. 'Here's two books,' he said to a junior employee one day. 'I'd like you to read them.' One was *How to Apply Yourself*; the other, *Do Right By Everybody and You'll Get On*—and these were preachings he practised. In 1924, for instance, he bought out of bankruptcy what became Hardie Rubber, and ran it for years before it made a shilling. When colleagues complained during the Great Depression that it had become an expensive indulgence, he asked how many people it employed. Upon being told that the number was 240, he stated: 'I presume that would mean a thousand by the time you took wives and children … We're feeding a thousand people. That's what we're doing. We're carrying on.'

On Andrew Reid's death in January 1939 the family line continued in three sons: Andrew Thyne, known as Thyne; John, known as Jock; and George, known as Doddy. The last preferred to run the family's pastoral interests near Yass rather than join Hardie, and would eventually perish in World War II, but the older boys were never other than keen to follow their father. Thyne joined Hardie in May 1927 when he had finished studies at Cambridge; Jock actually declined the offer of a sojourn at Oxford University, where his father felt that an arts course might make him 'more of a cultured gentleman'. He said instead: 'I want to start a business career now.' His father's only question was: 'Are you prepared to start at the bottom?' When this was confirmed, Jock was shipped off to serve an apprenticeship as an office boy at a Scottish firm, Watson Laidlaw.

Neither Thyne for Jock seemed entirely cut out for commercial life. Thyne was a gifted engineer, with an aptitude for nutting problems out mentally without recourse to pen or paper, and an avid traveller, especially at the controls of his DeHavilland Drover and Dragon Rapide aircraft. He seemed uncomfortable in suits, never wearing a belt, favouring hob-nailed boots and a tatty old tie that he often knotted round his waist, and happiest when pulling machinery apart. One veteran employee, Stan Strachan, who spent half a century with Hardie, recalled being sent to find Thyne one day at Camellia and kicking an anonymous pair of legs under a machine. 'Do you know where I'd find Thyne Reid?' he asked. 'I'm Thyne Reid,' answered a muffled voice. 'What do you want?' He would personally distribute Christmas bonuses, with the advice as he handed them over: 'Now, spend it wisely.'

Jock Reid, low-key and soft-spoken, a Freemason and Rotarian, seemed almost too gentlemanly for business. He joined the board when his elder brother resigned the chairmanship in order to join up in December 1939, and made a disarmingly inconspicuous successor. Another veteran employee, Don Warden, fell into an enjoyable conversation with him over a cup of tea at Asbestos House the first time they met, and got used to yarning with him about sport. Finally Warden was accosted by a secretary, who said excitedly:

'You met him. You met him.'

'Yes, he's a nice chap,' replied Warden. 'What department is he in?'

She was shocked. Didn't he realise that 'Mr Reid' was the founder's son?

When they next met, Warden was abashedly deferential: 'How do you do, Mr Reid?'

Jock Reid looked disappointed: 'Somebody spoilt it. Who told you?'

His tastes were at the puritan extreme of Presbyterianism. He would screen Mickey Mouse films at Brooklyn's Christmas parties until eyes glazed; on one occasion, the wife of assistant factory manager Harry Holman fell asleep and slipped loudly to the floor. One had to mind one's ps and qs when the family were involved. A story is told of Sandy Reid, son of Doddy, visiting the Birkenhead plant in his school uniform and asking at the cashier's desk for a cheque to be cashed. When the cashier refused, a colleague remonstrated with him: 'You see that young kid over there? He's going to be your boss one day. You've got your choice now of walking down to the bloody bank, getting his money for him, or you can go home tonight and not come back.'

The extent of the Reid family influence on James Hardie is difficult to measure. For as long as it was a private company, it was probably significant. Not only was Andrew a source of immense loyalty, but Thyne and Jock were hugely interested in all operational aspects of the business. Thyne personally initiated the company's first attempts to use asbestos in clutch plates and brake linings, and could be forceful. Gordon Reeve, who worked in the office at Camellia, remembered the spectacular scene when Cyprian Truman quit as works manager in April 1937 after an argument with Thyne about how best to shift pipes. Truman stormed into the office, ripped off the hat he normally wore inside and out on account of his baldness, and started jumping on it. He then began emptying his desk and shoving papers into a bin; when that was full, he asked for another. Finally he asked Reeve: 'Would you do something for me? Would you burn all these papers and make sure they're completely destroyed?' He never came back.

Such scenes, however, were rare. While substantial family presences on share registers can be problematical, the Reids seem to have wielded their voting power with discretion. Thyne was a relatively active chairman; Jock Reid, who acquired a slate of company directorships in the 1950s and 1960s, and became an ABC commissioner, was a more distant successor. Executive turnover was startlingly low, some enjoying careers of half a century and more. In the first half of the century, the backbone of management was a triumvirate of Stewart D'Arrietta, George Sutton and Chisholm Cameron.

D'Arrietta, the Australian-born son of Italian parents, was a busy, bristling, noisy man who would sweep through an office pointing out the cobwebs, and whose approach to most business problems was: 'Give them half of what they want.' He 'loved a drink', a contemporary recalled, and for the time blasphemed freely: 'Too right!' and 'My oath!' were favourite ejaculations. Sutton, a taciturn chain-smoker, was D'Arrietta's numbers man. Jock Reid recalled that he could 'look at a balance sheet and tell you the colour of the chairman's eyes'. Sutton and D'Arrietta talked business incessantly. One day, the story is told, they were at Circular Quay farewelling a departing liner. 'There must be a lot of profit in these streamers, Stewart,' said Sutton. 'Yes yes, I suppose there would be,' replied D'Arrietta at once. 'A marginal profit of 150 to 200 per cent.' Just then a gantry crane stooped and cut the streamers off. 'Well, there you are, George,' D'Arrietta continued. 'Another lot of streamers sold as soon as they can get them out!' Sutton agreed: 'Wonderful market for streamers.' Cameron, meanwhile, became Hardie's institutional memory, after joining as an accountant in September 1913. As company secretary, he ensured that everything passed through his hands. He would personally sign every cheque, throwing them over his shoulder for minions to catch as he did so, and complete every tax return; later, he would write the company's first history in two volumes.

D'Arrietta, Sutton and Cameron were slow to relinquish their executive duties, and by the Second World War were probably becoming an obstacle to change, running the company with little appreciation of its growth in size, and holding back the next generation of managers. Jim Rhys-Jones, one of that generation, recalled:

> They always struck me as men who'd brought a small company up to a middle-sized company, but were getting out of their depth as far as handling a big company was concerned ... I wouldn't dare say it at the time. But they had little idea of organization and they fiddled around with small things, you know. They fiddled around with the petty cash when there were big things to worry about.

After the Second World War, the Reid brothers could see the need for Hardie to begin acting as a big company should, and appointed 33-year-old Jonah Adamson, formerly with the British Colonial Service, as Thyne's assistant. Adamson, a bear of a man standing six feet four inches and weighing seventeen stone, was a kinsman of the Reids; like them, his mother had been a Thyne, while his father had been a senior executive at Hardie Rubber. Appointed chief executive officer on £1000 a year in November 1948, Adamson took to the job with relish, bringing the new religion of budgeting, formal reporting lines and financial controls to Hardie's antiquated structures. He promoted a new generation of technocrats to senior management roles, including chief engineer Frank Page, personnel director Tom Tidey, salesman Alan Woodford, and industrial chemist Ted Heath. He also drove the company's November 1951 decision to go public as James Hardie Asbestos: it listed in Sydney the following month, then in Melbourne in July 1953. But the family's aversion to confrontation confounded him. To avoid a showdown with their elderly retainers, the brothers kept them on the board, constituting instead an executive committee through which most daily decision-making could be steered. As Jock Reid explained:

And I remember Adamson, who was then managing director, saying: 'Look, why can't we get these chaps to retire? It's your job as chairman to get them to retire'. I said: 'No, I will not. If they want to hang on and get the little bits of fringe benefits that they can get' — which were very, very small — 'I'm prepared to let them do it. What we will do, we will form an executive committee and the executive committee will do all the business of the company and serve up to the board each month recommendations which, I can pretty well guarantee, will never be upset'. 'Well why won't you get rid of them?' I said: 'Look, these were the blokes who put into our hands a very prosperous company. I'm not going to kick them out. If they go of their own volition, that's fine — but death will resolve it for us in good course.'

The arrangement kept a lid on tension between old and new at Hardie, although not completely. The old-timers could sense their marginalisation. Stan Strachan recalled a conversation in which Cameron confided piteously: 'They want me to get out of the company. I'm not ready to go yet.' And Adamson's feelings of thwartedness eventually made him as much part of the problem as the solution.

BY THE 1950S AND THE 1960S, the outward stability of the Hardie executive was obscuring considerable inward tension and tragedy. Two members of its executive committee, Tidey and company secretary Allan Bennett, met untimely ends: Tidey suffered a heart attack while driving across the Sydney Harbour Bridge, and Bennett experienced a devastating mental breakdown that reduced him to a vegetative state for the last years of his life. A tradition of hard drinking also took its toll — including at least one life, that of Better Brakes boss Bob Butler, who finally committed suicide in May 1970. Thyne Reid's partiality to whiskey was aggravated by the medication he took to suppress his asthma. 'He couldn't take booze,' said a contemporary. 'That was his trouble.' The careers of both Adamson and Heath were also curtailed by their heavy imbibing, and their names at the company became unutterable. When writer John

Balmforth was involved in an oral-history project at Hardie in the late 1970s, he confided that Adamson and Heath were 'two names that more or less don't exist'.*

Adamson — intelligent, impulsive and intimidating — became a source of special sensitivity. 'Fundamentally,' said Page, with whom Adamson had rowed at Sydney University, 'he was a bit of a bully.' And under the influence of alcohol, recalled Don Walker, Bennett's successor as secretary, his animosities became almost radioactive: 'He was a wild man, he was a great drinker. Boy, could he put away grog … a real rampageous bugger when he got moving.' When he got moving, Adamson could be frightening: 'I went past it [the office] and he called me in. He said, 'Don, this bastard D'Arrietta, we're going to get rid of him … We'll shoot the bastard'. He had a great big hunting rifle behind his door, I thought he was going to shoot me for a while.' He was prone, too, to abrupt disappearances. Neil Gilbert, who managed Brooklyn in the 1950s, recalls one:

> He came down to Melbourne once and we brought him to the factory, and I had a counter lunch with him and a few beers. Then I said I had to get back to work and I'd drive him where he needed to go. And he said: 'Just drive me back to the hotel. I'll be catching the plane tonight.' And he wanted me to stay with him, but I wasn't going to get involved in that … Next thing I got a ring from Alan Baird who says: 'Where's Jonah? I went to pick him and he's not here.' We didn't find him for two days.

Adamson was protected, however, by the old code of silence about workplace behaviour, to which even Walker was a subscriber.

---

* Jock Reid's diary entry for 11 April 1978 records sadly: 'Ted Heath's retirement from H Tdg [Hardie Trading] board and JHA [James Hardie Asbestos] board as Mg Dir for 'health' reasons. The circumstances are very sad — an able and likeable chap destroyed by alcohol.' When Hardie came to write its company history, there was considerable awkwardness about Heath. R. V. Bolton, community affairs manager, advised writer Brian Carroll in January 1987: 'As you know, Ted Heath left the company under sad circumstances and it will be necessary for you to discuss with John Reid how you are deal with Ted.'

He recalled:

> Eventually Thyne said: 'Walker, you got a minute?' I said: 'Yes'. So I
> went back to his office. He opened a bottle of whiskey ... very good
> whiskey ... cream whiskey, no water ... and he said: 'What's the matter
> with Jonah? Is he causing a lot of trouble round here?' I said: 'Not really
> Thyne ... the senior staff know ... he's got a bit of a problem but we're
> accustomed to it. We live with it. I don't think there's any reason, you
> know, for anything else'. So that was that.

That *was* that. To a remarkable degree, the strains at the top of
Hardie were contained. Adamson's 'retirement' in August 1971 and
Heath's in April 1978 were effectively managed. At factory level for
most of the twentieth century, relations were remarkably serene,
even cordial. Labour turnover, for a period of full employment, was
low. The company won immense loyalty from workers in the
Depression, for instance, when it declined to make cutbacks. 'I'd go
into the office and start work at 8.30 Monday morning and at 12.30
I'd finished the day's work and we had nothing else to do,' recalled a
worker at Newstead. 'But they never put you off. They never stood
you down ... No, we never suffered any cuts because of Hardie's.'
Workers themselves made sometimes extraordinary contributions to
the company's growth. Brooklyn expanded so fast in its early years
that it outstripped the capacity of the water pipe that supplied it
from Williamstown Road; it was rescued by an employee who
moonlighted as a water diviner and located a bore.

The war was another crucial climacteric. Hardie was declared a
'protected undertaking', and was proud of its contribution to the war
effort. Fibre-cement pipes and sheets were widely used in military
encampments. The company's new business in brake linings was
harnessed for Bren gun carriers and Beaufighters alike. Sutton and
Jock Reid oversaw the opening of an insulation factory at Camellia,
pouring out fireproof lining for naval bulkheads, and a new fibre-
cement joint venture with Wunderlich at Birkenhead in South
Australia. 'How typical it was of their British faith that, even while
German armies occupied almost all Europe and the very fate of

England appeared in the balance, these three men went confidently about extending their company's activities,' hymned Chisholm Cameron in his company history. Thyne himself saw action at Tobruk, and his brother George was killed in New Guinea. Noel Hill, who had run the company's Camellia laboratory, ran the workshops at Changi. Hardie even set up a scheme to help employees buy war savings certificates, the company paying 80 per cent of their face value and allowing repayment by monthly instalments.

Above all, the war strengthened the affinity of employer and employed. Thyne revered the military. He insisted that jobs be held open for the four hundred who enlisted. Senior management after the war was chock-full of former fighting men. Ashby Hooper, who ran Brooklyn, was a former artillery officer in the British Army; Lester Henning, who ran Camellia, had been a Battle of Britain pilot; Neil Gilbert and Warwick Lane, who succeeded him, had both been air gunners; and Frank Page and Alan Baird had both been army officers, Page reaching the rank of major, Baird of captain.

Tremendous loyalty was the result. By 1952, Hardie had no fewer than eight-one existing staff with more than twenty-five years behind them. A Long Service Club founded in May 1953 honoured those who reached that milestone with a silver cup — to graduate was known as 'stopping a pot'. To quote 'An Old Timer's Ode to the Company', published in the Camellia staff newsletter in October 1957:

> It's a quarter century now — and more
> Since first I walked in Hardie's door.
> I'd 'ardly left me cot!
> 'twas the very first job I'd ever copped;
> Since then I've stopped — and stopped — and stopped,
> And now I've stopped a pot.

The staff newsletters of New South Wales (*Camellia News*) and Victoria (*Trimmings*) enumerate a remarkable variety of social activities: balls, socials, picnics, sporting events (cricket for the C. P. Truman Cup, table tennis for the D. C. Cameron Cup, an annual athletics competition organised by Tidey between Camellia and Brooklyn), and lunchtime talks (either on subjects like fishing and astronomy, or by well-known visitors like cricketer Ben Barnett and conductor Sir Bernard Hinze). The Newstead plant featured a nine-hole putting green, and played records over the public address system at lunchtime on a wind-up gramophone player. A group insurance scheme operated in conjunction with the AMP Society from May 1934, and Hardie became in July 1946 one of the first companies to establish a system for cumulative sick pay to employees: workers were credited annually with a week's sick pay at their current award wage, with the accumulation not taken credited on departure or retirement. The 1950s and 1960s, of course, are in some respects the golden age of industrial paternalism. But Jock Reid, in particular, seems to have been held by workers in uniformly high esteem. Jim Trevillyan, for thirty years the personnel officer at Brooklyn, recalled that Jock Reid often lent money to staff out of his own pocket on no surety save character:

> And he would say to me: 'What's the chap like?' 'You know, good man and so on'. Bang, you'd have a cheque for four hundred dollars or whatever it was … It was his money. No one ever rescinded on the payment either. He always got the money back … He'd never knock you back. He'd only ask what's my opinion of the man.

Perusal of Jock Reid's diary reveals the store he set by personal connection. Most individuals encountered are annotated with comments like 'has 2 daughters 3, 7'; 'wife Helene and 2 girls at MLC'; 'lives at Mt Martha, grows Aust. shrubs'. One worker, Eric Anthony, recalled being visited by Jock Reid's daughter, a nurse, while convalescing from illness in Royal Melbourne Hospital. 'My father asked me to call in and see how you are,' she explained. 'I'll try to get around and see you again. If I can I will. I wish you luck.' The regard in return was unfeigned. Phillip Morley, born in Parramatta, married a girl from two streets away whose father worked for Hardie at Camellia for forty-five years, before and after World War II. One of his father-in-law's prized possessions was an AMP Society life insurance policy that the Reid family took out on his behalf when he enlisted, worth £50 to his widow in the event of his death. When Morley joined Hardie as its chief accountant in October 1984, his father-in-law confided: 'I can now officially welcome you to the family.' Morley had at this stage been married to his daughter for thirteen years. It is at least ironic that such a company should have authored one of Australia's costliest public health disasters. But in some respects this environment of benevolence was part of the problem: Hardie saw itself as having its workers' best interests at heart, and its workers shared that belief in its good intentions.

4

'Pain so dreadful'

'We claim to be as efficient as any overseas company and in some technical aspects ahead of them. This has not only been achieved by a large expenditure in travel, research and development. As a result of our achievements, the two largest asbestos companies in the world, Johns-Manville of the United States of America and Turner & Newall whose headquarters are in the United Kingdom, both of whom because of their great size spend larger sums on technical development than ourselves, are happy to have formal agreements with us for the full exchange of technical and production "know-how" in asbestos cement manufacture. Since James Hardie "gives as good as it gets", no royalties or "know-how" payments are involved by either party. These agreements are unique in our industry.'
—Jonah Adamson at the Tariff Board inquiry, June 1954

MEDICAL KNOWLEDGE ABOUT THE EFFECTS OF ASBESTOS did not advance significantly during World War II, least of all in Australia. During his Listerian Oration on 29 May 1941 to the South Australian branch of the British Medical Association on 'Changes in the Lungs in Various Industries', Dr J. G. Edwards dismissed asbestosis as 'uncommon in Australia owing to the limited number of men engaged in the industry' — a state of affairs to which he had partly contributed two years earlier by testifying for James Hardie against the claim of the widow Jones. The Dreessen Standard of 5mppcf ruled (officially enshrined first in February 1945 in the Harmful Gases, Vapours, Fumes, Mists, Smokes and Dusts Regulations that were added to the Victorian Health Act) but was seldom enforced. And were one to judge Hardie according to the state of cognisance in Australian industrial hygiene of asbestos' toxicity, the case for the company to answer would not be formidable. As Jonah Adamson himself made plain before the Tariff Board, however, James Hardie regarded itself as an international presence in the asbestos market—indeed, it boasted of its connections, and of punching above its productive weight. It is only right to see it as a participant in an international story.

Hardie had long bought fibre from both Johns-Manville and Turner & Newall, but relations grew closer in the immediate post-war years, after a five-month overseas trip by Ted Heath from June 1947 when he spent considerable time at Johns-Manville and at Turner & Newall's American arm, Keabsley & Mattison. These links were then formalised by Heath and Frank Page on a similar trip through the US, UK, Italy, Switzerland and Denmark from August 1950. Both the British and the American companies had warded off threats to their profitability—Turner & Newall from the legislative restrictions that had been threatened by the Merewether report, Johns-Manville from a short-lived wave of common law compensation suits. Their cynicism where workers' health was concerned was deeply ingrained. Turner & Newall maintained a pose of candour, admitting to six deaths from asbestosis in 1942, even though subsequent analysis has suggested that the number was more than forty; Johns-Manville, according to Kenneth Smith, the medical officer who twenty-five years later would become a star witness against his erstwhile employer, practised a policy that kept the ill in ignorance. When a 1948 survey of 708 workers in the town of Asbestos found only four with normal, healthy lungs, Smith himself helped shape the policy:

> It must be remembered that although these men have the X-ray evidence of asbestosis, they are working today and definitely are not disabled from asbestosis. They have not been told of this diagnosis for it is felt that as long as the man feels well, is happy at home and at work, and his physical condition remains good, nothing should be said. When he becomes disabled and sick, the diagnosis should be made and the claim submitted by the company. The fibrosis of this disease is

irreversible and permanent so that eventually compensation will have to be paid to each of these men. But as long as the man is not disabled it is felt that he should not be told of his condition so that he can live and work in peace and the company can benefit by his many years of experience.

The temptation to impute the foregoing sentiments to Hardie should be resisted; a corporation should not be damned simply by the company it keeps. There was also, it should be noted, an abiding personal tension in the relations between Hardie and Turner & Newall, for Thyne Reid simply did not like his contemporary Sir Walker Shepherd, who had succeeded to the chairmanship on the death of the company patriarch Samuel Turner III in 1944, and who awed contemporaries with his 'power of thinking on the vastest scale'. He referred to Shepherd as 'Bloody Bill', and warned: 'You cannot take the word of the so-called English gentlemen.' But the companies also had too much in common — Turner & Newall's Manchester headquarters was even called Asbestos House — not to collaborate. When Shepherd arrived in Sydney on the *Orcades* in May 1951, for instance, he was met at Circular Quay by Jock Reid and feted at the Australian Club. Relations with Johns-Manville were so cordial that the American company declined to assist the Tariff Board when it was solicited for information three years later, 'as our relations with the James Hardie company are very friendly and they are, of course, one of our good asbestos fibre customers'. James Hardie was not, therefore, simply a company that used asbestos; it was an asbestos company.

The significance of this is that, for fifteen years after World War II, medical research into the effects of asbestos was not occurring in remote laboratories and being published in esoteric journals: it was under the aegis of an industry of which James Hardie was a proud and fully fledged member. In one way, this makes perfect sense: the industry had the records and ran the facilities in which the conditions concerned arose. But it was also, of course, a situation fraught with conflicted interests. Discussing the spectre of liability as a motive for the under-reporting of occupational cancers in a 1943

Bulletin of the American Cancer Society, Wilhelm C. Hueper of the National Cancer Institute committed to print an observation that seems as true now as then:

> Industrial concerns are in general not particularly anxious to have the occurrence of occupational cancers among their employees or of environmental cancers among the consumers of their products made a matter of public record. Such publicity might reflect unfavourably upon their business activities, and oblige them to undertake extensive and expensive technical and sanitary changes in their production methods and in the types of products manufactured. There is, moreover, the distinct possibility of becoming involved in compensation suits with extravagant financial claims by the injured parties. It is, therefore, not an uncommon practice that some pressure is exerted by the parties financially interested in such matters to keep information on the occurrence of industrial cancer well under cover.

A famous example of science's uneasy coexistence with industry are the Saranac Experiments, so-called for the prestigious tuberculosis laboratory in upstate New York where Dr Leroy Gardner and Dr Arthur Vorwald from February 1943 exposed as many as 450 animals to a new insulation product called Kaylo, manufactured by Owens-Illinois. The industry seemed to have gotten its money's worth when the researchers issued their preliminary conclusions in October 1947 that 'Kaylo alone fails to produce significant pulmonary damage when inhaled into the lung.' The prognosis was premature, however, for the animals shortly began to develop fibrosis consistent with asbestos exposure, and Vorwald had to advise: 'I regret to say, our tentative conclusion … must be altered'.

Although Vorwald now felt that Kaylo, 'because of its content of an appreciable amount of fibrous chrysotile is capable of producing asbestosis and should be handled as a hazardous industrial dust', his conclusion sounded a hopeful note:

> I realise that our findings regarding Kaylo are less favourable than anticipated. However, since Kaylo is capable of producing asbestosis, it

is better to discover it now in animals rather than later in industrial workers. This the company, being forewarned, will be in a better position to institute adequate control measures for safeguarding exposed employees and protecting its own interests.

But by the time the results of the experiments appeared in September 1955, written up finally by Vorwald's successor, Dr Gerrit Schepers, they had been cleansed of any reference that might have identified either Kaylo or Owens-Illinois.* A version of Kaylo, furthermore, was also being sold by James Hardie under the name K-Lite, with the reassuring lines in its advertisement: 'The material can be cut, scored and sawed with the normal tools of the trade. It is non-irritating to the skin and non-toxic.'

This was a gauntlet all researchers of the period ran, especially in probing the possibility that asbestosis was not alone among asbestos health risks. In the 1947 *Annual Report of the Chief Inspector of Factories*, Edward Merewether published the fruits of a remarkable survey of 235 autopsy reports between 1924 and 1946 that hinted at an abnormally high incidence of lung cancer among asbestos workers. Cancer of the lung and pleura were present in 13.2 per cent of asbestotics — ten times the rate in silicotics. As the medico-legal scholar Barry Castleman explains: 'The chance that as many as 31

---

* South African Schepers had already had some experience of the industry's self-protectiveness. In August 1950, he had been startled to find on the desk of Johns-Manville's Vandivar Brown a copy of a highly critical technical appraisal of the company's Quebec operations. Many years later, under examination by the American plaintiff lawyer Stephen Kazan, he would recall the dialogue that transpired:

> *Kazan*: And what, if anything, did Mr Brown tell you with respect to that report?
> *Schepers*: He asked me to suppress it and not publish the information in it.
> *Kazan*: Did he explain why?
> *Schepers*: He said it would be harmful to the economic interests of his company ... he suggested that I had been their guest, their privileged guest, and therefore should respect the confidence of the company, and not mention what I had seen.

Schepers insisted that he was duty bound to give the report to the South African government, who had commissioned it, and did — it was also suppressed there.

lung cancers in 235 would occur if their real likelihood was only the same as that of the general population (1 per cent) is remote—less than one a million'.

Testing Merewether's thesis became a preoccupation of industry and investigators, until they finally collaborated. In April 1953, Turner & Newall's company physician John Knox invited Richard Doll, a 40-year-old medical statistician at the London School of Hygiene and Tropical Medicine, to perform a joint epidemiological study of the company's deceased workers. But when Doll's study of 113 autopsies suggested that asbestos workers faced eleven times the risk of lung cancer found in the general population, the company's board panicked, withdrew its permission to publish, issued legal threats, and tried to dissuade the editor of the *British Journal of Industrial Medicine* from accepting the submission. This time, the industry was less successful. While Turner & Newall's and Knox's name were deleted, 'Mortality from Lung Cancer in Asbestos Workers' was otherwise unchanged on publication, and caused sufficient of a storm to attract its own story in *The Times* in February 1955.

Still more chilling research was even then on foot in South Africa, involving Cape Asbestos—with which, as we shall see, Hardie also had close and cordial links. In about 1952, physician Kit Sleggs, medical superintendent of West End Hospital in Kimberley, became aware of a number of cases of pleural malignancies of an unexampled size and extremity, mostly among coloured patients and exclusively from the west. The patients usually arrived appearing tubercular, wracked by chest pain and shortness of breath, with an excess of fluid in the chest cavity that called for draining—often in copious quantities. Autopsy would reveal that the lungs had been crushed by enormous tumours, which in some instances had also compressed the heart, diaphragm and liver into a single mass. Eventually, Sleggs passed some lung biopsies to a colleague's brother-in-law, Chris Wagner, who was a research fellow at Johannesburg's Pneumoconiosis Research Unit.

In February 1956, Wagner was then asked to autopsy a 36-year-old Bantu male who had been the shower attendant at a mine in

Witwatersrand, from whom the life had been squeezed by 'a huge gelatinous tumour completely filling the right chest cavity'. The technician suggested he take a section of lung, which to Wagner's surprise proved to be full of asbestos bodies. He called a professor of pathology from the University of Witwatersrand, who invoked a one-in-a-million cancer called mesothelioma. It wasn't to be rare much longer: in the next two years, Wagner saw sixteen cases. When Wagner visited Europe between September 1957 and April 1958, he shared his preliminary results with Turner & Newall's John Knox and Cape Asbestos's medical officer Walter Smither. Coincidentally or not, both companies were prime movers at around the same time with British Belting & Asbestos in the formation of the Asbestosis Research Council: a means by which the asbestos industry could sponsor medical research more amenable to its needs, and of which James Hardie would in time be an eager associate member. The ARC, thanks partly to Wagner, would have its work cut out. The paper he prepared with Sleggs and their colleague Paul Marchand had by August 1959 been read by Turners executives as senior as managing director, and recognised for what it was: a bombshell.

'Diffuse Pleural Mesothelioma and Asbestos Exposure in the North Western Cape Province', finally received for publication in the *British Journal of Industrial Medicine* in April 1960, concentrated on thirty-three histologically proven cases of this hitherto incomparably rare tumour, twenty-eight of which had some association with crocidolite mining in the Cape Province. Asbestos was not entirely incriminated, for there was no evidence of comparable mesothelioma incidence associated with amosite mines in Transvaal. But the scientists also implied that crocidolite was dangerous even in small quantities, and that risks did not stop at the gate of the mine or mill: among their cases were a 56-year-old social worker who had been exposed as a child, a 42-year-old woman who had once lived near a mine and a 50-year-old farmer who had transported asbestos in donkey wagons. The disease lay in wait for decades then killed in months, and its prevalence was widening. A postscript revealed that, by the end of June 1960, crocidolite exposure had been ascertained in forty-five of forty-seven cases.

If the epidemiological picture was bleak, so was the political one. Between November 1960 and February 1962, Wagner's Pneumoconiosis Research Unit, with support from Turner & Newall, Cape Asbestos and the South African government, undertook a survey of work areas round mines at Prieska, Koegas, Kuruman and Penge involving X-rays of a sample of 3000 subjects, and of which mesothelioma was one of the focuses. Four cases were found—a plague proportion, given its usual incidence. Statistics suggested that even one was too many, mainly because of the disease's natural rarity, but also because a sufferer must live to a reasonable age to accommodate mesothelioma's latency period, and silicosis, malnutrition, physical defects and communicable diseases hereabouts had considerably reduced life expectancy. But the really limited life expectancy was that of the report itself. This was South Africa just months after the Sharpeville massacre. Few concerns ranked lower than the health of black and coloured workers in a profitable industry. 'In terms of civil rights, access to the law and health care,' notes Jock McCulloch in his history of the South African asbestos industry, 'those people could not have been further removed from the British and American citizen who used asbestos-based products.' Commentary on mesothelioma in the final version of the report was winnowed away to a few lines.

IT IS HERE WORTH DISTINGUISHING, simply, between the diseases of asbestosis and mesothelioma, as indeed researchers began to in the early 1960s. Asbestosis is a disease of fibrosis (scarring), caused by the lung's response to its infiltration by asbestos fibre. The tendency of scar tissue to gradually shrink reduces lung function, with damage concentrating in the posterior (lower) zones of the lungs; the scarring also hampers pulmonary blood flow. The disease is dose-dependent (that is, the risk of incidence rises as exposure is prolonged) and progressive (it may slow down, but it is irreversible). The lung is astounding resilient, and its natural surplus capacity can make up for partial incapacity for long periods. But after ten or fifteen years' breathlessness, dry coughing and weight loss usually set in. Swelling of the fingers and toes called clubbing, and eerie crackles at the end of inspiration called rales, are held to be most reliable indicators.

The lung is surrounded by two thin membranes called the pleura, separated by the pleural space; the abdominal cavity is surrounded by another membrane called the peritoneum. These provide the lubricated surfaces that keep the internal organs from chafing. They are also the battleground of mesothelioma. The condition of the parietal (external) pleura, in fact, is a litmus test of asbestos exposure, as it is usually marked by collections of calcified collagen called plaques — generally benign, and suggestive mainly of somewhat increased risk of developing disease later. But tumours that break out in these areas are invariably lethal, crushing all in their path, and increasingly excruciating, thanks to the number of nerve endings trespassed on. In the words of a judgement by Justice O'Meally of the Dust Disease Tribunal:

I have been at the bedside of many men and women dying of mesothelioma. I have seen many people present in court, at their homes, at hospitals and at hospices dying of mesothelioma. It is a dreadful and a devastating disease, accompanied by pain which is uncontrollable. Those who suffer it reach a stage where it is necessary to fight for every breath, with every breath accompanied by pain so dreadful that the only way to avoid it is not to breathe. The choice between breathing and not breathing is no choice at all. Constant and exquisite pain is all that one may expect in the struggle to exist. My own experience is that in eighty to eighty-five per cent of cases, plaintiffs with mesothelioma reach a stage where they suffer pain which is uncontrollable.

More common is the pleural mesothelioma; more invasive and destructive is the peritoneal mesothelioma; a third variant is the pericardial mesothelioma, which attacks the sac surrounding the heart. These afflictions are, too, almost as psychologically destructive as physically. Mesothelioma is not dose-dependent, and stalks the body insidiously: after a latency period of up to forty years, it usually overwhelms the patient in a year. It can arise from exposures only dimly recalled, and confound decades of hard work and life planning. The DDT, Australia's main clearing-house for compensation, turns over cases daily that read like the torments of the underworld.

> The plaintiff's mental distress is apparent, he is often in tears. His wife says he is getting more emotional because he has more pins and needles higher in his body and he is increasingly frightened by the inexorable progression of his tumour. He shakes; whether that be from fear or some organic cause is not clear. It does not matter much. The plaintiff will probably die about the end of April 2000. The remaining month of his life will be marked by an increasing struggle to breathe, each breath at the cost of increasingly relentless and incessant pain. (*Stephen Smith v Sydney Water Corporation Ltd (2000)*; from the finding by Justice Curtis).

The life of a person diagnosed with asbestos-related disease quickly becomes a blur of medical appointments, despite the fact that the prognosis is always bleak, and legal processes, where the most intimate details of one's physical life are laid open. And because the diseases naturally tend to be concentrated among those lower on the socio-economic scale who have worked in factories, on building sites or in older offices, financial strains add to complications:

> The plaintiff himself describes the biopsy that did not happen on 20 August 2002. 'I was supposed to go into Prince Alfred on 20 August for a further biopsy. Jenni drove us again, it was a terrible trip, I was very sick and I was vomiting. It was my first day out of bed since I went into Bowral Hospital apart from going to see Dr Bayfield. We got there at 8.00AM. We had to walk from the Medical Centre in Carillon Avenue to the Page Chest Pavillion. They didn't give me a wheelchair. I was extremely weak and I almost passed out. I was in a lot of pain and I was quite anxious. I didn't really know what to think. Then at about 1.00PM Dr Bayfield came down and said 'There are too many emergencies and not enough beds, a lot of staff have called in sick. Are you a private patient, if so we can make a definite appointment? But if not then you can either come back the following morning and try again or make

another appointment.' I didn't have private health cover, we didn't want to be mucked about again so we made another appointment and I had a surgical procedure the following week.' (*Bob Muyt v Wallaby Grip Ltd & Amaca Pty Ltd (formerly known as James Hardie & Coy Pty Ltd) (2002);* from the finding by Justice Maguire).

When not at the disposal of doctors and lawyers, patients face a waiting game, with their capabilities shrinking daily, and death in doubt only as to the date.

In November 2003 Dr Scroop undertook a biopsy at St Andrews Hospital during which fluid was drained from the plaintiff's lung. It was following that procedure that he was advised that he had an inoperable lung cancer. He said that his shortness of breath is getting worse. His evidence today was that when he was advised that he had inoperable lung cancer he was ready to kill himself. At the time he was notified of the diagnosis he was told he had 12 months to live. As regards his breathing difficulties the plaintiff said that he is breathing 50 per cent at the moment. He said he lives his life in bed. He cannot do anything now and it is killing him.

He kept his electrician's licence on foot in the hope that he might get better. He still hopes that that might happen although all the indicators are that the hope is in vain. He said of himself that he is as white as a ghost from chemotherapy. That treatment started in January this year. He has had three weeks on chemotherapy each month and a week off. During the week off he has attempted to take some medication to deal with emotional upset but that also makes him sick. His weight dropped from 107 kilograms to 80 kilograms. It rose again and has dropped again so that he is now at about 82 kilograms. He said that he went fishing last weekend and did not have the strength to put the bait on his hooks.

The plaintiff said that in recent times he is always crying. During the course of giving his evidence today he was in tears. It is not something that he is able to control very well. He said at home he and his wife used to do things together but now she does the domestic things. Just before he became aware of the diagnosis which was offered to him he had bought the second of two buses. He likes to modify them so that they are a mobile home which he can use to go away for fishing holidays and the like. Just before the diagnosis was made he had commenced beekeeping with his brother at Kapunda as a hobby. His comment about that was simply 'that's gone now'.

He is able to shower himself. Sexual intercourse with his wife has now finished … He takes drugs every night and every morning to stop back pain. In addition to back pain he has some discomfort around his stomach which he attributes to the fluid in his lungs. When trying to sleep he said he wakes every half hour. Counselling has been suggested to him but he said he does not want to go yet because he gets too upset. The plaintiff said that his wife had had a stroke three years ago and that it was hard for her to cope. At present she is doing all the caring for him. The plaintiff said that when his wife takes a break and goes to Bingo a couple of times a week he simply lies on the bed. They have been married for 40 years.

His brother in law comes and cleans up the garden about once a month, spending something like three hours doing it. He has not had to use oxygen at this stage. The plaintiff said, and I accept this, that his whole life has become doctors and lawyers. 'It just drives you nuts'. (*Kerry Allen Hurst v Amaca Pty Limited (2004)*; from the finding by Justice Duck)

The sense of futility is so profound that it can overwhelm even those who have led the worthiest lives.

The plaintiff was for many years married to a builder who made extensive use of the defendant's products. She inhaled asbestos fibres in the course of cleaning his work clothes. She also inhaled asbestos dust thrown off by asbestos products when she at times was present while her husband carried out the work. Exposure commenced in about 1966 and continued at least until 1984. As a result of this inhalation the plaintiff contracted the fatal disease of mesothelioma …

The plaintiff was born on 18 February 1939 and is now 62 years of age. On 15 February 1958 the plaintiff, then just 19 years old, married her husband and embarked upon a lifetime of service. She initially kept house for her husband, his father, his brother and her brother. She has borne seven children ... In addition to these children the plaintiff in 1966 adopted Michael, then aged four and Patrick aged two. As if that were not enough the plaintiff also raised two grandchildren born to her daughter, Kathleen, after the breakup of Kathleen's marriage. In addition to caring for her children and ultimately seventeen grandchildren, the plaintiff was active in charity, working with Crisis Care for babies and children in distress, helping out the Red Cross, Meals on Wheels and the Anti-Cancer Council. In pursuit of parish activities she regularly visited the sick and the lonely.

In 1996 the plaintiff saw her local doctor, Dr Pace, complaining of cough and shortness of breath. She was misdiagnosed as then suffering from asthma. In 1998 the plaintiff endured an appalling year. In that year her husband was diagnosed with terminal bone cancer and five of her children were diagnosed as having contracted thyroid cancer. The plaintiff at the time, unknown to her, suffered from the insidious growth of her mesothelioma. The breathlessness continued to get worse while she cared for her husband.

In October 1998 X-rays showed fluid on her lungs. She did not do anything at that time because she was more concerned with her husband. As her breathlessness increased she finally in 1999 agreed to have the fluid drained and attended upon the Burnside Hospital on 9 February 1999 when a litre of fluid was drained from her lungs. Her breathlessness continued to worsen. On 19 April 1999 she went back to Dr Robinson for another X-ray which showed that the fluid had re-accumulated. Dr Robinson referred the plaintiff to Dr Peacock. She did not see him straight away because she was very worried about her husband. Eventually she saw Dr Peacock on 18 May 1999 and CT scans were taken.

On 14 July 1999 Dr Peacock performed pleural biopsies and a right video-assisted thoracotomy. Following upon those procedures Dr Peacock informed the plaintiff that she had mesothelioma. The plaintiff was told by Dr Peacock that she only had 12 months to live and it was suggested that her symptoms may be relieved by a talc pleurodesis. The plaintiff decided not to have that procedure because of her understanding that following the procedure she would spend some time incapacitated while recovering and she wished to remain relatively well in order to look after her husband.

When given the diagnosis the plaintiff was stunned and in disbelief. She understandably became very angry. She felt the unfairness of her circumstance as someone who had always thrived on being busy, working 18 hours a day, looking after 15 people in the home and assisting in running her husband's business. Her life, as she says, was productive, rewarding and worthwhile.

In early 2000 again the plaintiff's breathlessness increased and she commenced to have some pains in the right chest and night sweats. She understood her breathing difficulties were occasioned to her by further fluid build up in the lungs. Again the plaintiff refused to have the necessary treatment until the death of her husband. He died on 22 March 2000.

After the death of her husband the plaintiff's condition deteriorated. On 22 December 2000 she had a fall and the shortness of breath became severe. She had swelling in her back and a marked increase in pain. It was only then that the plaintiff submitted to the talc pleurodesis. On 10 January 2001 the plaintiff was admitted to Calvary Hospital where the pleurodesis was carried out. She was released home on 19 January 2001. She was in a lot of pain following that surgery and has continued to experience severe pain. Although she takes some medication it is the advice of Dr Peacock that she should remain off medication as far as possible to save it for later when she really needs it.

The plaintiff now cannot walk more than 10 metres without becoming breathless. Her breathlessness increases. She is in constant pain. She experiences nausea in the morning and does not have much appetite. She has a painful cough. She is becoming increasingly anxious. She is no longer able to carry out activities involving her family, the church or her charities. She presently lives by herself because, as she says, she does not have the patience to have other people around her. She does not wish to be around other people. She wishes to spend the last period of her life in St Mary's private hospice. Her overwhelming emotions, she says, are anger and sadness. (*Winifred Brennan v James Hardie & Coy Pty Ltd (2001)*; from the finding by Justice Curtis).

Once the collaboration of Sleggs, Wagner and Marchand was published, it was not long before mesothelioma was noticed here. Dr Jonathan Streeton, probably Australia's most experienced respiratory physician, recalls arriving at Melbourne University for his usual autopsy and learning that there'd been a change in programme: 'Our pathology teacher said: 'We're not going to do an autopsy today. We're going to talk about some work that's just been published'. He had this old easel covered in butcher's paper, and started to write things on it about this disease called mesothelioma.'

In November 1960, a prospector called Joseph Sawyer was admitted to Kalgoorlie hospital exhibiting all the hallmarks of asbestos disease: he was emaciated, breathless and duly lived only another eight months. Chest physician Jim McNulty, who had read of Wagner's work, diagnosed mesothelioma, and published a case study in the *Medical Journal of Australia* in December 1962. McNulty, too, thought instinctively of the Australian Blue Asbestos mine at Wittenoom, whose conditions he knew to be hot, harsh and exceedingly dusty—much like those found in the north-west of Cape Province, where they also mined crocidolite. His letters to its owner, Colonial Sugar Refining Company, went unanswered. They were too busy serving the interests of their clients—the greatest of all of them being James Hardie.

5

'A very unpleasant and profitless war'

'An ill-advised mining speculation'.
—Hardie managing director Jonah Adamson on Wittenoom

WHILE AUSTRALIA IS FAMOUSLY RESOURCE RICH, its economic deposits of asbestos are small. Consequently, James Hardie was haunted for much of its seven decades as the country's foremost manufacturer of asbestos products by its vulnerability to disruptions in the flow of raw materials. Hardie's warm relations with Johns-Manville and Turner & Newall were seasoned with a certain envy— both the American and British giants were vertically integrated, their manufacturing facilities fed by their own mines. So, even though Hardie's first foray into mining at Barraba was to no avail, it continued to nourish dreams of secure supply. The fruition of those dreams also encompasses its involvement with Wittenoom, Australia's most infamous asbestos mine, which is like a tale of fatal attraction. Hardie never meant to become involved. Its board scorned the site itself, believed the mine would lose money, and loudly ridiculed its owner. But in the end a relationship between Australia's biggest miner of asbestos and Australia's biggest user was inevitable.

The long courtship began in the late 1920s, when Hardie, troubled by rising fibre prices, evaluated two asbestos-mining prospects before settling on a third. The first was a chrysotile deposit at Takaka in the north-west of the south island being mined by the New Zealand Asbestos Company, which proved too small to be worthwhile; second were the large crocidolite outcrops in the Pilbara, including Wittenoom, which the distinguished geologist Sir

Edgeworth David advised Andrew Reid would simply be too expensive to exploit. Hardie resolved instead to take an exotic plunge into Rhodesia, where it leased the Pangani mine in return for a royalty agreement with its owner, Johannesburg's Hancock Asbestos Company. Andrew Reid looked forward to Filabusi Asbestos Co Ltd 'turning out quite a nice mine' and, equipping him with a mosquito net, sent Cyprian Truman to Africa for almost two-and-a-half years to work it up. It was an uncharacteristically romantic adventure for a company as pragmatic as Hardie, with a touch of Rider Haggard. 'I hope you are enjoying your African trip and find a certain amount of time for shooting etc,' wrote Thyne Reid from Camellia in January 1929. 'You should adopt my philosophy that life is not all asbestos cement and bring home a few lions skins as floor decoration.' But then the Depression hit, Rhodesian fibre prices plunged from £30 to £10 a ton, and cheap fibre became so plentiful as to obviate the need for a dedicated raw-material supplier: the enterprise was abandoned in August 1930.

Hardie's contempt for the Pilbara, too, was not shared by one young and ambitious prospector. Lang Hancock had noted veins of fibrous material threading the red ironstone cliffs that are the area's chief feature, pegged them, invested in a primitive crusher and hammer mill, and tributed asbestos from other prospectors. It was a brutal business—the ore had often to be gouged out by hand, and the only transport to Port Samson was by dray—but others became interested.

For some years, the venerable Colonial Sugar Refining Company had hankered to diversify away from its traditional monopoly, and identified building products as an opportunity. At a new facility at its Pyrmont refinery, CSR had begun producing a low-density wallboard called 'Cane-ite' from megass—the fibre left over when the juice has been crushed from sugar cane. When it was then steered towards asbestos by the rising cost of freighting the megass, its two senior executives, Keith Brown and Malcolm George King, were sent overseas in 1938 to study the mineral and its applications, only to suffer in advance the same supply anxieties that plagued Hardie —Brown was in Vienna the day that the Nazis annexed Austria.

This caused CSR, like Hardie, to fantasise of an Australian mine.

So began a long, complex, sometimes combative, often cool relationship between Hardie and CSR. The former enjoyed a comfortable mainland duopoly with Wunderlich and wasn't about to welcome a newcomer. When CSR went into partnership with Hancock in a venture called Australian Blue Asbestos at Wittenoom, Thyne Reid was privately furious; when CSR acquired a small fibre-cement plant, Asbestos Products Pty Ltd in Alexandria, equipping it with two antique Fourdrinnier machines, he was openly sarcastic. In an extraordinary unsolicited letter in June 1944, Reid essentially warned his opposite number at CSR to stay out of the industry: 'The present antagonism to your company, which is becoming fairly general, should not be further encouraged without justification, and I, personally, do not like the thought of a very unpleasant and profitless war when there is so much else to be done.' His advice about crocidolite was even more explicit:

> In regard to the West Australian Blue Asbestos, there is no doubt an overseas market, though very small compared with chrysotile, but should your officers be under the impression that blue can be economically used in asbestos cement, it is probably because they are not aware that South African amosite can be obtained for about half the price and is used in asbestos cement for the same purpose for which blue is sometimes used.

One can only imagine how CSR's chairman, Edward Knox, perceived such a colossally condescending letter, although he contented himself with a polite reply: 'We can see no reason for any such unpleasant developments as you foreshadow in your closing lines'. One wonders, too, whether Knox ever revisited it—because, gallingly, Reid was right.

Thyne Reid should have been feeling confident at the time. Between the mid-1930s and the end of World War II, Australian consumption of asbestos grew 700 per cent. Hardie lines like Fibrolite, Super Six and Tilux ruled unchallenged; the rival Fibrock range made by CSR's Asbestos Products had little impact. The market was at Hardie's mercy—if only it could obtain the fibre it needed. And when the Department of Import Procurement took over asbestos importation at around this time, Hardie started to encounter supply difficulties. Fibre had been in ready supply because of the number of manufacturing facilities in Europe out of action; now, supplies began dwindling.

Again, Hardie went mine hunting. Thyne Reid retained a consultant geologist, John Proud, a protégé of Edgeworth David's from Sydney University, to review a number of prospects, including the Pilbara again. Hardie even contemplated going head-to-head with CSR in Western Australia when, in October 1945, it was offered leases at Yampi Gorge, adjacent to Wittenoom, by the De Fernales Group. But when it forwarded a proposal for a joint venture to Turner & Newall, the return telegram was a terse negative: 'Cable received not interested writing.' After abortive tests at Hardie's old mine near Barraba, Proud urged investing in an exploration that Wunderlich had commenced of chrysotile outcrops near Baryulgil, 80km from Grafton, on the upper Clarence River—of which more later.

Thus it was that CSR—Hancock having by now also opted out—plunged alone into one of Australia's greatest industrial and occupational health disasters ... and a byword for the horrors of asbestos poisoning before Hardie became subject to scrutiny. The engineering challenges of Wittenoom had been grossly underestimated. The host rock was too hard, the seams too narrow, the ersatz mill from Youanmi gold mine too frail to withstand the friction toll that asbestos exacts, the conditions inimical to safety and comfort—as vividly described in Ben Hills' landmark book *Blue Murder*:

> Down the mine the dust from drilling and blasting the asbestos was bad enough, but in the mill it was blinding. One-hundred watt light bulbs hanging from the ceiling of the tin shed looked like candles, one worker recalls. When you walked in, you had to get within a couple of feet of a man to recognise him, because their faces were coated with dust like pancake make-up. In later years the management did provide little masks for the workers, but the men couldn't wear them because

within minutes the filters would choke up with dust and breathing would become impossible. They didn't know, of course, that the dust they were breathing could kill them. So ignorant were they of the dangers that one worker recalls his mates using strands as dental floss after they had eaten their lunch on a table so coated with dust that you could write your name in it.

Hardie, nonetheless, was about to invest in a venture perhaps even uglier.

AMOSITE'S NAME BETRAYS ITS ORIGINS: it is derived from an abbreviation for 'Asbestos Mines of South Africa', the country to which it is peculiar. Cape Asbestos PLC, formed to mine crocidolite in Cape Province, diversified into amosite in the north-east of the Transvaal in 1925. When the US Navy designated amosite its insulation of choice during World War II, Cape's Penge mine rode the crest of the wave. John Proud, who visited just before the cessation of hostilities and who was clearly the source of Thyne Reid's conversance with the fibre in his letter to Knox, came away hugely impressed by amosite's potential. Like Johns-Manville and Turner & Newall, Cape had its own manufacturing operations, near Johannesburg and in Britain, including a large factory at Barking opened in 1914. But it was not in fibre-cement—and wouldn't be until it acquired Universal Asbestos Manufacturing Company in 1967. The Penge mine, too, was set to undergo a substantial expansion, both in production, ramping up output six-fold in six years, and amenities, with the building of new houses, a recreational hall, tennis courts and a hospital—at least, for the white workers.

For the profitability of Penge, like Cape's crocidolite mines, was built on cheap black labour—by 1953, the workforce there would reach 5000. While a parsimonious board based in London insisted on scrutinising all expenditures of more than £30, employees worked under abominable conditions for wages so poor that they could not afford soap. They dwelt in hovels, suffered from malnutrition, were weakened by scurvy, and sacked if their health did not permit them to work. Even by South African standards, Cape was a brutal employer, appalling local inspectors of native labour — although they were helpless to do anything about it. 'I agree with the assistant health officer that the practice of discharging native labourers the instant they show any signs of developing any disease is most despicable,' reported one, 'but owing to the lack of any proper control and medical services one can hardly do anything.' When Dr Gerrit Schepers was sent to the Transvaal in 1949 to make the first radiological and clinical survey of the industry, he found barefoot Bantu children spending days inside huge jute bags trampling fluffy amosite fibres that came cascading over their heads, forced on by whip-wielding overseers; he found that many of these children had developed asbestosis with *cor pulmonale* (right-sided heart failure) before the age of twelve.

Of how much Hardie were aware is unclear and contestable. While Proud was a regular visitor on Cape, he is unlikely to have reported on working conditions. Mind you, it is doubtful whether knowledge would have made any difference. Jonah Adamson's Colonial Service background had left him with some pretty unambiguous views of the white man's burden. He confided to a colleague one day: 'If I wanted to make a fortune quickly, I'd go over to South Africa and I'd grow tobacco. You can get land over there for a song. You stick in one crop of tobacco and the ground's buggered. You have more land, and you work the niggers to death, and that's it.'*

---

* Cape Asbestos, to be frank, was an appalling employer of everyone, not simply of blacks. Conditions in Cape's biggest factory at Barking in London were little better: a 1928 survey of eighty workers showed that almost all were suffering some degree of asbestosis. Its urban location was an uncomfortable reality for the neighbourhood. A council medical officer in 1945 was a prescient voice in what was as yet a wilderness:

> I am firmly of the opinion [that] it [asbestos] is a deadly and dangerous commodity, and that unless those who are charged with the responsibility of safeguarding the health of the people in the industry can give positive assurances that they have now after all these years removed every possible danger, the processing of asbestos, except so far as its products are essential to the national economy, should be barred.

What mattered was that Cape had fibre, and the potential to deliver much more. Because Hardie — and Australia — were desperate. The company had relied during the war largely on fibre from Turner & Newall's mines in Rhodesia and Swaziland. Then, as Frank Page recalled: 'We got a cable that there would be no contracts for next year. And we just lost two-thirds of our supply in one go.'

It is forgotten today how acutely short of essential raw materials were Australia and New Zealand after World War II, and how depleted were foreign exchange reserves. Hardie felt it sorely as it strove to handle pent-up demand for building materials in the face of its vanishing supplies. The in-house journal *Trimmings* reported such developments as the plaint of a customer at Newstead: 'We've been trying for months to get a house built but they tell us there's no fibrolite, and we're still living in a leaky tent. Any chance of getting four sheets of corrugated to put over the floorboards, so that when the water comes through it will run down the grooves and leave us the ridges to stand on?' It recorded, too, what purported to be 'the coming national song of New Zealand', to the tune of 'Show Me The Way to Go Home': 'Show me the way to get a home/I'm tired of living in a tent/I placed a little order 'bout two years ago/But they ain't got no cement.'

When the Chifley government decided to review all the licences issued for asbestos importation in consequence of the dollar position, both Hardie and Wunderlich entreated New South Wales' newly appointed minister for building materials, C. H. Matthews, to intercede on their behalf. The situation was judged serious enough for a letter to be sent directly from Labor premier James McGirr to Ben Chifley in October 1947:

> Strong representations have been made by the industry, and the point has been stressed that supplies which have now been arranged from Canada will now be diverted into foreign channels where there are heavy demands, and that as a consequences it may be extremely difficult to obtain further quotes. I am advised that both Hardie & Co and Wunderlich Ltd ... have agents abroad trying to locate fibre but with very little success.

Australian asbestos production reached a record 191 million square feet in 1946–47, then could not get beyond 177, 167 and 171 million in the next three years; the industry was operating for much of that time, despite overwhelming demand, at half its rated capacity. And although commonwealth price control was relinquished in September 1948, the industry would need for some years to apply to state authorities for permission to raise prices.

Both Thyne Reid, in Europe, and Ted Heath, in North America, made extensive tours of companies and laboratories exploring asbestos substitutes. History could have been very different had their investigations borne fruit. Slag wool was used experimentally in flat sheets for a time at Camellia, and conference of executives there in November 1947 learned from Reid that 'there appeared little prospect of increased supplies of asbestos, and it is possible that the position may become worse', countervailed slightly by word that 'Cape Asbestos were expanding and might be able to supply 2000 tons per year of amosite'. Relief, in fact, was at hand. What appears to be Cape's very first invoice to Hardie—levied by Egnep Pty Ltd on 19 June 1948 for 1000 100lb bags of amosite, and stamped by customs when it arrived in Perth on the *SS Tournai*—survives among a collection of artefacts from Rivervale at the Mitchell Library. Someone thought it marked the beginning of something important—and they were right.

It was the start of a beautiful friendship, secured in December 1948 when Hardie acquired its first shares in Cape 'as a gesture of goodwill'. The stake would swell to half a million shares over the next decade. The relationship may have run even deeper, for in that time as many as eighteen investors with the surname Reid appeared on the Cape register. It was certainly struck at a most opportune moment. In January 1949, the asbestos market was disrupted in unprecedented fashion by the Montreal newspaper *Le Devoir*. A series of tragic and graphic reports by Burton le Doux of working conditions in the mines of the Quebec Asbestos Corporation, owned by the Philip Carey Manufacturing Company of the US, began with the headline: 'Asbestosis at East Broughton—a village of 3000 suffocated by dust'. Le Doux accused the company of running a 'charnel house', the government of condoning 'criminal negligence', and local doctors of collaboration. 'If we told the workmen … that they were affected by asbestosis,' one said, 'it would cost the company too much money'. This, it has since emerged, was quite common practice in North America. A New Jersey attorney would later testify to a 1942 conversation in which Johns-Manville's Vandivar Brown spoke of the policy with the utmost enthusiasm: 'Yes, we save a lot of money that way.' But it was news to unions: award negotiations collapsed, precipitating strikes at Asbestos and Thetford Mines that crippled the industry for five months. Hardie board papers show that its immediate response was to place an additional order for 7000 tons of amosite from Cape; John Proud paid a four-month visit from July 1949.

By 1950, as much asbestos was coming to Australia from South Africa as from Canada. And by the mid-1950s, about a third of Australia's imported asbestos was amosite from Cape — an extremely high proportion, considering that chrysotile has tradition-ally represented 95 per cent of the world industry. The burgeoning relationship between Hardie and Cape guaranteed the fulfilment of Thyne Reid's prophecy. After buying one small quantity of Wittenoom's 'WA blue' for what the board called 'policy reasons' — probably to check its quality — Hardie scorned it. Australia's biggest user of asbestos, controlling 70 per cent of the market for asbestos-containing products, would not deal with Australia's newest mine.

The fact is that, even with generous freight subsidies and housing grants from the West Australian government, Australian Blue Asbestos was uncompetitive on price. The reason for this was simple. Cape's labour was dirt cheap and docile. There was also a ready supply of women for the gruelling and extremely dangerous custom of cobbing the ore — beating it from the ironstone with flat-faced hammers, and separating long fibres from short — which improved the economics of processing. Australian Blue Asbestos's workers, though mostly migrants, were paid over the odds to entice them to their remote destination, and in the enervating heat usually lasted only so long as it took them to save some money. When Brown and King pitched their product at Hardie again in November

1952, one imagines that the rebuff they were issued gave Thyne Reid some satisfaction. Jonah Adamson shared his contempt for CSR. When King rang to ask for some amosite to examine 'in the interests of science' at his company's Alexandria works, Adamson dismissed him: 'I told him it was a waste of time sending it to him since we considered Asbestos Products to be technically incompetent.'

CSR wasn't finished yet. In May 1953, Hardie received a direct approach from the West Australian government urging them to use WA Blue. Reid, Adamson and Proud protested to Robert Menzies' national development minister William Spooner that they should not have CSR's fibre foisted on them (Hardie had, after all, put £1000 toward the Liberal Party's successful 1949 election campaign). Then, in February 1954, came a bombshell. Hardie directors learned that asbestos fibre was to be subject of a Tariff Board inquiry. They resolved to 'oppose this to the fullest extent'. The plant journal *Camellia News* told Hardie workers very clearly where their loyalties lay:

INCREASED COSTS OF HOUSING
New Tariff imposes
Additional burden on nation's future homebuilders

These are the newspaper headlines we could expect to read if a famous Australian company achieves its aim at a Tariff Board inquiry now being heard.

The famous company is the Colonial Sugar Refining Co Ltd and they're up for tariff on asbestos.

They are virtually asking the Australian man in the street—you and me and everyone who buys 'Fibrolite' products—to subsidise an asbestos mine which never has been and never will be a paying proposition.

The inquiry's proceedings, hearings for which were held at Dalton House in Pitt Street, were lengthy, detailed and technical. CSR proposed that Australian Blue Asbestos be protected by a 40 per cent duty on imported foreign fibre, which at the time ran to about 30,000 tons per annum, with the only concession that there would be no duty levied on companies using WA Blue to the extent of 15 per cent of their total usage. But it was also extremely personal. The Tariff Board noted: 'As a result of antagonisms which had arisen, there was little evidence of a willingness to compromise and what, in easier circumstances, might have been minor points of difference, were contested with a vehemence more appropriate to major points.' When Proud gave evidence that WA Blue was at the time up to three times as expensive as amosite, Adamson deplored Wittenoom as an 'ill-advised mining speculation' and the 'careless expenditure of £2 million'. He insisted:

> While ... every source of locally produced asbestos has been thoroughly investigated by us, it has always been our policy that local operations to produce asbestos must be on an economic basis in competition with world prices. The company has always sought to secure the cheapest source of raw material consistent with quality.

The clinching argument, however, was probably the dark consequence for costs in the housing market at which Hardie hinted. The report was not tabled in parliament until September 1955, but it utterly vindicated Hardie's position, calling the extra cost 'unjustified' and the protective duty 'coercive':

> Allowing for the possibility that some of the hostility stemmed from earlier discussions between the parties involved, the Board believe that the largest user of asbestos in Australia would not reject the opportunity of an assured supply of portion of its requirements without having given serious consideration to the long and short-term advantages and disadvantages.

Hardie, in fact, had not rejected the opportunity out of hand. Mysteriously, something shifted in the relations between Hardie and CSR between an extraordinary general meeting of Hardie shareholders in November 1955, at which Thyne perfunctorily dismissed WA Blue, and about a year later when Hardie undertook to buy it.

The deal's precise terms have not come to light, but Hardie made the most of its position of strength. CSR agreed to vacate the fibre-cement market in return for Hardie buying a minimum quantity of WA Blue every year at what was very probably a considerably reduced price. It was an ignominious check on CSR's building-products ambitions, and merely prolonged the life of a marginal mine that still was only profitable for two years of its lifespan; Hardie seem to have found the arrangements most advantageous, buying comfortably in excess of the minimum for the duration of the contract, to a total 50,000 tons. The stain of Wittenoom on CSR will probably prove indelible. It has even insinuated itself even into the lines of one of Midnight Oil's most famous songs, *Blue Sky Mine*: 'And if you blue sky mining company won't come to my rescue/If the sugar refining company won't save me/Who's gonna save me?' Yet it's seldom noted just how much of this crocidolite found its way into Australian homes and hearths.

6

'We don't have to worry about that one any more'

'When Pliny referred to asbestos as "the funeral dress of kings", he failed to consider the practical application of asbestos to the needs of modern industry. For James Hardie Asbestos Ltd—dynamic and very much among the living—this fabulous stone, which once set on fire could not be quenched, has proved a veritable money spinner. James Hardie Asbestos, exploiting asbestos to the seams, turns out an earnings fabric, silken lustred, rich in profits, crusted with bonus issues and powerful through and through with reserves backing.'
—'Wild Cat' of *The Bulletin*, July 1961

ASBESTOS PROTECTED THE BURNING BROOMSTICK in the *Wizard of Oz* and provided the artificial snow in *Citizen Kane*, but by the end of the Second World War had long ceased being exotic. In Australia, in fact, it was fast coming into its own. After the fibre bottleneck cleared in the early 1950s, the market seemed unappeasable. From the mid-1950s to the mid-1960s, fibre imports grew almost three-fold, and as many as six in 10 houses were being clad in fibro. In a hot land, it did not retain heat. In a big land, it was light and easy to transport. In a land where Jack was allegedly as good as his master, it was as suitable for handsome California bungalows as it was for working men's cottages. More important even than its fire resistance was its durability. For Fibrolite, James Hardie adopted the motif of Father Time wielding a scythe and cradling a globe, while its advertising stressed not its novelty but its antiquity:

FIBROLITE is made on a laminated process, being built up, layer upon layer, like the leaves of a book. Each of these layers is strongly and rigidly reinforced throughout with the long, indestructible Asbestos fibre, and are finally united into one homogenous, rock-like mass — forming a dense sheet of great tensile strength and durability.

ASBESTOS is the most remarkable mineral known to science. It is older than any life on earth. Found in massive serpentine rock, it is heavy and dense as marble in its crude state, yet as light as thistledown when treated mechanically. It is immune to fire, unaffected by time, impervious to moisture, and possesses a remarkably high tensile strength.

PORTLAND CEMENT dates back to the time of the early Romans. Besides being insoluble, indestructible and weather and fire resisting, it possesses the peculiar property of increasing in toughness and strength upon exposure to the elements. Its crystallising or setting action continues for many years, ensuring permanent durability.

Formidable but friendly Fibrolite suited the get-ahead mentality of the times, when architect design and professional construction was yet to become the rule, and *Australian House and Garden* was preaching that 'any amateur handyman who has ever put a bookcase together, built a shed, knocked up a fence or made a dog kennel is capable of building a home'. The proletarian suburbs of Sydney and Perth swelled into fibro oceans; for the hero of John O'Grady's *They're A Weird Mob*, a fibro shed was the culmination of his sub-urban idyll. In Melbourne, Brisbane and Adelaide, fibro was har-nessed mainly for weekenders and outbuildings. Barry Humphries, whose builder father himself hammered together a fibro retreat, recalled:

The outskirts of Melbourne … pullulated with low-cost fibro construction. Not just working men's houses, but garages, sheds, parades of shops, and in the Dandenong range — soon to be smothered in stag-horn ferns and morning glory — the ubiquitous Devonshire Tea Room. By painting the strapwork black in contrast to the cream or off-white exterior walls, a bogus half-timbered look was often attempted, investing the team rooms and cafes of Melbourne's more picturesque environs with an Elizabethan or olde worlde look.

Gough and Margaret Whitlam lived in a fibro home. The wealthy retailer Henry Marcus Clark built his rambling Blue Mountains mansion from fibro. For some, it was even a symbol of hope. Robin Boyd chose fibro for his House of Tomorrow at the 1949 Melbourne Modern Home Exhibition, and designed a celebrated fibro mansion in Eltham in 1960 as an antidote to the condition he diagnosed in his bestseller of that year as *The Australian Ugliness*. Fibro's quality was also improved by a new process called autoclaving, in which finely ground silica was added and the sheets steam-cured in giant cylinders called autoclaves: a chemical reaction between the silica and the free lime in the cement produced much greater stability. There were also more and better concessions to fashion. 'Asbestos cement goes glamorous,' promised the headline in *Australian Home Journal* in January 1960: 'With the new types of asbestos cement on the market, every room in the home can look like a picture out of a glossy magazine.' Channel Seven's *Your Home* gave away a fibro home in Forestville to a lucky viewer in January 1961; Channel Nine's *Pick-a-Box* presented a fibro home in Macksville to its champion Frank Partridge three years later.

In addition to its new residential popularity, asbestos maintained its industrial applications. Fibre-cement roofed Woolworths's giant Silverwater warehouse, the Blacktown bowling centre, the Royal Agricultural Hall at Sydney's showgrounds, and the Housing Commission Flats at Redfern. Twenty-three acres of sheets prevented evaporation at Geraldton's Wicherina Reservoir; thousands of yards of panels composed the fences of the Commonwealth Games Village in Perth. Post-war industrialisation also opened new avenues for expansion in insulation. Giant refineries were equipped: Anglo-Iranian at Kwinana, Vacuum Oil in Altona, Caltex at Kurnell. Then came a golden era of power-station construction, especially in New South Wales: Wangi Point and Wallerawang, then Vales Point and Munmorah, were larded with '85 per cent Magnesia' and 'K-Lite'. 'As the years race by, the insulation business becomes bigger and brighter,' reported *Camellia News* in December 1957. 'Generally speaking in an expanding country such as ours the demand for electricity becomes greater and greater and since insulation is so closely tied to power generation there is an assured market in this field.'

Pipe plants were opened at Meeandah in Queensland, Elizabeth in South Australia and Penrose in New Zealand; a challenge in pipes by a joint venture of Wunderlich and Humes in Victoria was warded off, acquired and closed. Hardie moved to market leadership in brakes by acquiring Better Brakes in January 1959; the company had been a major user of Hardiebestos brake lining, but its founders, Noel Leddin and Sir John Storey, had lately died. Its assets were thirty months later assigned to a joint venture with Turner & Newall called Hardie-Ferodo, which came to dominate the trade. Relations had also thawed sufficiently with CSR for the companies to pool their insulation business in September 1964 as Hardie-BI. It was, in short, a glorious time to be in business: contented workers, quiescent unions, and expanding markets for a product of remarkable ubiquity.

POST-WAR INDUSTRIALISATION had entirely different ramifications for worker health. More manufacturing meant more fumes, more toxins and more illness. Unfortunately for authorities, it seldom meant more inspections, more powers or more resources. Asbestosis, as we have seen, was acknowledged to be a problem from the 1930s onwards. The first recommendation that workers be informed of its risks seems to have been issued as early as December 1939 by Dr Douglas Shiels in the journal *Health Bulletin*. Shiels, medical officer for industrial hygiene in Victoria's health department, was also way ahead of his time in realising that the risk was not simply to those manufacturing products from asbestos, but also to those using them. In October 1943, for instance, his division issued explicit advice to the Department of the Navy with regard to its Garden Island shipyard at Williamstown:

> There is no doubt that the inhalation of asbestos dust may produce damage to the lungs, the condition being known as 'asbestosis'. This

condition, which may be incapacitating, may take years to develop, the time required, depending among other factors on the concentration of dust in the air breathed, usually 7-12 years … Cases have occurred within as little as one and a half years.

Shiels, however, was inhibited by the inexactness of knowledge, the imprecision of his testing instrumentation, and not least by the rigidity of entrenched interests. Although tests he performed at Williamstown in January 1944 found that 'in certain cases the concentrations of asbestos dust in the air was above that which could be regarded as a safe limit for continuous exposure', he was finally persuaded that a policy of cutting asbestos in the open air should mitigate its effects—a judgement which would prove too conservative. Likewise when he toured Yallourn power station six months later, he was thwarted by a combination of apathy and intransigence. His recommendation of water sprays for dust suppression, use of respirators in dusty corners, and periodic medical examinations did not take root. Victoria's State Electricity Commission claimed that workers disliked the spray, and preferred 'their old method of mutton cloth over the mouth and nose', while medical examination was 'a matter for the employees themselves'. The commission's attitude was summed up by a June 1945 memo from a senior official to Yallourn's manager: 'My personal view is that this bogey was raised only in the context of getting working hours reduced.'

At James Hardie, the bogey was scarcely raised at all. One radiological survey was carried out during World War II and produced evidence of 'seven doubtful cases', but it could be given little weight because the procedure was voluntary and it was noted that there was 'a tendency for the older employees not to report for examination'. In the late 1940s, Camellia's factory manager Jock Henderson introduced a policy of rotating workers through different areas. After a few years in a dust-heavy role, like mixing, an employee could expect a period in a cleaner part of the factory, like stacking. Otherwise, efforts to reduce manual involvement in processes were desultory; indeed, at Camellia, Brooklyn and Rivervale they had remained essentially unchanged since the 1920s. As cement arrived by rail wagon and truck, bags of fibre were manhandled by the 'asbestos gang' to disintegrators. The asbestos was then mixed and shovelled into pug or hammer mills, and blown through ducts by the 'blower men' into storage hoppers called 'fibre rooms'. Raked into barrows for weighing, it was wheeled on trolleys to the 'tide mill' where water, cement and silica were added. This liquid mix was fed by gravity to the agitator then laid on the felt belts of the Hatschek sheet-making machine, where water was removed by filtration and suction, and the sheets stacked and trimmed; pipes were manufactured by wrapping the flat sheet round a collapsible mandrel. Dry areas of the process — particularly manhandling, shovelling and mixing — were of a particular dusty deadliness.

Such supervision as existed was light. When Cecil Roberts and Harvey Whaite of the division of industrial hygiene in New South Wales undertook a survey of workers at Hardie, Wunderlich and Asbestos Products (CSR) in 1952, their results were suggestive. While only nine asbetotics were identified among 175 surveyed, the case rate was one in nine for those who had been employed more than five years, and another twenty-two workers were found to be suffering respiratory illnesses like bronchitis and tuberculosis. The authors also warned that dry-area dust concentrations 'were high enough to lead inevitably to the development of asbestosis, provided the employees remain long enough in these particular jobs'. The effort, however, as would become customary, was wasted. Changes of personnel at the department ensured that these findings were not shared with Hardie for another four years, when they were published in the *Journal of Industrial Hygiene*. Under no pressure to change, Hardie did not.

It was possible, nonetheless, to make a difference, and at least one man tried. West Australian Neil Gilbert had a personal interest in pneumoconiosis. His father, a gold miner on Kalgoorlie, had died of silicosis; Gilbert himself started his working career in the mines, and as a labourer and rigger for Lake View & Star. He decided to bring his pregnant wife and engineering degree east in 1951, and after helping design a silica grinding plant at Camellia was posted to Brooklyn to do the same. When he was appointed deputy to factory manager Ashby Hooper in August 1954, he had a simple idea. Even if the exact risk of the dust was unclear, why not do the best you could?

Gilbert was dissatisfied with the needless labour-intensity of Brooklyn's processes. He introduced an automatic mixer and a skip hoist under negative pressure with a low opening where the bags were opened, and eliminated the reselling of bags, which had been widely used for fruit and vegetables at the Victoria Market. He had spike rollers installed on conveyor belts; he reduced numbers of workers manning the Hatschek machines, and insisted on wet trimming; he redesigned two of the three Mazza pipemaking machines with extractors at every point that dust might escape; and he modified the plant's four dust collectors. At times, he was confounded. The Federated Miscellaneous Workers Union would not hear of air-wash masks in the blow room because it would incommode smokers. On other occasions, he found it difficult to convey urgency. 'You had to make sure people didn't just say, 'Oh, it's only a little leak',' says Gilbert. 'And unfortunately that did happen.' There were always complications. Hardie was proud, for example, of its efforts to assimilate new European migrants. The first were hired at Brooklyn in August 1949; within three years there were fifty there; within a decade, they would be a majority. 'We used to meet the boats offering them jobs,' Gilbert recalls. 'We had a stall down there [at Port Melbourne]. That's how short of labour we were in those days. And these people wanted to work, and would work very hard.' Yet barely a thought was given to instructing them in safety in general, or asbestos in particular: 'Some of them couldn't count. A lot of them couldn't talk English.' In retrospect, Gilbert has few illusions:

> I was just an engineer. I got interested really. I read whatever I could get a hold of, so I knew asbestosis was a problem — perhaps not as bad as silicosis, but it was bad enough. The problem for us was that there were very few dust reduction systems round. We really had to design our own. And some parts of the process we never got right. For instance, we never worked out how to get dust out of the accumulation bags [in the dust collectors]. We'd mask the men before they went in, but their

clothes would always be covered with dust. At the time we thought our dust control was pretty good. In hindsight, it was only fair, and not as good as it should have been. But we did try.

Nonetheless, Gilbert was proud of the plant, and when he succeeded Hooper as factory manager in November 1956 thought it ahead of the curve.

At odd times someone would appear from the state government and take [dust] readings … Then we'd be told the count was up or down, and they'd disappear for another two or three years. People say now that the department was telling us we should do this and we should do that. It's absolute cock. They came and went because that was what they were paid to do. What they told us was always in passing, like: 'It's very dusty down there, you should have a look'. And we usually did.

If anything, in fact, Gilbert's efforts show up because of their isolation. If it was in the power of an alert, concerned manager to take remedial steps, it was in the power of the company. But while Gilbert says he enjoyed the support of Frank Page, neither the Reid brothers nor managing director Adamson was greatly exercised by dust. When Gilbert was promoted to succeed Lester Henning at Camellia in February 1965, he was surprised to find how backward the plant was compared to Brooklyn: 'They still had their manual systems and their blow rooms. No one was wearing airwash masks. I'd been to factory managers' conferences at Camellia, but I'd not been through the plant for a long time and there was a lot of cleaning up to be done.' In general, too, opportunities to reduce asbestos use were overlooked. In the late 1950s, for example, Page asked Gilbert to develop a water-cured board in which half the usual asbestos was replaced by cellulose pulp and autoclaved. Using only five-grade chrysotile — the cheapest asbestos variant — it became the hugely successful Hardiflex.

We got the asbestos down from 27 per cent to 15 per cent, and I said to the production manager, Jim Rhys-Jones: 'Look, I think we can get the asbestos down further.' He said: 'No, don't. I have to buy a certain amount of five-grade asbestos to get the three-grade for the pipes.' So we kept it at 15 per cent. Now I wasn't that upset at the time, and I could see his point. But it was almost twenty years before they began reducing the asbestos in the board, and it could have happened much earlier.

Much else could have happened earlier besides. When a company is making money, the future always seems a far-off place. But just occasionally there was a glimmer of the health crisis that asbestos would become. In September 1953, Dr Douglas Shiels commissioned a radiological survey of workers in all the 'dusty trades', including asbestos, which he rated 'one of the most dangerous'—preliminary investigations had revealed nine cases of asbestosis in fifty workers. Shiels set one of his ablest men on the case, Dr Leslie Gordon Thomas, whose results were foreshadowed in *The Age* in January 1956:

> The survey found a disturbingly high incidence of asbestosis among workers regularly handling asbestos. A third of the asbestos workers showed signs of development of the disease … Dr Thomas said some of the stricken workers in advanced stages of the disease were in a pitiful condition. They were unable to continue working and the slightest effort made them gasp for breath.

Thomas' seminal paper 'Pneumonokoniosis in Victoria' in the *Medical Journal of Australia* the following year, still the most thorough of its kind, encompassing 3823 workers from stokers to spray painters, should have filled readers with foreboding. A third of the 300 asbestos workers examined had asbestos bodies in their sputum; 15 per cent showed lung damage on X-rays. Thomas also reiterated Shiels' view that this 'grave threat to life and health' was not confined to those who handled asbestos in its raw state, but anyone 'sawing, cutting and finishing any product containing asbestos—for example brake linings, asbestos sheeting and various insulating materials'. Asbestosis in Australia, Thomas added, should be compensable:

When this survey started, eight cases of asbestosis had been reported and the disease was regarded as a rarity. It will be seen from the figures that the incidence of the disease is far too high. In addition to those found in the investigation, there must be many older folk suffering from the complaint in whom it has not been diagnosed, and who are incapacitated and very poorly off financially, and should be receiving adequate compensation.

Stringent regulations on the asbestos industry drafted in November 1955, however, were never gazetted, despite obtaining Health Commission approval, and the impetus for reform petered out when Shiels retired in July 1956. His successor, Allen Christophers, had been overseas during the survey, and did not regard asbestos with the same urgency; likewise Thomas's successor, Jim Milne.

It is known that Jock Reid distributed copies of the Thomas report among senior executives because Ashby Hooper forwarded one to Page with a dismissive covering note: 'I do not think there is anything in this which we do not already know.' When Jock Reid himself sent the report to a Turner & Newall executive, he referred to 'the supposed danger of asbestos dust', and generally asserted that victims of asbestosis were primarily culpable for their own condition: 'We have always been conscious of the possible risks in our own works and have taken what steps we could to minimise any danger to men working in the vicinity. The provision of masks and other protective methods fall down to a very large extent due to the refusal of the men to wear them.' What happened once the product left the factory, moreover, was still less his concern. As for compensation, that was to be resisted at all costs.

Just over fifteen years after the thwarted 'widow Jones', compensation again reared its potentially expensive head. The Anti-Tuberculosis Association's mobile X-ray unit paid its annual visit to Camellia in April 1955, and detected a case of asbestosis in an insulation worker called Weyman. Then two other workers, Percy Leabon, also in insulation, and F. M. Kirchen, in the tide mills, were also diagnosed. Leabon, from Wentworthville, became the first to take action. He had spent thirteen years at Hardie, the last seven filling bags of asbestos that had collected against the sleeves of its giant blowers, where the dust was so thick that 'sometimes you could not see a hand before you'. Leabon had noticed his declining health: accustomed to cycling to work, he began struggling to ascend upgrades. When his doctor informed the company that Leabon was 'dusted', he was given a new job making paper clips. But when Leabon reached the age of sixty-five in July 1955, executive Athol Higgins was sent to see him. 'It is the usual thing to put men off at sixty-five,' Higgins reminded him. 'If it comes to retiring,' Leabon replied, 'you can have the pleasure of putting me off'. After serving his three weeks' notice, Leabon ended up at home, increasingly incapacitated. He could potter round the garden, but the exertion of using a spade made him cough violently and even vomit. When a doctor confirmed that he was suffering 'fibrosis of the lungs, which is caused by the inhalation of asbestos dust', he decided to file a claim for workers' compensation.

Hardie and its insurer, Manufacturers Mutual, fought the claim tooth and nail. They asserted that because Leabon had been capable of making paperclips — although 'not maintaining the daily quota ordinarily expected of him' — he could not be considered totally incapacitated. Hardie's counsel, Monahan, insisted: 'We take the stand we are not liable and if we can escape liability on any ground without unfairness to the applicant, we are entitled to do it.' He pressed a doctor from Westmead Hospital to agree that 'idleness isn't the best thing for a man in Mr Leabon's condition, is it?'

Doctor: He has got a condition which is usually progressive and they have to live within their capabilities. They are not capable of doing very much.

Monahan: I don't mean that he could do heavy work, but he would be better off working within his capabilities than being idle.

Doctor: Only insofar as anybody is better off occupied if they are able to be.

Monahan: His general health would be better?

Doctor: I don't think it would influence the chest condition.

Under cross-examination by Leabon's counsel, Jenkins, MMI's medical officer Dr Bert Hughes insisted that Leabon should still be capable of work if he just showed a bit of spunk.

Jenkins: Might I put this to you, that the most desirable thing that could happen so far as employment would be concerned would be if he were picked up at his door in a car and delivered to a place at work and then brought back at night in a car?

Hughes: That would be very nice. I would like that myself ... There are plenty of means of transport that are easy without being picked up at the door in a car.

Jenkins: Suppose he were to go into town and get a job, when he had to negotiate the steps of Wynyard station that wouldn't be an easy task for him, would it?

Hughes: No. It is possible he might be able to do that slowly.

Sixteen years since the widow Jones had tried and failed, asbestosis gained a modest legal recognition. Justice Conybeare found in April 1956 that Leabon had 'sustained injury by contracting the diseases of asbestosis in the course of his employment, and to which the conditions of his employment were a contributing factor'. He dismissed the arguments of Hardie and MMI: although Leabon 'might have some small residual capacity for work', it was 'so insignificant as to be negligible'. The award was a paltry £11 a week, plus medical expenses and costs, but he'd started something. Kirchen made his own claim and also received a small pension; Weyman, who it was noted suffered 'a fair degree of disability', was given a job as a storeman. MMI began supervising another series of X-rays, and the division of Industrial Hygiene came to follow up their 1952 survey. Between October 1956 and June 1957, a further 200 workers at Camellia were examined, and extensive dust counts taken by midget impinger.

Again, the results were suggestive rather than conclusive. Six workers were sent for further tests to Maurice Joseph, a respiratory physician at Royal Prince Alfred Hospital, all of whom proved to be suffering from asbestosis ranging from 'very slight' to 'marked'. But such testing, given the dose dependency and latency period of asbestosis, was of limited efficacy, because two-thirds of the workers had been at Camellia less than five years, and because it revealed little about the effects of their current exposure. The midget impinger, too, a four-cylinder rotary hand-pump drawing air through a 1mm nozzle, was a notoriously imprecise measuring instrument. It could not, for instance, differentiate between asbestos and other dusts, and all it could demonstrate here was that not much had changed in five years. The department's Alan Bell largely reissued the warnings of five years earlier: 'The manual handling of asbestos if carried out for any appreciable time is potentially dangerous. I consider that in many instances its handling can be either eliminated or the amount considerably reduced.'

The 1950s, then, were an opportunity for both Hardie and its bureaucratic scrutineers—an opportunity mostly squandered. With the honourable if partial exception of the endeavours at Brooklyn, such efforts as were made to remediate the dust hazard through ventilation and mechanisation barely kept pace with the growth of the company.

Justice Curtis of the Dust Diseases Tribunal has summarised as follows:

> The dangers were real and grave. Notwithstanding this knowledge it is also apparent that at the time ... little was done to limit such inhalation. It seems to me that the explanation for this state of affairs is to be found not only in the want of care by employers in obtaining and disseminating information but also in the nature of the risk. Though the risk was real and grave it was not immediate; it did not call attention to itself as did risks posed by more immediate dangers such as fire, unguarded machines, defective scaffolding and the like. The liability of employers was triggered because the risk was not far-fetched or fanciful, but in human terms it may have been seen as improbable or remote. The men on site remained ignorant of the risks and the need for caution in working with asbestos products. It was the duty of James Hardie to address these perceptions.

Why did it not? It is empty rhetoric to call Hardie's directors and senior officers 'evil'; they were not even notably malign. They were limited men who thought they knew best. Safety in the workplace was considered a matter for foremen. For all its paternalism in other respects, in fact, 'occupational hazard' was at Hardie a very meaningful phrase. At Camellia in 1954, for example, there were no fewer than 129 work accidents—one in seven employees lost time due to injury. The July 1955 edition of *Camellia News* sported what would prove an eerily prophetic slogan: 'Give a hazard enough time and it will present you with an accident'. But Hardie, a company rich in engineers from Thyne Reid down, sought engineering solutions that minimised commercial disruption, even where human beings were concerned. The practice of rotating workers through different areas, for instance, bespoke a mechanistic view of the challenge, in which the worker was scarcely differentiated from other components inclined to wear and tear.

The attitudes also evoke the times. It was such a hearty, heady period of opportunity. No wonder it was felt that those problems which couldn't be out-engineered could be outlasted—like Percy Leabon. When he died in November 1959, his wife made a claim for a lump-sum allotment, alleging that asbestosis was a contributory factor in his death. Then she died, too, and the matter lapsed. When news of her death reached him, Hardie's personnel manager Don McDonald was observed to move the Leabon file to the back of his filing cabinet. 'We don't have to worry about that one any more,' he said.

7

'What are we going to do with you?'

'In the light of our recent investigations, there is no doubt that asbestosis is very common in the industry, that it helps develop much more quickly than silicosis, and that once established is a killer of the most vicious type. We have found that 30 per cent of those working in raw asbestos have some stigmata of the disease.'
—Dr Gordon Thomas, *Safety News*, March 1962

'Staff: I want to make special reference to the loyalty and efforts of the executives and employees throughout the group. They have, in this quite difficult year, brought to their work enthusiasm and skill which have produced the results you have before you. They constitute a major asset of the Company not appearing in the Balance Sheet. I know you will wish to join with me in thanking them.'
—Thyne Reid in the 1963 James Hardie Asbestos annual report

THE TWENTIETH CENTURY'S gravest industrial disasters—the like of Seveso, Aberfan, Minimata Bay and Bhopal—can be dated to a shattering instant when normality was overthrown or menace was revealed. The toll wrought by asbestos, however, accreted stealthily, over decades, not always at the same rate, and not without resistance. If James Hardie's objectives were sometimes barely fulfilled and its determination fluctuated, an increasing amount of its management time in the 1960s was devoted to dust emissions and worker welfare. Having tried essentially to adapt the employees to the dust, Hardie began for the first time to try and adapt the dust to the employees.

There is no doubt that Hardie's safety standards, even on a conservative reading of the epidemiological evidence regarding asbestosis, fell badly behind the scale and scope of its business in the 1950s. Such medical attention, hygiene surveillance and engineering control as there was fell to factory managers—and, with the partial exception of Neil Gilbert at Brooklyn, that was little. Camellia, a plant with almost 1000 workers, did not even have a resident medical practitioner: between weekly clinics by Dr Darcy Croll, whose presence was announced by the appearance of his Rolls-Royce in the car park around morning teatime on Wednesday, first aid was dispensed by an ex-army nurse, Sister Herd.

The safety officer's duties were restricted to cleaning up oil spills and keeping walkways clear: dust was not part of his responsibility. When Peter Russell took the job in November 1960, he had no occupational health and safety background. He had joined Hardie twelve years earlier as a cadet chemical engineer with three other young men, Rex Torzillo, Warwick Lane and Clyde Waugh, reporting to senior chemists Ian Archibald and Jack Simpson. Russell's only real brush with asbestosis had been when a 'dusted' employee, Jack Hamilton, had been made a general assistant in his laboratory as respite from the tide mills. Prior to his appointment as safety officer by personnel director Tom Tidey, he had been factory superintendent in the insulation section of Camellia.

Tidey wanted to give safety a profile. He believed that dust was Camellia's 'most pressing problem', and promised Russell his support. The sum total of Russell's background information on asbestos and health was contained in the 'dust file'—a slim manila folder that he shared with personnel manager Don McDonald consisting essentially of the two health department surveys, articles about hazardous materials by Harry Whaite and Bert Hughes, and information about the staff rotation policy: 'It was certainly not a very voluminous file because dust was something we didn't want to hear about'. Russell was undeterred. To steep himself in asbestos' health risks, he instead became a regular at the Mitchell Library in Macquarie Street: 'It was a friendly place in those days. You would thread your way past groups and individuals squatting on the vast step area. You got to know the cloak attendant on a first-name basis and the staff inside were all familiar faces.' It was here that he became probably the first person at Hardie to learn of mesothelioma, from Wagner's work in the *British Journal of Industrial Medicine*.

Tidey had warned Russell to expect to 'encounter resistance', and it wasn't merely at Hardie. His reception by Harry Whaite and Alan Bell at the health department was chill: 'They basically showed me where their bookshelves were then went into a huddle in another part of the open plan research area. They could not have been less helpful and I did not stay long.' When he confided to the departmental inspector Trevor Jones that the authorities did not seem 'up to speed with the asbestos problem', he was disturbed by Jones' reply: 'We consider you the experts in that area.'

The scale of his challenge was made apparent by his first monitoring efforts early the following year. Russell's midget impinger readings found that Camellia was spectacularly non-compliant even with the 23-year-old Dreessen Standard, achieving readings as high as forty million particles per cubic foot in areas where 'men work continuously in the conditions without wearing masks'. Those in the personnel office 200 metres away would regularly telephone the works to complain about 'snowstorm conditions'. 'A dust situation could be reduced one day,' Russell recalls, 'but would reappear overnight.' It was not unknown to receive complaints from the local bowls club about dust settling on their greens, and Russell was told that dust readings in excess of 5mppcf had been detected at distances up to two miles from the plant: 'At the time I was taken aback to learn of that information, I can recall saying to Trevor Jones ... that surely that would be nuisance dust or road movement. However, he said, "No — it is asbestos dust".'

Russell's initial report in May 1961 to what would be called the dust control committee, chaired by the branch manager, Alan Woodford, and including Tidey, was the first enunciation of a coherent strategy to reduce dust rather than merely mitigate its effects. The rotation policy for workers performing dusty tasks on which Hardie had relied, Russell explained, was a waste of time:

This time limit in dusty areas is not the answer and creates problems in labour movement and administration. The aim is, of course, to use methods and equipment which do not create dust. This is obviously not always practical and so once having created the nuisance we must check it to a safe level by suitable exhaust ventilation. The lungs must be guarded by refusing to allow contaminated air to be inhaled. Overseas, asbestos dust is classified as one of the most dangerous of industrial poisons and regulations require ventilation equipment associated with asbestos dust removal to be maintained under six monthly certification.

When Tidey died suddenly of a heart attack two months later, however, Russell lost an important champion. The role of personnel director was not filled until the following year; and when it was, Ted Pysden, formerly a manager at an alpine holiday lodge at Thredbo of which Thyne Reid was a director, 'didn't have the same sort of concern' with dust. Woodford was a fiercely loyal company servant. 'I remember once when a guy left Hardie-Ferodo to join a competitor,' recalls Warwick Lane. 'As far as Alan was concerned, it was as though he was a convicted felon.' Woodford was especially anxious that the Federated Miscellaneous Workers' Union not become involved.

Russell continued to tackle individual engineering problems, and made some headway. But he gradually sensed that while nobody in management 'was happy to have dust around', nor was anybody 'encouraged to create any undue concern among the workers'. He was impressed with Neil Gilbert's work, and thought the Brooklyn manager was 'on the ball'. Otherwise, he felt he was a lone voice, and took increasingly extreme steps to confront his superiors. Frank Page, for instance, was famous for his habit of walking round Camellia with his head down, avoiding eye contact. On one occasion, Russell positioned himself near the tide mills and intercepted him in order to issue the reminder that it was now a decade since health officials had asked for modifications which still had not been carried out. He also accosted Ted Heath in the canteen at Camellia and suggested that the company make contact with Gordon Smith of the School of Tropical Medicine at Sydney University. 'We don't have anything to worry about from that direction,' Heath replied. 'They value our annual grant'.

Nor did anyone seem even vaguely conscious of the company's responsibility to users. In a Johns-Manville publication on asbestos entitled *Miracle Fibre of the 20th Century*, Russell found a pie chart which, dividing up the mechanical, chemical, thermal and other properties of asbestos, documented its scores of applications in the field. This he took to meeting of Woodford's committee, where the application of wet treatment of fibre was discussed as a means of dust suppression. When Russell agreed that this would be a commendable initiative, all the other committee members suddenly picked up their papers and made for the door. 'Hold on, hold on,' said Russell. 'It's necessary to consider that we do not store a wet product and we do not sell a wet product.' Referring to the pie chart, Russell commented that Hardie's responsibilities did not stop once product passed out the factory gates: at the very least, users of asbestos products should be warned. One of the meeting participants commented that this was not Hardie's affair. Woodford asked Russell to stay after the meeting, complained that he was becoming an embarrassment, and finally sighed: 'We don't know what we're going to do with you.'

The company seemed intent on leaving asbestosis to Don McDonald, who would organise such compensation as was deemed necessary, and would also attend funerals. He would issue periodic updates. In February 1962, he noted twenty cases with three deaths; by March 1964, this had become twenty-three cases, and five deaths. These, of course, were only those incidences brought to Hardie's attention. No effort was made to survey former employees, or to ascertain the degree of awareness among existing workers. Russell's frustration gave way to feelings of futility; he agrees he 'could have been obsessed or a bit even paranoid about the problem'. His contemporary Lane recalls: 'Poor old Peter, he took it very seriously, took it to heart. I got the impression that all reports on dust circulated around the senior managers, but that when they saw the word "dust", they passed it onto the safety officer.'

Russell decided to have one last try. In November 1964, he

prepared what he called a 'hard hitting' report on the problem, which he addressed to Jock Reid himself. 'Millions of men, women and childen will in the future die from the harmful effects of a hazard of which they are unaware,' he began. 'We are committing genocide on a race of asbestos workers.' The alarmism was deliberate. Because Hardie was now active in so many different products — fibro, insulation, pipes, brake linings — its exposures were potentially huge. He concluded with a chilling flourish: 'My final paragraph outlined that anyone knowingly administering or allowing people to ingest a deadly material such as arsenic over a long period resulting in death would be liable to a charge of murder, and I am not prepared to be an accomplice.'

This was obviously an ultimatum — but it was never issued. After reading a draft of the report, Russell's colleague Rex Torzillo commented: 'Are you sure you're not obsessed with this problem? You give us no credit for our efforts to control the dust.' Russell hesitated, and decided to start again, choosing a tone less obviously antagonistic, recognising that Hardie had 'taken a positive approach to this dust problem' and devoted to it 'considerable effort and money'. But he was still unambiguous about asbestosis being a crisis waiting to happen:

> As knowledge of this disease becomes more widely spread, the Company could, in the future, become a 'sitting duck' for claims not only for ... asbestosis, but for cases of lung cancer and possibly heart conditions. These cases will be strengthened if the Company does not keep abreast of current knowledge and developments in this field ... It has to be realised that asbestos dust is one of the most dangerous of all industrial poisons.

Russell then took seven weeks' holiday, during which Ian Archibald dissuaded him from resigning with the offer of a less-demanding job as quality controller at Hardie-Ferodo's new Smithfield plant, and the redrafted report seems to have stopped with Woodford. Russell has wondered since if his original report would have made a difference. The answer is probably not. The tragedy's momentum was already irresistible. Torzillo and Woodford, in fact, would be part of it: both would die of mesothelioma.

OTHER REPORTS COULD BE IGNORED nearly so easily. In October 1964, Dr Irving Selikoff from the Environmental Sciences Laboratory at Mount Sinai Hospital convened a conference at New York's Waldorf-Astoria innocuously entitled 'The Biological Effects of Asbestos'. The audience was the elite of occupational health and safety, ranging from the foremost respiratory clinicians to representatives of Turner & Newall and Cape Asbestos. Selikoff's interest in asbestos had been aroused in 1953 when he had founded a medical clinic in Patterson, New Jersey, and his early clients featured a group of seventeen men from UNARCO who had been installing insulation in ships in the 1930s. As steadily they began to die, he asked UNARCO to let him analyse its employment records. They refused. Then he became really interested.

Selikoff turned instead to the relevant trade unions — who, it transpired, were already concerned about the mortality rate among their membership — and surveyed 1117 asbestos-insulation workers in New York and Newark with the help of their union. The results were literally breathtaking. Among insulators with twenty years' experience, the rate of asbestosis was 87 per cent; insulators in general faced 92 times the risk of contracting lung cancer than non-smokers. Selikoff would become the asbestos industry's public enemy number one: a charismatic, gregarious expert prepared to damn asbestos from dawn till dusk.* New Yorker's Paul Brodeur described him as a man who 'rattled off statistics about asbestos disease the way some baseball fanatics recite the batting averages of big-league ballplayers'. And, as Brodeur also noted, the proceedings of 'The Biological Effects of Asbestos' marked 'a turning point in the views held by doctors and health officials round the world', fur-

---

* A Turner & Newall internal memorandum in 1972 from research manager David Hills to director Harry Hardie sums up the industry view: 'This man Selikoff has got to be stopped somehow ... He almost needs certifying.'

nishing 'incontrovertible evidence that industrial exposure to asbestos was extremely hazardous'.

The first news of the conference reached Frank Page in January 1965, through a letter from a colleague at Turner & Newall. Page convened a meeting at Asbestos House with his opposite number from Wunderlich, and circulated a clipping from the *Australian Financial Review* about current medical opinion among Pysden and all the company's branch managers with a covering letter: 'Quite apart from any legal requirement, the Company accepts the moral obligation of ensuring that the health of its operators and staff is adequately safeguarded. To this end, the quest for better dust control and working conditions will continue. At the same time it will cooperate actively on any programme which will provide early detection of impending trouble.' He also redoubled efforts to join the industry's captive scientific body, the Asbestosis Research Council, whose importance had increased with the Selikoff findings.

Developments at Hardie that year were disturbing enough. In April, for instance, Don McDonald was advised of the death of an employee, Edward Field. Only 47, Field had spent eight years making pipes, then thirteen years as a fitter's assistant, neither of which were considered heavy dust jobs. But he had been suffering respiratory symptoms for a few years, which had latterly turned to coughing blood. An autopsy by Maurice Joseph showed 'ample evidence of pulmonary asbestosis, there being considerable thickening of the pleura, widespread diffuse fibrosis, and numerous asbestos bodies'. As McDonald wrote to Woodford, the finding was highly disconcerting:

> There had been no suggestion that he was suffering from asbestosis and because of his employment record we had not considered that possibility. Apart from humane considerations, the diagnosis is disturbing because we have not regarded the occasional exposure to which maintenance people are subjected to be significant or dangerous. Indeed, we have considered the shop to be a good place to which other people can be transferred after exposure of production.

Epidemiological evidence coming in, however, was pointing only one way: to the conclusion that asbestos was deadly at far lower concentrations than the industry had hitherto believed. A few months later, the *British Journal of Industrial Medicine* published a painstaking study by Molly Newhouse and Hilda Thompson, 'Mesothelioma of the pleura and peritoneum following exposure to asbestos in the London area'. Newhouse and Thompson had pored over the pathology records of 76 mesothelioma deaths at London Hospital between 1917 and 1964. To nobody's surprise, 31 victims had worked at Cape Asbestos' Barking works, but another eleven had simply lived within a mile of it. Of nine others who were relatives of asbestos workers, seven were women who had washed their husbands' clothes, and two were men who as children had had sisters employed by Cape.

'Urgent probe into New Killer Dust' read the front-page headline in the *Sunday Times* on 31 October 1965, which impelled a new bout of investigation into asbestos. In a briefing note to managers at Turner & Newall, managing director John Waddell would complain that this article 'set light to a powder trail, which had already been laid by the medical conferences and by the rising statistics of asbestosis from the insulation industry, with the result that MPs, trade unionists and many others with both good and bad motives began to fan the flames'. Hardie was anxious lest the powder trail wend its way to Australia. In February 1966, Thyne Reid's son John Boyd Reid, now a young executive, forwarded to Pysden a copy of the *Sunday Times* story; he had been sent it by a business contact in Tasmania who was 'concerned about this sort of information getting around Australia'. Pysden recommended containing the damage:

> The article is not new. It is merely one of many reports of world studies which have been conducted since 1935 when the association between exposure to dust and carcinoma of the lung, mesothelioma of the pleura, tumour of the bladder and uterus and other fatal complaints was first recognised ... The only preventive action is to eliminate the presence of dust. Moving employees around between 'dusty' and 'clean' jobs is not necessarily effective. Some people seem to be affected more

readily than others—the reason hasn't yet been discovered. The *Financial Review*, many state newspapers and a large number of union papers have all featured reports from time to time. If you look for them, there are about a dozen or so articles a year in Australian newspapers … The best advice you can give your friend is to (1) ignore the publicity—dust is a fact—denials merely stir up more publicity; (2) do something positive about engineering the dust hazard out of existence.

There were several reasons to be concerned about publicity. Hardie was perpetually anxious about sales. In a memo to executives soon after Pysden's, Woodford warned that customers might be driven away by 'ignorant fear of asbestosis', and complained that 'already manufacturers of competitive products in the insulation field which do not contain asbestos are using the bogey of asbestosis as a factor to boost their own sales'. There was also regulation. On 31 March 1966, Camellia received a visit from Dr Alan Bell, director of the Public Health department's division of industrial hygiene, accompanied by another doctor and a dust technician. Neil Gilbert, who had just taken over as factory manager at Camellia after his years at Brooklyn, reported to Woodford that the tone of the encounter had been unexpectedly combative:

> Dr Bell believes that the accumulating mass of evidence in regard to asbestosis and lung cancer caused by relatively short exposure to asbestos is such that more stringent regulations applying to dust control within factories handling asbestos will have to be formulated and applied by his division. He believes that these new regulations could even go as far as requiring zero asbestos dust within the factory as has been laid down in some other countries … Two points of interest which should be noted came out in this discussions, the first being that the tests would be conducted on all long term employees, not only on those that have had a known exposure to asbestos dust. Secondly, Dr Bell made it quite plain on several occasions that if we did not cooperate in the tests he would be quite prepared to force us to …
>
> Dr Bell stated that in his opinion any of our older employees who were found by the proposed tests to have lung cancer or asbestosis

would be compensation cases. He felt that sufficient evidence existed, and he would be prepared to state in court, that, in his opinion, the disease at least in part was caused by exposure to asbestos ... Dr Bell expressed concern regarding the hazard from asbestos dust which could exist to families living within three miles of the factory. Overseas evidence he believed had in some cases shown that a hardening of the chest lining had been caused by the very mild exposures to asbestos dust.

Gilberts says now that he slightly exaggerated Bell's concerns. 'That was me trying to get attention for the problem,' he says. Page encouraged him with his own memo: 'The control of dust in the Camellia area must be regarded as urgent and important. It is not possible nor is it, I feel, desirable, to try and define a safe concentration. All dust is harmful so that we must regard the best we can do as still inadequate.' At the time, in fact, Page and Pysden were reading the conference papers from 'The Biological Effects of Asbestos', which had been forwarded by Johns-Manville (Pysden complained that 'the big words are slowing down my reading speed'). And it was to this company that Gilbert turned for a solution.

In October 1966, he and Page's deputy Eric Cohen undertook an extensive tour of Johns-Manville's plants in order to study its approach to the dust hazard, in particular its elaborate health scheme and dust-count system. Gilbert thought it was impressive but improveable: 'On the surface, the scheme was very good. They weren't applying it as they thought they were, because they hadn't really convinced their factory managers it was necessary; it was lip service, really. But Frank Page gave me permission to do something here.' Gilbert coopted a figure of growing stature at Hardie: Dr Stanley Forster McCullagh, known universally as Terry, who had begun visiting Camellia in the early 1960s as Croll's locum, but steadily became part of the furniture, and finally been made chief medical officer in August 1967.

For several years at Brooklyn, Gilbert had been sending employees for radiological examination by Dr Bryan Gandevia at Royal Melbourne Hospital. Gandevia warned him that this alone wasn't enough, and Gilbert told McCullagh that he favoured a far more comprehensive approach at Camellia. The first thing he wanted was to really understand 'The Biological Effects of Asbestos'. Forty-year-old McCullagh's specialty was actually tropical medicine. He once confessed that his entire prior experience of pneumoconiosis before coming to Camellia had been a two-hour lecture as an undergraduate at Sydney University. Nonetheless, he wrote with considerable elegance, after the practice he had obtained from composing reports during a spell as a district medical officer in New Guinea. McCullagh's précis of the New York conference's papers, in fact, reads at times like a book review rather than a scientific analysis: 'There are … wide areas of disagreement … at times such as to detract from the objectivity and detachment customary in the learned journals. The editing is poor and on occasions lacks clarity, in one instance at least achieving an opacity that defies comprehension.' But it established McCullagh as the company go-to guy on asbestos-related disease.

McCullagh is an enigmatic figure in the Hardie story. He was a skilful and versatile medical practitioner; he was also an utter pragmatist, who never needed reminding that Hardie was a commercial operation. When Russell once remonstrated with him that the only way to eliminate dust risk was 'stop using asbestos', McCullagh retorted that 'asbestos pays yours and my salary'—one might have expected the advice between a company man and a doctor to flow the other way. In one memo, McCullagh even proposed that 'for dusty jobs, James Hardie should employ older men, because the older men will not live long enough for cancer to develop'. The idea was not his—it had been advocated by Cape Asbestos' medical officer, Walter Smither—and wasn't adopted 'because it was not possible to be so selective given the labour shortage at the time'. But he was always the kind of doctor with whom one could do business. When the company finally acquired its own Seriphos X-ray machine at Camellia, McCullagh stuck it in his office and used the lavatory as the dark room. He later served as a director of Hardie-Ferodo.

The scheme which Gilbert and McCullagh designed was a genuinely significant upgrading of Hardie's commitment to industrial hygiene. It had four elements: every worker in Australia and New Zealand was to be examined clinically and radiologically at least every three years and preferably more often; regular programs of dust sampling would commence at all operations; extensive analysis of existing literature would be undertaken; and expert external advice would be solicited. Gilbert and McCullagh went on the road to promote it, addressed every shift at every Hardie factory over a period of months, talking to unions and the various state health departments. After trials at Welshpool, the program commenced at Newstead in March 1967. Other states, with external doctors, followed.

There was opposition. 'I got some interesting letters back,' says Gilbert. 'Anything new gets resistance, especially when it involves in someone being elevated to a point where he's telling you what to do. Hardie-BI was one of the ones we got a very bad reaction from. Their manager [Ron Hinton] wrote what he thought was a justified but very critical letter back. In general, though, we got co-operation.' McCullagh insisted that the company not fall back on past practices, like the pretence of masks: 'Masks don't work because people don't wear them [and] … they encourage people to do nothing about a problem.' Nor is there evidence that Hardie indulged in the American practice of sparing workers the unpleasant information that were afflicted by an asbestos-related disease. 'I would always tell the men my findings,' claimed McCullagh. 'If somebody had asbestosis, I would always tell them. I would tell them they were "dusted". They knew what that meant. A man was always told; the company was always told. The man was always told first.' Dust counts became the responsibility of a young engineering draftsman, John Winters, who had previously worked at ACI.

By the time the scheme got underway, however, it had lost its champion. Gilbert was made federal manager of research and development. He managed to retain oversight of industrial hygiene, but eventually ran foul of Ted Heath, who had positioned himself as Adamson's successor. In so doing, he lost the ability to monitor McCullagh, whom he saw increasingly as motivated by personal ambition:

When Ted got the nod, of course, he was going to chop everyone's head off that looked like it was going to be raised. I got taken out of the industrial hygiene area—I was a bit annoyed because I was due to go a conference in Dresden—and they put the personnel manager in charge. Now, he [Ray Palfreyman] was very nice bloke, but he'd never been interested in the area. And Terry McCullagh, I thought, was more intent on the running of the scheme than on getting the desired effects. He wanted to write a paper on how the only people who got cancer were smokers. And I said to him: 'We're not interested in bloody papers. We're interested in getting the dust down so people are all right. And besides, we don't have the information to write a proper paper anyway.' I wouldn't let him, which annoyed him. So I resigned [in January 1971]. My promotion path was blocked, and I wasn't happy with the asbestos problem because I felt Ray didn't have the background to do the job.

And while the scheme represented an improvement on the piecemeal approaches of the past, medical examination was an inexact means of assessing hygiene standards. In the 1967 survey, McCullagh found fourteen asbestotics. In the 1968 survey, he found twenty-four, plus fourteen cases of pleural plaques. By early that year, too, he knew of four mesothelioma cases—the company's first. But what did this mean? Whatever peace of mind examinations offered individually, they were essentially meaningless as a guide to present conditions or trends; McCullagh, indeed, made clear his belief that 'the incidence of disease reflected past periods of exposure and did not reflect the adequacy of industrial hygiene measures taken by the company after I arrived'. Hardie was driving by looking in the rear-view mirror—a rear-view mirror, moreover, that looked back decades into the past.

Hardie's approach was motivated only partly by the cause of worker welfare: this was a pre-emptive placation of potentially hostile parties like health departments and unions. Hardie was closely monitoring the travails of Cape Asbestos, in which it remained a substantial shareholder, and of Turner & Newall, with which it was a joint venture partner. The scandal following the publication of the

Newhouse and Thompson paper had resulted in Barking's closure, while Turner & Newall's managing director John Waddell was complaining that smears on the industry were 'as difficult to combat as McCarthy's political smear campaign on individuals in the USA ten years ago'. The response at Turner & Newall to tightening regulation was a pretend compliance: 'If ... we demonstrate, by a token effort only, an ostensible intention to comply with the regulations, it is conceivable that we can ward off the evil day when asbestos cannot economically be applied ie 'hold on' until 1972–1973.'

Australian newspapers were incurious, but as there was always the risk that something would break through from overseas, Hardie had to improve its state of media readiness. When *The Australian* burst into print with a long article quoting Irving Selikoff extensively in October 1968, Hardie had to cannibalise a Turner & Newall public relations document in response. The following month, a dossier was circulated, written by McCullagh, which it was intended would be 'sufficient to answer the average questions that may arise from time to time'. It began on a note of cheery mockery:

> Asbestos is by no means alone in having suspicion directed at it of being a possible health hazard. There are hundreds of substances as mundane as fuel oil, charcoal-grilled steak and iron rust which are known or suspected of being cancer causing agents under certain experimental conditions.'

It acclaimed the work of the Asbestosis Research Council, to which Hardie had been 'admitted to membership'. At a factory conference in September 1969, McCullagh was buoyant: 'You are aware of the wave of bad publicity that the industry has suffered over the last few years both in the USA and the UK. This wave has not yet reached Australia and I believe we are in a position to prevent it doing so'.

Hardie's new procedures offered something else, too: a hint of the potential quantum of compensation. In about June 1967, Gilbert commissioned from McCullagh an estimate of Hardie's liabilities. McCullagh projected about one hundred compensable cases group-wide, a similar number among former employees, and a bill 'perhaps as much as $1.5 million' — a not insignificant number compared to shareholders' funds of about $30 million.[†] And while it was only a back-of-the-envelope calculation, it was also the crystallising of a thought. Hardie had a liability. What should — or could — be done about it?

---

† Others were alive to this threat also. On 13 June 1967, Jim Milne of the industrial hygiene division in the Victorian Health Department, who was helping Hardie read its X-rays, wrote to Brooklyn's manager Wally Williams suggesting that he arrange bulk radiological services and send the company the results 'because your company is then in the position of having precise details of the health of its employees', knowledge of which 'may be of no little assistance should future litigation occur.'

8

'A dirty job that had to be done'

'All in all, I believe we are good corporate citizens and will continue to be so.'
—James Hardie managing director Ted Heath in James Hardie newsletter, 1977

ONE REQUEST DR TERRY MCCULLAGH MADE of James Hardie in the 1960s that was complied with involved crocidolite. It could not be said that anyone had rushed to judgement after Wagner's 1960 incrimination of blue asbestos in the development of mesothelioma. Eight years had elapsed by the time McCullagh arrived at his view, and by then a senior medical inspectors' panel had recommended to British companies that they substitute other fibres for crocidolite where possible, and the Industrial Hygiene Foundation of America was proposing a threshold value of zero 'since no safe limit can be established for this form of asbestos'.

In a memo to Frank Page in January 1968, McCullagh asked outright: 'Could consideration be given please to ending the use of crocidolite in the company's plants?' McCullagh, it turned out, was pushing at an open door. After decades of losses, CSR had finally closed Australian Blue Asbestos at Wittenoom.* Hardie actually thought briefly of buying the mine. But by this time, the company had bigger ambitions where its perennial anxieties about supply were concerned.

---

* There is some evidence that Hardie used small, possibly leftover, quantities of crocidolite for another five or so years. Not until May 1973 did the James Hardie & Coy board officially resolve not to use further blue asbestos.

The Cassiar region of British Columbia had been the scene of gold rushes in 1861–62 and 1873–74. It was known as — and remains — one of North America's outstanding big-game districts. The asbestos in which it abounded was a trophy no one had been hunting. The prospectors who staked the original claims were working on the Alaska Highway, only did so because of a chance encounter with a party from the Geological Survey of Canada, and quickly sold it on to Conwest Exploration. Tests by Raybestos-Manhattan, however, found the chrysotile to be of high quality, and geologists proved up a deposit of six million tonnes. Cassiar Asbestos Corporation was formed in December 1952 with development funds raised from a group of manufacturers, including Turner & Newall's Bells Asbestos subsidiary.

From 1953 to 1962, Cassiar was a seasonal mine, extracting ore for only nine months of the year, stockpiling it for when the ground became too cold, too hard and covered by up to 300 centimetres of snow. It was served by a company town whose population peaked at 1000 but whose only boulevard was named for the company's boss, Jack Christian, and whose town doctor was also coroner, magistrate, judge of the juvenile court, and registrar of births, deaths and marriages. Hardie's links were established in the early days, when it bought a sample from the mine and found it to be 'beautiful fibre'. Jonah Adamson's production manager, Jim Rhys-Jones, paid the first of a series of regular visits in 1956; other representatives followed, conveying the specific technical requirements of fibre-cement manufacturers. It was genuinely a journey into the wilds. Neil Gilbert recalls his chauffeur's excited remark when he was being driven into town on his visit: 'Thar's a bar! Thar's a bar!' Gilbert was musing that he quite fancied a drink himself when he followed the chauffeur's pointed finger: a grizzly bear and cub were foraging by the roadside.

When Cassiar also acquired leases in the Yukon at Clinton Creek, close to the Alaskan border, Hardie's relationship deepened. In December 1964, it acquired a stake of 40,000 shares 'to cement the friendly relations existing between the two companies', then took up its *pari passu* entitlement in a fund-raising for Clinton Creek. Hardie became a staunch supporter of this new mine after its opening in October 1967, and within five years its share of Cassiar Asbestos Corporation had grown to 12.5 per cent. The acquisition was partly funded by Hardie's sale of its Cape Asbestos shares to the mining and finance house Charter Consolidated, which had made a recommended bid, in September 1969.

Cassiar was Hardie's most important overseas foray. In his chairman's review dated 30 July 1970, Jock Reid spoke of the 'very close association', the 'tie that it provides with a source of raw material' being complemented by the 'most valuable free interchange of technical and fibre research information'. But of an investment which soaked up as much as $24 million, shareholders learned very little. They weren't informed, for instance, that from November 1969, Hardie's Bahaman subsidiary, Independent Brokers and Contractors, was Cassiar's distributor in south-east Asia.[†] Nor did they learn anything about conditions at Cassiar's mines, which, as one account by a mill-hand suggests, were classically filthy:

> There was no orientation that I can recall, and I was handed a broom and an aluminium grain shovel and taken upstairs and shown a floor to sweep. It was a large floor ... It was covered in asbestos dust about two inches deep. I was shown a wheelbarrow and where to dump the dust. I was left on my own then, so I tackled the floor with gusto, thinking that this floor must not get too much traffic to get such a heavy layer of dust and there weren't too many footprints in the dust. I worked steadily, the dust sweeping up easily on the nice hardwood floors and I dumped many wheelbarrows full of dust. After about two hours of this, I stopped to turn around and survey my work and was shocked to discover that the area where I had started already had about half an inch of dust again.

---

† Independent Brokers and Contractors, a mysterious entity in the Hardie accounts from the mid-1960s, had been a subsidiary of Purpull, an independent petrol importer, which Hardie had acquired from H. C. Sleigh. It became a means of accumulating US dollars offshore to fund Hardie's foreign ventures, and also of minimising Australian tax.

Shareholders also heard next to nothing—despite the fact that by this time Hardie was represented on Cassiar's board by Ted Heath—when Cassiar's industrial relations began to deteriorate markedly after a sixteen-day strike in November 1972. In a period of widespread labour unrest, Canada's asbestos industry would become the scene of particular militancy, and rolling stoppages disrupted many producers through 1973 and 1974. Nor did companies get much sympathy from prime minister Pierre Trudeau, a veteran campaigner against the industry who had edited a collection, *La Grève de l'amiante,* concerning the earlier strike wave of 1949.

Cassiar wasn't spared: it could not pay its usual quarterly dividends in June or September 1974, after which Hardie foreshadowed a write-down of the value of its stake with the ambiguous comment that its raw material position was 'secure, if not completely comfortable'. Tension boiled over in 1975 when a theology student who worked as a union official, Paul Formby, tired of picking asbestos fibres from his beard at Thetford Mines and smuggled in measuring equipment. He found dust levels up to fifty times the newly recommended threshold levels in the UK of two fibres per cubic centimetre. The events achieved only minimal coverage in Australia—one syndicated *Financial Times* story about industrial unrest in the *Australian Financial Review*—but there was one very anxious Australian spectator. And worse was to come. Cassiar received its first claim for compensation from an employee of a Texas textile manufacturer, who had named it among defendants in an action seeking $C750,000.

After union officials smuggled measuring equipment into Cassiar itself in November 1975, that company's workers also went on strike. The union was defiant ('Men and women did the only lawful thing they could do to protect their health and get attention to the health problems at Cassiar'), the company intransigent ('The strike is illegal and improper in every way'), and the Labor Relations Board sided with the latter. The strikes in general, which lasted up to eight months in some places, accomplished almost nothing. The unions did not obtain the right they sought to monitor their own air, and the price of fibre rose about 25 per cent in 1974, then another

40 per cent in 1975. For all its fibre, Cassiar had been another reminder of asbestos' increasingly malign reputation. Hardie's most ambitious international play was never mentioned again, even when Clinton Creek closed in August 1978. The chapter mentioning Cassiar in the draft of Hardie's official history, *A Very Good Business*, was deleted from the final version.

A Very Good Business, in fact, is at its most selective in this period of Hardie's history. It gives very thorough coverage, for instance, to Hardie's Asian manufacturing operations, perhaps because these were closely associated with its chairman at the time the book was written: John Boyd Reid, son of Jock. These began with an opportunistic investment in 1964, Hardie stepping in when Johns-Manville withdrew at the last moment from a pipe joint venture in the Malaysian town of Ipoh planned with Turner & Newall and Eternit, and became the first significant task delegated to Reid, then a coltish 34-year-old. *A Very Good Business* offers this as a rosy story of entrepreneurship in action: after Reid and Ted Heath rang Jonah Adamson in London to ask if they could present their feasibility study personally, 'the line was so bad they could not be sure whether he had said "Yes" or "No", so they decided to go anyway'. Hardie became UAC Berhad's managing partner, designing the plant's machinery, providing it with research and development support, and devoting it a chairman (Reid), a director (Heath), and a general manager (David Macfarlane) when it became operational in August 1967. A second investment was made in Indonesia two years later with local partners, PT Harflex Asbes Semen acquiring an existing fibre-cement factory and a manufacturer of sheet and pipe.

Hardie was generally happy with its investments — happy enough to feature a homely photograph of two Indonesia boys amid a pile of Fibrolite pipes on the cover of its 1972 annual report. In south-east Asia, of course, it was not troubled by unruly unionists and inhibiting health regulations. A third investment in making similar products was undertaken in what became PT James Hardie Industries, a partnership with the wealthy Bakrie brothers at Tangerang in West Java, opened in October 1976 by prime minister Malcolm Fraser and Indonesia's General Soeharto. In truth, the

businesses did not amount to much. The markets were too embry-
onic, the currencies too volatile, and the economies too dependent
on foreign aid and oil and gas revenues to make them especially
lucrative.

A Very Good Business, by contrast, overlooks altogether another
investment at home that was far more significant — perhaps because
it is so difficult to explain. Asbestos Mines Pty Ltd, formed to mine
and mill chrysotile near Baryulgil, eighty kilometres from Grafton in
the Northern Rivers district of New South Wales, is one of the
strangest and least-accountable ventures in which Hardie became
involved. It produced comparatively little fibre, scarcely earned a
profit, and became a source of acute, if not perhaps entirely well-
deserved, embarrassment.

The land on the upper Clarence River is traditionally home to
the Bandjalang people, who lived in unusual harmony with an indul-
gent squatter, Edward Ogilvie, from the 1840s. It was an aboriginal
man, Bill Little, who in 1918 received a bottle of rum and a plug of
tobacco for leading prospectors to an asbestos outcrop, which
became the source for a short-lived mine. The site was not revisited
until wartime concerns about security of supply provoked an exploration program by Wunderlich's Asbestos Mines subsidiary. Hardie's
half-share was acquired in November 1944 at the urging of Thyne
Reid's consultant geologist John Proud, although Wunderlich
retained management control.

Perhaps because of its size, and perhaps also because little was
expected of its largely indigenous workforce, Baryulgil was from its
inception a decidedly primitive operation: the simplest open-cut
arrangement where men in bare feet smashed ore with 14-lb sledge-
hammers. Sorting was manual, processing was done in Brisbane
until a crusher and separator were trucked in, and almost all the
output was sent the shortest possible distance to Newstead. It was,
furthermore, always dirty. A 1952 report of the Public Health
Department's industrial hygiene division recorded excessive dust
concentrations where ore was crushed and fibre bagged, and
recorded that 'the two men who worked at these points were subsequently X-rayed and found to have increased lung markings'.

Matters did not improve significantly when Hardie bought Wunderlich out in April 1953, with Stewart d'Arrietta becoming chairman of the Asbestos Mines board. The antiquated mill was not replaced until January 1959, and hygiene standards received precious little attention. A memo from March 1960 reports another visit from two government inspectors who remained thoroughly inscrutable: 'They had lunch here and altogether were very pleasant but left without giving any opinion of the tests or the mine conditions generally.' When a chief draftsman tried to take a photograph in the dirtiest part of the mill in February 1966, the enveloping cloud meant that nothing came out. Not until September 1970 was Baryulgil included in the new cycle of dust surveys, and company hygienist John Winters immediately reported 'alarmingly high dust levels'. McCullagh noted that at one point the site hit levels hundreds of times the recommended limit: 'With counts of this order the fact that an operator is only so exposed for about an hour a day provides only grossly inadequate protection.'

Critics of Baryulgil have since looked with horror on the apparent exploitation of an indigenous workforce, who were not even provided with showers and had to wash in the creek. At least as significant, however, was the mine's precarious profitability: manager Gerald Burke was told candidly that a mine so marginal didn't merit a proper dust-extraction system, and came to think of his task as 'a dirty job that had to be done'. 'The mine manager is well aware of the necessity for controlling asbestos dust,' reported Winters in September 1971. 'However, the dust control programme for Baryulgil has been hampered through a lack of a decision by management as to the future and likely life of the mine. Consequently all modifications performed to reduce dust levels have been stopgap measures and planning for major modifications has not been possible.' Steps were taken. Winters insisted, for instance, that the mine cease reusing the sacks that came back from Newstead, which often imported more dust than they'd left with. But Baryulgil's remoteness also limited what the workforce could do for itself: a water-spray system to damp down asbestos in the tailings hopper did not work, for instance, because of insufficient mains water pressure.

In essence, Baryulgil was just too small to bother with. The mine never employed more than forty people, and was seldom visited by senior managers, as it entailed a flight to Grafton and a 60km inland journey on an unsealed road. If a director ever visited, a record of the occasion has not yet come to light. Had they done so, they might have been confronted by the 'deplorable' sight reported by McCullagh's assistant, Dr Vincent Gerrard, in February 1972: 'I inspected the mine on a mild still day after much recent rain. Nonetheless billowing clouds of fibre could be seen coming from this building and Mr Burke tells me he has, on occasion seen such clouds from distances of several miles'. That distance from Hardie's decision-makers, however, probably also contributed to Baryulgil's longevity. Closing it would have required an expenditure of management time. Perhaps the perspective would have been different had there been complaints. But, ironically, as Jock McCulloch has pointed out, the local community liked the mine:

> For Baryulgil, the mine allowed the community to break away from the chronic unemployment which was the shared fate of other aboriginal communities in New South Wales. It also gave the people a feeling of pride and independence in being able to do work which was difficult and often highly skilled. The only Europeans employed at the mine were the manager and the fitter. All other jobs were performed by aborigines. They worked with jackhammers, as mill-hands, as powder monkeys and as drivers. They did repair work on the machinery and they laid the benches in the quarry. It was aboriginal labour which did the bulk of the work in the construction of the new mill in 1958 … The men of Baryulgil compared their situation with that of other aboriginal workers in Kempsey, Grafton and central New South Wales towns. In comparison with so many others their lot was that of a labour aristocracy. They lived and worked on traditional land, free from outside interference. But, in truth, their choice was to work for Asbestos Mines Pty Ltd or to work for no one.'

By the early 1970s, two asbestos mines operated in northern New South Wales, the second being the old Woodsreef mine near

Barraba at which Hardie and Wunderlich had been near neighbours half a century earlier. Hardie had considered reviving the mine itself, but the feasibility study that Jim Rhys-Jones had taken to Johns-Manville, Asbestos Corporation, and Cassiar had been rejected: 'Two of them said it wasn't a goer. One said it was marginal'. Now it had been revived by Chrysotile Corporation of Australia, a subsidiary of a Canadian firm, and these prophecies were coming true. Woodsreef was much larger than Baryulgil, costing $17.9 million and employing as many as 400 men, and dirtier, its mill achieving astronomical dust counts because it had been designed for the sub-zero temperatures of the northern hemisphere. Woodsreef, nonetheless, had two characteristics in common with Baryulgil. There was an abysmal lack of dust consciousness, with workers being transported to the mine from dormitories twelve miles away in buses that later took the children to school, while no dust-counting took place until Hardie offered to send John Winters on an instructional visit. The mine, too, scarcely made a cent, and operated under the control of receivers Irish, Young and Outhwaite from November 1973.

The two mines only came to public attention thanks to the visits of an enterprising young journalist. On ABC radio's *Broadband*, Matt Peacock painted a vivid portrait of Woodsreef:

> Even to a casual observer, there were serious safety hazards. There were vast quantities of asbestos dust throughout the floor of the mill, which were being swept up, shovelled into wheelbarrows and tipped down a shute by men who—with one exception—were not wearing respirators. Dust from the tailings was blowing into the mill, on a comparatively windless day, so strongly that it was impossible to look into the face of the breeze.

At Baryulgil, Peacock was shocked to find workers without the faintest clue of the hazards of asbestos, and wives who thought of dust as their houses' natural coating:

> When he comes home of an evening, he's covered from head to foot in white dust. It's on his clothes; he's got it all through his hair! You can

see the fine pieces of fibro all through his hair and in his nose and in his
ears, in his clothes, and when I wash his clothes you've got to soak them
and rinse them about ten times. You get fibre and it gets into your
fingers and you've got a hard time trying to get it out. It's like glass. All
the women are the same. Oh, the wind just blows the dust and it comes
in on your clothes and in your window and in on your cups and plates
and everything, because the housing facilities are no good, you know.

By that stage, while it continued buying fibre from both mines,
Hardie no longer owned Baryulgil, having the year before sold out
to Woodsreef. In fact, it was indifferent to their futures. A year later,
CCA lobbied business and consumer affairs minister Wal Fife for
the imposition of licences on imported fibre or a bounty for local
producers that would make its output more competitive. It was a
very similar action to that instigated by CSR twenty-five years earlier, and Hardie took a very similar attitude to it.

The Industries Assistance Commission hearing was about jobs,
not lives. Ironically, in view of later attitudes, CCA's application was
supported by four trade unions. Hardie was represented by director
Athol Higgins and legal manager Lionel Denmead, an accountant
who had been secretary of Asbestos Mines. They stated that there
was 'no price at which it would be induced to increase the quantity
of CCA fibre used', and the commission concurred that 'local consumption of CCA fibre cannot be increased without incurring significant technical problems and/or increased costs'. It was another
highly satisfactory result for a company accustomed to them. But it
wouldn't be so long before technical problems and increased costs
were the least of Hardie's worries.

9

'Asbestosis House'

'The asbestos story demonstrates that the process of hazard identification can unravel slowly and that regulatory responses can lag behind the knowledge that slowly accumulates while a mounting toll of disease and death is borne by workers who are thereby cast in the role of human guinea pigs.'
—Report of the Royal Commission on Matters of Health and Safety Arising from the Use of Asbestos in Ontario, 1984

FOR THE INTERNATIONAL ASBESTOS INDUSTRY, 1973 was as good as it got. Competitors had suffered a litany of bad publicity, especially in Britain, with a rash of television documentaries concerning all the principal players.* But sales were holding up: American consumption ascended a peak of 800,000 tonnes. In a speech in June, Matthew Swetonic of the industry's newly formed public relations group, the Asbestos International Association,

---

* The first significant television treatment of asbestos was in August 1969, when the BBC's *Twenty-Four Hours* presented 'The Health Hazards of Asbestos', which included such scary information as the fact that 10,000 British Rail passenger coaches were asbestos-lined, and that an estimated 600 of 15,000 workers at the Royal Navy's Devonport dockyard were affected. The program was considered so epoch-making in the industry that Turner & Newall's W. P. Howard sent Frank Page a transcript. The latter was bemused: 'I am rather surprised at the attitude which has been adopted by the BBC.' The British media, in fact, would give more cause for bemusement. ITV's *World in Action* ran documentaries attacking Cape in June 1971 and Turner & Newall in October 1974; BBC2's *Horizon* had its own stab at Cape in January 1975. In Australia, the first of many episodes of *Four Corners* devoted to asbestos, accented mainly to Wittenoom, went to air on 23 November.

insisted: 'The good news is, despite all the negative articles on asbestos-health that have appeared in the press over the past half-dozen years, very few people have been paying attention'. When Jock Reid presided as chairman over his last Hardie annual meeting at Asbestos House the following month, the seventy shareholders attending asked exactly one innocuous question. He was shortly to be knighted, in the same list that created Sir James Foots of MIM, Sir Thomas Webb of the Commercial Bank of Australia, Sir Theodore Bray of Queensland Press, and Sir John Parker of Western Australia's State Electricity Commission.

Yet if they did but know it, the participants had reached their industry's zenith. American asbestos consumption would plunge to 300,000 tonnes by 1982, being replaced by fibreglass, ceramics and silica. Even Australia, mostly sheltered from the worst of previous publicity, began generating mainstream media critiques. 'Is This Killer in Your Home?' asked *The Bulletin* on 6 July 1974, promoting a wide-ranging article by Tim Hall; Hardie grumpily responded that the same issue carried an advertisement for its products, money for which the publishers seemed happy to accept. Harder to ignore was *Expendable Americans*, in which *New Yorker's* Paul Brodeur covered the so-called Tyler case, concerning a class action by workers exposed to asbestos dust while installing insulation. Even Hardie bought a copy, on the recommendation of Cape Asbestos' chief medical officer Richard Gaze, who had provided sensational evidence in the case to the effect that he had known of asbestos's dangers since joining his company in 1943. 'It makes *The Bulletin* attack sound like a Sunday school text,' commented Frank Page. Other books followed, including *Asbestos Kills*, the first laymen's guide, written by Nancy Tait, a civil servant whose husband Bill had died of mesothelioma, which became the bible for an emergent network of asbestos disease victims' group.

The publicity caught Hardie at an awkward moment in its dust-control efforts, when it was running hard simply to stand still. After Gilbert's departure, personnel manager Ray Palfreyman had constituted what Hardie called the environmental control committee, which featured medical officer Terry McCullagh, industrial hygienist John Winters, and chief engineer Eric Cohen. They worked on new standards, and McCullagh pushed for adoption of a threshold limit of four fibres per cubic centimetre mooted by the National Health and Medical Research Council (which was twice the three-year-old British standard). They also designed new measurement protocols, finally retiring the old midget impinger in favour of the membrane filter method recommended by the Asbestosis Research Council. Winters came up with an ingenious new device based on a $10 fish pump used for keeping pilchards alive while deep-sea fishing, on which the valving was reversed and a nickel-cadmium battery installed to create a portable sampler that workers could carry with them.

The trouble was that more accurate measurement made compliance tougher. In September 1972, McCullagh noted that not a single Hardie facility was meeting its new standards. Some sites had deteriorated. When Dr Jonathon Streeton visited Brooklyn in the early 1970s with Jim Milne from the Victorian Health Department, he was 'a little horrified':

> They weren't terribly keen on people like me visiting. They did their in-house checking, took x-rays over at the Epworth, did a form of spirometry out there. But there's no doubt that in the early 1970s, things were not remotely as they should have been. The bag room was just mind-boggling. A corrugated iron structure, ten or twelve feet square, with a bunch of guys lifting bags, tipping it out, and shovelling raw asbestos down a hole. They couldn't see each other.

One facility in particular, Hardie-BI, the insulation joint venture with CSR on the other side of the railway line from the main plant at Camellia, was notoriously intractable, after what McCullagh called 'many years of exhortation and inaction'. Insulation is, by nature, a low-density product; Hardie-BI became, by nature, a very dusty place. 'It was a disaster,' says Winters. 'Well, maybe not a *disaster*. But it was pretty bad.' Warwick Lane was amazed by the conditions when he succeeded Ron Hinton as factory manager:

The dust there was terrible. Insulation is very light substance and the only way of getting the shape was to either plane it or cut it, in which case you left residual dust on the surface. Transportation was by pushing a trolley on iron rails, and the slightest bump would raise dust. I'd heard stories that at one time the dust was so thick the guys would put up bits of string to help guide them from this place to that place, because otherwise they couldn't see where they were going. When they did the sweeping, they raised as much dust as they removed.

In a memo to his superior Athol Higgins in October 1972, he could find little good to say:

There can be no doubt the factory itself is a contained storehouse of accumulated dust. Every horizontal surface above ground level, the tops of dryers, purlins, conduit pipes etc has inches of dust on it...Even assuming that all vented systems were perfect, the fact remains that dust clings to every cut surface, is generated every time a block is moved, even in transportation on barrows, and no doubt great quantities are produced in packing and in the subsequent transport and unloading by the end user. I see no real solution to these problems except by use of an asbestos substitute.

The key problem, however, was design. The plant was almost antagonistic to safety — even those features installed to mitigate the dust threat, as foreman Colin Marshall would recall:

The dust collection units were useless. Taking, for example, the men who made caposite [an insulation manufactured under licence from Cape Asbestos], they would tip out amosite fibre into a tray three inches high. They would then fluff up the asbestos using a stick. They would get it nice and woolly. They would spray silica over the asbestos. They would then apply more asbestos over the top of that layer and roll it. The dust collection unit was above their heads. Before the dust could get to the unit it had to go past their faces. Consequently, they were permanently covered in dust.

Apocryphally, the dust alarm was switched off; otherwise it would have worn out.

Lane, who had been Neil Gilbert's deputy at Camellia, pushed for changes. He adopted trollies with rubber wheels, insisted on the floors being carpeted with sawdust during sweeping, and on filling bags of fibre with water. Strangely, the Hardie-BI workforce still enjoyed a strong sense of camaraderie. Bernie Banton, a leading hand, recalls that they compared themselves favourably to those at the adjacent Hardie fibre-cement works: 'It was them and us. We were up here and they were down there. We made lots of different products—bits for heaters, hair driers—instead of the run-of-the-mill Super Six sheets. And they worked a lot harder, every minute, where we would have time while they changed the product we were making.' There was even, strange as it sounds today, a strong regard for Hardie as an employer. 'Bluey Hunt, who made the clips that were put around larger pieces of lagging, had a lung removed,' recalls Banton. 'But at the time there was a fair bit of talk about how terrific it was that as soon as he was able to come back to work there was a job for him. The inference was what a great company Hardie was.'

What dust could not stop, the market did. Demand for industrial insulation petered out. 'The bread and butter of Hardie-BI was really big jobs like powerhouses and refineries,' explains Lane. 'Production on one of those would keep you going for years, but there were no more big projects on the horizon.' Closure was announced in December 1973. But the challenge to Hardie was hydra-headed: for each one removed, two grew back. Long-deferred, regulations on asbestos emission were finally being gazetted round Australia: in Queensland (1971), South Australia (1976), New South Wales (1978), Victoria (1978), Western Australia (1978), and Tasmania (1979). And Hardie was getting bigger. In May 1977, it acquired the fibre-cement operations of its erstwhile rival Wunderlich for $19 million. More rules at more places were being policed than ever before. Hardie's real problems, in fact, were destined to be at Brooklyn, and owed themselves to acts of vigilance that were nothing if not belated.

Trade unions in Australia have not covered themselves in glory where asbestos is concerned. Honorary officials were ill-equipped to deal with a public health issue of such complexity, and protection of jobs and wages tended to take policy precedence over safety. The Australian Workers' Union even publicly deplored the closure of Wittenoom: 'The closure of Wittenoom gorge asbestos mine by its parent company, Colonial Sugar, is seen by many workers as a bitter foretaste of the callous treatment they may expect at the whim of the consortiums and foreign companies gouging out iron and other minerals in the north-west.' In fact, as Ben Hills points out in *Blue Murder*, the Wittenoom workers scarcely knew they had a union:

> They never knew who their shop steward was. They never saw a representative from head office. The only way they knew they were even in a union (those who could read English that is) was when they saw the few bob a week membership dues compulsorily deducted from their weekly pay.

The union that had the coverage of asbestos workers in New South Wales and Victoria was the Federated Miscellaneous Workers Union (FMWU), which had swept them up among the rich range of occupational groups—including spruikers, greasers, ferrymen, commissionaires, bill posters, luggage porters, laundry workers and ice-cream makers—that it had come to represent since being formed in 1910 in a small room at Trades Hall in Sydney. For many years asbestos was significant only insofar as its immediate discomforts could be parlayed into additional benefits, like the 'itchy money' eagerly sought for members constructing power stations in New South Wales. They took a strangely detached view of disablement. Peter Russell recalls advising Jim Braid, an FMWU official, that he had been classified as suffering the onset of asbestosis:

> He said he wasn't concerned because he would be in line for an ex-serviceman's pension. I don't know whether it's bravado or an Aussie trait but many adopted the attitude that they had a job and something that might cause problems twenty years down the track wasn't an immediate priority.

In the mid-1960s, that began changing. When he started making site visits, New South Wales branch secretary Doug Howitt was amazed at what he found. 'It was just like walking into a factory that had been inhabited by cobweb spiders for centuries,' he recalled of Wunderlich at Redfern. 'There were festoons of asbestos fibres and dust hanging off the rafters, the ceilings and the windows ... There were a couple of exhaust fans out there spilling asbestos dust every-where and there was no attempt whatsoever to protect the workers.' Hardie wasn't much better, as Howitt advised Gilbert after an inspection of Camellia in December 1965:

> During our inspection it was noticed that there appeared to be no improvement in the older section of the mixing floors and that workers are being subjected to unreasonable exposure ... While we appreciate that a large part of your factory has been in operation for a long time and that modifications are difficult and costly, and whilst we have also found your company to be cooperative in helping to find solutions our mutual problems, we ask the company to appreciate that we have a great responsibility to safeguard the health and interest of our members and that urgent priority be given to replacing and improving the unsatisfactory plant and working conditions.

The FMWU was mollified by Hardie's initiative to begin regular employee examinations and dust counts. Federal secretary Ray Gietzelt even promised to put aside a union claim for dust money so long as the company continued its medical surveillance and indus-trial hygiene improvements. One official, though, wasn't so sure, and when he became the FMWU's Victorian branch secretary in 1973, Ray Hogan decided to do something about it. 'When they started the medical program, Gilbert and McCullagh came down from Sydney and talked about it,' Hogan recalls. 'And we thought: 'Well, maybe they're doing something decent for a change'. Then I decided to ask for the X-rays myself, and they fought tooth and nail to keep them out of my hands.' Hogan's chief handicap was that his own membership at Brooklyn was almost as uncooperative as Hardie management: 'The workers there thought it was as safe as making

ice cream. And it was difficult, because there were so many nation-
alities there, to make them understand that they were dealing with
something very dangerous. I remember a man saying to me: 'There's
no other job for me.' I said to him: 'There's no other life for you
either'.'

It was a slow process of building credibility and concern. The
workforce gradually soaked up Hogan's circulars on asbestos on
health, which were eventually translated into Greek, Italian,
Yugoslavian, Serbian, Croatian, and Arabic, and which always finished with the slogan: 'The Union Puts Your Life Ahead of All
Other Considerations of the Industry.' Hogan finally instigated
some industrial action in April 1976, pulling employees out when
malfunctioning asbestos-ducting filled the plant with dust, and
insisting that nobody would resume until the Health Department's
okay. A five-day stoppage followed seven months later after the
death of one worker and the dismissal of another who it was thought
may have suffered lung damage. Then, just before Christmas, Hogan
threw down a gauntlet, submitting a claim for special consideration
in respect of any employee losing their health, or the dependents of
anyone who died. The proposal was based on a deal the FMWU had
just struck for security guards injured in the line of duty, and was
without prejudice to workers' compensation or common law rights.

Hardie did not reject the proposition outright, indicating instead
that they might consider discussing something similar on a national
basis. This was shrewd politicking, as it dealt into negotiations
national secretary Gietzelt, who was felt to be more malleable, and
who nursed disagreements with Hogan on other matters: on the
perennially divisive issue of uranium, for instance, Gietzelt favoured
mining, while Hogan was ardently opposed. But Hogan and his
assistant John Neil had their auxiliaries, too. The Victorian Trades
Hall had just initiated a first of its kind. The Workers' Health
Resources Centre, intended to help in formulating health advice and
policy for workers in industry, was run by an unusual duo: Richard
Gillespie, a Trotskyist, and David Kilpatrick, an industrial hygienist
from the CSIRO. They collected information on asbestos and the
epidemiology of asbestos-related diseases from all over the world—

even writing to Irving Selikoff, who responded promptly and volu-
minously—and applied it to scrutiny of Hardie's policies for dust
suppression and medical testing. Their initial meeting at Brooklyn,
Kilpatrick recalls, showed them the extent of the challenge:

> As we went from the admin building to the main sheet production
> plant, there was a huge cloud of white dust that you almost couldn't see
> through, and one of the directors who was on the guided tour said: 'Oh
> God!' Each of us got turned round by a Hardies representative and they
> tried to lead us off in a different direction. There was a roofing plumber
> who was cutting up a piece of Super Six with a power saw. It was so
> embarrassing for them. They'd just spent an hour telling us how
> wonderful was and it all fell apart in twenty seconds.

Gillespie was stunned by the degree of ignorance among workers,
which was in its own way a reflection of the indifference among
management. He encountered a builder bleached white by the dust
from his work unaware even of what fibro contained:

> He had worked as a builder for thirty years, and had cut and sanded
> cement sheeting all that time. He had no idea that he was working with
> asbestos ('It's just fibro-cement') and was unaware that there was any
> danger to his health from inhaling the dust ... One of the directors
> escorting me through the factory hurried over to explain that the man
> worked for a sub-contractor and that the company had no control over
> these workers; then excused himself as he had a meeting in Sydney that
> afternoon. The builder resumed his sawing ...

After a fairly sheltered academic and research life, Kilpatrick
found the grind hard at first. Where Gillespie enjoyed the hurly-
burly of union politics, Kilpatrick found senior unionists 'arseholes'
almost to a man, and had to take assertiveness classes before he
could stand up to them with confidence. But he liked the even-tem-
pered and meticulous Hogan immediately, never forgetting the first
meeting he attended at Hardie with him where the official commenced proceedings by passing round a ruled sheet on paper on

which everyone had to write their name and title. Kilpatrick began to relish parts of his toughening up. At a meeting with the state health minister Bill Borthwick, he found the Hardie line being towed by the Health Department's Jim Milne, who then insisted on following him to his car.

'You know, David, you should get off Hardie's back,' complained Milne. 'They're good guys.'

Kilpatrick replied: 'You're on the wrong side, Jim.'

Less official but more surprisingly in the FMWU's corner, was an anonymous Hardie executive who began feeding Hogan information in telephone calls that he would begin with the salutation: 'Idi Amin here ...' Hogan was never sure of 'Amin's' motivations, but his information was always sound: 'I don't know whether he had a genuine concern for the people there, whether he'd fallen out with the management, or whether he supported what we were doing and just thought it was right. But I gave him my private line, and he'd tell me what was going on, what Hardie's position was and what he'd heard about the other factories, and it was very helpful.' The FMWU began to feel a sense of crusade about their endeavours. John Neil saw a number of former Hardie employees brought low by asbestos, and his reports were bleak. In March 1978, for instance, he met a 21-year Hardie veteran whose health had curtailed his employment at the age of sixty. The first that Theodor Karakash had known of mesothelioma was shortness of breath, which had caused him to complain that there was 'not enough air in the bedroom', and to sit through the night in the kitchen so as not to disturb his wife. Neil was struck by his selflessness. After the removal of a huge pleural tumour, Karakash had weeks to live, but spoke only of what risks his former colleagues might be running:

> Mr Karakash's main concern was not in regard to himself but for the future wellbeing of his workmates at the James Hardie factory. He stated that he did not want to see others suffer or develop a condition similar to his own and indicated that the company should be stopped from inflicting irreversible medical conditions. At this point he and his wife became very emotional and disturbed. I explained the union's

policy that if the industry could not be made safe it should be closed down with which he agreed wholeheartedly. From my observations he appeared to be a very sick man with hardly any flesh on his bones. He would be six feet tall and weigh approximately nine stone. I was surprised at the clarity of his speech and his clear thinking. I was of the opinion that his life expectancy would not be very long.

When the FMWU state secretaries for Victoria, New South Wales and South Australia finally met Hardie officials at Camellia the following month to discuss a national special consideration scheme, they could point to valuable precedents being struck elsewhere for compensation and communication. CSR was negotiating establishment of the Wittenoom Trust, a charitable institution to help former employees; VicRail, whose Harris trains had recently been revealed as asbestos-lined, had just agreed to provide the Australian Railways Union with details of all dust counts. When Hardie proved hard bargainers, workers at Brooklyn and also at the old Wunderlich plant at Sunshine went out for three days, and a modest but noisy protest at Asbestos House followed to coincide with Hardie's annual meeting on 27 July. Directors arrived to find that the building's name plate had been graffitied to read 'Asbestosis House', and the entrance picketed by twenty protestors, two of whom gained admittance to the meeting.

The opportunity to ask questions was mostly misspent. When one interlocutor tried to raise worker fatalities at Baryulgil, chairman John Reid easily declared him out of order, by pointing out that Hardie no longer owned the mine. But the stoush did provide something reportable, and Reid was forced to give assurances that, if not evasive, could have been better informed. He airily claimed that the company had had 'about one hundred' asbestotics in its history, and wasn't sure how many had died; in fact, Hardie had been in regular correspondence with the Dust Diseases Board for six years, where it was accustomed to sending workers who were 'dusted' to seek pensions, and had been advised in April of figures of twenty-nine deaths and 116 certified sufferers. Reid dismissed the possibility of a health risk to users: 'Asbestos cement building products have been used, without known damage to health, by building tradesmen, home-owner builders and handymen in Australia for more than seventy-five years ... We believe that the general public is not at risk in the use of asbestos cement products manufactured by the company.' But he also acknowledged that Hardie was negotiating with health authorities about health warnings on its products.

It was another nine months before the scheme was agreed after a nationwide vote in March 1979. Hardie undertook to voluntarily pay a maximum lump sum of $14,000 to all with a compensable asbestos-related disease as recognised by the Dust Diseases Board; the first beneficiary was Theodor Karakash's widow. But Hardie was circumspect. It would not provide Hogan with historic dust-count figures, as there were 'legal actions underway'. It was loath, too, to turn over medical records to the union, and only complied after a string of stoppages in the second half of the year.

As for efforts at education, these were spasmodic and selective. One tended to find out about asbestos health risks around Hardie by chance. Russell Chenu, then a young finance executive, remembers his first intimation one day at Brooklyn: 'I remember this old guy coming in, I think to get his compensation cheque. He was having a great deal of difficulty breathing, and he looked really, really ill. Afterwards I asked the personnel manager what had given rise to his condition and I was told: "He's contracted asbestosis, because of materials in the factory." I thought, gee, that's pretty grim.' A workers' education program was approved by the Hardie board in July 1977 and a brochure, 'Asbestos and Health', was produced in January 1979 which insisted that 'improved dust control techniques and safety procedures now in force will in time be reflected in a con-tinuing fall in the occurrence of asbestos related disease'.

Whether this made a genuine difference to workers is debateable. In an FMWU survey of Hardie workers the following year, which amounted to an exam on asbestos-related health issues, marks ranged from 85 per cent at Elizabeth to 56 per cent at Camellia. Four in ten workers in the group thought asbestosis was or might be curable. After examining ten Hardie workers feared to be suffering lung abnormalities in September 1980, Jonathon Streeton offered a colleague good news and bad. The good news was none of the workers were suffering from asbestos-related disease; the bad news was that their understanding of the risks involved was poor:

> I do find it as a chest physician very disappointing that despite the fact they are all in a recognised hazardous industry the majority of them continue to smoke in varying degrees. There is not the slightest doubt of the relationship between smoking and asbestos-induced lung disease and I would have thought it proper that consideration be given to an education program among the men to try and make them more aware of the long-term hazards of smoking in its own right let alone their additional asbestos-induced risks. On the other side of the picture there is not the slightest doubt that in years gone there were very gross exposures of the men to asbestos dust.[†]

One artefact of the shortcomings of employee awareness at this time was collected by Hardie itself. In April 1979, with its centenary in view, Hardie commissioned a documentary writer, John Balmforth, to oversee an extensive oral history project, which eventually contained more than one hundred interviews. Many long-standing employees were sought out, some going back as far as the 1920s. For himself, Balmforth believed the health concerns about asbestos were pure alarmism. But employees, even if unclear on detail, were less sure — workers such as Ray Whitehorn, thirty-one years a Hardie man, who had retired as a foreman at Birkenhead in 1975:

> It's just a pity that there's so much controversy about that thing there — you know with the dust and things like that. This is what used to muck us fellows up. We could stand up to them [unions], but as soon as they

---

[†] The closest that Hardie seem to have come to such an acknowledgement was in the letter to workers for the 1983 health survey which mentioned only that smoking was bad for you: 'If you are a smoker I strongly urge you to kick the habit. Smoking not only causes nearly all lung cancers but also many other diseases such as emphysema and arterial diseases etc'.

mentioned dust we were sunk. We were sunk. I was, anyhow, because I realised—well, they told me later in life that it was a bad thing … and if a person is complaining about that and it's affecting his health, you've got to listen to him. And everything was too dusty … well, we used to eat it on our sandwiches at dinnertime. Well, I've seen fellows that would have been working—it would be hanging out of their mouth—and they're eating sandwiches … Well, firstly I didn't know it was a dangerous industry you see? But as I say I did try and prevent dust. I just put a handkerchief over my mouth.

There was a good deal of nervous laughter around the topic. In December 1979, Balmforth was talking to three New Zealand workers with a hundred and twenty years at Hardie between them when the subject turned to the health risks of asbestos:

Balmforth: What's the real gut feeling that people have about asbestos?
Bob Douglas: I've never heard anything.
Jack Pollard: They don't seem to be worried. Occasionally when some discussion comes up, you know, when we get, say a visit from … McCullagh or something and get everyone together, you'll get a few questions asked about it. But I've had more questions asked about it outside the company than inside
Balmforth: Yes … does it ever worry you?
R. H. Evans: Oh it worries me now thinking about it, but then…
Bob Douglas: I was buried in it once and thought nothing of it, but I'm thinking now (laughter) … Familiarity breeds contempt with some people, they live with it for so long they accept it. It's strange to someone outside who has all these emotional …
Balmforth: Much more scary when you hear about it than when you experience it?
Douglas: That's quite true.

Sometimes even Balmforth was shocked by what he heard, as when he interviewed Dick Carter, a foreman at Penrose with forty years behind him:

Balmforth: Good God! The storage of the asbestos and where you ate was the same area? Does it still exist?

Carter: Yeah, I'll show you. It's changed now, of course, but it's still there … See the blue pile? That they were more worried about than anything. They don't use it here now, but they used to have a lot of it in those days. But nobody gave asbestos dust a thought in those days. We used to eat in it, play in it … we didn't worry about the dust at all. You got covered in it … It's only been in the last few years that people have started to realise … anything about it here.

Ted Bell, the first New Zealander employed at Penrose, who had joined as a fitters' labourer, said that, even if he didn't 'blame the people because I don't think they knew how bad it was', was surprised he hadn't been told more:

> We weren't even told the stuff was dangerous until very much later in the piece when possibility [sic] all the damage was done to my contemporaries. There was little or no form of dust collection or prevention … About half a dozen of my contemporaries have all died of something to do with lungs … It wasn't until much later in the piece that we got people moving in, the health department moving in, and that sort of thing. And from there it started to improve. But up until that time the damage was done … You've got to aerate the asbestos, you know, and they used to be in an enclosed room and nobody even told them to put a mask on. I suppose as a foreman I should've told them but nobody told me.

Under criticism, Hardie's former paternalism began giving way to a general truculence. In January 1980, an FMWU organiser called on Hardie at Brooklyn and found workers upset that nothing had been done about the death that morning of a 17-year-old apprentice in a fall. An executive said airily: 'He worked for a contractor'. Told that this was 'typical of James Hardie', the executive said that if workers intended downing tools he would be pleased if they cleaned their machines first. Hardie tried reining Hogan in with increasingly pettifogging restrictions. When he arrived for a visit previously cleared with management in April 1981, for instance, factory manager Brian Thompson informed him that he would have to be chaperoned. The FMWU report achieves a certain deadpan humour:

> Hogan informed Thompson that he would not be accompanied by a representative of management. Thompson then telephoned [state manager Eric] Charles and informed him that Hogan insisted on going into the factory unaccompanied. Charles confirmed that in accordance with policy, Hogan would have to be accompanied. Hogan then informed Thompson that he intended to proceed and it would be up to the company to call the police if they wished to stop Hogan from entering. Thompson again telephoned Charles and Charles informed Thompson that he had spoken to [executive director Tom] Hore in Sydney and that the policy would have to stand. Charles asked Thompson to go to his office. When Thompson returned he said that Hogan could go in but insofar as policy was concerned, Thompson would be keeping an oversight but at a distance. Hogan told Thompson that he would be going in accordance with past practice and if Thompson were to hang around in the distance that was up to him … When Hogan returned to Thompson's office, Thompson was still in his office and commented that he had not left his office.

Sitting tight, indeed, was about all Hardie could do. And the battleground was about to spread beyond Brooklyn.

10

'Next time you are speaking to the Lord ...'

'I note ... that the mere fact of a company surviving one hundred years, particularly in the corporate climate of the past decade is something of an accomplishment. It is worth restating that this year we completed a long, expensive and difficult transition.'
—James Hardie chairman John Reid at its centenary annual general meeting, August 1987

THE ANNUAL MEETING OF JAMES HARDIE ASBESTOS at Asbestos House on 2 August 1979 was less eventful than the previous year's but at least as significant. Shareholders effectively did away with both company and venue, their votes approving name changes to what became James Hardie Industries and James Hardie House. By that time, in fact, a corporate makeover was in motion with few Australian precedents: one of the great Australian one-product business dynasties was turning its back on that product.

This had been a long time coming. In the 1970s, under chairman John Reid and managing director Ted Heath, Hardie had drifted. Reid, as active in his role as his father Jock had been inconspicuous and retiring, seemed more interested in doing deals than the quotidian concerns of operations; Heath's effectiveness was curbed by alcohol. It took Heath's successor, David Macfarlane, another protégé of Reid's who had worked with him in South Australia and Malaysia, to face the future.

Macfarlane had been born in Iching where his mother had worked as a missionary, fleeing China just ahead of the advancing

Japanese. In his new role, he became a kind of missionary, too, lighting the way to a promised asbestos-free land. He had two exit strategies. The first was a long-term effort to develop a form of fibre-cement reinforced by something other than asbestos. Hardie had always experimented with the composition of its products, but effort now could no longer be avoided. Hardie began reducing the asbestos content of its products little by little, with zero as its objective, and set up a pilot plant at Welshpool in Western Australia, run by veteran fibre-cement executive Harry Hudson, as the centre of its research efforts—the reason being that the state used more corrugated sheet, subject to greater stresses than flat, than any other. It was a painstaking process in which the hero was a boisterous engineer with an MBA in his mid-thirties called John Pether, who smoked, drank and thought freely. Most companies seeking to replace asbestos in products had chosen glass fibre; Pether preferred fibrous kraft cellulose. Perth's hot, dry summer of 1979–1980 proved a stern initiation for the new sheets which, at first, cracked badly. The physical bond with the cement could be replicated, but not the chemical bond—the use of pine, it is said, although not by Hardie, who remain coy about it, proved the solution.

The second key strategy was a relaunch of the company that put a distance between itself and its asbestos past. The name change emulated similar initiatives among Hardie's overseas peers such as Cape Asbestos (which became Cape Industries); Johns-Manville (which created a new holding company Manville Corp); Cassiar Asbestos Corporation (reconceived as Cassiar Resources); UNARCO (henceforward UNR Corporation); Raybestos-Manhattan (rebadged as Raymark); and, eventually, Turner & Newall (which waited longer than most, but finally became T & N from 1987). But the main change was in Hardie's asset base, which became increasingly diverse.

In October 1978, Hardie plunged into the future by lavishing $52.1 million on Reed Consolidated Industries (RCI), an Australian-listed arm of the British conglomerate Reed International. It was at the time Australia's biggest takeover, and brokered by the Ord Minnett corporate financier Keith Halkerston, who understood Hardie's keenness to branch off from the core product that at this stage provided 90 per cent of its profits, and Reed's eagerness to get shot of a subsidiary that they essentially could no longer afford to fund. 'Go away!' said Macfarlane when he first heard the Halkerston proposal in June. Then it occurred to him that it was a way to tide the company over while Hudson and Pether toiled away in Perth—with, it should be said, no real certainty they would come up with anything.

RCI, nonetheless, was a curious target for Hardie, a company that was as freewheeling as its suitor was focused. Its main operations were in plastic pipes, but it was also involved in irrigation, packaging, and leisure and entertainment, with its subsidiaries including Hanna-Barbera Australia, maker of *The Flintstones* and *The Jetsons*. For all its expense, the acquisition was a strategically diffident affair. Hardie needed rather than wanted to diversify, and RCI offered a range of options rather than committing them to any single one.

The diffidence became apparent almost immediately to RCI's senior executives: Jim Brookes, Keith Napier, David Say and David Luke. 'The wine people?' Say recalls asking, when told that RCI had been sold to James Hardie. It might as well have been. After a meeting in London with John Reid and David Macfarlane at which cheques were exchanged, RCI heard nothing. 'We went into a kind of phoney war period,' says Say. 'Nothing happened. David and I went out to lunch. After four weeks we got the phone book, looked up their number and rang them and said: "You've taken us over. Would you like to find out what you've bought?" ' In fact, as it emerged when RCI's various divisions hosted a presentation of their wares at Dee Why, the cultures of the two companies were oil and water. As each division did its party piece—the animators presenting a cartoon, the administrators performing a sketch in which a manager enumerated the company's assets to such a degree that two men in white coats bearing stethoscopes appeared and removed him—the guests from Hardie sat stony-faced. And after the first joint Christmas party, Hardie's Ray Palfreyman said: 'We must never have those people at our party again.'

When the RCI senior executives relocated to Asbestos House,

they were appalled. 'It was a grey company with grey people,' Say remembers. 'Nobody said boo to anybody. At one stage I went into the corridor and just shouted as loud as I could, just to see if anything happened. Nothing did.' Brookes and Napier took divisional responsibilities, Say eventually found a job working with then succeeding chief financier officer Fred Loneragan, while Luke remained in a planning capacity. But none would ever feel entirely at home. And at Hardie, after so many decades of certainty and continuity, change seemed convulsive—the more so, because some felt it was unnecessary. For the fact is that Hardie was exiting asbestos only with the greatest reluctance.

Macfarlane's low-key manner—he had begun his business life as a fitter and turner at pump-makers Kelly & Lewis—wasn't for everyone. 'I think he was over-promoted,' says Neil Gilbert. 'I mean, everyone is. I was. I was a good engineer, and always struggled a bit with being a manager. Macfarlane was a good salesman. But the main reason he got the job was that he agreed with John Reid on everything. A nice man, but I don't have a huge regard for him ... At one stage he was on the board of the National Bank, which was absolute nonsense.' Others warmed to him. 'David was a really astute, shrewd, talented guy,' recalls Russell Chenu. 'Very understated. Don't think I ever saw him lose his temper, although he was very clear. He said: "We have a limited time with asbestos cement. We must find another fibre as substitute, and in the meantime we must have businesses that can get us through the interim period". It would be fair to say that some of the die-hards in the asbestos cement operations found it pretty challenging.' Tensions emerged. When James Kelso joined Hardie as its public affairs manager from McPherson's around this time, he found that Macfarlane wasn't exactly surrounded by true believers:

A lot of the old hands said you couldn't get out of it. I can tell you, there were plenty in the company, at very high levels, who'd say: 'You can't get rid of the asbestos. That's what giving it the flexibility.' In about 1983, I remember the production manager looking at this new board we'd made and saying: 'Y'know, this'd be a lot better if we had 5 per cent asbestos in this product.' They'd grown up round asbestos and nothing had happened to them. So David really had to stick to his guns.

Thanks to Pether, Hardie sold its first asbestos-free products, a new flat sheet styled Hardiflex II, and an insulation board called Harditherm 700, in 1980. Its new SX fibre-cement sheets were launched in Perth in May 1981 after two years of trials. The James Hardie Industries board formally resolved in April 1983 to 'cease production and sale of building products and friction materials containing asbestos as quickly as possible', and production of asbestos-containing Hardiflex, Hardiplank, Versilux and Villaboard duly ceased that year. But it didn't hurry. There is even evidence that Hardie used asbestos, albeit in small quantities and not perhaps advertently, after it purported to have ceased. In 1983, the Teachers' Federation sent David Kilpatrick some samples of asbestos-free Villaboard in use at their new health centre. He alerted them to traces of chrysotile. Hardie, both irked and concerned, asked him to a meeting at Camellia on 11 October 1983 with John Winters, where the Villaboard was examined microscopically. Kilpatrick recalls:

I said to John: 'See that bundle there, pal? That's chrysotile.' Winters took a look, and said: 'Yes, unfortunately it is. There's not much. Could be a little over half a per cent.' I said: 'I agree with you. Maybe three-quarters of a per cent. But it is there.' So that was fine and we went in and had lunch. Then, midway through, one of the Hardies directors produces a document and says: 'We wondered if you'd sign this.' It was a statement in which I said: 'I believe that the asbestos in this product would not constitute any threat to health.' It was a full page. I said: 'I'm not signing this. This has got asbestos in it.' So that was the end of lunch and I got the early plane back [to Melbourne]. They kindly typed up the minutes of the meeting and sent them to me. Nowhere in the minutes was there any mention of what I'd refused to sign.

Hardie's eventual explanation, not implausible, was that it had been reusing water from a dam previously used in the manufacture of asbestos cement. And there is no reason to suspect that Hardie was other than in deadly earnest about eliminating asbestos from its products as soon as it could. Even Kilpatrick felt the urgency of the effort: 'Every meeting I had with them suggested to me that they were pulling out all stops to get the asbestos out of their sheet.' But it gave little away willingly. After Selikoff and two colleagues finished their pioneering study of the *Mortality Experience of Insulation Workers in the United States and Canada*, suggesting that mesothelioma was caused by amosite as well as crocidolite, McCullagh and Winters became convinced that Hardie would have to cease using it. It took, Winters recalls, a lot of persuasion:

> For a while, the place became divided between people who were saying we should get out of amosite, and the older production guys who were saying: 'No, we need it 'cos it makes the machines run faster.' There was a fair amount of discussion, and for some, I think, it was almost [an attitude of] 'bugger the consequences'.

Concessions to advertising asbestos's health risks — like the agreement from October 1978 to the appearance of warnings of its products — were grudging at best. And to the outside world, Hardie maintained a chorus of denials. Future Hawke government minister John Kerin recalls being escorted around the former Wunderlich factory at Rosehill by a courteous but disarmingly obstinate Hardie medical officer:

> What I saw shocked me, the worst being men using giant vacuum-cleaners to suck up asbestos from a concrete floor which was covered with dust and asbestos fibre. They wore no protection. I quizzed the doctor and expressed my alarm. He took the tobacco lobby's defence and stated that there was no proven link between asbestos and asbestosis. I couldn't believe I was hearing this! It was like saying that lepers don't have leprosy.

The official was perhaps only echoing his chairman's sentiments. John Reid told the *National Times* in January 1980 that the replacement of asbestos in fibre-cement was motivated by finite asbestos supplies: 'Over a long period of time — 25 years or so — we could see a possible shortage and rising costs which would make asbestos products uneconomic'. Did it have anything to do with the health risks of asbestos? 'Definitely not. The controversy has its origins in the United States and United Kingdom and there is a very important distinction between their industries and ours. Asbestos textiles and bagging were the great problems — industries we don't have here.' This was, frankly, misleading. Insulation, in which Hardie had been heavily involved, was as risky as either textiles or bagging; Hardie had used widely the same crocidolite that was beginning to haunt CSR; and Hardie had even, by this stage, been advised of risks to end-users, having in October 1976 received from Johns-Manville a copy of its new guide to precautions for cutting and fixing fibre-cement, and had been experimenting itself on the dust released by hand and power saws.

Whatever the manner of the end — too quick for some, too slow for others — it was coming. Between 1980 and 1984, as Australian asbestos consumption fell from 70,000 to 10,000 tonnes, Hardie's workforce shrank by 2000, and it took a $15 million charge for decommissioning and divestments. The group structure was simplified by a bid for its associate, Hardie Trading, from February 1980 that reunited the companies after their 54-year separation, the acquisition of Turner & Newall's stake in Hardie-Ferodo two months later, and the sale of the company's share of Cassiar Asbestos to Canada's Brinco Ltd six months after that. In the meantime there were a host of bite-sized acquisitions — R. Fowler (sanitaryware), Besley and Pike (envelopes), Rigby (publishing), J. Fielding (fibreboard), Cameron Irrigation — and the formation of a joint venture with APM, James Hardie Containers, in October 1980. For such a staid company, such activity was frenetic.

As though to compensate for its internal identity crisis, Hardie was also cultivating a public profile as at no time in its history. It ran a national advertising program, devised by Coudrey Dailey, promoting itself as 'The Name Behind the Names'. The 500-mile touring car race at Bathurst's Mount Panorama circuit had since 1968 been the Hardie-Ferodo 500; now, metricated as well as wholly owned, it became the James Hardie 1000. Hardie became the major corporate backer of the *Life: Be In It* program and the Parramatta Eels rugby league football league, premiers in 1981, 1982, 1983 and 1986. It sponsored activities as diverse as *The Michael Parkinson Show* on the 0-10 Network, the Australian Opera Company production of *Fiddler on the Roof,* and a musical version of *Seven Little Australians.* There may also have been the suspicion that Hardie had never had greater need of its good corporate name. A worst-case scenario was that a populist politician would seize the commanding heights and unilaterally ban asbestos. As David Kilpatrick recalls, asbestos was finally coming into focus as a socio-political issue:

> Back in 1978 when it was looking as though Labor was in with a chance in Victoria, I used to have one Labor Party preselection candidate after another coming through my office [at the Workers Health Resource Centre] to talk to me about what they'd do if they were elected and became Minister of Labour and Industry. All of them — bunch of bloody stooges really, none of whom would have been any good in the role — said they wanted to either control or shut down James Hardie. My suspicion is that Hardies knew that.

The last products containing asbestos manufactured by Hardie rolled off production lines at Welshpool in Western Australia and Meeandah in Queensland in March 1987. By that stage even Hardie's Indonesian businesses had been sold, to its joint-venture partners Bakrie Brothers, and its remaining shares in UAC Berhad followed in July 1987. By coincidence, it was the company's centenary year, and John Reid used the company's annual meeting the following month to muse on its survival:

> For almost seventy years asbestos fibre has been an important raw material in our manufacturing process. It was essential in terms of the known technology of the times ... since March no asbestos fibre has been used in any of our products ... There is no doubt whatsoever that if this transition had not been handled intelligently and with great care, the damage to the company could have been very serious indeed.

IT WASN'T, OF COURSE, to be so simple. Even as it groped to find its future, James Hardie was shadowed by the ghost of the company it had been. Asbestos had been prized as a substance for its indestructibility; in the story of those previously involved in its mining and manufacture, its traces would prove similarly ineradicable.

In August 1961, Claude Tomplait, a 40-year-old asbestos insulator recently diagnosed with pulmonary fibrosis from inhaling asbestos fibres, visited the offices of Stephenson, Stephenson & Thompson in Orange, Texas, to lodge a claim for compensation. Legal satisfaction would take more than twelve years — by which time Tomplait would be dead — but it detonated the greatest explosion of tort litigation in the history of American jurisprudence. In a landmark judgement in the Fifth Circuit Court of Appeals in *Clarence Borel v Fibreboard Paper* in September 1973, Judge John Minor Wisdom confirmed a principle of torts in which, in a sense, the whole *raison d'etre* of asbestos litigation is contained: a manufacturer must disclose the existence and extent of reasonably foreseeable risk involving the use of his product.

> Under the law of torts, a person has long been liable for the foreseeable harm caused by his own negligence. This principle applies to the manufacture of products as it does to almost every other area of human endeavour. It implies a duty to warn of foreseeable dangers associated with those products. This duty to warn extends to all users and consumers, including the common worker in the shop or in the field. Where the law has imposed a duty, courts stand ready in proper cases to enforce the rights so created. Here there was a duty to speak, but the defendants remained silent. The district court's judgement does no more than hold the defendants liable for the foreseeable consequences of their own inaction.

Twenty-five thousand lawsuits would be brought in the US over the next decade, with plaintiff lawyers landing some knockout blows. In April 1977, for instance, an attorney visiting the headquarters of Raybestos in Trumbull, Connecticut, was pointed to a pile of boxes containing the 'personal documents' of founder Sumner Simpson. These proved to include correspondence to and from Johns-Manville discussing the health risks of asbestos, and their own efforts to suppress knowledge of same, as far back as the 1930s. When defendant companies protested their use as evidence on grounds they were prejudicial, Ron Motley said: 'Darn well right, it's prejudicial. So were the Watergate tapes.'

It was a far cry from the derring-do of American plaintiff lawyers when the Melbourne labour-law firm of Slater & Gordon ran its first asbestos case in May 1978: *Ryan Carlisle Thomas v Waldorf Appliances and the Gas & Fuel Corporation* involved an applicant who had developed asbestosis after three-and-a-half years placing asbestos sheets between the outer and inner coatings of cooking utensils. The Limitation of Actions Act, laying down for legal action a six-year limit after cause of damage, loomed as an obstacle, but expert testimony from David Kilpatrick on the history of health risks from asbestos did the trick. When Justice Grey finally decided that he was 'satisfied that he [Thomas] did not know about the dangers of asbestos and I do not believe that he could reasonably have been expected to become aware of such dangers', the Gas & Fuel Corporation settled swiftly.

Slater & Gordon, founded in 1935 by a former Labor attorney-general in Victoria, and associated with the Communist Party of Australia throughout its travails in the 1940s and 1950s, was an heir to all the local left's lofty ideals and bitter prejudices: it championed the cause of the common man, but would not employ Catholics, even as cleaners. Slightly less doctrinaire by the 1970s, it was still a home for lawyers with an affinity for the poor and disenfranchised: Mike Higgins had been self-supporting since fifteen, when he had left home to escape the violence of an alcoholic father, and only studied law thanks to scholarships; his young protégé Peter Gordon, the son of a clerk and factory worker from Melbourne's working-class west, had founded a legal referral service there while still at university. Their colleague Geoff Jones had provided legal advice to Ray Hogan during his recent argy-bargy with Hardie over the special payment; Higgins and Gordon suggested now that the Federated

Miscellaneous Workers Union bankroll a common law test case involving a Brooklyn worker.

A year earlier, Cornelius Maas become the first Wittenoom worker to sue Australian Blue Asbestos, now renamed Midalco by its owner, CSR, only to die in the attempt.* Slater & Gordon needed someone who would stand the course. In March 1978, Triantafillos 'Theo' Meletis, who had worked at Brooklyn from 1956 to 1974, had been undergoing routine tests for a cold when an X-ray showed evidence of asbestosis. Now he was chosen from a number of potential cases. Writs were issued in November.

The wheels of justice, of course, grind exceeding small. A *papierkrieg* ensued. A Limitation of Actions case had first to be fought and won in February 1979, Justice Clifford Menhemmit deciding that there was a *prima facie* case of negligence, and that Meletis could not have taken action earlier. In August, Hardie's lawyers Ellison Hewison & Whitehead stated that their client would only participate in discovery if Slater undertook that documents would not 'be used in subsequent litigation on behalf of other workers'. Higgins held his ground, claiming that this was 'outrageous and ... lacks any legal basis', and Hardie eventually surrendered 117 exhibits. Then, a few months later, the Brooklyn factory manager Brian Thompson walked into the milk bar owned by Meletis's brother-in-law and said that Hardie wanted to talk. When the family's Greek Orthodox priest was suggested as an intermediary, a meeting was duly held at the Saint Nicholaos Church in Murray Street, Yarraville, on 6 February 1980.

The James Hardie story has contained many extraordinary meetings, but few so unusual as that between Theo Meletis, Saint Nicholaos's Father Amanatidis, Hardie legal manager Lionel Denmead, plant secretary Cliff Mott and an unknown insurance

---

* Maas had been receiving a tiny pension from the State Government Insurance Office. 'Thirty thousand dollars isn't much for a man's life when he's got twenty-five years of working life left in him,' he told the ABC's *This Day Tonight*. CSR retorted that it had 'discharged its legal requirements by insuring the men for workers' compensation and the question of moral responsibility was not relevant'. Maas died ten days later. His family lost even his pension.

company representative. Meletis's own account reads:

> The man from Sydney did the talking. He told me they didn't want a
> bad name. They wanted to settle it. I said I wanted $150,000 and $180
> per week until I die. They said you are asking too much and why are
> you asking this amount. I said I am a sick man and I don't believe I will
> live any more than two years. I said if I was healthy and could work to
> sixty-five, I would make double the money. He said you ask more than
> we had in mind.

Meletis seems to have asked for more even than his spiritual
adviser had in mind. After the Hardie representatives had left,
Father Amanatidis told him: 'The Lord does not like people who are
greedy.' Meletis replied: 'Next time you are speaking to the Lord, tell
him that for $150,000, I won't be'. Peter Gordon flew into a pre-
dictable outrage, upbraiding Ellison, Hewison & Whitehead for
'this highly unethical and contemptible conduct'. Ellison offered a
predictably glib response that there was 'no rule of ethics known to
us which prevents people coming together to discuss their problems'. The reply, which it took Hardie's state manager Eric Charles
a month to draft, was nothing if not sanctimonious: 'Any employer
who has concern for the interests of his employees and former
employees' health and well-being should at all times be able to discuss these matters personally, with a view to assisting in the resolution of problems which may arise and this is simply all that was done
in this case.' *Meletis v James Hardie & Coy* was in some respects a
cheeky case: the applicant had only a relatively mild form of
asbestosis, and was still gainfully employed at Containers Packaging.
The proceedings would take more than four years to play out, finally
settling in October 1982 with Meletis receiving $65,000. But the
bigger win was the feeling that the action gave for Hardie's vulnerability. As Higgins reported to Hogan, the company steadily gave
way on its awareness of asbestos's dangers:

> It is fairly clear that the insurance industry is accepting that the danger
> to asbestos have been well known for many years. The James Hardie

defence shifted ground during the currency of the action. The emphasis became that it was known that the produce [sic] was dangerous, but the company had taken all reasonable steps to protect their employees from the danger. We might add that we were told by Counsel acting for James Hardie that the company was very keen to fight the action but that the insurance companies involved took the view that it could not be successfully defended.

One of the ironies of Hardie's position where asbestos-related liabilities are concerned was revealed very early: it would become a victim of its own prior domestic dominance. If a product contained asbestos in Australia between the 1920s and the 1970s, chances are that at some level Hardie had been involved — a state of affairs that, as late as the company's 1978 annual report, John Reid was celebrating: 'Every time you walk into an office building, a home, a factory: every time you put your foot on the brake, ride in a train, see a bulldozer at work ... every time you see or do any of these things, the chances are that a product from the James Hardie Group of Companies has a part in it.' The legal significance of this became apparent from July 1981, when Ronald Thomas Baker, a lagger with three insulation companies at the Vales Point and Munmorah Power Stations in the 1960s, brought his mesothelioma to the Sydney labour law firm of Turner Freeman.

Turners had been founded in 1952 by Roy Turner, who had returned from service as a bomber pilot in the RAF as a Trotskyist, and was now a member of the Legislative Council in the Wran government with strong union links: Baker had come on the recommendation of the Australian Manufacturing Workers' Union. His case was split initially into a common law product liability suit to be led by a senior partner, Peter Tyson, and a workers' compensation claim by a graduate solicitor who had been at the firm only nine months, Armando Gardiman.

Gardiman, raised by immigrant Italian parents near Nimbin, had been inspired to pursue law when the British human rights lawyer John Lynes, recently expelled from Ghana because of his opposition to its genocidal dictator Kwame Nkrumah, settled on a nearby farm.

The challenge here, however, was not so much fighting the opposition as finding it. There was no one to sue. The three companies for which Baker had worked — Bells Asbestos & Engineering, Australian Asbestos Insulation, and Quality Insulation — were respectively departed, defunct and deregistered. The junior counsel acting for Baker, Peter Semmler, then had a good idea: *faute de mieux*, sue Electricity Commission of New South Wales, who had been principally responsible for his working conditions. Gardiman then advanced an even better one when Baker remembered the name on most of the products: sue James Hardie. 'Had we had a company that was live and with unlimited insurance cover,' recalls Gardiman, 'we probably would never have gone after Hardies.'

When the workers' compensation claim was won, attention turned to the Supreme Court; like Meletis, Baker needed to win relief from the Limitation of Actions Act. And again, the case proved as important in what it added to the sum of human knowledge as its outcome. 'We had no idea what we were doing,' Gardiman says. 'No idea at all. No one had ever run one of these cases before; hardly anyone had ever sought an extension of time. We needed to show that there was a *prima facie* case of knowledge. That was when we stumbled on to Maurice Joseph.' Joseph, the respiratory physician who had been asked to examine Hardie workers with asbestosis more than two decades earlier, testified accordingly. After appealing unsuccessfully against the extension of time, then consulting with insurers, the company settled.

The litigation pressure on Hardie, in fact, was causing significant friction with its longest-standing insurer, QBE. The pair had a relationship going back to 1933; QBE insured Hardie for public liability from 1952, and for product liability from 1965 — until, in both cases, 1977. It had also insured Hardie-BI. On their face, the QBE policies provided very substantial cover. But unhappy with the course of litigation, QBE now purported to cancel all of the policies on grounds that Hardie had failed to disclose to it all available information about asbestos's risks. Hardie, QBE said, referring to the growing corpus of scientific data on the subject, had 'adopted a course of deliberately attempting to conceal facts known to it relating to the asbestos hazards', arguing that, even if the policies were valid, the claims did not constitute an 'accident' as required. Only legal action averted an embarrassing *froideur*. Going to court was becoming, for Hardie, a regular occurrence. One morning in September 1982, toward the end of the Baker case, Armando Gardiman and Peter Semmler arrived at the Supreme Court to find a group of sheepish, middle-aged men almost indistinguishable in grey suits. 'I was told it was the board of James Hardie,' Gardiman recalls.

11

'I think we're fucked'

'Here's a roomful of people who are dying, and no one's doing anything about it.'
—Peter Gordon, on his first meeting with Wittenoom survivors

THE CHALLENGE CONFRONTING potential litigants and plaintiff lawyers in the early 1980s could be condensed to four words: who knew what when? Yes, health alarms about asbestos dated back to the 1920s. But when did people *really* know it killed you, killed you in different ways and after relatively low dosages? Frankly, too, this was not only a problem for applicants; defendant companies faced the same question. CSR executives had traipsed regularly through Wittenoom; senior managers were among the victims of its lethal dust. Thyne Reid had been a familiar face at Camellia, as had Jock Reid at Brooklyn, and Jock's son John was state manager for South Australia from 1960 to 1965, based at Birkenhead. Perhaps they were studiously looking the other way, but these were not the behaviours of men harbouring a dark secret.

These same questions resonated with judges—who preferred to take no chances. The second case by a Wittenoom worker was taken against Midalco by Joan Joosten, a typist at the mine between 1950 and 1953 who defied her mesothelioma for three years after an initial prognosis that she would live six months. CSR prevailed, Justice Wallace of the West Australian Supreme Court finding that Midalco could have taken no precautions against mesothelioma because its association with crocidolite was not proposed until Chris Wagner's pioneering paper of 1960. 'I do not condemn as negligence,' the judge concluded, 'that which, in my opinion, was a sad misadventure'. Lawyers, too, remained inexperienced where such litigation was concerned. In February 1982, the blue-chip Adelaide firm of Finlaysons took to the state's supreme court the case of T. A. Footner, who had developed a pleural mesothelioma after working for Broken Hill Associated Smelters as a boilermaker and fitter from 1944 to 1952. Again, David Kilpatrick provided expert testimony, stating that 'a responsible employer' should have been aware by 1944 that asbestos dust was hazardous, and should 'by simple expedients' have been capable of remediating work processes. The case, however, was a debacle:

> I interviewed Mr Footner by telephone and sent his statement [recalls Kilpatrick]. Then when the case didn't settle, they rang me up and flew me over on the first plane. I was meant to have a barrister's conference and interview the client personally, but the lawyer had me sitting in reception for two hours. Then the barrister came down, spoke to me for thirty seconds, and said sorry, he had to go. A secretary took me down to the court where I introduced myself to Mr Footner—he was obviously Mr Footner because he looked so crook. Then they said: 'Oh, you're on'. When the barrister for Mr Footner started saying stupid things I had to correct him. Then the BHAS barrister tried to turn around the Fleisher report to make it look like it said how safe lagging was when it was actually damning—which he did very skilfully but was actually outrageous—and I just stuck to my guns, from which the judge concluded that I was partisan.*

Justice Jacobs' finding echoed that of Justice Wallace, giving heart to all potential defendants: 'It is more than usually important, in a case such as this, to guard against the wisdom of hindsight, or an emotional response—of which I detected some sign in the evidence of Dr Kilpatrick—to the predicament in which the community now

---

* The 'Fleisher paper' refers to a 1946 contribution to the *Journal of Industrial Hygiene and Toxicology* by W. E. Fleisher who noted many very high dust counts from asbestos lagging operations on naval vessels, and three cases of asbestosis among laggers.

finds itself by reason of what are now known to be the medical hazards of any exposure to asbestos.' Hardie's legal redoubt was then assaulted from a different angle when, following representations by the Aboriginal Legal Service, a House of Representatives standing committee was constituted to investigate health and working conditions at the Baryulgil mine.

Rightly anticipating a lengthy siege, Hardie immediately raised the drawbridge and lowered the portcullis. When the committee sought documentation, it received instead a letter: 'I regret to advise that the company has received legal opinion that because of litigation pending against companies in the James Hardie Group and the difficulty that the committee faces in controlling the use of material presented to it, I am unable to comply with the request.' (This did not prove an obstacle to investigation because the mine manager, Gerald Burke, turned over kilograms of internal company documentation). Then, at the first hearing, public affairs manager James Kelso had to read out a statement saying that he was not authorised by James Hardie 'to make admissions on its behalf of any fact or any matter'. As Kelso recalls: 'Frankly, Hardie didn't know whether I'd be able to handle it and they didn't know who else would be called. So they weren't going to have anybody admitting anything on Hardie's behalf.'

Kelso, with the assistance of legal manager Lionel Denmead and a new company solicitor, Mark Knight, had done a good deal of preparatory work. He had even managed to track down Burke's predecessor as mine manager, who arrived at their meeting in Kalgoorlie driving a 1965 Buick, polished off a bottle of whisky as they talked, and scoffed at the claims: 'It's all bullshit. The aborigines wouldn't do anything they were told. Half of them were drunk when they turned up.' Kelso was actually dismayed by the visit: 'No point using that; would've sounded like we'd paid him'.

The other evidence he sifted was more promising. There was documentary and anecdotal support for the idea that Baryulgil had been chronically undercapitalised, extremely dirty, and should never have remained open so long. But there wasn't empirical proof of a superabundance of sick workers. A 1977 Health Department clinical and radiological survey commissioned by minister Kevin

Stewart had reported a high rate of bronchitis among workers but no problems among residents: 'Except for a few cases of non-related lung disorder, all non-miners were shown to be free from asbestosis or any other lung abnormality which could be attributed to the mining and milling of asbestos.' This may have been because the generally low life-expectancy of the indigenous population ensured they did not live long enough to develop diseases; perhaps also because if one must work with asbestos at all, a small, open-cut chrysotile mine is probably best. Asbestos is unusual in growing more dangerous, because it is becoming more fibrous, as it is processed. Mines that have proven particularly dangerous have tended either to be mining crocidolite, worked underground, or both (like Wittenoom). The Baryulgil community, moreover, remained oddly proud of the mine. 'They had a beaut little school, in the courtyard of which was a selection of minerals from the area,' Kelso recalls. 'And the biggest and most prized was a big lump of serpentine with an asbestos seam running through it, which you could brush away with your fingers.'

For months in Grafton and Canberra, Kelso sat alone at a table facing the ten members of the committee. Occasionally he sounded glib, as when he claimed that it was 'inconceivable that employees were unaware of the dangers of asbestos' because they would have seen dust counts in progress. Sometimes he sounded facetious, as when evidence was produced that the mine had deliberately slowed down operations while inspectors ascertained dust levels: 'Your wife puts all the dishes out of the sink into the dishwasher before somebody comes and I believe that would happen at Baryulgil as well'. But mostly he sounded reasonable, picking holes easily in a poorly organised and presented case by the Aboriginal Legal Service.

The question inevitably arises of racism, and there were some flashes of it, though not from Kelso; rather, they came from National Party member Ian Cameron who, on one occasion, ridiculed a suggestion that aborigines had a special attachment to the land: 'That is garbage ... How would you know? You're as white as I am!' But the committee's finding, while equivocal, was hard to avoid: while Baryulgil had been 'run in such a way as to be capable of producing asbestos-related disease', such illness 'was not widespread'. Within Hardie, Kelso became a kind of hero, the man who spoken truth to power, warding off the greatest threat yet to Hardie's reputation.

For there were threats, and they were to more than reputation. The worldwide asbestos industry found that the early 1980s were years of living dangerously, especially in the US. In February 1982, a congressional inquiry into asbestos was told by an insurance official that product-liability suits would likely cost about $US90 billion, and the growing scale of damages awards, as a Raybestos lawyer complained, threatened to 'turn punishment into annihilation'. Hardie's American ally, Johns-Manville, had embarked on a similar course of restructuring and diversifying. Less than one-fifth of its sales were now from asbestos; a third now came from fibreglass, centred at Defiance, Ohio. But while it was the 181st-largest industrial corporation in the US, with assets exceeding $US2 billion, Johns-Manville was also receiving as many as 500 law suits a month — and bore the title, conferred by Ron Motley, of being 'the greatest corporate mass murderer in history'. Its strategic response was to withdraw into Chapter 11 bankruptcy in August 1982, a month after another asbestos manufacturer, UNR, freezing all payments to creditors, including litigants.

The decision reverberated round the world. Australia did not offer companies the sanctuary of Chapter 11, but Gerry Gardiman was reminded of the limits of corporate resources. Turner Freeman was running a succession of common law actions for insulation workers who had been employed in the construction of power stations, along with one for Peter Calkin, a senior executive of the fire-protection company Wormald International. In each case, Gerry Gardiman also sued Hardie. In each case, Hardie settled, usually picking up roughly half the damages in return for confidentiality. Gardiman was content with this arrangement: 'My great fear was the Johns-Manville experience. You had to ensure that the primary defendant didn't get whacked so hard that you pushed them over the edge.' For the time being, Gardiman accepted the small target offered by Hardie's solicitors, a firm called Diamond Peisah: 'Ashley Neilson [from Diamond Peisah] was a very decent man. He tested things at the edges, and concentrated on contribution. The attitude was: you settled claims, you kept a lid on it, you kept it quiet, you kept material out of the public arena, minimised any media attention.' In his finding in the Hardie case against QBE in November 1984, Justice Rogers concluded that the claims 'must be of immense consequence to the future financial well-being of the parties'. It was in no one's interest if any of the parties ceased to exist.

In the meantime, Gardiman was learning. He opened a Turner Freeman office in Parramatta in June 1985, and began to eat, drink and sleep asbestos. 'I have a deep-rooted love of history, and the work suited me,' he recalls:

> The years from the 1950s to the early 1970s were a period of Australian history where the country was being constructed. The guys who worked at the power stations were going from Vales Point to Munmora to Liddell … If they worked for ICAL they went one way. If they worked for Babcocks they went another. The insulation companies would move from power station to power station, from chemical works to chemical works. We put that story back together.

That year, too, a foot-slogging official from the Australian Manufacturing Workers' Union, Tom Cook, tramped round Parramatta seeking as many past and present workers from Camellia as he could, advising them of their legal rights and flushing out more litigants, including a group from Hardie-BI. 'Up until the time that I spoke to Tom Cook I was not aware of the fact that I could take legal proceedings against James Hardie,' recalled one, Colin Marshall. 'The practice had been that we would all be herded like sheep down to the Dust Board. As far as we were aware, the Dust Board provided us with our only avenue of compensation.' Hardie-BI's former foreman, Alf Hinton, who himself would die of mesothelioma, brought many old workmates in himself.

Slater & Gordon's more aggressive approach in Melbourne was somehow embodied in the burly, bustling figure of Peter Gordon, who took over common law litigation in August 1985 when his old boss Mike Higgins joined the bench. Slater & Gordon went to court

146

a month later on behalf of Harold Pilmer, who had contracted mesothelioma almost fifty years after joining the hardware firm McPherson's as a fourteen-year-old general hand. The company's admission that it taken 'no effective measures to prevent or reduce or minimise exposure to asbestos' undermined its defence that there was 'no consensus' of medical opinion regarding mesothelioma for most of Pilmer's career, and eventually cost them $222,500 damages — the first time a common law action had been seen through to a verdict, rather than settled.

Not everything Gordon tried worked. So moved was he by the impoverished circumstances of one former SEC worker, James McEwan, a victim of mesothelioma contracted over a career at Yallourn power station, that he tried to make the man's brief stay in Melbourne memorable, booking him into a lofty penthouse at the Regent Hotel for the night, and leaving him with a six-pack of Crown Lagers. Gordon found him the next morning cowering as far from the fortieth-floor window as possible: terrified of heights, he had not slept a wink. In court, Gordon had more luck. In February 1986, the SEC settled with McEwan for $140,000 plus costs. Six months later, compensation proceedings obtained a new dimension when Slater & Gordon successfully sought leave to videotape the evidence of a former employee at APM's Fairfield paper mill, Bill Hyslop, confined to his hospital bed by lung cancer; no sooner had the harrowing recording been played than the defendant settled for $120,000. And that same month, Gordon received a telephone call that would alter the course of Australian tort history.

The caller, a Croatian man called Robert Vojakovic, had been spared a long stint at Wittenoom by a lucky win at cards. The sensation of blessedness had never left him, and he had become president of Perth's Asbestos Diseases Society. Now, to Gordon, he poured out his frustrations, from legal indifference to test cases thwarted by untimely deaths. Brian Burke's government had relaxed the statute of limitations for asbestos cases, allowing a three-year window for claims for all illnesses occurring prior to January 1984, but time was running out. Gordon soon found himself in Perth surrounded by some very ill people and thinking: 'What the fuck is going on here?' By the deadline, Slater & Gordon had lodged more than 300 writs.

The initial test case, which opened in July 1987, was a disaster. Wally Simpson, an indigent labourer who had spent four years at Wittenoom and now claimed asbestosis, was an uneasy, erratic plaintiff. His contradictory testimony was savaged by CSR's silks. Finding for the company, Justice Brinsden described Simpson as 'a person who is inclined to exaggerate his symptoms, give false information to those examining him, and engaging in seeking hospital and medical assistance through some personality disorder'. Some aspects of proceedings smacked of parochialism, but Simpson's use as a standard bearer for asbestos litigation was like Bottom's casting as Pyramus. The result was deeply demoralising, and Slater & Gordon might well have retreated had it not already committed to two other interleaving actions. The first, in the WA Supreme Court, involved two mesothelioma sufferers diagnosed in 1986: Peter Heys had worked at Wittenoom for two months as a plumber's assistant and hand in the bagging mill; Tim Barrow had spent three years there as a timekeeper and tally clerk. The second, in the Victorian Supreme Court, was taken by Klaus Rabenalt, who had worked six months at Wittenoom twenty-seven years earlier as a young German émigré, and after a highly successful business career had been diagnosed with mesothelioma in October 1987.

Enough material had come to light by now for CSR to be concerned, from a 1944 memo in which Keith Brown had noted that 'the mill is so dusty that it is definitely hazardous to health', to a 1948 letter by a young doctor, Eric Saint, prophesising for Wittenoom 'the richest and most lethal crop of asbestosis in the world's literature'. Looking up from five documents that Slater & Gordon requested the day before the Rabenalt trial began, CSR's counsel, Alan McDonald QC, announced: 'I think we're fucked.' To sheet its advantage home, however, Slater & Gordon needed to cope with a concept as economically quaint as it is legally robust: the corporate veil.

The cornerstone of limited liability is the idea that companies are legal entities separate and distinct from their shareholders — the 'corporate veil' refers to the protection inhering in this principle, confining a company's liabilities to those sums recoverable from *its* assets rather than those of its members. Thanks to the veil, shareholders can invest without fear of covetous creditors. Thanks to the veil, a company can set limits on its legal responsibilities by the straightforward expedient of arranging its businesses in self-governing entities within a larger group—as indeed, CSR had done by steadily winnowing Midalco away to a $337 shadow of its former self.

The veil was regarded as all but impermeable, having been upheld in numberless judgements since the 1897 finding of the Law Lords in *Salomon v A. Salomon & Co Ltd*, in which Lord Herschell stated unambiguously: 'In a popular sense, the company may in every case be said to carry on business for and on behalf of its shareholders; but this certainly does not in point of law constitute the relation of principal and agent between them or render the shareholders liable to indemnify the company against the debts which it incurs.' Most recently, and seldom more explicitly, it had been found in *Bank of Tokyo v Karoon* by Sir Reginald Goff: '[Counsel] suggested beguilingly that it would be technical for us to distinguish between parent and subsidiary company in this context; economically, he said, they were one. But we are concerned *not with economics but with law*. The distinction between the two is, in law, fundamental and cannot here be bridged.' Peter Gordon, however, intended not a frontal assault on CSR's legal fortification, but a siege. In chagrined appreciation, his quarry, CSR's in-house lawyer Ian Mutton, explains:

This was Gordon's brilliance. He sued CSR and Midalco, and bet everything on the emotion. Here were people who had obviously been injured by the inhalation of asbestos, and who might go without compensation if the court did not find proximity between the two. Piercing the corporate veil is next to impossible, so Gordon didn't even try. What proximity says is: 'Sure, they're not jointly liable. But it's a bit like being a murderer and a murderer's apprentice: the two of them move together. So that, if the subsidiary has no money, then the parent provides.' You put all the corporate veil niceties to one side and go back to old-fashioned criminality, and say: 'What matters is that they were in the car together.'

The emotion *was* acute, especially in the case of Rabenalt, who turned out to be an utterly charming and decent man, and who sent a shocked silence through the court when his counsel, Richard Stanley QC, asked that he open his shirt to reveal the ravages of his chest surgery. The cases also proved complementary. The Melbourne jury handed down the first verdict for a former Wittenoom employee, laying on top of $426,000 damages for negligence a further $250,000 in exemplary damages for a 'continuous, conscious and contumelious disregard' of the plaintiff's safety, in May 1988. Four months later — after 131 sitting days, sixty-nine witnesses, 730 exhibits, 11,000 pages of transcript and probably emboldened by events across the continent — Justice Rowland in Perth awarded $116,000 to Heys and $216,000 to Barrow. He explicitly vindicated Gordon's proximity argument by concluding that 'it would be completely unrealistic to suggest that ABA (Midalco) controlled its own destiny in any real sense', and that it was 'impossible ... to believe that standards have changed to extent that an industrialist would not be obliged to find out all there was to know about the properties of a mineral which he intends to mine and mill, and to find out the industrial dangers of such an enterprise'. The verdicts were still tinged with tragedy: within six months, all three men were dead. But a simple gesture by CSR's instructing solicitor, Philip Rowell of Russell Kennedy, on the day the Rabenalt verdict was upheld on appeal, proved to have lasting consequences.

> Mr Rabenalt was the most delightful man [Rowell recalls]. We were at our barrister's chambers and after I'd rung the client I said to my articled clerk: 'OK it's over, we lost, but we should go round and wish him well.' Peter [Gordon] wasn't there — he was doing his media things. But everyone else was at Dick Stanley's chambers having champagne ... I congratulated Dick and asked if I could speak to Mr Rabenalt. He said: 'Sure'. So I just went in and said: 'Well done, Mr Rabenalt, and all the best.'

Anyway, Peter [Gordon] rang the next day and he said: 'Did you really come in and say 'all the best'? After the way this case was fought?' I said: 'Peter, I'm a lawyer, you're a lawyer. You won, I'll beat you next time, but we're all trying to do the best for our clients. We should have lunch.' So we did. Over lunch, Peter said: 'Well, now that we've got liability established, how about we try and settle all the other claims? I said: 'Do you want me to explore the possibility with my clients?' He said yes, and within a week we were.

What became known as the global settlement, negotiated in Melbourne and Perth in the first half of 1989, and made possible by an agreement on insurance coverage splitting the bill between CSR and the West Australian State Government Insurance Office, was signed in October. Essentially, CSR handed over about $20 million, leaving it to Slater & Gordon to apportion amongst 200 existing claimants. It was a gamble on CSR's part, because it voluntarily lifted the corporate veil. James Hardie showed no such instincts. In June, Diamond Peisah had successfully defended it from an action brought by a Baryulgil worker, a 71-year-old asbetotic Kumbaingeri aborigine called Briggs. As a result, it was feeling secure enough to offer CSR some gratuitous advice.[†] 'In the late 1980s,' recalls Mutton, 'Hardies came to me and said that we were doing it wrong, that the issue of proximity was an incredibly important issue, that we should be doing all in our power to maintain the separateness of our asbestos subsidiaries.' Mutton felt, on the contrary, that he was rectifying an earlier mistake:

---

† Justice Rogers' finding in *Briggs v James Hardie & Coy* explicitly recognised that the corporate veil flew in the face of commercial reality, but left it intact:

> In the result, as the law presently stands, in my view the proposition advanced by the plaintiff that the corporate veil may be pierced where one company exercises complete dominion and control over another is entirely too simplistic. The law pays scant regard to the commercial reality that every holding company has the potential and more often than not in fact does exercise complete control over a subsidiary ... It remains to be seen whether the time has come for the development of a more principled approach than the authorities provide at present.

CSR was an engineering company. We managed the asbestos liability badly early on; we tended to look at the evidence clinically and say: 'This is what should and shouldn't happen.' I'd include myself in that. It's an approach that gives rise to good research papers which not many people read. It's vital to keep your strategies in line with community expectations, and at the beginning ours were disconnected ... We went from the high moral ground to thinking: 'How do we manage this?' The upshot was that our settlement costs rose slightly, but our legal costs plunged, and the transaction costs were reduced on a net basis.

The upshot was also that while CSR and James Hardie ended the 1980s paying out essentially similar amounts on compensatory damages, their liability positions were quite distinct — CSR having conceded theirs, Hardie still protecting theirs. CSR's problems were largely confined to its cohort of affected miners; Hardie's were spreading from the original group of insulation and fibre-cement workers to those who had used its products, which, given its market share, was vast. CSR had disgorged most of its secrets; Hardie had not. In fact, it was intent on keeping them. Neil Gilbert recalls a telephone call from David Macfarlane on the subject of litigation:

I was rung up by Macfarlane and asked would I look after the asbestos investigation side of the company? And I said: 'Well look, I've got nothing against the company. I believe that while we were there we did what we could. I'd be happy to help anyway I could.' He said: 'Well, that would be worth quite a bit of money to the company. I'd like to offer you a salary. What would you like?' I said: 'I'm not interested in being paid. No thanks, but I'd quite prepared to help.'

What he meant, I think, was that I should keep quiet about anything I knew about asbestos. And he wanted to pay me to keep me on side. I know Terry McCullagh was paid $10,000 a year as a consultant after he left, because I was in contact with Terry just before he died of stomach cancer about five years ago and he said: 'Y'know they're still paying me. I don't know what they're paying me for.' They paid several others, but they're still alive so I won't mention their names. Anyway I did appear for them in several cases as you know, but

I gradually realised … that they were tending to try and push the problem under the counter. That's when I started to get difficult about appearing. I was asked to appear in one case and the solicitor asked me what was it like at Camellia. I told him and never heard from him again. That fixed that problem.

The policy of containment had pluses, but also minuses. It was not learned until *Graham Courtney Phillips v Concrete Constructions Victoria* in 1988, for instance, that Hardie had for a decade used crocidolite from Wittenoom. This wasn't entirely bad news for Hardie, as it gave the company the chance to force a contribution to settlements from CSR, but its generally defensive posture seems to have made it reluctant to take advantage. 'I can remember talking to Diamond Peisah in the late 1980s about the blue,' recalls Gardiman. 'I said: "You know, you blokes have got a really big cross claim against CSR." They said: "We'd rather not know." Hardie didn't want a brawl about blue asbestos out in the public domain. They'd rather pay the compensation and make 'em go away.'

At the end of 1989, Hardie found itself tackled by *Four Corners*. Host Andrew Olle topped the show by brandishing a copy of *A Very Good Business;* reporter Chris Masters proceeded to depict a very bad business indeed. Standing at a picnic for sufferers of asbestos-related disease in a park across the Parramatta River from Camellia, Masters commented on how successful Hardie had been at avoiding public odium:

If there was a factory explosion where hundreds of people died and it occurred somewhere in the western world, then it would be considered in the west to be a disaster of international proportions. Across the water at the James Hardie factory a similar disaster has occurred with an extra dimension to the tragedy. This has been a drip-fed disaster. The workers have died quietly and at discrete intervals, so there've been no headlines, no public monuments, and no conspicuous public mourning.

James Kelso, so effective in dealing with government, had found the media altogether less tractable, and was scathing of the program.

But Masters' title was not an inappropriate description of Hardie's legal strategy: 'Dirty Secrets'.

-12-

'If you don't achieve it, you are gone'

'We are undemonstrative and inarticulate and in some ways we are not
a very powerful thinking people either.'
—James Hardie Industries chairman John Reid, of Australians, in May
1979

ON THE AUSTRALIAN FINANCIAL LANDSCAPE IN THE 1980S,
little changed in decades, broke waves of innovation. Some
developments were welcome, some not: deregulation, leverage,
takeovers and entrepreneurs. They were forces, however, of little
immediate relevance to James Hardie Industries. It was a dull,
workaday company, clear only about what it was leaving behind—
asbestos—and vague as to its future direction.

It ran a blur of businesses from paints (Spartan), paper (Spicers),
packaging (James Hardie Containers) and publishing (Paul
Hamlyn, Rigby, Lansdowne Press) to animation (Hanna-Barbera
Australia), irrigation (RIS, Cameron), engineering (Horscroft,
Acme, Duraform) and envelopes (Besley & Pike). It made the mini-
series *Return to Eden*. It published *The Complete Works of Banjo
Paterson*. It distributed Bullworkers in Australia. It even imported
tropical fish through Pets International, originated in a suburban
fishpond by an amateur aquarium-builder in 1923, and acquired by
Hamlyn.

It was everywhere: a listing of its various offices, plants and
warehouses in January 1982 showed up 214 separate addresses. But
it was also nowhere, adding little of value to any of its businesses. As
for the new genus of corporate predator, chairman John Reid simply
disdained it. 'If someone offered $50 a share for Hardie,' he

harrumphed in *Australian Business* in June 1986, 'the directors would have to think about it.'

Nor was the company simply dull on the outside. 'Within three months I was looking for a new job,' says Stephen Gellert, who joined the company in 1984 as a 28-year-old lawyer from Sly & Russell. 'I hated it. I thought they were all deadheads.' Realising that a brief stay might look a little odd on his resume, he reconciled himself to staying, and found that his job had its stimulations, if for mainly bad reasons. 'I like solving problems,' he says. 'And Hardies was resplendent with problems.' The overarching challenge, as Gellert saw it, was that the sheer diversity of the company's operations had made central control very difficult, strengthening the hand of the already strong divisional bosses.

Gellert's first job was taking care of the company's legal work unrelated to asbestos, which was now the sole task of Mark Knight, and it gave him a good vantage point on Hardie's hidebound culture. The first commandment he heard was not an instruction but a prohibition: 'Don't turn up anywhere without clearing it with the relevant executive general manager first'. The executive general managers not only ran their businesses like fiefdoms, they also predominated on the board. For most of the 1980s, the only non-executive on Hardie's board, aside from chairman John Reid, was his pastoralist cousin Sandy.* Otherwise the table was occupied by managing director David Macfarlane, deputy managing director Fred Loneragan, Harry Hudson (in charge of fibre-cement), John Roberts (in charge of the company's nascent American operations), Bill Butterss (running Hardie Trading, wholly owned from 1980) and David Say (finance director). It is a mystery, for instance, what any of them knew about the running of an amusement park. Yet Hardie cheerfully took a shareholding in Australia's Wonderland at Michinbury, west of Blacktown, on which Neville Wran turned the first sod in November 1984. The arrangement changed Say's mind about board practice:

---

* Alexander Thyne Reid, known as Sandy, was the son of George Reid, youngest son of the patriarch Andrew. He joined the board in 1973.

As a younger man I was all for executive directors, especially in finance; as I grew older and more senior, I realised what a bad forum it is for debate when a board has too many executives. What tended to happen at Hardie was that the executive who put up a plan at board level was seldom cross-examined because the other executives wanted him on side when their plan came along. Worse, you only had a small minority asking questions.

Hardie's only truly new frontier was the United States, to which it had been an exporter of fibre-cement sheet since 1969, but never had a presence on the ground. That changed in October 1983 when Hardie paid $10 million for HRM Inc, an irrigation company in California. After buying a paper merchant in Oregon in April 1985, it began replicating its diverse local structure abroad with ventures into security, fine-paper trading, and two gypsum wallboard operations acquired for $100 million in July 1987. The advance, however, seemed ill-starred from its inception. The first full-time executive it sent over, Roberts, suffered a lethal heart attack within months of arriving, and was succeeded by Butterss. Worst of all was a relationship into which Hardie slipped with a young San Francisco businessman, Arthur Trueger.

Quite against type, Hardie wanted a piece of the burgeoning technology and services sector. John Reid foresaw the alignment of antipodean ingenuity with American capital, and invited Trueger, a high-tech investment guru running a Jersey-incorporated, NASDAQ-traded financial services firm called Berkeley Govett, to join the Hardie board in May 1987. Though the sharemarket crash five months later knocked the stuffing out of small-cap stocks, Trueger shortly involved Hardie in the restructuring of a hard-hit British trust, Touche Remnant Technology. Fifteen per cent of TRT was acquired by a Hardie-sponsored entity called Firmandale, whose $US160 million loan from UBS would be guaranteed by Hardie in return for a nominal 1.25 per cent: in essence, this was a means by which Hardie could acquire an interest in the trust without breaching its negative pledge covenants to other banks.

When TRT became the American Endeavour Fund with

Berkeley Govett in the investment adviser's role, however, matters started to get out of hand. The value of the AEF portfolio dwindled in the nervous, illiquid, post-crash equity market, placing stress on Hardie's guarantee; it was also later alleged that Berkeley Govett was receiving kickbacks in return for its investment attentions at companies including Integral Systems, AMI Acquisition, Evans Rents and Franchise Enterprises. Certainly, Trueger's name would become a dirty word at Hardie; he quit the board in May 1992 on the pretext of being unable to find the time for board meetings. But the intricacies of Firmandale are less important than the malaise of which the investment was symptomatic. 'We've come a long way from being a one-product company,' boasted John Reid at the company's annual meeting in August 1989, as though the distance was somehow more significant than the destination.

In fact, as investors recognised by paying it increasingly scant regard, Hardie was strategically lost and financially inert. Building products, the core of the company's activities for most of its history, was now one business among a dozen. Recession prevented further significant divestments after the spin-off of Spicers Paper in May 1988, and the big acquisition that might have re-energised the company was never a possibility because of the dilution risk it posed to the Reid family shareholding. So Hardie limped along. The executive general managers were always going to 'get it right next year'; earnings appeared to advance, though mainly because of extensive efforts to reduce Hardie's tax bill. Ironically, it may in this time have been the ghost of asbestos that preserved the company's independence. For all its enticements to a raider as an asset play, Hardie's presumed asbestos liabilities constituted what on Wall Street would have been called a 'poison pill' — a large, indeterminate nasty with which any owner would eventually have to contend.

Even then, oddly enough, a future was in the offing. Amongst all the dross Hardie acquired in the US was what would prove a diamond. At the end of 1987, the Hardie board signed off on the construction of a 190,000-square-foot fibre-cement plant at Fontana, near Los Angeles. The $70 million facility would manufacture asbestos-free siding, backing boards and roofing products using the company's new proprietary technology. By the time Reid and Macfarlane attended its opening in February 1990, Hardie had also acquired land for an east coast facility near Tampa in Florida at an industrial park called Plant City. It was also losing money—lots of it. Courageous enough to renounce Hardie's asbestos birthright, Macfarlane had left a blurred bequest. Now the US would become a huge headache, consuming capital insatiably and failing to make inroads against the entrenched timber and masonry products to which fibre-cement was the alternative. The pay-off would be handsome, but a long time coming.

CORPORATIONS ARE ALWAYS TUGGED one way and another by personal tensions, especially when under financial pressures. Hardie was no exception. Chairman John Reid, grandson of Andrew, son of Jock, nephew of Thyne, was a classic patrician—impeccably mannered, immaculately tailored, permanently tanned. Someone building an identikit of an establishment figure would have arrived at an image resembling Old Scotch Collegian Reid, marked out for public eminence since his days at Melbourne University in the late 1940s when he had made himself conspicuous, even in more formal times, by wearing a suit to classes.

Reid did not at the time hint at an aptitude for business, excelling instead at debating, and graduating in law in a class including a future attorney-general (Ivor Greenwood), an ambassador to Moscow (Murray Bourchier), a head of ASIO (Ted Woodward) and four judges-to-be. In his first job at James Hardie, the self-created one of legal officer, his *de haut en bas* air infuriated Jonah Adamson, who roared at company secretary Don Walker: 'Look, get rid of this little bastard. Do what you like with him ... build him a bloody office up there ... Spend all the money you like, but for Christ's sake get him out of my hair!'

It wasn't difficult, of course, to infuriate the choleric Adamson, and Reid's money was visible really only in his manner—he worked, always, extremely hard. 'His primary interest in life is work, they [friends] say,' wrote Hardie's historian Brian Carroll, in a description excised from the final version of *A Very Good Business*: 'He arrives in the office at 7.30AM, leaves between 6.30 and 7.00PM, goes home, has a simply meal, then works in his study until midnight or later. Lunch is usually sandwiches, fruit and orange juice eaten at his desk.' He inhabited an unostentatious home in Waiwera Street in McMahon's Point with his wife, the former Patricia Ferrier, whom he had married in 1954. A member of the Australian Club and Royal Sydney Yachts Squadron, he occasionally fished from a twelve-foot dinghy on Pittwater. Otherwise his life was a bulging diary of board meetings—when it was not Hardie's board, it was BHP's, or Qantas's. His *pro bono* works were accented to youth: he was chairman for many years of the Pymble Ladies College council, deputy chairman of the Queen Elizabeth II Silver Jubilee Trust for Young Australians, and a generous benefactor of the Boy Scout and Girl Guide movements. 'Am I a conservative?' he responded to one journalist in August 1974. 'I suppose that's fair comment.' Although it was the Order of Australia that he held from June 1980, he was sometimes erroneously knighted in newspaper stories, probably for the simple reason that he behaved like one.

Reid became a favourite of the Fraser government, leading a range of committees and administrative reviews, culminating in his elevation to the chairmanship of the Australian Bicentennial Authority in May 1979. This he marked, somewhat unusually, with hearty admonitions of his countrymen, especially the cultural phenomenon of the ocker: 'I think it is the outward manifestation of the fact that we are an instinctively undisciplined people. And I think sadly that, despite their travelling and world exposure, Australians in many ways are not a civilised people. In many respects we are ungovernable.'

But it wasn't the people about whom Reid had to worry; it was his political masters. When the authority was criticised for over-generosity with itself in travel and entertainment expenses, Reid was forced to seek the resignation of his chief executive, former academic Dr David Armstrong, in August 1985. When the terms of Armstrong's $500,000 severance package were criticised for their exorbitance, Reid was then defenestrated by Bob Hawke himself. To the serene progress of John Reid it was an undignified interruption, with the personal dimension that he also left Patricia for Armstrong's wife, Virginia Henderson, a fund-raiser for the Australian Opera. When they married in January 1988, Reid seemed to lose such interest as he had had in the public spotlight. In March 1990, he also suffered the blow of the death of his cousin Sandy, who perished with his wife Georgina when their light plane crashed in Queensland.

Reid's reputation as an autocrat at Hardie, too, may not have been entirely deserved. The authority of Hardie's executive in the 1980s suggests otherwise, as does his initiative of introducing a mandatory retirement age of sixty-five for board members at a time when he was two years from the landmark. Indeed, Reid grew concerned to remedy the under-representation of non-executive directors on the board, appointing several more as opportunities arose, beginning with former Trade Practices Commissioner Bob McComas in May 1988. Some of the new appointments were on a matey basis: lawyer turned pastoralist Alan MacGregor, who joined in March 1989, was Sandy Reid's brother-in-law, and as a fellow board member of the Australian Bicentennial Authority had publicly defended Reid; and former Queensland deputy premier Sir Llew Edwards, who joined in August 1990, had welcomed Reid onto the board of World Expo 88 after his ABA retrenchment. Others who came later—BHP Petroleum's Peter Willcox and Bond Corporation's Meredith Hellicar from May 1992, and Renison Goldfields CFO Michael Brown from September 1992—were genuine independents with excellent credentials. Willcox was recruited by Reid himself; Hellicar and Brown, by search firm Russell Reynolds.

David Say, who succeeded David Macfarlane as managing director shortly after the Fontana opening, was cut from another cloth: intelligent, worldly, whimsical and, by executive standards, decidedly eccentric. Executives grew accustomed, for instance, to receiving cryptic memos in Say's inscrutable scrawl, sometimes in verse. Stephen Gellert found the habit endearing, and because he had the advantage of being able to decipher Say's script became a go-to guy among perplexed colleagues. James Kelso found it infuriating, and would return memos with the annotation: 'Can you please type this out and use words I understand?' And, as another executive recalls, Say also soon ran foul of one of Reid's new appointments, MacGregor: 'David couldn't abide MacGregor, and that became a huge problem. And, frankly, MacGregor was not an easy man to get on with ... He was part of the South Australian aristocracy, a yes-sir, no-sir, three bags-full sir type. He never said an encouraging word to anyone.' MacGregor had a seigneurial air and independent wealth: he was a Lloyd's name. He had also won a reputation for outspokenness on boards, skirmishing with John Elliott when he had been a director of Elders IXL. Some felt he had come to relish the role of provocateur.

The big problems for Say lay on the other side of the Pacific, in Hardie's offshore fibre-cement business. 'We were making it,' he recalls. 'We just weren't selling it.' In February 1991, Hardie recruited an ebullient plant manager for Fontana, Louis Gries, a veteran of USG with an outstanding sales sense; yet Say could also see that Hardie would make little headway until he was given some discretion:

> When you know everything there is to know about a product, there is usually the assumption that you know something about the market. We had known enough about the market to export product to the US. Then we decided to go there and set up a manufacturing business, which had to be run by our fibre-cement people here, and they wouldn't let it go. And once it was operating, they insisted on doing everything from here, including sales and marketing.

Even as he was trying to lighten the yoke on Gries, Say was being asked searching questions by the board—especially, in a manner he found carping and insulting, by MacGregor. He commissioned for board consumption a strategic review of Hardie's US operations by the tony management consultants Boston Consulting Group, and asked them specifically to brook the possibility of closure: not disposal, or downscaling, but shutdown. The first meeting attended by new directors Willcox and Hellicar was by no means a gentle introduction. Profit for the year ending 31 March was a paltry $5.9 million, after heavy writedowns. 'After ceasing to use asbestos, Hardie was in serious trouble,' Willcox recalls. 'It had had the whole foundation of its business removed, and there's an argument that it should have gone into liquidation at the time. My picture of the company when I joined a few years later was that it was still thrashing around trying to find a way to make the business work without asbestos.' Hellicar was persuaded by the conviction with which Gries evoked the American market's possibilities: 'We were all hugely impressed with the vehemence with which he prosecuted the argument of staying in the US. He was this young plant manager, serious and intense, and loved the business.' Willcox took a more pragmatic view: 'The reason we did not shut it down was that there was nothing else. They had just to succeed or the company, I think, would have failed. We had to make it work.'

Say would not be around to do so. Between July and November 1992, Hardie's share price plunged almost a third, culminating in the assignment of a credit rating below investment grade by Moody's. Say had simply lost the faith of investors. After another skirmish with MacGregor at a board meeting, Say complained to Reid that he could not foresee working with him further — especially if, as was likely, MacGregor eventually succeeded to the chairmanship. That meant only one thing. Reid described Say's early retirement in December as 'a combined decision'. There was an equally ready consensus about his replacement.

DR KEITH BARTON's *curriculum vitae* is not untypical of his executive generation: educated at Toowoomba High School, he joined BHP as a teenager while completing his BSc part-time, then moved to Ajax Chemicals after finishing his PhD in chemical engineering, leaving there as general manager in 1979. He joined CSR when in November 1981 it acquired the construction company Farley & Lewers, where he was business development manager, and served tours running its chemicals, timber products and concrete businesses before two years in the United States. It was the preamble to a career as a chief executive; but, when the vacancy at Hardie emerged, not only had Barton not yet risen to that level within CSR, but the incumbent, Ian Burgess, had just anointed Barton's rival, Geoff Kells, as his successor. 'We will be eternally grateful to Ian Burgess,' says Willcox. 'We would not have hired Geoff Kells,' says Hellicar.

Barton seized the opportunity to run a public company with alacrity; part of him, no doubt, felt the urge to prove Burgess wrong. His initial impressions were scathing. 'What the fuck have I gotten myself in for?' he asked his wife after a week. 'This is a much bigger mess than I thought.' His formula in speaking to executives was, by standards at Hardie, where problems were often politely fenced around, brutal: 'I have a very fair system. There are no agendas. You will be expected to achieve X. If you don't achieve it you are gone. What we won't be doing is accepting X-50, which is what we have been doing.' Nor was he above publicly criticising those who failed. At his first presentation to analysts, Barton was asked about the bathroom division's performance. 'It's bloody dreadful,' he replied. 'Next question.' Asked about prospects by *Business Review Weekly*, he snapped: 'I think this year will be lousy.' For many, Barton would come as a breath of fresh air. John Winters recalls his first visit to the laboratory at Camellia: 'We'd never seen Say out there. But Barton just walked around on his own, talking to people. He was so bright he took in what you told him and could have an intelligent conversation with you about it straight away. I ended up talking to him for half an hour.'

He was also a magnet for executive talent. When Ken Boundy was approached through the headhunters Amrop in November 1994, he met Barton at Sydney Airport expecting a forty-five minute chat. 'Barton and I spoke for two hours,' Boundy recalls. 'The chemistry was so good with him. Even though this was a building-products company, and my training was as a scientist, I thought: "I want to work with this guy as CEO".'

Barton was to enjoy all the good fortune that Say had been denied. As recession lifted, he was able to divest Hardie of all the surplus businesses with which it had burdened itself, including Hartec, a manufacturer of printed circuit boards, by public float.

Hardie in the US, too, was even then experiencing the good of two ill winds. A fire in Alameda County destroying 2900 homes in October 1991, and floods in southwest Florida in August 1992 had exposed vulnerabilities in homes that made extensive use of timber, prompting a number of builders to examine alternatives, including fibre-cement. But Barton was determined to introduce to Hardie some of the management rigour he had helped inculcate at CSR, retaining an organisational-development specialist from New Zealand, Gerry Harloss, to run his executives through their paces. Harloss preached a five-point approach to corporate purity, summarised by the abbreviation CTFMP. Executives were to think of the business as a Coherent whole; of themselves as Team-based; of their objective as Fitness, a forty-minute walk four times a week being better than a last-minute sprint; of their focus as the Market, both shareholder and customer; and of their *modus operandi* as a Planned approach.

Some found the approach an anathema, not simply out of conservatism. While himself frustrated by Hardie's adhocracy, Gellert would complain that the opposite approach was equally absurd: 'This is replacing one madness with another.' He recalls: 'Barton had completely black-and-white views. He didn't attempt to understand anything that had gone before. He didn't want to know what had happened or how things had been done the day before he arrived.' Others found the Harloss disciplines refreshing. Philip Morley, then financial controller, believes they revolutionised the company: 'It was a complete change to the way the company had run, which was very individual, pretty hierarchical, based on who you knew at senior levels, looking after your own patch … At the time, cultural change wasn't something they were singing from the rooftops, so it was pretty confronting for some people.' The old guard were fading away anyway; others were pushed. Within five years, Barton could boast that there was 'not one person reporting to me that was reporting when I started'.

Barton's new praetorian guard was hand-picked. Morley, who usurped John McFadden as chief financial officer, was the only long server, his silvering hair and silver glasses lending him a faintly ecclesiastical air. When he arrived at one management retreat in a black polo neck, Ken Boundy quipped: 'Here comes the monsignore'. He was privately known, a little less kindly, as 'Mr Teflon' — a born management survivor. But he was smart and adaptable, and also not ambitious for the top job, which made him an ideal lieutenant.

The rest were all recent or new arrivals. Robert Middendorp, a former management consultant who had joined Hardie in January 1991, was to take over building products from Haitham Ghantous. John Moller, who had come from Honeywell in April 1992, was sent to run building services. Don Cameron, a finance executive who had joined Hardie soon after from Rheem and Southcorp, succeeded Rod Wilson as company secretary. Louis Gries, having seen Fontana into the black, became responsible for all fibre-cement operations in the US. Don Merkeley, a former colleague at USG, joined in August 1993 as his offsider, based at Plant City in Florida; his twin brother Dave arrived the following year. Noel Thompson, previously at BHP, AAEC and the University of New South Wales, joined in September 1993 as head of product development in fibre-cement.

Boundy, previously boss of Goodman Fielder in Asia, built a strong international department, starting with former colleague Greg Baxter as head of corporate affairs in November 1996. Greg Stanmore, formerly at LEK Consulting, became business development manager a year later; John Ballass, a senior finance executive at Procter & Gamble in Europe, joined as a merger and acquisitions specialist a year after that and ended up running the company's new business in the Philippines.

In this top-to-bottom management makeover of quite unHardielike proportions were also two figures disrupting all the previous lines of patronage. Recruited within days in August 1993, just as they were destined to leave together, were Peter Macdonald and Peter Shafron: the future stars of what would become David Jackson QC's inquiry into Hardie's attempts to cast its asbestos liabilities adrift. New Zealander Macdonald completed his undergraduate studies at Wellington's Victoria University, but for twenty years had travelled as his commercial career had demanded.

His first decade had begun at CSR, starting as a junior accountant, where he had been one of the first of a new generation of executives introduced to leaven the company's traditional mix of engineers and chemists: his speciality became sales and marketing. He had then filled divisional management roles at Metal Manufactures and Tyco International. Shafron, just thirty-two, had been a prize-winning law graduate at Sydney University after undergraduate studies at ANU, and come to Hardie from being an associate at the blue-blood law firm Allen Allen and Hemsley, where his speciality had been trade practices law.

Macdonald and Shafron were models of the kind of executive Barton was seeking: technically proficient, hugely diligent, exceptionally disciplined, and owing no fealty to old and discredited ideas. Macdonald's first important task, in fact, was closing the old Camellia site once and for all, and overseeing the consolidation of operations at a new administration, warehouse and manufacturing facility at Rosehill, which he completed by February 1994. And in October, he took his Irish wife Deirdre and their boys Liam and Rory to California, and became Hardie's senior US-based executive, reporting to head of international operations Boundy.

In the US, Macdonald soon became thoroughly acculturated. Boundy encouraged him to undertake an MBA from the George L. Grazidio School of Business and Management at Pepperdine University in Malibu, and Macdonald would encourage Shafron to do the same.† In Hardie, in fact, the United States soon became where the action was, as a house-building boom began to reverberate. Over the next three years, Hardie would pour money into Fontana and Plant City, as well as new building-products

---

† Pepperdine University was founded in 1937 by George Pepperdine, founder of Western Auto Supply Company. He envisioned a college with the highest academic standards guided by the spiritual and ethical ideals of Christian faith. Pepperdine University is affiliated with the Churches of Christ, of which George Pepperdine was a life-long member. The Grazidio School was founded in 1969, and named for its benefactor, the co-founder and former CEO of Imperial Bancorp. Its mission statement expresses the following sentiment:

facilities at Cleburne in Texas and Tacoma in Washington. Macdonald staged a particular coup in January 1997 by paying $US121 million for Boral's gypsum wallboard operations. So buoyant was the market for corporate assets by this time that virtually all this expansion could be funded by about $540 million in proceeds from divestments.

One figure who remained amid all this change was Reid who, because he was now officially beyond the retirement age, stayed on at the board's request on a year-to-year basis. His presence lent events a reassuring sense of continuity, although it was fast becoming clear that the character of the company was being changed by the influx of new management and by the geographic origin of an increasing proportion of its profits. As staggering as the speed of the turnaround was the potential for further growth that it was creating.

In October 1995, Reid and Barton took the Hardie board on an extensive tour of the company's American operations, from Fontana to Plant City, threading El Cajon, El Paso, Las Vegas and Dallas en route. They learned, for example, that Hardie's American fibre-cement production would soon exceed its Australian output, while its mooted plasterboard line at Tacoma would shortly be making more plasterboard than the entire Australian market. 'There's no doubt,' recalls Sir Llew Edwards, 'that at the end of that trip the board saw the future of the company lying in the US.' Barton jested in December that the company might one day 'move its head office to Dallas'. The only question was how they were going to get there.

As a professional school growing out of the tradition of a Christian University, we seek to positively impact both the society at large, and the organizations and communities in which our students and graduates are members. Therefore, we affirm a higher purpose for business practice than the exclusive pursuit of shareholder wealth. We believe that successful management seeks collective good along with individual profit and is anchored in core values such as stewardship, compassion, and responsibility.

13

'Plucking figures from the clouds'

'Asbestos-related claims are expensed as incurred and a provision is made for the ultimate cost of settlement of known claims. While certain Australian subsidiaries recognise that they will continue to be named as defendants in litigation in Australia as a result of past manufacturing and marketing of products containing asbestos, James Hardie cannot reliably measure its exposure with respect to future asbestos-related claims. The directors rely upon various internal and public reports and seek expert actuarial advice in assessing the ongoing exposure to claims. A contingent liability exists in respect of the ultimate cost of settlement of any claims yet to be made which cannot be measured reliably at the present point in time.'
—Note to the accounts of James Hardie Industries, 31 March 1998

JAMES HARDIE HAD STRIPPED ASBESTOS from its product range, its name and even its head office, but could not unwrite its history. 'They make asbestos, don't they?' friends and colleagues said to Meredith Hellicar when she was contemplating joining the Hardie board in May 1992. When she was being interviewed by John Reid, David Say and Alan MacGregor about the directorship, she asked anxiously: 'You don't have anything to do with asbestos, do you?' Their assurance otherwise was not disingenuous, nor was it wholly accurate. Hardie still had a great deal to do with asbestos—the only question, an unanswerable one, was how much.

The New South Wales government of Neville Wran had already ensured that the depth of involvement would not diminish, by establishing the Dust Diseases Tribunal for the expeditious processing of common law compensation claims for industrial pneumoconioses in

1989. The Supreme Court of New South Wales had been struggling to process claims in the twelve months that mesothelioma commonly allows its victims, while the nature of claimants had lately broadened from those who had manufactured products to those who had used them, such as carpenters who had spent lifetimes power-sawing sheets of Super Six through hazes of asbestos dust: a disturbing development for defendants, as users usually had higher incomes than workers, and produced greater estimates of future economic loss. The creation of the DDT stirred the first estimate of the final toll that asbestos might wreak. At the Institute of Actuaries in Australia's third accident compensation seminar at Ballarat in November 1991, Tim Andrews and Geoff Atkins of the actuarial firm John Trowbridge forecast a quantum of up to $881 million.

By this time, Hardie was making its own prognostications. Legal manager Lionel Demead commissioned from his in-house asbestos lawyer Mark Knight a 'conjecture' about future claims, prepared in cooperation with Diamond Peisah and two other firms involved in the area, Melbourne's Arthur Robinson & Hedderwicks and Perth's Northmore Hale Davey & Leake. In his April 1992 report, Knight foresaw an imminent peak, it being twenty years since the period of maximum risk (1972–75) and asbestosis cases being toward the end of their latency period, although he noticed CSR's very different view: 'A different view, expressed by the legal department of CSR, is that the asbestos litigation peak is not due until 2000–2010. I do not know the reasoning they have adopted.' Of his 'best intuitive guess' of $40–45 million, moreover, Knight made clear it was for the want of anything better: 'The three firms agreed that trying to determine expected claims numbers and quanta was like plucking figures from the clouds but also agreed that this attempt to put on paper a distillation of their combined thoughts and rheumatic knee-type weather forecasting was as good as any other.'

At this quantum, asbestos was actually somewhat overshadowed by Firmandale. In 1992–1993, Hardie paid out only about $4.24 million in compensation to victims of asbestos-related disease. The Firmandale liability seemed bottomless. Its structure, with its American businesses, Jersey domicile, and intermediate trusts in

Hong Kong and Malta, was like a haunted house—all dark rooms, creaky corridors and trapdoors. 'Compensating asbestos at least was simple,' recalls Meredith Hellicar. 'Firmandale was the bane of my life. I tried to understand it, but I'm not sure I did. I constantly had to ask the same questions in the next meeting, and frankly that not a comfortable position to be in. If there was ever an opportunity to get out, unwind, sell, I would say: "Yes, yes, yes".'

With the removal of Arthur Trueger's Berkeley Govett, now called London Pacific, as manager of the American Endeavour Fund in March 1995, the story became a veritable *Jarndyce v Jarndyce*. London Pacific had at the time been negotiating a merger with another financial services firm, Duff & Phelps, which now fell through. It responded to AEF's $US67 million suit alleging mismanagement, negligence and fraud with its own $US446 million suit for compensation arising from the failure of the deal, joining Hardie as a party and alleging that it had 'conspired to terminate' the contractual arrangements between AEF and London Pacific, had 'acted in breach of good faith and fair dealing', and defamed Trueger; both sides, in fact, would end up issuing defamation proceedings against the other. Worse even than the tit-for-tat cross-claims, however, was the continued diminution of AEF's portfolio. Firmandale's share at June 1996 was worth $US39 million compared to outstanding principal on its borrowings of $US86 million. In October, Hardie was obliged to underwrite the refinancing of the loan, Firmandale issuing $US22 million of preference shares to another Jersey entity, Toucan Holdings, to enable Firmandale to meet three years of interest payments to UBS. Toucan borrowed the money from Natwest, and Hardie not only had to guarantee this repayment but also put up a cash deposit to cover the shortfall between net assets and the UBS loan. Hardie buried the bad news story in time-honoured fashion by announcing an increase in its provision on Melbourne Cup day.

There were other works afoot in this period that in time would cause even greater consternation, depending as they did on a hith-erto-insignificant aspect of Hardie's corporate structure. For most of its history since incorporation in 28 May 1937, James Hardie & Coy had been the principal operating entity of the Hardie group and the legal owner of the bulk of its plant and equipment. It was established as a wholly owned subsidiary of James Hardie Industries, formerly James Hardie Asbestos, which became the listed vehicle from December 1951 and was essentially a holding company. Between them hung the same curious legal membrane as reposed between CSR and Midalco: the so-called 'corporate veil'.

The reasons for the 1937 restructure are lost in time. There is a historical tendency among former asbestos companies to quarantine their former operations in undercapitalised subsidiaries to limit their financial exposure. But no document has ever emerged to prove that this was the case at Hardie, and its reconfiguration was more probably to accord with the requirements of a new Companies Act. Whatever the case, by 1995 what henceforward will be called Coy was largely inactive, save as the owner of about $250 million in assets and property (for the management of which it paid an annual fee to its owner of about $20 million), and as the party traditionally named in claims for compensation. The only other party sometimes named in actions was Jsekarb Pty Ltd, the mortal corporate remains of James Hardie Brakes, formerly Hardie-Ferodo, whose operating business had been sold eight years earlier to Futuris.

There is no escaping the detail of these intercompany transactions; fortunately, what actually took place is not in dispute. On 1 April 1995, Coy sold its 'core technology' (certain intellectual property rights), to a new entity, James Hardie Research, for $75 million. Shortly after, Coy also sold a group of 'controlled entities', crystallising a net profit of $38.25 million, so that by August it controlled net assets worth $385 million, $166.73 million of which was 'available for appropriation'.* From this, JHIL drew dividends of $100.9 million, some $60 million directly, and $40.9 million through a subsidiary called Winstone Pty Ltd. Coy was then further diminished by a change of policy with regard to building-products

---

* The controlled entities concerned were James Hardie Building Systems Pty Ltd, Bondor Itex Pty Ltd, Bondor Itex Hungary Kft, Fibre Cement Contracting Pty Ltd, Fibre Cement Technology (Australia) Pty Ltd.

assets, under which it was decided that new acquisitions were to be made by James Hardie Fibre Cement Pty Ltd and leased to Coy for an annual rental equal to the assets' depreciation. In October 1996 a further dividend of $43 million was upstreamed to JHIL.

What would later be disputed was not what occurred, but what the process should be called. To counsel assisting the Special Commission of Inquiry held in 2004, the raising of cash within Coy and its routing to JHIL through exorbitant dividends and management fees looked suspiciously like a 'stripping' of Coy's assets, and thus a diminution of the resources available to those who sued it. Keith Barton contended that all the sales were for valid commercial reasons and that 'there was never any suggestion that we wouldn't be able to meet our claims', although he admitted it was also about preserving 'flexibility for the future' in dealing with Coy.[†] Commissioner David Jackson QC decided, after a disapproving glance at the management fees, not to peer deeply into the matter. The purpose of the capitalising of new acquisitions in James Hardie FC, he said, was clearly so that 'those assets could not be available to asbestos creditors', but the individual transactions were all legal. This is a view about which Peter Gordon remains indignant: 'Jackson takes them transaction by transaction, but when you look at them over a period it's clear that they're being done with the final structure in mind, and it's clear what the overriding intent was.'

There is a context to which the inquiry did not actually penetrate. Hardie's general counsel, Stephen Gellert, was examining the

---

† Barton's evidence ran as follows:

> *Q:* Can you explain the purpose for adopting that structure?
> *A:* Well it was simply to maintain flexibility for the future in terms of dealing with those assets. Should we ever want to sell them, it was much easier if they sat in a company such as James Hardie Fibre Cement.
> *Q:* Why was that?
> *A:* Well we had alternatives, we could sell the company, or we could sell the assets et cetera. Had they been sitting in Coy we clearly couldn't sell the company.
> *Q:* And you couldn't sell the company because Coy had asbestos liabilities?
> *A:* Correct.

company's asbestos liabilities closely throughout the relevant period, and recommending a significant revision of its approach to their management. He was an unusual choice to do so. His reputation in the company was as extremely talented and rather volatile. 'Stephen and Mark Knight used to have the biggest rows I have ever seen,' recalls John Winters. But the decision seems to have been not so much because Hardie's senior managers were deeply interested in the asbestos problem; it seems to have been because they were barely interested at all. With the exception of Morley, Barton's inner circle of Robert Middendorp, Ken Boundy, Peter Macdonald, Don Merkeley, Louis Gries and Greg Baxter were all new arrivals, which Gellert feels had a subtle impact on attitudes to asbestos: 'All of a sudden there were all these new individuals, who had less and less time, less and less patience, and less and less tolerance for hearing anything about asbestos. What I got was: 'Yeah sure, go away and do what you have to do'. Which made it pretty clear that you weren't going to enhance your career by hanging round and trying to solve asbestos.' A review, however, was probably long overdue. Nothing much had changed about Hardie's litigation strategy over the years, recalls Slater & Gordon's Ken Fowlie, with Diamond Peisah continuing to offer the smallest possible target:

> Hardie's approach to litigation was to resolve most claims, to eschew high-profile defences of their conduct, and in settlements to seek confidentiality. And, at the end of the day, any lawyer who's advising a client where there is confidentiality attached to a settlement will tell you that very frequently that suits clients fine. Mr Smith who's dying of cancer doesn't really want his neighbour to know that he's $200,000 richer. Hardie took advantage of the fact that people are private about their personal financial circumstances ... We used to joke that Diamond Peisah would never let you tender a Hardie's document in court. As soon as you threatened to put a document into evidence, they'd settle the case.

Gellert's study suggested that this approach was no longer saving Hardie money. The Dust Diseases Tribunal was very quickly seen as inclined to generosity, out of sympathy with sufferers of asbestos-related disease. And Hardie's cost of claims was rising relative to other defendants, because it was perceived as a soft touch. The company's processes of claims handling were also wasteful, because they were geared to nothing except settlement:

> For instance, we were always finding new documents. And every time we did that, we had to advise the court, and it cost a fortune. My proposal was that we should have a final, absolutely final, never-to-be-done-again document search for all remaining information. We should have a document room that plaintiffs could visit, and we should actually set about destroying documents that weren't related to asbestos. It was ridiculous, really. The attitude at Hardie's was always to take the soft option and pay for things to be stored. No one had the guts to just get rid of stuff … I can't tell you how many depositories I had cleaned out.

Gellert wanted to try some new defences, to run some cases to verdict to at least scope out liabilities, and to take a more aggressive approach to cross-claims against CSR and employers like the State Rail Authority so that they paid their share of contributions — which would require greater legal resources than those of Diamond Peisah. That anything as explicit as spinning off or somehow eliminating the asbestos-related liabilities was on the agenda, however, seems unlikely. Some form of legal separation had been seen as a possibility since the example of Johns-Manville's restructuring in 1982, says Gellert, but he doubts it was seriously entertained:

> It was well known that the profile of asbestos liabilities was going to get worse, much worse, before it got better. I made various recommendations for curtailing costs, including changing the settlement mentality that had set in with our lawyers. But none of it involved getting rid of the liabilities altogether. That lurked in the background as it always had — I mean, they'd been talking about that when I arrived in 1984 — but I started from the premise that we would pay every claim.

The other part of the review, which Gellert commissioned in April 1996, was a thorough examination by the actuarial firm Trowbridge of 'the potential liability of [JHIL] and its subsidiaries for personal injury claims arising from asbestos-related diseases' to 'provide background for the conduct of asbestos-related litigation'. Hardie's first brush with the arcane art of actuarial calculation would be a harbinger of its later experiences. Several estimates were made over a period of months, hedged with qualifications regarding 'considerable uncertainty over the future cost of asbestos-related disease claims', finally concluding with the presentation of a figure of $230 million to the board in November—considerably more than the Knight review of four years earlier.

The mercurial Gellert found the process stimulating but infuriating. He was losing patience with Barton's rigid Harloss prescriptions—even more so when his first report revising the company's litigation strategy was rejected because it did not meet the house style. 'That really pissed me off,' he says. 'They simply would not receive it. But, recognising the importance of the issue, I was granted one-on-one tuition in the new format by the new guru [Robert Middendorp].' In the end, he got somewhere: 'It was a report designed to get an honest answer to an honest question. Did the answer surprise me? Yes it did, and it surprised the board, too. But they didn't go into shutdown mode. And once I'd put it into Harloss format—after I'd been Middendorped to death—they did give me the go-ahead to implement my recommendations.' Peter Willcox says: 'The general opinion was that we weren't doing a good job of managing it [the liabilities], because we were so busy on other things.' Michael Brown explains: 'In recognition that the Dust Diseases Tribunal was deciding on cases not only on their merits but also because of sympathy with asbestos sufferers, it was considered appropriate to ensure that cases were settled on the basis of appropriate liability rather than a feel-good contribution.'

Gellert wasn't around to see his recommendations in action—he would quit in March 1997. But the greater vigour he envisaged became the Hardie way. Allen Allen & Hemsley, Sydney's most prestigious and powerful law firm, suddenly started putting a bit of stick about. Accustomed to softly softly Diamond Peisah, Allens' legal opponents were momentarily shocked. Gerry Gardiman of Turner Freeman thought that plaintiff lawyers themselves were the target: 'There's no doubt that they thought if they squeezed us on costs and forced us to litigate every step of the way that they'd exhaust us. They didn't. They underestimated our capacity to fight. We've been in this from day one and we weren't going to go away.' Ken Fowlie of Slater & Gordon formed the view that it was a crash through-or-crash strategy: 'I didn't really understand what Hardies were doing: previously they'd been inclined to settle. Later I came to see it as the precursor to the strategy of 2001 — a last throw of the dice to see if they could curtail the liability, after which they formed the view that they were just lining their lawyers' pockets and that they should try and isolate the liability.' It may not be so straight-forward, but the changed strategy was definitely an evolutionary step. As Gellert says: 'The only plan left after mine was the auda-cious one. The people who enlisted in that solution were the ones who did very well.'

Mention of one case fought under Allens' new dispensation is here compulsory. New Zealander Desmond Putt was diagnosed with mesothelioma in January 1997, fifty years after he'd begun a four-year career lugging Fibrolite at Penrose. Putt's lawyers, McLaughlin & Riordan, sought damages not from JHNZ in New Zealand, where common law rights have been restricted since 1972, but from both Coy and JHIL in the Dust Diseases Tribunal. When the expedited trial began on 5 January 1998, they relied on a recent precedent, *CSR v Wren*, in which it had been found that CSR owed a mesothelioma sufferer, Norman Wren, a duty of care by virtue of its 'direction, control and involvement' in the operations of Asbestos Products Pty Ltd, its old manufacturing plant at Alexandria. The finding had brushed roughly against the corporate veil without dis-turbing it: CSR managers were actively involved in the subsidiary's management; Asbestos Products had been deregistered in 1960; and no finding against CSR would have meant no compensation. The judge in *Putt*, O'Meally, was the same as in *Wren*, and his decision on 23 January to award Putt $151,500 followed like logic: 'It is plainly true that the first and second defendants and JHNZ were separate legal entities, but it is equally as true that the enterprise was one and significantly and actually influenced by the board of the first defendant.'

Hardie could scarcely let this result stand, and a fortnight later appealed. Then Putt died on 13 April with his verdict in limbo, the case being carried forward by the administrator of his estate, Michael Hall. It turned out to be a coup for Hardie. When the NSW Supreme Court of Appeal set aside O'Meally's orders on 22 May, it found firmly for the concept of a subsidiary leading a self-contained life:

> There was nothing to suggest that those responsible for workplace safety at the Penrose plant were employees of the defendants (JHIL or Coy) rather than employees of JHNZ and that the separate corporate identity of JHNZ was a mere façade. The most that could be said, and this was certainly true of the Holding Company, was that the defendants were in a position to insist that proper workplace standards were maintained. Did the defendants owe a duty to the plaintiff to do so when they were neither the occupiers of the premises nor the employers of those responsible for the safety of the workplace or of the plaintiff? While the way in which the case was put and apparently accepted by Judge O'Meally gives lip service to the integrity of the corporate veil, implicitly it lifts it by saying that the control of the workplace was not that of the subsidiary company occupier or employer but, through their influence or control, that of the defendants ... Ultimately the question was whether the control or influence which his honour found to have existed was such as to impose a duty to the plaintiff of which there was a breach. None of the cases referred to support such a conclusion. To suggest that such a duty existed is to ignore JHNZ's separate legal identity and the absence of any evidence that this was a mere façade.

Putt's lawyers failed to obtain leave to appeal the judgement to the High Court on 7 August, and 'the Putt case' would provide the legal undergirding for much of the restructuring that followed. It is also worth citing the identity of the silk on the losing side of the Putt argument: David Jackson QC.

THROUGH 1994 AND 1995, while Barton began shaking the company up, Hardie was a largely friendless stock, burdened by imponderable liabilities. It had, however, one big fan. Peter Pedley, the senior industrial analyst of Brierley Investments, was a veteran of the securities market. He had left Sir Ron Brierley's circle in August 1987, when the famous sharemarket trader had declined to accept his advice that shares were riding for a fall, but rejoined six years later. He was now doing what he did best: spotting oversold industrial stocks with undetected growth potential. BIL bought its first Hardie shares in February 1994. They came readily. By August, BIL owned 10 per cent; by February 1995, BIL owned 20 per cent; and by April 1996, it had eclipsed the Reid family as the biggest presence on the register, speaking for more than a quarter of the shares.

Two months later, Hardie welcomed Pedley onto its board. It was an uncharacteristic level of commitment for BIL, which has traditionally eschewed board representation because of the legal restrictions it places on trading. But Pedley believed there was value embedded in Hardie that could be released by restructuring. Hardie was in the final stages of undoing its 1980s diversification misadventures: in the second half of 1996, it sold its irrigation division to Toro for $150 million and its building-services division to Chubb for $220 million. Fibre-cement was taking off in the US, and the company's gypsum wallboard operations were throwing off cash faster than it could be spent. Something had to be done to recognise this shift in Hardie's centre of financial gravity. In a far-reaching report to his fellow directors in January 1997, entitled 'Considerations for the Reconstruction of James Hardie', Pedley mooted 'a change of domicile or its equivalent' involving the relocation of senior management to the US, which would 'need to occur within the next twelve months'. This, he recognised, would not be easy: 'So far, so simple. But, of course, there are hooks and these are the Australian asbestosis and Firmandale liabilities. However, I believe that the commercial logic for the operating businesses is so compelling that a way must be found to circumvent these problems so as to continue to maximise the potential of the operating assets.'

Carriage of Project Scully, as it became in honour of the sceptical half of *The X-Files* duo, was given to two mergers-and-acquisitions partners of the global investment bank SBC Warburg, Anthony Sweetman and Ian Wilson. Pedley's proposition that the Australian operating businesses be transferred to the group company holding the American businesses, leaving a 'USCo', and JHIL operating as an Australian 'legacy company' containing its asbestos and Firmandale liabilities, became their starting point. By May, they were ready to share the fruits of their lucubrations with the board: they presented plans for a listing in the US, a return of surplus capital to shareholders, and an 'organisational realignment' positioning the executive in the US. In December, Hardie officially initiated what became Project Chelsea — all the entities involved were code-named after football teams, with Chelsea being the moniker of JHIL, Newcastle for Newco, and Arsenal for what Hardie demarcated as the 'Rump' of non-core assets.

The idea involved reconceiving JHIL as an Australian investment company (containing non-core assets and liabilities) steadily selling down its interest in a US-listed Dutch holding company called James Hardie NV (containing the operating businesses) after an initial public offering of 15 per cent. JHNV would henceforward be the hub of the Hardie group, conducting treasury operations through a Dutch finance company, JH Finance BV. Wilson and Sweetman now answered to a Project Chelsea sub-committee constituted by Barton, Pedley, Morley, Hellicar and Michael Brown.

To documant all the plan's iterations is probably too deep a level of detail, but two observations are worth making. Tax was a paramount concern for Hardie. Australian companies pay tax at 36c in the dollar, with the tax paid credited to shareholders when they receive franked dividends. At the time, however, Australian companies earning a large proportion of earnings in the US were hit at three levels: they paid tax to the US government on their earnings and foreign withholding tax when they repatriated the profits to

Australia, and then their Australian shareholders could not claim franking credits and ended up paying their top marginal rate. By the time the foreign profit was passed to the Australian shareholder, as much as three-quarters of it had been consumed by various public exchequers. Hardie's tax situation wasn't quite so severe, its tax rate having been mitigated by losses in the early 1990s and its Australian earnings base being sufficient to cover its dividend obligations. But higher tax bills and payout expectations loomed, in which event dividends from earnings would have to be routed a different way: on the advice of Coopers & Lybrand tax partner Tony Clemens, the most promising involved use of the US-Netherlands tax treaty, which granted favoured status to Dutch-registered companies in the US.

The other observation is that Project Chelsea amounted to a deferring rather than a reckoning of Hardie's asbestos burden. The structure of having JHIL sell down its interest in JHNV rather than detach completely was a flexible response to the chronic inexactitude of actuarial projections which Hardie's annual report now specifically recognised in the note prefacing this chapter. Barton himself had been struck by the imprecision of Trowbridge's calculations: 'One of the things that amazed me at the time was the quality of the data, so it was extremely difficult to get anything reliable.'

In order to achieve the coveted tax advantages, however, the committee needed to get its hands dusty, as it were. JHIL shareholders would need an explanatory memorandum; the American and European investors who, it was envisaged, would own the 15 per cent of JHNV after its listing on Wall Street, required a Securities & Exchange Commission registration statement. Hardie obtained one fillip in March 1998 when it finally groped its way out of the haunted house of Firmandale, agreeing to settle the liabilities outstanding on its guarantee and voluntarily liquidate the American Endeavour Fund at an all-up cost of about $US72 million. More precision was also needed where asbestos was concerned. As the restructuring was seen as culminating in a return of surplus capital to shareholders, for instance, it was crucial to know how much it was prudent to distribute. At the end of that month, Trowbridge was invited to update their now two-year-old quantification of liabilities

—albeit carefully. Minutes of the relevant Chelsea sub-committee meeting end with a coda suggestive of a good deal of apprehension: 'There needs to be a strategy for managing Trowbridge and they need to be informed that parts of the report may become public. It is expected that the Trowbridge report will be heavily qualified.' In hindsight, of course, the most innocent of comments can arouse suspicion, and it would be tendentious to regard this as an injunction to mislead or deceive Trowbridge. The perceived need for a 'strategy to manage' the work of an independent expert, nonetheless, seems an early acknowledgement that Hardie had a vested interest in what might be found.

The other reason for the significance of Trowbridge's findings was longer term. Although Project Chelsea did not specifically involve an elimination of JHIL or Coy, an exit was clearly envisaged in the ensuing twelve months. It was at this stage that a dedicated stand-alone fund to cope with asbestos litigants was first mooted, in a dense but lucid piece of legal advice composed by Allens chief mergers-and-acquisitions partner Peter Cameron. The respected Cameron—who joined Allens in February 1976 and made partner in July 1983—was by this time a veteran of more than one hundred takeovers. He was brought in not by Hardie but by Warburg, with whom he had worked on the creation of BHP Billiton, and his first distillation of the issues, entitled 'Ultimate Resolution' showed the penetration of his intellect. Two choices existed: Cameron called them 'compromise' or 'cushion'. One was addressing the issue 'head on', with a formal determination of all claims at a stroke, perhaps by winding up Coy, JHIL or both; the other involved the creation of a fund to meet creditors' claims as they arose:

> The directors, acting reasonably on the basis of the best available advice, would need to be satisfied as to the adequacy of that fund to ensure that insolvency will not result ... To provide a degree of comfort, the fund would include a safety margin or cushion, in excess of the estimated maximum liabilities. The fund would be held (perhaps by a trustee) for both creditors and (once the proper claims of creditors had been exhausted) for shareholders.

This was, as yet, the epilogue to a story that hadn't yet played out. But Hardie's board could now glimpse their far-off future, and begin working towards it.

14

'Canberra on steroids'

'The reality is other than the fact of being a public company on the
ASX, its operations, its income and the weight of the company is in fact
American.'
—James Hardie Industries' chief operating officer, Peter Macdonald,
May 1999

JAMES HARDIE'S PROFIT TO 3I MARCH 1998 amounted to what
an Australian treasurer once called 'bringing home the bacon'. Net
profit of $83.3 million was up 62.4 per cent. The American
operations that the board had countenanced closing six years earlier
now generated seven in every ten dollars of earnings; revenues had
grown an annual 46 per cent for three years. Through the result,
however, protruded the horns of a tax dilemma. Dividends for
distribution outstripped the scope of the Australian operations to
provide them, compelling costly repatriation of funds from the US.
Likewise, most of the company's debt was in the US and most of its
cash balances from asset sales in Australia, earning historically low
cash rates. Project Chelsea could now not fructify fast enough, with
Coy being hastily cleaned out in preparation. On balance date itself,
James Hardie & Coy officially sold all its plant and equipment to
James Hardie Fibre Cement for what netted off, after a valuation by
Gray Eisdell Timms, at $37.05 million — a $12.5 million profit on
book value. On 30 June, Coy's trademarks were also sold to James
Hardie Research for a sum, as later calculated by Grant Samuel, of
$139.5 million.

The chief executive himself was in transition. Barton had by any
measure proved himself. He had become a wealthy man, raising

more than $9 million the previous July by selling Hardie stock, then paying $2.42 each to turn 2.5 million executive options into shares. He had caused CSR's board, which had sacked Geoff Kells after an unhappy reign, to rue their choice. Now he was contemplating an exit strategy, constituting a CEO sub-committee composed of himself, MacGregor and Peter Willcox, advised by a head hunter from Spencer Stuart. Barton had brought Ken Boundy to the company four years earlier with hints that he was the dauphin; Robert Middendorp had some fans. But the strength of the US operations had changed the company's executive dynamics: Peter Pedley had commented as early as January 1997 that it was 'glaringly obvious that the group CEO will have to be a US resident (if not a US national)'. Two external candidates were interviewed: Ron Mathewson, with thirty-three years behind him at Owens-Corning and Johns-Manville, among others, and David Oskin, a 22-year veteran of International Paper. And another figure came to the fore: Peter Macdonald, in charge of the company's American businesses for three-and-a-half years.

At the time, Macdonald was in an unusual position. Project Chelsea would make his role redundant. He had been asked if he was interested in heading Hardie's gypsum wallboard operations, and rejected the clear demotion; he would accept only the role of CEO. There was even the prospect that he might leave. Minutes of the CEO sub-committee for April 1998 specifically envisaged his departure: 'If Macdonald does decide to leave, it is imperative that suitable restraints are in place given his significant knowledge of the US fibre cement business'. The fact was that a Macdonald succession would represent a very big change for Hardie. As one executive comments, good relations between Macdonald and Barton had always been helped by the distance between them:

> The funny thing is that I think if Peter had worked in Australia and been a direct report to Keith, it wouldn't have worked. They were monumentally different in personal style. Keith's a pretty knockabout sort of bloke. He's very intellectually sharp, but he's also capable of relaxing, and he's pretty casual. Peter is a very early-to-bed, early-to-rise

kind of character. He'd be up first thing in the morning, on the exercise bike. He looked after himself, watched his weight. Then he'd be on the email sending off messages at ridiculous hours. His whole personal style was very disciplined: no PA, no secretary, booking his own travel, sitting in the back of the plane.

Project Chelsea was already causing upheaval in executive ranks at Hardie. When the plan was finally shared with management during a retreat in the Blue Mountains over Easter, Phil Morley, Greg Baxter, treasury executive Stephen Harman, human resources chief Brad Bridges and Stephen Gellert's successor as general counsel, Peter Shafron, all learned that they would be relocating to Hardie's American HQ, Mission Viejo, while treasurer Don Cameron would be packing his bags for Amsterdam. In the end, whilst loath to redomicile himself, Barton decided to remain another year, with Macdonald appointed to the role of chief operating officer so both he and the company could get a feel for one another.

The board itself — Keith Barton, Alan MacGregor, Peter Pedley, Peter Willcox, Michael Brown, Meredith Hellicar and Sir Llew Edwards — approved Project Chelsea on 30 June after reassuring words from their advisers, Warburgs, Allens and Coopers & Lybrand. The voluminous board papers touch on all possible concerns, from adverse publicity to possible legal action on behalf of asbestos claimants to injunct the restructuring. They adamantly articulate the view that asbestos is of 'limited relevance' to Project Chelsea, and merely 'a derivative issue from the proposal'. If this was so clear it is perhaps surprising that it required restatement, although again this need not have been a deliberate attempt to mislead. The likelihood is that it was made explicit just in case the document was ever sought in a legal action; Warburg's Anthony Sweetman had warned as early as the previous July that 'plaintiffs lawyers in the DDT may attempt to subpoena all documents relating to the proposal'.

It is as well to remember here that the strategic reasons for seeking a US listing and a Dutch domicile were in a commercial sense entirely sound. Foreign companies explain the enticements of Wall Street as Willie Sutton used to explain why he robbed banks:

'Because that's where the money is'. Hardie's disequilibrium—earning four in five dollars in the US, but having barely one in fifty shares held there—made the attraction still more acute. Nor is the wish to quantify and manage more effectively a large but shadowy liability inherently wrong. In fact, it would be one of the stranger aspects of the Special Commission of Inquiry that Hardie witnesses devoted so much effort to asserting that asbestos liabilities had not been a paramount concern in the company's restructurings, with semantic quibblings of the most hair-splitting kind.

Peter Macdonald, for instance, was asked by counsel assisting about an April 1998 letter to the Securities and Exchange Commission stating specifically that 'the Newco structure has been designed to insulate Newco from asbestos related claims', and a November 2001 memo in which Project Chelsea was described as a procedure 'to ring fence assets of JH and Coy'. He responded that any such insulation or ring fencing was 'an outcome of the design to list a company that didn't have legacy issues in North America rather than being a primary driver'—a distinction without a difference. For what was merely an 'outcome', the board papers lavish attention on asbestos, with explicit recommendations for 'managing' Trowbridge, and the report it was preparing:

> There may be pressure to make public the results of the Trowbridge analysis to Allens. The pressure to make that disclosure will be increased to the extent that the analysis is directly referred to in any public document, including, say, the independent expert's report [to be prepared for shareholders by Grant Samuel], although at this stage there is not contemplation to do so. Pressure for further disclosure may come from the ASX or ASC or any creditor intent on derailing any further selldowns. This risk can be minimised in two ways:
>
> First, continue to limit accessibility of the Trowbridge advice. For example, it may not be necessary for the independent expert to review the advice. Maintenance of legal and professional privilege should be a primary goal.
>
> Second, to the extent that disclosure of the advice, or reference to it, must be made, the report must be capable of withstanding critical review …

Perhaps the key contributor to board debate that day, however, was Greg Baxter, known for pungent realism, and a manner with journalists alternately affable and acerbic. Now he provided a clinical guide to selling Chelsea. There was, warned Baxter, 'a reasonable risk that the New South Wales government may attempt to interfere in the project', especially as the proposed day of the announcement was a sitting day in the Legislative Council and Legislative Assembly, which increased the possibility of 'political grandstanding'. Even the federal government might become involved:

> The project will be implemented in an election environment, whether the next federal election has been called or not. It provides an easy platform for an opportunistic opposition to claim that the economic environment and the tax and regulatory framework is forcing Australian companies to relocate. The asbestos issue may be linked with such an attack. The opposition may claim for example that not only is the company abandoning Australia, it is leaving behind liabilities. Both are spurious claims but could play well in the media. These issues have the potential to transfer media coverage from the business pages to the news pages. Both issues have potential, fuelled by political comment, to become topics of talk back radio discussion ... Newcastle will need to schedule one-on-one meetings with reports at major national business magazines that offer the opportunity for prominent profiles on the company and its management. Much of the success in having such a story published will be determined by the personality of the CEO.

Some of Baxter's comments on the business and commercial media, in fact, show a keen sense of its weaknesses:

> On the day of the announcement, the story will attract widespread interest from newswire services such as AAP, AP and Reuters etc. Experience shows that these agencies will assign junior reporters to the story who have virtually no knowledge or understanding of even the most rudimentary facts about the company. These people will be filing their first stories on Chelsea and this project within 1–2 hours of being assigned to the story. Given the above, many of the interviews will be

unpredictable in their scope and approach. Some of the more colourful media personalities may try to attack the project without really understanding it, because it will feed the prejudices of their audience (the sustenance of their ratings).

The asbestos gauntlet to be run was not the only source of concern. Baxter also feared tabloid tub-thumping about Hardie turning its back on Australia: 'We have not ruled out the possibility that members of the 'family' will publicly oppose or criticise the project as 'unAustralian' and not in the best interests of the vast majority of Australian resident shareholders. We recall the media's sympathetic treatment of Alice Oppen's campaign to save Arnott's from the Americans.' Baxter's recommendations stressed the need to 'influence key decision makers in the New South Wales government on this issue', to make 'strategic use of influential newspaper columnists and Channel 9's *Business Sunday* program to provide positive, independent third-party analysis', and MacGregor bringing John Reid 'into the loop and securing his early support.'

If anything, Baxter was needlessly thorough. Governments were too mired in their own machinations to worry about Hardie's, journalists proved malleable, and Barton was even able to flag his intention to retire. 'At this stage I'm not relocating to the US,' he told *Business Sunday*, 'so probably I won't stay on after that.' The Reid family, too, fell in line. When MacGregor addressed the annual meeting a week later, he was able to tell shareholders that his predecessor was an enthusiastic supporter of the plan: 'It is the only proposal I have ever seen that didn't have some minus in it.' MacGregor, of course, wasn't looking all that hard. For one thing, the company was foregoing $100 million in future tax benefits. For another, it was hardly being forthcoming about the implications for asbestos liabilities. On 10 September, Trowbridge presented its long-awaited report. Although occluded by the usual haze of qualifications, it figured the net present value of the liabilities at $254 million: a total quantum of $501.47 million discounted at 7 per cent. This was encouraging for Hardie, at least superficially vindicating its changed legal strategy, and consistent with the report of two years earlier. Yet it was far higher than most analysts' estimates. When Baxter's new assistant, Steve Ashe, reviewed broking research, he found estimates as low as $90 million, and the highest at little more than $150 million. When Grant Samuel's valuation of Hardie was included in the information memorandum a week later, it was so vague as to be entirely useless, if not misleading:

> The future liabilities for asbestos-related illnesses are quite uncertain as they involve both existing claims and claims yet to be made. JHI provides in its accounts for the cost of existing claims based on actuarial and other expert advice. However, while the directors have taken expert advice, the population of potential claimants is unknown and there is no reliable basis on which to assess at the present point in time the likely cost of settling potential future claims. In any event, in terms of comparing market valuation parameters, it is the market's assessment that is most relevant. Analyst estimates of the present value of the liability vary widely but appear to range from $50 million to $120 million.

The market was underwhelmed by the information memorandum. Even the building-products analyst at Warburgs was bemused:

> No one truly knows what asbestos is worth. The independent expert valued the liabilities at $80-120 million based on brokers' estimates (you really wonder about that document). Our own valuation of $115–130 million is a best guess based on discounting ten more years of $12–18 million (basically what it has been over the past five years) with a further ten years asymptoting towards zero, giving a total stream of liabilities of 33 years from the time the company ceased production. A viable alternative was to ask my nine-year-old for a number somewhere between a fair bit and lots.

Ord Minnett went further, rejecting the plan outright: 'Your analyst believes shareholders should seriously consider not supporting this proposal. Also we don't believe it is in shareholders' best interests to sell at the moment. US profits are only just getting into their stride.' By this time, exogenous factors had also come into play. The day of the formal announcement of Hardie's initial public offering coincided with the third-largest point drop in Wall Street history—357 points, or 4.1 per cent—in response to Russia's default on its sovereign debt. European and Asian markets also reeled, and Hardie's share price with them, slumping as low as $3.47, a fall of a third from its peak shortly after the announcement of Project Chelsea. By the time the company obtained the *fiat* from its shareholders at its 16 October extraordinary general meeting, it was unclear whether the opportunity to implement the IPO and capital reduction would present itself within the permissible six months.

Parts of the project continued. Hardie's debt was refinanced, existing borrowings being extinguished by new facilities worth $340 million at maturities up to fifteen years and rates of about 6 or 7 per cent. James Hardie NV was ushered into existence, formally acquiring control Coy's remaining operating businesses for $30.13 million on 28 October; Coy henceforward would be nothing but cash, receivables, the properties Hardie had or was occupying at Camellia, Rosehill, Welshpool, Meeandah and Carole Park—and, of course, liabilities. But Christmas passed with investors still fretful, and not until early in the New Year did Barton began to feel confident again. Engagements were organised for an investment roadshow through the US and Europe to spruik the 15 per cent of JHNV that Warburg was trying to sell. On 8 February, the day JHNV filed its registration statement with the Securities & Exchange Commission, Barton flew to New York to begin the tour with Macdonald, Baxter and Morley: a gruelling three weeks entailing more than sixty presentations to institutional fund managers.

The tour itself was an introduction to the hard-driving American culture that Hardie hankered to embrace, embodied in the thoroughly assimilated Macdonald. Baxter could scarcely credit his work ethic. One leg of the team's journey involved a five-hour American Airlines flight to Los Angeles leaving at 6.00PM on a Friday. Baxter was astonished to see Macdonald flip open his laptop with a cheerful: 'C'mon buddy. We'll do some work on this presentation.'

When Baxter looked askance, Macdonald was perplexed: 'We've got time for five hours of productive work.' Baxter laughed: 'That's one good meal and two movies.' But after a relatively cordial welcome in Europe, the US proved hard to crack. The market for building mid-caps was crowded; and while there was some concern about Hardie's residual exposure to asbestos, there was at least as much apprehension about its exposure to gypsum. Tapping into the US building boom, Hardie's gypsum business had been a stellar performer, making more money in the previous financial year than either the US or Australian fibre-cement operations. But analysts detested gypsum, considering it a commodity product with a volatile earnings cycle. Then, in the last week of February, as Warburg began its book-build preparatory to setting the price on the Hardie shares, the yield on thirty-year US Treasury bonds began rising. Hopes of a price between $US15 and $US18 were dashed; even at $US12, the stock was hard to get away. The team's last day of presentations, 4 March, ended with a dinner at the exclusive Maloney & Porcelli steakhouse on 50th Street between Park and Madison Avenue. But the Hardie team were only tourists.

Late in the evening, the group met at the Warburg office to participate in a teleconference with the board: MacGregor in Adelaide, Willcox in Melbourne, and Hellicar, Brown and Pedley's replacement as BIL representative, Jonathon Pinshaw, in Sydney, with Peter Cameron and John Martin from Allens. Barton reported that interest rate rises had affrighted investors in building stocks. Warburg's Tom Piper felt the issue might get away at $12, but that the aftermarket would then be soft; he suggested another cut in the issue price to $US11. After two hours' to-ing and fro-ing, the board concluded that neither prospect was enticing, and kiboshed the issue.

With the benefit of hindsight, this was a severe blow to Hardie. The Chelsea structure was far more robust and flexible where asbestos was concerned than the deal with which the company eventually proceeded. Even at the time, it was an immense frustration. Barton had been due to ring the New York Stock Exchange's bell the following morning; instead, he and Morley took a flight west. 'It was pretty tough,' recalls Morley. 'We'd put in a lot of work. When Keith and I flew back from New York to Sydney, I reckon we said maybe three words to one another. I think we were both thinking: "Where do we go from here?"' Of this, though, there was never any real doubt. Hardie's American destination was the same — it would simply be finding another route.

ALTHOUGH THE IPO AND CAPITAL REDUCTION would not now take place, some of Project Chelsea's aims had been achieved. In everything but listing and investor base, in fact, Hardie had already ceased to be an Australian company — it even quit being a member of the Business Council of Australia. While Baxter returned to Sydney because there would now be no investors for him to service, Morley, Shafron, Bridges and Harman went ahead with their relocations. Two new American non-executive directors, based in San Francisco, were appointed to the board: Michael Gilfillan, a former deputy chairman of Well Fargo, and Martin Koffel, executive chairman of the engineering and construction company URS Corporation. When Barton formally announced that Macdonald would succeed him on 20 May, there was no doubt about from where the company would now be run.

James Hardie Industries ended up headquartered in California's Orange County quite adventitiously: Mission Viejo, 80km south of Los Angeles, had been the location of the head office of HRM Inc, the irrigation company Hardie had acquired fifteen years earlier. Nonetheless, if a location had been sought to represent the opposite of everything stood for by the former Asbestos House, Hardie could have done little better. Its exotic name, with the Californian soft 'j' pronounced as an 'h', is inherited from Rancho Mission Viejo, a 52,000-acre Christian mission taken over by a successful trader when Mexico won its independence from Spain in 1821. This passed down through many wealthy hands, until the area's transformation from a semi-arid zone into a residential area began when Los Angeles was threatening to burst its urban boundaries in the 1960s. On the land now controlled by Irvine Company are scattered a host of gated communities, from large ones of about a thousand homes, like

Laguna Niguel, to small ones of around thirty homes, like Chelsea Point, all set in a landscape of theme restaurants, sprawling satellite shopping centres and fifty-screen cineplexes that would nonetheless revert to desert in weeks if the water supply from the Colorado River was cut. The then chief information officer, Dennis Cooper, recalls:

> It's an unreal environment, really. You have bands of Mexicans more or less continually tending the verges and making sure everything is growing beautifully. As you lie in bed at night, you hear the sound of the irrigation system sparking into life. It's very pleasant and very strange. Like Canberra on steroids. The way Americans do things, if there's a hill and they don't want a hill, they get rid of the hill. If they want a hill, they build one. The landscape is totally manufactured. Yet I remember being told that if I turned right having exited Freeway 5, rather than left to the airport, I would end up in a place no one should go to, where there were regularly murders.

Every member of a gated community must choose a password; Cooper's endowed his with a tinge of Australia by deciding on 'wombat'. There was less flexibility in other matters, even in mores: 'As you're driving up to come home you press your remote control in perfect time so that the door rises just in time to accommodate you and closes behind you immediately. It's like no one was ever there. To have your garage doors open is frowned on.'

Macdonald lived in Laguna Niguel; Morley preferred Chelsea Point; and Shafron, Harman and Cooper stuck to Mission Viejo itself, while the company began to hold board meetings at the Ritz Carlton in Dana Point. The location was ideal for traffic from LAX, and Fontana was about 100km east. Where the old Asbestos House had always seemed dark and formal, the head office at Mission Viejo was light and low-key. Hardie occupied only half of the rented, four-storey building. Macdonald, Morley and Shafron enjoyed the indulgence of small offices on the ground floor surrounded by nine other finance, tax and legal staff—young, healthy and tanned white-collar workers with complimentary 'sodas' seemingly grafted to their hands. Senior operating executive Louis Gries sat on the floor above in a 'six pack' working station with his building-products colleagues, the Merkeley brothers and production manager Dave Kessner; Noel Thompson, appointed chief technology officer in January 1999, squeezed his team into another half a floor.

It was an impersonal and rather sterile environment. The building was indistinguishable from the other two in the anonymous office park: one was occupied by a bank, Washington Mutual; the other, by a medical centre. But the differences were more than cosmetic. The American style, of which Macdonald was the standard bearer, was a significant departure from the more staid Australian mores and the personnel-development culture that Barton had sought to instill. 'Keith's expression was always: "Get the conditions right and the outcomes follow",' recalls one executive. 'Peter was much more of the opinion that conditions and processes get in the way of outcomes.'

In this set-up, Macdonald leaned more and more heavily on Gries and his cohort, a tight-knit group that played ice hockey together and tended to hold aloof from the Australians. Rumours abounded about how hard Gries had been prepared to drive for a dollar at USG, and he enjoyed living up to his reputation for relentless drive. On one occasion he presented a padlock to each member of his sales team with the advice: 'Your objective has got to be to put a padlock on the gate of one of your rivals.' He condensed his slogan for the spread of fibre-cement in the US into four simple words: 'Make wood go away.' If it did not go away fast enough, someone else would be found: staff turnover at sales and retail level is reported to have reached 70 per cent.

It became a running joke at Hardie to call Macdonald the 'BLO': the 'board liaison officer'. This was an exaggeration. Macdonald was always formidably well-briefed and well-informed about all the company's endeavours, in the US and Australia. But there is no doubt, at least in an operational sense, that he relied on an important *eminence Gries*. As one former executive puts it:

> The cultures are very different. The US culture is very performance-oriented. There's less respect for people, more putting them into roles

then moving them on if they can't add value. I mean, American business is like that. Relationships are more fleeting. There's much greater depth in management and markets, which means companies are more prepared to churn and burn.

Says another:

It's management by fear and intimidation, really. The system is that the people there just say what management want to hear … 'Yes, boss. What a great idea, boss'. People are constantly reminded that they could be out the door tomorrow, and a lot of them are.

But, as Morley says, it worked. If the pursuit of shareholder value was your measure, Hardie was a gold medalist. The banality of the surroundings suited the clinical approach:

Mission Viejo's not a city. As a location, it's a bit like working in Wollongong or Newcastle. You were probably more cocooned from things that happened than if you'd been in Los Angeles. As far as Australia was concerned, you came down once a quarter, did the results, got the first plane out. When you got back to Mission Viejo, the local press didn't cover Australia. The closest you got was reading the website. The idea was to keep it very matter-of-fact. The business units would send in a one page summary of financials and one page of commentary every month. As a result, the decisions tended to be more black and white, because what you were doing, whether it was looking at a plant, or where to locate it, was driven by statistics, models, and focused on capital returns. But I mean, look at the returns! It was pretty intense stuff, but that's OK. That's business nowadays.

There was no immediate attempt to reprise Project Chelsea. It had been a costly exercise. Extinguishing debt early had cost $24.4 million; professional fees, to Warburgs, Coopers, Trowbridge, Allens and New York lawyers Gibson Dunn & Crutcher, were $5.3 million in the third quarter alone. James Hardie Finance BV had to be collapsed, and a new Australian-domiciled JH Australian Finance Pty

Ltd created to make use of local tax losses. But at least one party wanted the issue on a front burner. Since Pedley had led its push into Hardie, Brierley Investments had come under the influence of a consortium of Malaysian, Singaporean and Indonesian investors, who had acquired a fifth of the company for about $US700 million —just in time for the Asian currency crisis. The chairman and chief executive had been ousted in favour of former New Zealand treasurer Sir Roger Douglas in April 1998 who, within a few months, had himself fallen foul of key investor Tan Sri Quek Leng Chan while preparing to reveal an annual loss of $904 million.

Urgently in need of cash, struggling to bed down a refinancing, and seeking a chief executive officer, BIL dumped its stakes in Central North Island Forest Partnership, W.D & H.O Wills Holdings, John Fairfax Holdings and Creative Publishing. The failure of Hardie's IPO and capital return had been a grave disappointment. As Hardie considered its next move, so did BIL. Pinshaw was succeeded on the Hardie board in July by BIL's new chairman, Sir Selwyn Cushing. As Peter Macdonald settled into his new role after Barton attended his last board meeting the following month, it was pretty clear he could rely on whole-hearted support from his biggest shareholder for anything that extracted cash from the group.

The first stirrings of interest in finishing the process that Chelsea had begun were reports by Morley and John Martin of Allens responding to a restructuring proposal devised by Tony Clemens of what was now PwC, involving a share swap between JHIL and a newly incorporated Dutch entity. But these might have remained of academic interest had the federal government not at that moment providentially adopted a key recommendation of the Ralph Tax Reform package, foreshadowing scrip-for-scrip rollover relief for the purposes of capital gains tax, removing the risk that a Hardie share swap would crystallise gains on which tax would be payable. 'Suddenly, what we wanted to do was viable,' Morley recalls. 'In the old days, if you did what we were intending, you had a new piece of paper for the same company, and another new piece of paper called a tax assessment that they had to pay in cash. And the shareholder's going: "What's gone wrong here? I haven't done anything and someone's clipping my ticket for 25 per cent".'

This was promising. If the tax impost was removed in doing so, Hardie could finally shed its old identity, like a snake sloughing off a layer of skin. The company could be officially reborn. As 1999 ended, Shafron, Morley and their retinue of advisers were hard at work on what would become known as Project Green.

-15-

'Wow. That's much more than I was expecting'

'The environment in which James Hardie's asbestos related liabilities are determined is unfavourable to JH.'
—Hardie general counsel, Peter Shafron, in report to board, 17 February 2000

PROJECT GREEN, THE SCHEME BY WHICH Hardie would become a tax *émigré* and attain its coveted New York Stock Exchange listing, soon developed a dark-green parallel project: the lifting of the company's asbestos burden. The failure of Project Chelsea had been a grave disappointment to management, and an awakening to the board. Meredith Hellicar, so insistent when she had joined on determining that Hardie had nothing to do with asbestos, now found that the assurances had, albeit inadvertently, been hollow:

> Chelsea was really the first time I'd realised that asbestos could be a problem for us. Mr Investment Banker had come along and said: 'Hey, do a 20 per cent IPO, that'll really put some value in your share price. Oops, sorry, forgot to tell you that with gypsum you won't do as well. And by the way, this asbestos thing is a problem, too.' It was really post that when it dawned on me that asbestos was a liability in a corporate-valuation sense.

Asbestos, in fact, was becoming more than a line in the board papers. Hardie was now devoting considerable resources to its claims processing. A dedicated department was being run by Wayne Attrill, who brought with him a Harvard masters degree when he was recruited from Mallesons in January 1998. It had a broader remit, including legislative activism. That year, it was involved in lobbying the New South Wales government to prevent detrimental amendments to the Dust Diseases Tribunal Act, and commissioned the editor of the standard tort law text *Accidents, Compensation, and the Law*, Australian National University's Peter Cane, to report on alternative means of compensation resolution. For Hardie, the ideal would have been something like Sir Geoffrey Palmer's Accident Compensation Act 1972, which abolished work-related personal injury claims in New Zealand. The lobbying bore no fruit, but the savvy political machine of premier Bob Carr was toying with reform of compensation regimes in New South Wales, and might in the long term be a useful ally.

Hardie was also forced to reopen legal hostilities with its recalcitrant insurer QBE, whose allegation that Hardie had 'adopted a course of deliberately attempting to conceal facts known to it relating to the asbestos hazards' had caused such grief a decade earlier. Since the court skirmish in November 1984 following QBE's decision to cancel its insurance contracts, an Asbestos Claims Facility had operated under which QBE paid half the amount Hardie claimed to be entitled to, and under which the parties consented to 'consult and use their best endeavours to negotiate a new arrangement' when it expired in June 1995. These endeavours had failed in early 1996, when Hardie had refused QBE's offer of $5.8 million in full and final settlement, and stalemate ensued. Hardie had then received some surprising legal advices, from Philips Fox and Bret Walker SC, to the effect that more was at stake than suspected. Both parties had been assuming that the maximum amount recoverable under the policies had been around $25 million. But epidemiological evidence that 'bodily injury' occurs immediately on inspiring asbestos, long before disease develops, implied that the quantum recoverable might be closer to $100 million — an intelligence Hardie had forwarded to QBE in March 1999. After nine months, QBE came back with an offer of $25 million. Hardie rejected it, and argy-bargy began.

Above all, claims flowed unabated, with the bigger legal stick that Allens wielded now tending to make them more unpleasant. In June 1999, for instance, Hardie elected to fight a case brought by a carpenter with mesothelioma, Peter Thurbon. Melbourne's Jack Rush QC and Gerry Gardiman's Turner Freeman protege Tanya Segelov lured the former Hardie safety officer Peter Russell from his retirement residence at Queensland's Airlie Beach, and his testimony was devastating. Thurbon's wife was astonished at the lengths to which Hardie went to fight the case out: 'The Asbestos manufacturer … tried to undermine Peter's case that he had a successful business so that they could minimise the compensation they would have to pay. They even employed a private detective to interview Peter's clients and sub-contractors.' When the case was settled on the third day with an award of about $800,000, Hardie's silk, Jack Forrest, made a point of wishing Thurbon well. 'The detective had reported back that there was no such dirt to be found, everyone they interviewed had told them Peter was a hard-working, honest and decent bloke,' said Elizabeth Turbon. 'We all have choice as to how we earn a living; this barrister certainly made the wrong choice when he decided to defend this lot!'

In a landmark case two months later, the High Court awarded $800,000 to the widow of Brian Crimmins: a waterside worker diagnosed in May 1997 with mesothelioma as a result of handling asbestos at the Port of Melbourne between 1960 and 1964. Slater & Gordon's Margaret Kent had sued the waterfront statutory authority, the Stevedoring Industry Finance Committee, arguing that the body it had succeeded in 1977 (the Stevedoring Industry Authority) had owed Crimmins a duty of care. The law firm shortly advised Hardie that they would be bringing another 284 claims for compensation on behalf of former waterside workers, and a proportion of costs would be borne by Hardie as the principal consignee.

In the year to 31 March 2000, Hardie resolved 135 claims at a net cost of $18.56 million, an increase of 8.5 per cent on the previous corresponding period: $16.74 million in damages and plaintiff legal costs, $6.36 million in its own legal costs, offset by $4.54 million recovered from insurers. It was also paying an increasing proportion of claims to which it was party: almost three-quarters compared to just over half. Asked for an overview of Hardie's litigation practices, Forrest cast doubt on the company's direction:

> The stark reality is that most claims against James Hardie will be successful. No amount of exotic legal defences or the ingenuity of solicitors or counsel will affect this fact of life. In my view, James Hardie's resources are best expended investigating claims on a case by case basis to determine at the earliest possible time the viability of any defence and if impractical to defend, then to achieve settlement if possible. The scope for [further] large projects to reduce James Hardie's current level of liability is minimal. The task at hand should be to endeavour to concentrate on ensuring that James Hardie's position does not deteriorate to a point where its very existence is threatened.

Some cases, especially those where the plaintiff was not a lowly paid worker but had had a brush with asbestos before pursuing a lucrative career, were of the scale to rock almost any company. Roman Judzewitsch, a 52-year-old specialist endocrinologist, had been expecting to work another twenty years when asbestos exposure from his father, who had worked at Camellia in the 1950s and 1960s, caught up with him. 'They [Hardie] didn't see it coming,' recalls Gardiman. 'Or if they did, they were completely ignorant of its potential.' Calculating his economic loss on the basis of a $275,000 annual income, the Dust Diseases Tribunal in April 2000 awarded Judzewich $3 million damages, net of insurance claims and before costs.

Macdonald had not long met QBE's chief executive Frank O'Halloran at LAX to personally negotiate a settlement of their company's dispute. Neither man was budging much, but neither was keen on the alternative of court. Peter Shafron and Wayne Attrill specifically warned their boss of the way that any action could blow up in their faces even as Project Green took shape, providing grist for the mill of 'spoilers' — litigants, lawyers, lobbyists and trade unionists under whose cosh Hardie seemed to fall at the least provocation:

Any hearing could in effect amount to a 'commission of inquiry' into the manner in which JH conducted its asbestos operations during the 1950s to the mid-1970s. JH's knowledge of the risks posed to consumers of its products and its failure to place warning labels on those products, would all be minutely examined ... JH is now around ten years old in asbestos litigation and believes that most adverse material has been discovered. However, additional adverse material could surface, and in any event the proceedings may provide a forum for a further airing of existing allegations against JH (eg it steadfastly refused to label its products, putting third parties at risk, for fear of losing sales) ... Litigation would not be helpful to JHIL as Project Green may require a court-approved scheme of arrangements or other public process that provides an opportunity for asbestos claimant 'spoilers'. Spoilers may be able to take advantage of litigation between JHC and QBE to underscore a claim that the level of James Hardie's asbestos liabilities is inherently uncertain, and quite possibly worse than it has been leading the market to believe.

To the most disturbing development of all, however, Shafron was alerted by an email on 4 November 1999 from Steve McClintock of what was now PriceWaterhouseCoopers: a mooted accounting standard deriving from ED88 would compel more detailed treatment of Hardie's contingent liabilities. Hardie's accounts carried only a boilerplate note concerning potential asbestos damages, and imputed them a value of $43 million; as we have seen, analysts estimates varied widely. Promulgation of a standard based on ED88 would force the publication of an accredited actuarial estimate, which might exceed the net assets of Coy and Jsekarb. In this period and for much of 2000, Hardie fell extremely quiet, even in the DDT, where it was decided that the test cases and appeals were perhaps not such a great idea. Attrill specifically recommended 'a period of relative stability in the litigation' while two options were pursued: the restructuring initiatives on foot, and perhaps a settlement agreement with plaintiff lawyers. 'To achieve this state,' he noted, 'will require James Hardie to significantly improve its relations with external stakeholders who have traditionally been opposed to James Hardie, including plaintiffs' lawyers, trade unions and victim support groups.' Attrill would not have known that Hardie was by now too committed to the former to even consider the latter.

HARDIE DID NOT HASTEN to this judgement. The first Hardie board meeting of 2000, on 17 February at the old Asbestos House, devoted two hour-long sessions to what was now Project Green. Between those presentations, Shafron presented a paper containing as many as ten options for asbestos, ranging from insurance defeasance like the kind adopted (unsuccessfully) by Turner & Newall in the UK to a company split like those engineered (unblinkingly) by Louisiana Pacific and W. R. Grace in the US. Again, perhaps with legal posterity in mind, Shafron noted how publicly disastrous might be a restructuring mishap, given the fervency of the company's detractors:

> In sum, the US experience has shown us thus far that a carefully planned reorganisation that makes fair provision for the asbestos claims has some chance of succeeding. But any attempt at reorganisation that does not leave significant assets for the asbestos claims will, at a minimum, spawn lengthy and costly litigation with the plaintiff bar, and may ultimately be unsuccessful.

This was not the most emphatic of endorsements, but 'some chance of succeeding' was better than none. The paper was more emphatic about the unsustainability of the status quo, originating a refrain within the Hardie's executive that, while the company was committed to helping what it called 'legitimate claimants', the DDT was running amok. The cost of running cases in New South Wales —which was, of course, where most cases were run against Hardie —was considerably greater than in other states. Although they usually settled, cases ran longer, involved more court time and institutional expense. Shafron had become a disciple of the distinguished British law professor Patrick Atiyah, who argued in his *The Damages Lottery* (1997) that the tort system had left people unwilling to take responsibility for protecting themselves against misfortune, leading them instead to go looking for an object of blame when something went wrong. Hardie, Shafron felt, had become such an object; in fact, it wasn't merely plaintiffs doing the blaming. 'There is a strong institutional bias against JH and the other asbestos product manufacturers,' he argued. 'It is apparent in courts, juries, and in government, and is especially well developed in New South Wales.' This was 'a distraction to senior management and an uncertainty factor in the JH share price'. He was keenest on a company split, with perhaps a trust thrown in to 'create a buffer between JH and asbestos claimants and could provide some sense or apprehension among claimants and/or the market that the litigation was no longer a company problem or distraction but an issue for the trust.'

The Hardie board shared their general counsel's loathing for the DDT. 'We were very disparaging of the DDT,' says Hellicar. 'We felt —and we knew the government felt this too, even though they wouldn't say it—that the tribunal ran itself somewhat lavishly, was prone to overseas trips for death-bed hearings, etc. I don't remember the view that the amounts of compensation being awarded were wrong, but more that the system was not well controlled and run efficiently ... Money was being thrown around on unnecessary things.' Shafron was gratified by the response to his paper. 'On the A issue,' he emailed Peter Cameron and John Martin of Allens, 'there is plenty of support to do something with finality.'

'Finality': from its antecedent, Project Chelsea, Project Green would be distinguished straight away. Chelsea had been aimed merely at shutting the door on asbestos; Green was imagined as locking the door and throwing the key away. Tackling the challenge gradually drew ahead in significance of the general corporate makeover. At the Hardie board meeting at Dana Point's Ritz Carlton on 13–14 April, it was top of the agenda, with shareholders envisaged holding equity in two entities, a Newco and an Oldco, with Oldco to carry sufficient assets to meet an actuarial assessment of asbestos liabilities.

The different extremities of intent between Chelsea and Green are crucial but mysterious. There is an operational raison d'etre. In the preceding few months, Macdonald had been reviewing a number of acquisitions and deals, including a merger with the British giant BPB, a joint venture with the Belgian fibre-cement and gypsum group Etex, and the acquisition of the American gypsum manufacturer Republic Group.* An asbestos liability was no small matter for an acquirer; using equity in a takeover was likewise problematic. The outline of ED88, which might compel explicit quantification of the contingent liability, was also distantly visible.

The difference, however, also seems analogous to the personalities of the chief executives involved. Barton, while tough, was innately conservative. 'Keith is one of those very hard-nosed business people who will do anything but breach an ethic,' says a long-time colleague. 'Very driven and quite difficult to deal with, but dead straight. He'd push you to the limit, but he'd never ask you to step over it.' Macdonald was temperamentally drawn to total solutions, complete exits. 'Peter comes across as an exceptionally decent and hard-working guy,' comments an adviser who has worked closely with Hardie. 'But when he was there, it became a breakthrough environment. That's something you need operating in foreign markets. You just have to break through. But the whole culture became very black and white. No grey.' In some respects, it may be as simple as the fact that Chelsea was largely designed in Australia, where a vestigial connection to the asbestos past remained, and Green in the US, where corporates operate on more Darwinian principles.

A total solution, however, would not be easy. The emails that bounced around even as the Hardie board met in California provided Shafron with an immediate headache — and a headache four years later when he had to explain them to the Special Commission of Inquiry. The first, on 13 April, was a heads-up from Trowbridge's David Minty:

---

* Macdonald had a meeting with Etex's CEO, Canio Corbo, and a member of the controlling family, Jean-Marie Emsens, in Brussels a few days after this board meeting. He, MacGregor and representatives of Warburgs also visited BPB on 8-9 May to discuss an agreed paper bid, which would have created the world's biggest plasterboard and gypsum products producer, but BPB satisfied its acquisitive itch the following month by acquiring gypsum and ceiling tile businesses from Celotex for $US345 million.

Please excuse the cryptic nature of this email given the non-secure nature of the internet! Despite the time frame and some issues with data interpretation we have managed to get to a first cut of an estimate. Our 'first draft' conclusion is that the discounted present value of the liability lies between \$A300 to \$A350m at 31 March 2000 compared to our estimate of \$254m at March 1998.

'Major drivers', confided Minty, were increased settlements for mesothelioma from the factoring in of loss of voluntary services to family, increasing cross-claims, and the new stream of settlements to flow from *Crimmins v SIFC*. He concluded cheerfully: 'I trust your deliberations at the Board meeting go well and look forward to seeing you again soon. Kind regards.' They were not reciprocated. Shafron's unsigned reply was terse in the extreme: 'Wow. That's much more than I was expecting.' He alerted Macdonald at once: 'See below—much higher than we were expecting.' Oldco, it seemed, would have to be a considerably larger entity than imagined to cover Coy's obligations. At the weekend, after the board meeting had concluded, Shafron called Attrill in:

Wayne, I am off next week, but can you stay close to Minty? I am appalled that the number is so high, no fault of anyone of course but deeply disappointing. I mean, \$100m more? A 40pc increase? Are the legals more or less than last time? (We were expecting less of course). Can you test his logic—his short note was not convincing. The next critical date is the May Board meeting. Can we get David to agree to have a draft executive summary, read and commented upon by us first, ready for that meeting? How much longer does he need? See what you can do and make this a high priority.

Attrill duly rang Minty on the Tuesday to stress that he would 'like to go through the assumptions with them before it is finalised', and expressed solidarity in his email reply to Shafron: 'I expected the figure would go up (given the wharf claims and JHC's increasing settlement share) but I must say not by this much.' Shafron was grateful but rueful: 'Thanks Wayne—still not a great story. If it went up 25 per cent over the last 2 years, why wouldn't it go up 25 per cent over the next 2 years, so the argument could go?' Attrill thought the position might well deteriorate:

> Yes, Peter. This is definitely a problem. As you know I had thought that JH's investment with Allens in working up test cases would yield us long-term dividends in the form of lower settlements. That has not proven to be the case. The legislature intervened to nullify some of our key advances, the plaintiffs' lawyers improved their own performance, and the courts did their bit by expanding and increasing the level of damages (a quite common, but unhelpful, feature of the tort system) as well as our share of them. What we have told QBE — that the litigation always gets worse — is quite correct. And unfortunately there is more potential downside in the system yet.

When Attrill met them two weeks later to ascertain 'the status of, and assumptions underlying' Trowbridge's report, Minty and his colleague Karl Marshall had moderated their views somewhat: they were now talking of an estimate of $294 million, including $10 million for wharf claims, which Attrill felt 'reasonable'. But Shafron was now on guard. Slim, handsome, rapid in speech and often humorous in tone, he was a popular executive — an altogether warmer personality than his boss Macdonald. 'Peter was a great guy to work for,' recalls John Winters. 'A really nice guy, very principled, very encouraging. If you had a good idea, he just let you do it.' But he had a flair for secrecy and a cognisance of security risks that would not have disgraced a spymaster. His emails were always assigned the importance 'high' and the sensitivity 'confidential'; he advised colleagues to mark all documentation 'private and confidential' or 'confidential and attorney-privileged' on every page, and warned against 'leaving information on desk tops where visitors can or may find it' and against sending faxes 'unless you know someone is waiting to pick up the document at the receiving end'.

Now he acted to sanitise and bowdlerise the Trowbridge report. 'Don't let them go to final whatever you do,' he advised Attrill. His intention was to keep the report in draft form, so that it did not commit Hardie to anything if it happened to become public. The addressee, he felt, should become Roy Williams, the Allens partner in charge of asbestos litigation. But he, Shafron, would still be dictating the terms of the report. In extensive marginalia on the final draft, he insisted that Trowbridge firm the conclusions up, by deleting all qualifying references to the imprecision of actuarial calculations, and 'tone down the speculative risks', including deleting a whole section on areas of exposure not encompassed by the report. There were even factual deletions, such as a reference to an increase in mesothelioma claims, and mention of ED88. The report was presented *mutatis mutandis* to the next board meeting, but even then was never signed off on. When Trowbridge's 'sensitivity analysis' ventured a range from $167 million and $420 million depending on 'low or high' claim numbers, Shafron again sought a veto: 'When I saw the sensitivity analysis, I thought it wasn't, you know, based on anything—there didn't seem to be any logic behind it, so it seemed to me that a cosmetic change that I could make, which I suggested, was: "Let's go keep this under 400".' Trowbridge baulked, the argument could not be resolved before events moved on, and the report remained in draft.

Because much of this remained obscure to the board, who saw only a summary of the report in August, Trowbridge's figurings began to lead a strange double life, arbitrary *and* precise, provisional *and* definitive. Evidence would later be presented that Trowbridge wildly underestimated the liabilities by a number of means, such as an unsupportably low figure on settlements, and too high a discount rate. Even at the time, they encountered criticism from Allens' Roy Williams, who faxed Attrill an astringent assessment, noting the 'excessively optimistic assumptions' of no 'superimposed inflation', which is the phenomenon in the compensation of torts that claim sizes increase faster than general wage inflation, and no change to the legal environment, ignoring the probability of further 'landmark or precedent-setting cases'. Shafron dismissed this assessment with the comment that Williams was always on 'the doom and gloom side'.

The main problem, however, was the sheer lack of clarity about what the figures represented. Shafron, in particular, understood their elasticity full well. When director Michael Brown posed a question about the continuous-disclosure implications of the Trowbridge report—that is, whether Hardie was obliged to inform the market now that it was in possession of such calculations—Shafron assuaged his concerns: 'The Trowbridge work is very uncertain. It is based on very imperfect epidemiological models and very uncertain predictions of future claims numbers and claims costs. On the basis of the sensitivity analysis, the liability could be up to $384 million higher or $220 million lower'. But to this self-same sensitivity analysis he had himself objected, and at all other times acted to make the calculation seem as precise as the time on an atomic clock. He was happy, for instance, for the report to be used by Hardie's London-based insurance brokers, Jardine Lloyd Thompson, when they shopped around the company's asbestos risks to reinsurers in June. Indeed, he insisted on it. When Minty confessed to being 'extremely nervous' about this use of the report, Shafron obtained Macdonald's approval to 'beat him up a bit', and remonstrated by email: 'I have just finished talking to the CEO and wanted to convey how unhappy we are with the position you have taken in demanding an indemnity in return for us being able to use your report for the purposes I outlined to you in February.' But he preferred not to deal with the implications of the reinsurers' response that, after examining Trowbridge's calculations, their own undiscounted base-case esti-mate of Hardie's liabilities was $675 million.[†] As David Jackson

---

† In his evidence at the Special Commission of Inquiry, Shafron airily dismissed the initial responses from insurers, indicating that they would want up-front premiums of $400 million for taking on Hardie's liabilities, as commercial argy-bargy:

> *Michael Slattery QC* [counsel for the Medical Research and Compensation Foundation]: So what the insurers were telling you was that their view were that $675 million was the appropriate undiscounted base case number rather than what was in the Trowbridge report?
> *Shafron*: Well they were saying that was going to be the assumption they would make in terms of the programme they were going to write.
> *Slattery*: As you understood it, that was in their opinion a more realistic view of

summarised: 'The 2000 Trowbridge report was used by James Hardie when it suited it to do so, but was denigrated when it did not'.

While Jardine Lloyd Thompson's efforts to buy cover for Hardie's liabilities eventually came to nought, June brought some good news on the insurance front. Five years after the expiry of its facility, QBE agreed to pony up $47 million in fourteen equal annual instalments of $3.13 million secured by a Commonwealth Bank letter of credit. The 'QBE receivable' was a coup, at a time that Hardie was rehearsing an old line of argument anew: the 'corporate veil'. To fund Oldco to the extent of its actuarially assessed liabilities would clearly be very awkward. But there was another way to look at the same problem. In a steady flow of legal advices to the board, Allens' Peter Cameron had advised of a tension between directors' possible inclinations and their legal duties: 'Directors need to be cognisant of the rights and interests of shareholders who could legit-imately argue that it is not part of the business of the company to give money away to unproven potential creditors nor to lock up cap-ital indefinitely'. Hardie, Cameron contended, owed no legal duty to claimants not yet identified. Strictly speaking, in fact, setting aside monies on top of Coy's net assets might be found in court to be unduly generous; likewise, periodically topping up Coy's funds if cir-cumstances dictated. The lawyer Shafron took this advice very seri-ously. Notes of a meeting at Philips Fox on 18 July record a telling exchange between Shafron, on the phone from Mission Viejo, and insurance partner Michael Gill. Any provision, Shafron insisted, would only be set aside once. Gill sought clarification: 'The pressure point will be—if the funds prove to be inadequate, will JHNV#2 put in more money?' Shafron's reply was one word: 'No'.

---

the future of the asbestos liabilities which were the subject of the quote for which they were asked?

Shafron: Well I think they had an interest in having a higher number than a lower number.

Slattery: But you certainly understood that they were the terms upon which they were prepared to deal?

Shafron: At this point yes.

Whether the board would be prepared to sign off on a proposal so categorical, however, was another question. Shafron knew it. When investor relations chief Greg Baxter and his offsider Steve Ashe listed the stakeholders in any proposal, some appeared especially daunting, especially the much-loathed plaintiff lawyers. As he confided to them, Shafron personally doubted that his directors had the cojones:

> In relation to the stakeholders, judging by the Board last time they are unlikely to agree to anything that is not 'guaranteed not to fail'. It seems to me that if that is right (and let's talk tomorrow) then we need to assume that we will have to talk to the major stakeholders, in detail, early. We will effectively need to report back to the Board that they are all OK before we press the button. It follows that we will need inducements.
>
> Greg, you said that the board needs to understand that they may have a fight. I think that if we have a fight they are likely to go to water, and if we tell them that they may have a fight (albeit one we should win) they will not proceed (a sufficient number will not have the heart).

Shafron was particularly dismissive of the board's tendency to lean on external advisers. To a suggestion that the company retain professional crisis managers, Control Risk Group, he commented: 'I don't think we should underestimate the value the Board will place on <u>outside</u> third party advisers (as insulting as that is to the company's internal advisers — myself included).' Notes of the next day's conference call record Baxter reading the signals from government and media with some trepidation: 'Even if you get four or five major shareholders on board, you can't stop everyone. Say an individual asbestos victim with an axe to grind. They will turn against us quickly and will use our material to marshal their resources for a media campaign … The Tele today mounted an extraordinary attack on Carr. Maybe the Tele has turned against the Govt. But the Tele would say — so what will Bob Carr do about this?'

Philips Fox's Michael Gill tried to sound positive: 'You're setting up a compensation fund for the future. You've gone further than most people would expect. If the company was taken over, the new owners may not be nearly so benevolent.' Shafron again shared his misgivings about the board: 'At this stage there are a number of directors who will want convincing that the completion risk is low.' Gill asked the simply question: 'You need to work out whether you can afford to fail.' 'At this stage,' replied Shafron, 'the answer would be "no".' The Trowbridge report, even stiffened and strengthened, had left them vulnerable: 'Don't underestimate potential for significant risk if a judge permitted a line-by-line analysis of the method for calculating the fund.'

The group decided they wanted a clearer risk-analysis, and Ashe, whom Baxter had recruited six months earlier from PwC where he had spent sixteen years in accounting and regulation, was commissioned to compile the group's collected wisdom on 'Stakeholder Management'. Ashe's *métier* was dealing with government and regulators, and he was here given a broad remit. Chancing on the Trowbridge report on Baxter's desk, he was appalled: 'Greg, if Turner Freeman or Slater & Gordon got this, they would tear it to pieces.' Baxter told him to add it to his brief. What he came back with was one of the most perceptive and trenchant documents compiled in the course of Hardie's manoeuvrings.

'The real issue,' decided Ashe, 'is whether we can convince a raft of potentially hostile and emotional stakeholders of the merits and integrity of our case, such that they will not act in a way that prevents us from separating the asbestos liabilities.' And that, as he pointed out, was far from clear; indeed, the 'possible allegations' that Ashe listed were uncannily prophetic:

- Now that the company appears to be doing well it wants to preclude access to victims (or their families) upon whom they have inflicted the asbestos related disease.
- Past experience suggests that JH is a company that cannot be trusted. The company has a history of not disclosing the truth — for its own gain. This can be seen in its failure to properly disclose the risks of asbestos exposure to employees and end users. They have also failed to disclose to shareholders and creditors the true extent of the

asbestos liability. They have done it before—and are doing it again.

- Their behaviour in court provides ample evidence that they will do whatever they can to avoid or minimise the amount paid to victims. This provides a good pointer to whether they are likely (without being forced by a court or legislation) to adequately provide for the victims.

- If JH thinks taking out additional insurance is the solution why doesn't the company merely take out the insurance itself—why does it need to separate? It is merely absolving itself of the risk—and asking the victims to carry it …

In support of these allegations the main area of attack by stakeholders will be the inadequacy of assets left behind to meet future liabilities. Particular allegations that insufficient assets are being left behind could include:

- The numerous disclaimers and assumptions contained in actuarial reports meant that no reliance can be placed on it for setting a finite amount to be available for victims. James Hardie should guarantee that there will at all times be sufficient funds to meet future liabilities.

- There is inadequate recognition of the potential for future legislative or regulatory changes which may expand the company's exposure to liabilities.

- There is inadequate recognition for the potential for future Court findings or medical scientific research to increase the extent of liabilies for JH. Evidence around the world suggests that the number of claims and amounts of settlements are escalating.

- The company has stated publicly that the full amount of its asbestos liabilites cannot be accurately determined. How can it now say—when it suits them—there is a specific amount that will satisfy all future liabilities?

All good questions—and ones for which Hardie would need an answer in time. In his appendix concerning the Trowbridge report, Ashe acutely anticipated lines of legal attack, too: 'The extensive qualifications provided by Trowbridge throughout the report suggest that in relation to estimating future asbestos liabilities reliance on the actuarial assessment provides questionable benefit. The report does not leave the reader with confidence that the amount of $294 million is sufficient. In fact, one could easily be left with the impression that the amount is insufficient'. Of the inclusion of alternative projections under a number of different scenarios, Ashe remarked: 'They appear to be saying you can pretty much take your pick. Stakeholders referring to the sensitivity analysis are invited to pick a higher number!' It was a devastating critique — Baxter would later joke that Ashe deserved a pay rise simply for prescience — and it almost changed the course of events. Because it very nearly killed the cause of asbestos separation stone-dead.

'Possible in future not solvent'

'What happens when the money runs out?'

'It runs out.'

'What guarantees can JH give that victims aren't going to be stranded?'

'None.'

'They are the two big questions.'

'Agree.'

—E-mail exchange between Liza-Jayne Loch of Hawker Britton and Greg Baxter of James Hardie, January 2001

JAMES HARDIE EXECUTIVES SPEAK OF PETER MACDONALD with more respect than affection. 'Peter was an excellent CEO but he was a driver,' says one. 'He wanted everything done yesterday. You were always under pressure to drop everything and work nights and weekends.' And in mid-2000, Macdonald was driving very hard indeed, on both aspects of Project Green: the change of domicile and the separation of asbestos.

The former, involving Ian Wilson and Anthony Sweetman from Warburg with Tony Clemens from PwC, was an ever-changing proposition; Clemens became known as 'the Lilypad Man' for the way, in his plans, he hopped from one tax jurisdiction to another. For the latter, enthusiasm waxed and waned. Macdonald found another good reason to proceed in a conversation on 2 August with Alec Brennan, a former workmate at CSR where he was now deputy to CEO Peter Kirby, who was visiting Hardie's operations in Orlando. Brennan confided that CSR would probably increase its provision against asbestos liabilities in its next annual accounts, sheltering it by an abnormal gain of $300 million on the sale of its aluminium assets.* 'We need to consider this information in light of Project Green,' Macdonald confided to his Project Green cohort. 'It would be preferable to "beat CSR to the punch" than to be on the back foot fending off questions about what our intentions were on asbestos following any announcement from CSR.' He had also just had word from PwC that ED88 was back before the Accounting Standards Review Board, and likely to pass in the foreseeable future.

The obstacles to separation, however, looked formidable. It would be very difficult to fund Oldco to the extent of its actuarially assessed liabilities, even after Shafron's efforts to whip the Trowbridge report into shape, not to mention the breach of directors' duties this might entail. To set aside funds only to the extent of legal liabilities, meanwhile, with the probability that these would be insufficient to fund all future claims, would be politically and socially risky.

In a report to the board, Macdonald worried aloud about the possibility that 'stakeholders' would 'place the issue onto the political agenda unless they are satisfied with the level of future payment security provided — that level may well be in excess of our legal obligations'. When Ashe's 'Stakeholder Management' document landed on his desk, Macdonald felt his worst fears confirmed. To the Project Green team's next conference call on 10 August, Shafron brought gloomy tidings: the boss had been 'strongly influenced' by Ashe's views, and 'the mood in the camp' was now 'very negative'. He admitted that there was now 'not much prospect of separation without a major portfolio acquisition or us coming back with a more positive story'. The deal was still 'doable', although carrying the risk, Baxter summarised, 'that we would totally disable the investment case for this company'.

Perhaps further legal advice on creditors was needed: Tom Bathurst QC was briefed. Perhaps another actuarial report would yield a happier result: Shafron pondered approaching Trowbridge's

---

* In its 2001 accounts, CSR did indeed increase its reserve from $110 million to $300 million, despite having perhaps a third of Hardie's exposure.

rival, Tillinghast. 'I plan to get these guys to help us handle Minty (an actuary in our corner),' he advised Attrill; a meeting was scheduled with the firm's Verne Baker and Dave Finnis. But support from the top had waned. Shafron reported another disheartening conversation with Macdonald on 12 August: 'Speaking to Peter today I think it is fair to say that separation is dead'. Attrill tried to buck up his spirits: 'Peter, I was surprised to receive your message. I would have thought it is too early to make this decision. Separation was always going to be a challenge, but it's certainly not impossible and we are still to receive some key data ...' Shafron was cheered: 'Yes Peter's attitude was as big a surprise to me as you. I agree, proceed with Verne as discussed for the time being.'

The Hardie board meeting at Newport Beach's Four Seasons Hotel four days later had two bob each way. Macdonald pointed to the need for change. 'Business as usual' was not an option. ED88, now expected to be promulgated from December, would require Hardie to increase its provision for asbestos liabilities from the present paltry $43 million to more than $250 million — in excess, in fact, of Coy's net assets. But the Trowbridge report, limited in scope and larded with qualifications and disclaimers, was barely usable 'as a tool for defending our position'. Inquiries, directors were told, were now proceeding down two avenues: the original 'restructure with separation', or a 'restructure without separation', under which JHIL and Coy would remain in the group cradling the liabilities, but still acquiring the desired tax benefits. The former, while preferred, was nonetheless at this stage taking two steps back for every one forward.

At a meeting on 23 August, Tillinghast's Baker and Finnis proved less tractable even than Trowbridge. Baker said they would only offer a range of plausible provisions for liabilities, not a precise figure: 'That is as far as you can go. Otherwise it's spurious accuracy.' Finnis's preference for scenario modelling would take in 'a lot of potential developments' excluded by Trowbridge. 'I'd be very edgy about picking a best estimate,' he said. 'That is not within actuarial capabilities'. It was a demoralising encounter: for more than a month afterwards, while preparations for restructuring steadily homed in on a court-approved scheme of arrangement, the separation cause was in limbo.[†]

What revived it was the power of two thoughts. To Peter Shafron occurred the idea of Oldco issuing partly paid capital to Newco to the extent of the $1.5 billion market value of the shares in JHNV previously held by JHIL. All of a sudden, Oldco's resources would look ample, its ability to pay creditors would be beyond question, and several legal and statutory obligations would be removed. There were risks. Steve Harman, Shafron's finance colleague at Mission Viejo, pointed out that it was a very large exposure for JHNV:

> My concern is that, with this partly paid investment in place, should circumstances arise where JHIL was found to be liable for JH & Coy's liabilities ... the directors of JHIL would have little alternative but to make calls upon the unpaid capital. Similarly, if JHIL was ever to find itself in liquidation, for whatever reason, I would imagine that an early action of the liquidator would be to call for payment of unpaid capital.

But it got the creative juices flowing. In the meantime, as the Project Green team explored 'restructure without separation', they were prodded to what would be the other crucial aspect of their final structure. While ED88 was not yet reality, Steve McClintock of PwC pointed out to Morley, on 18 October, that the American accounting standards which Newco would need to observe after its New York listing were very real indeed: detailed disclosure of asbestos liabilities would be necessary in its F-20 filing with the Securities & Exchange Commission. Perhaps, ventured McClintock helpfully, the liabilities could be somehow 'deconsolidated'. When Morley solicited further advice, a further helpful suggestion came back that this deconsolidation might be achieved by assigning shares

---

[†] It was certainly inert when on Attrill emailed David Booth Beers of the Washington law firm Shea & Gardiner on 26 September, soliciting advice about Hardie's American liabilities. By way of background he noted: 'The restructuring will produce tax and other benefits to the Group and its shareholders. There is no proposal at this time to separate the subsidiaries which hold the asbestos liabilities from the rest of the group.'

in Coy to a trust—the first time a trust had been mentioned in despatches since February.

IT WAS LATE IN THE DAY. The restructuring proposal was at an advanced stage, having reverted from a joint takeover to its original configuring as a court-approved scheme of arrangement. 'I look forward to presenting a major step forward for James Hardie's structure,' Macdonald wrote in his confident preface to the Hardie board papers for the meeting of 15 November. The latest iteration involved Newco (JHINV) acquiring all stock in Oldco (JHIL), the latter buying back its shares from Newco in return for the transfer of JHNV. Subsequent to the buy back, JHIL would issue partly paid shares to Newco NV to the value of the buy back: these would be paid up to $80 million, with an uncalled balance of $1.42 billion, with timing and the amount of future calls to be at the JHIL board's discretion.

Would it work? Who knew? By this stage, in fact, Macdonald, Shafron, and the Project Green team were tired—and anxious that the board was feeling the same way. It was now four years since Peter Pedley had set the restructuring ball rolling, but a host of plans had come and gone to little effect. Macdonald worried that 'deal fatigue' would get the better of his directors. Shafron wanted to take a number of alternatives 'as far as we can as soon as we can', even simply walking away from Coy, but was 'not sure the Board are ready for that'. Based at Mission Viejo, at the frontier of the company's future, they feared that the restructuring might not happen at all if not consummated soon.

At this crucial moment, Macdonald found in his chairman, MacGregor, a staunch supporter. In the year of Macdonald's steward-ship, they had formed a tight unit. As a chairman, MacGregor had shared board tables with a number of prestigious CEOs, including F. H. Faulding's Brian McNamee and Burns Philp's Tom Degnan, and his preference was to give executives their head. 'Alan wasn't one of those former CEOs turned chairman, part of whom still wants to be CEO,' says a fellow director at another company. 'And he was a big fan of Macdonald's.' For the minutes, MacGregor was noted as agreeing that 'the model appeared to have some merit' and requesting that the executive 'continue developing the concept for further discussion at the next meeting'. The request was met with alacrity.

The very next day, Morley, Harman and Peter Cameron met McClintock, Clemens and Leigh Minehan from PwC to begin realising a freestanding trust for the shares in Coy, involving an independent board of trustees, an insurance company processing claims, and the New South Wales Cancer Council as beneficiary. There were many questions to be decided. Would Hardie hold a residual interest? Would the trust also contain Jsekarb? Could the Coy shares simply be gifted to the trust? The answers were no, yes and a tentative maybe: in theory, Hardie was giving an asset away. But the trust was now firming to favouritism. Perhaps the Coy gift could be made, proposed Peter Cameron, if it was proved worthless: that is, if its net value was demonstrably zero. Corporate advisory firm Grant Samuel was retained to provide a most unusual independent experts' report, which proved that Coy stood to be entirely consumed by compensation payments, and that its shares could therefore be disposed of without shareholder approval, capital reduction or compunction.

Another aspect of the PwC meeting of 16 November also merits mention. The PwC file note includes an assertion, reprised on several occasions over the next few months, to the effect that Coy's net assets of $190 million 'on present estimations of likely future claims over the next 10 years should be full and sufficient to meet such liabilities', and even brooks the possibility that they will be 'in excess of the amount that is required to be paid as claims'. While a fund would be expected to accumulate for a period, the relevance of ten years to the former statement, and how the latter position could be adopted, in the light of the Trowbridge report, is puzzling—to say the least.

Such remarks, furthermore, were about to become rather more difficult to make. Not quite a fortnight later, two Trowbridge actuaries presented a paper at the VIIIth Accident Compensation Seminar of the Institute of Australian Actuaries, updating their firm's existing models of asbestos-related disease claims to take account of new epidemiological studies, increases in claim numbers and award sizes as recorded by the Dust Diseases Board and Tribunal, recent decisions like *Crimmins v SIFC*, and the growing proportion of product-liability claims. It also paraded new analytical tools based on the study of mesothelioma, lung cancer and asbestosis among former Wittenoom miners by Professor Geoffrey Berry of Sydney University. Bruce Watson and Mark Hurst discussed new models called Berry Medium and Berry High, based on different assumptions about latency periods, which radically ramped up claim forecasts — the same data that produced an Atkins & Andrews estimate of 4500 produced under Berry High a figure of 11,400 — and concluded alarmingly that 'many insurers and other parties exposed to asbestos-related disease liabilities may be significantly underreserved'. As the biggest 'other party' in the business, James Hardie was about to receive an untimely jolt.

Minty forwarded the paper to Attrill, prefaced by a light-hearted covering email: 'As you might expect, you should be sitting down and probably heavily sedated before reading it. The paper itself with the gory numbers and tables in it has not yet been finalised, but in any case we should probably talk about it next week when you've had a chance to get over the necessary urgent medical attention.' Hardie saw nothing to be light-hearted about. Shafron sent the report to Macdonald with the observation: 'Peter, we will need to consider whether a report to the Board on this is warranted.' Macdonald griped in his reply: 'This "hits the spot" — although I wish it didn't.' Both were irked that they had not been forwarned, and furious to learn that the paper had been posted on the actuary's website. Shafron informed Attrill:

> Peter Mac hit the roof when he saw the report, wondering how it was that our retained experts could publish something that implicates us so directly without any prior notice. He thinks the chairman will react the same way, and I am a bit that way myself, although I do wonder whether it's part of an ongoing program of some sort … I think we should feel David out on Trowbridge suspending it from their website

on the basis that it is based on an incomplete report and we haven't had time to consider it and how we would address possible questions.

Shafron enlarged on the matter in the monthly asbestos-litigation report he was preparing for Macdonald. It wasn't that Hardie differed with Trowbridge's conclusions, simply that they had been drawn so publicly. After all, wasn't Hardie paying Trowbridge good money?

The information in the report broadly accords with our own experience, although was based on information from insurers, the DDB and possibly other public information. To that extent its broad message is no surprise, either to us or participants in this area. However, the specificity of the findings and their broad public release could well attract wider attention. The report is based on a more detailed study, which is not yet complete. We are very surprised to hear of the report, given that we have Trowbridge on retainer on this very subject.

To Attrill was delegated the task of advising Minty of 'a reaction of extreme disappointment at this end', the complaint that 'we would like to know why we weren't given any advance notice so as to deal with media/analyst inquiries', and the request that the paper be removed from Trowbridge's website—which was declined. But there was a limit to his grounds for complaint. Hardie was living through verification of the trends Trowbridge had noted. 'November has been a poor month on the asbestos front,' Attrill noted in the monthly asbestos-litigation report, with settlements worth $4.65 million. Worse still were the figures that followed in Attrill's latest half-yearly Operating Plan Review, which reported a 56 per cent increase in cost of damages, a 58 per cent increase in the number of settlements, and a 70 per cent increase in new claims. This might be, he said, a 'temporary phenomenon'; it might also necessitate a 'rerating upwards of James Hardie's long-term expected claim number and liabilites'.

Reaction to Attrill's plan was to hunker down deeper. A teleconference involving Macdonald, Shafron and Morley at Mission Viejo with Attrill, Baxter and Ashe in Sydney minuted 'concern' about the Operating Plan Review. But the concern was private. Shafron spoke of Hardie being on its 'best behaviour', Baxter said the company should 'aim for no media coverage for a month or so', and Macdonald later disavowed specific knowledge of Attrill's report, claiming that he was at the time reviewing ten different operating plans for business units 'all of which were more important than Mr Attrill's operating plan'. Macdonald's perennially hectic work rate makes this not unbelievable. But his thoroughgoing insistence that only Trowbridge was positioned to 'take into account claims data' and 'form forward projections', while 'the company itself did not have such expertise', raises the question of why the report was compiled at all.

The trust was now taking shape. It was given a name, Claimsure Nominees. It was given a staff, thanks to a serendipitous discussion. When Shafron confided in Attrill his intention that the trust be managed principally by either a law firm or an insurer specialising in the area, Attrill adeptly proposed instead his own claims-management unit, which was otherwise to be disbanded. And it was about to get a board. Shafron knew that Sir Llew Edwards had already been sounded out by Alan MacGregor about the chairmanship, and drew up a short list of potential directors — from former Hardie auditor David Myles and former Hardie executive Don Cameron, to former GIO director Peter Lamble and Philips Fox lawyer Michael Gill. He started, nonetheless, rather closer to home.

On 15 December, Shafron and Morley walked into the Mission Viejo office occupied for the preceding eighteen months by chief information officer Dennis Cooper, and explained that they had a proposition for him. The following month, Hardie would be constituting a trust dedicated to the administration of asbestos-compensation claims. How would he feel about becoming a director? Cooper, a tall, softly spoken man with an air of wary formality about him, was momentarily puzzled. He knew nothing of asbestos, still less of Hardie's liabilities in the area. He was one of nature's boffins, having come to Hardie in June 1994 after a long career in information technology and management roles at Berger Paints and G. E. Crane. The terms of a thirty-hour week and a two-year contract, however, had appeal. He had been unhappy in the US, at odds with the get-ahead culture embodied in Macdonald, whom he found 'very organised, very efficient, very cold and insular', and Gries, whose aggression seemed to point the way to the future. 'I was happy to be leaving,' he recalls. Cooper was planning to return to Australia to do some consulting: 'When you're at a particular stage of your career, pretty employable and with relative financial security, you don't have to work for someone you don't want to work for'. This sort of gig might set him up. 'Well, think about it and I will speak to you next week,' said Morley. 'If you decide to become involved we will give you a more detailed briefing.' For the moment, all Shafron offered was a photocopied chapter from Patrick Atiyah's *The Damages Lottery*.

Morley and Shafron left soon after for Sydney while Cooper was busy packing for the return to his home in Beecroft currently occupied by his son, so it was a week before he confirmed his 'interest' in joining ClaimSure's board. Now he was given Shafron's copy of Attrill's Operating Plan Review and Asbestos Liabilities Management Plan, plus asbestos fact sheets and the financial accounts of Coy and Jsekarb. When he enquired about the legalities of the trust's position, Shafron invoked Putt's case: 'The effect of the decision in Putt is that there is a separation between a holding company and its subsidiaries. The trust proposal does not fundamentally change anything. It does not represent a separation from any corporate liability for JHIL.'

Shafron spoke with authority. Putt's case had just been the subject of a new advice from James Allsop SC, who had advised Allens that he was 'confident that if Putt's case was reargued today on the same basis and based on the same factual scenario, it would be decided in the same manner'. In answer to a question from Shafron in the same advice about whether the trustees of the new venture could 'covenant to procure' that Coy not sue JHIL, meanwhile, Allsop had also said yes, if only in return for a 'valuable considera-tion'. As a briefing to someone whom it was envisaged would be taking a general management role at the trust, then, this was passing strange. Cooper was informed of a legal precedent that the trust didn't 'fundamentally change anything', but was not informed of a legal manoeuvre that was under active consideration, involving the trust trading away its right to sue its former parent.

What became the 'deed of covenant and indemnity' had come up at intervals in Project Green meetings over the last year as another means of distancing Hardie from its former liabilities. Most recently, it had occurred to Shafron in an issues paper a month earlier, and in Cameron's last advice about the legality of gifting Coy to the proposed trust: this, he thought, might become easier if JHIL was to receive some sort of undertaking in return, perhaps a deed under which Coy and Jsekarb *covenanted* not to make asbestos-related claims against JHIL, and *indemnified* JHIL in respect of asbestos-related claims against it. How serious was the risk of either is debateable. Compensation claims were almost without exception against Coy or Jsekarb; efforts to tackle JHIL, like Putt, and also Briggs earlier, had been abortive. But for the previous year, Roy Williams' team at Allens had been involved in a work of legal forensics called the Discovery Project, aiming to ascertain the commercial and managerial connections between JHIL and its subsidiaries, Coy, Jsekarb and also JHNZ, just in case any plaintiff elected to join it to an action. An effective deed would lay such anxieties to rest. As the year 2000 ended with the trust still scheduled for board approval on 17 January 2001, there remained a host of unanswered questions.

When Attrill's litigation lieutenant Maija Burtmanis forwarded the last case-tracking record for 2000 to Shafron and Ashe on Christmas Eve, he chirped: 'I take the opportunity to wish you and your families a very Merry Christmas … and an exciting New Year!' No one suspected how exciting it would be.

HAVING BEEN A DEAD LETTER as little as two months earlier, James Hardie's plans to contain and cast off its compensation liabilities were now a red-hot priority. ClaimSure held forth the promise of a litigation-free future for Hardie. What it would represent for victims of asbestos-related disease was not, ultimately, Hardie's affair: if it failed, Hardie believed, the company would be under no obligation to remedy any shortfall. By year's end, three prospective ClaimSure directors on Hardie's list had ticks by their names. The two others, Edwards and Gill, had sounded receptive to briefings by Shafron and Morley on their quick trip to Sydney. Edwards, who had reached the board retirement age of sixty-five, was weary of the overseas travel involved in being a Hardie director; Gill, the 54-year-old managing partner of his firm's insurance and financial services unit, was eager to make new connections. A fourth tick was soon added. On 4 January, Macdonald faxed Edwards at his Noosa apartment, requesting that he telephone Peter Jollie, chairman of the Defence Housing Authority and a former president of the Institute of Chartered Accountants, in Sydney. When Jollie found Edwards' message on his answering machine and rang back, Edwards went carefully through a prepared script, indicative of the attention to detail in Hardie's recruitment: 'At the request of Peter Macdonald, I will be leaving the Board of James Hardie Industries to take up a position as chair of a new Hardie entity. I would be honoured if you would be involved and it would be a very interesting role. Would you take a call from Peter Macdonald … to discuss the proposed role?' Macdonald in due course invited Jollie to meet Shafron and Morley at the old Asbestos House at 7.30AM the next day.

What was said and left unsaid during the tutelage of the trust directors would be exhaustively debated at the Special Commission of Inquiry. Recollections varied. Edwards thought he was assured that there would be a surplus of assets at the end of the trust's lifespan. Jollie did not, recalling a straight answer to a straight question about solvency from either Shafron or Morley: 'We pay $20 million per annum in claims. There will be $200 million as investment and the net return on that will enable solvency now. Informally it is our belief that you will be fully solvent but it is possible in the future you will not be solvent and you will need to keep an eye on that as part of the normal director/trustee duty.' Jollie's notes include: 'Possible in future not solvent. NPV of future claims line ball. Not quite enough towards the end.' In an email later that day, Shafron recorded the exchange: 'Actuarial advice? Yes we get it, it shows there could be a shortfall'. But when Cooper presented for his own, somewhat more detailed, briefing with Attrill five days later, he unknowingly encountered the limits of Hardie's candour, being subtly stonewalled when he asked to see the most recent Trowbridge report:

> I could see the change in his attitude when I asked him. He said: 'I'll have to ask Peter Shafron.' And it was never provided. In hindsight, I should have followed it up more vigorously, although at this stage I was confident that we'd be getting a more up-to-date version. I now understand why I didn't get the report, given that the extent of Shafron's edits were so extraordinary.

Attrill recalled the exchange with his boss. 'Peter, Dennis Cooper would like a copy of the Trowbridge reports,' he enquired. 'Can you just hold off on that at this time?' Shafron replied. 'Tell Dennis we'll get back to him.' They did not. Hardie would even control the legal advice the prospective directors received. When Mallesons' Tony Bancroft was retained to advise them, Shafron instructed: 'Technically your client will be the proposed directors. However, your advice leading up to establishment of the trust will be paid for by JHIL'. Bancroft, Shafron told the young Allens lawyer David Robb, was to be given no information prejudicial to Hardie, least of all the Allsop advice, which included 'some views as to how a plaintiff may seek to bring a claim, if it could, against JHIL, and arguments that it may seek to press'.

The objective of exercising strict but subtle control over information flows also underlay Hardie's external relations policies. After discussion with the public affairs consultancies Hawker Britton and Gavin Anderson & Co, Baxter sent Macdonald, Shafron and Morley a draft communications strategy on 8 January. Its aims were, essentially, the dissemination of news without information:

- Attracting as little attention as possible beyond the financial markets
- Positioning the initiative as a 'business' news as opposed to a 'general' news story
- Having financial markets recognise and reward the certainty and finality of the separation

- Managing fall out and minimising damage to JH's reputation generally
- Minimising the potential for government intervention

The launch would take place at 10.00AM, for an 11.00AM conference, rather than 8.30AM, to minimise preparation time and 'the risk that non-business media and perhaps other stakeholders would attend and 'hijack' the briefing'. Hardie would not do its usual 'webcast', citing 'technical difficulties', and would review the recording for possible editing before putting it out—Allens were concerned about any deviations from the approved script which might arise during questions. Not everything, of course, could be controlled. Baxter pointed out that the planned date of the announcement, nine days hence, involved irreducible risks:

- There is no ready made forum in which to announce, making positioning the trust initially as a business story more difficult
- We would have to create a presentation forum for analysts as a 'special event' thereby drawing more attention to it from analysts and others
- In mid-January there will still be too many journalists chasing too few stories and therefore there is a higher risk that the trust will become a 'hot story' which would command more 'air time' than might be the case in February
- A mid-January announcement would ensure that the story was revisited and revived at the time the Q3 results were announced.

Pressure, he concluded, should be anticipated: 'We expect that notwithstanding our recommendations, the announcement of the trust will create a significant, negative 'news and current affairs' story which will run for 1–2 weeks in the news sections of the newspapers, and on news and current affairs programs on radio and television'. Baxter was even more candid three days later in a communication with Liza-Jayne Loch, a former Hardie's public affairs employee now at Hawker Britton. Hardie, in fact, had good cause to fear too much scrutiny of the creation of the trust. For all the pretence that the creation of the trust didn't 'fundamentally change anything' legally, it changed a great deal effectively. Loch was responding to a stakeholder study that Baxter had completed of the New South Wales government. Loch's comments, here bullet pointed, show that she had failed to grasp that Hardie fully countenanced the trust failing; Baxter's remarks, here bracketed, show him disabusing her:

Reactions to the Trust concept

- Sounds like a good idea—separate from JH, sounds a bit more caring
- Can probably sell the trust as being a more holistic approach given that it, unlike JH, won't be driven by the profit motive
- What happens when the money runs out? (It runs out). What guarantees can JH give that victims aren't going to be stranded? (None) They are the two big questions. (Agree) ...
- What's in this for JH? How do we know this isn't about JH pulling a 'swifty' and walking away from its responsibilities here? (Let's discuss our position on this)
- Is there some sort of safety net which JH could provide to guarantee that people aren't going to be left stranded? (No. Directors could actually be sued by shareholders if they vested more money into the Trust when they had no legal obligation to do so)...
- I think JH can be quite open about the corporate rationale for pursuing this structure. It makes sense. The big political question is what guarantees can you give me that victims aren't going to be left high and dry in 10, 15, 30 years—why just don't know how long there are going to be claims. (There can't be a guarantee under any scenario including the current scenario)...
- What can JH do to cover off on the 'what if' question? There must be some sort of certainty it can give? (There isn't)

The objective, then, was not merely to present news without imparting information, but to offer certainty without giving it.

-17-
'Lots of hairs on it'

Sheahan: The 2000 report was complete, wasn't it?
Shafron: Yes.
Sheahan: Why did you mislead the directors in that way, the proposed directors?
Shafron: Well, the 2000 report hadn't been signed so you could technically say it wasn't complete.
Sheahan: But this was not drafting a debenture, Mr Shafron, it wasn't necessary to be technical, was it?
Shafron: No it wasn't necessary to be technical.
Sheahan: The substance of what you said to the proposed directors was false in this respect, wasn't it?
Shafron: Yes.
—Peter Shafron asked by John Sheahan QC why he did not give the 2000 Trowbridge report to directors of the mooted Hardie asbestos trust who requested it, 15 January 2001

SOME DEALS FOUNDER because they are contemplated before a company is psychologically ready; some come too late, from a kind of *torschlusspanik* at the sight of other deals being done. Then there are those for which everyone is somehow in the mood, which are executed because their time has come, because their momentum is irresistible. As Sydney returned to work in sticky heat and uncomfortable winds in the third week of January 2001, two boards of directors, one to be and one extant, met to consider opposite sides of such a deal. Circumstances still weren't quite right; both pulled back. But, informed by the same group of executives, they ended their deliberations closer than ever to going ahead.

The prospective directors of ClaimSure Nominees — Dennis Cooper, Sir Llew Edwards, Michael Gill and Peter Jollie — were in a positive frame of mind when they arrived for their first meeting at noon on Monday, 15 January in PWC's Zurich Room on the tenth level of 201 Sussex Street. They were further disarmed by a social chit-chat over the light lunch that preluded the serious business of three hours of presentations. In the Hardie corner were Phil Morley and Peter Shafron, whom Cooper, for one, knew well: 'Phil had been my boss. Very intelligent, although he was all about business, and personal relations completely escaped him. Peter, I liked. Sometimes he talked so quickly you'd be left wondering what he'd said. But generally, I found him very personable.' With them were Wayne Attrill, who had already struck Cooper as very capable; Steve Ashe, the clever external affairs manager; and David Robb, a well-spoken young Allens lawyer. It was all very smooth, even comradely. But, in crucial ways, it fell short of the meeting needed.

All the issues were touched upon. After Edwards' welcome, Robb explained the trust structure and the legal documentation; Morley outlined the financial details; Ashe, the program of medical research that it was intended the trust endow; and Attrill, recent events in asbestos litigation. But for an organisation intending to start so soon, the program was far from comprehensive. Detail was scarce: the deed of covenant and indemnity does not seem to have been mentioned. Numbers were skated over: again, in the face of an estimate of liabilities of near $300 million, those present talked as though Coy's $210 million in net assets might somehow accumulate to adequacy. The directors began, perhaps unconsciously, to make compromises. Robb recalled Gill saying: 'We would not want to be directors of it if the money runs out in 5–7 years'. But notes taken by Attrill also record Gill's remark: 'If funds adequate for 10–15 yrs, OK. Question if funds less than adequate for 10–15 years.' Why '10–15 years'? Even Shafron was aware that claims would last far longer than that: 'I certainly knew that ten or fifteen years was unlikely to see out the claims. I believed they would last for a long time and possibly thirty years, yes.' The only reason that '10–15 years' was satisfactory and '5–7' not seems to have been that the former strengthened a Micawberesque assumption that something would turn up: an advance in medical science, perhaps, or a change to the compensation regime.

Shafron took more steps than saying nothing to ensure that the discussion did not trespass on detail. Asked about Trowbridge's calculations, he responded that their most recent complete report dated from 1998 — pedantically true, although the 2000 report lacked only a signature after the disagreement over the actuary's sensitivity analysis. Shafron's explanation, that he was anxious not to affect the report's legal privilege, was made to sound increasingly hollow in the face of questions three-and-a-half years later from Michael Slattery QC:

Slattery: They wanted the draft report from which you had been quoting, didn't they?

Shafron: Yes it appears so.

Slattery: And you never gave it to them, did you?

Shafron: No I didn't.

Slattery: You didn't want them to have it, did you?

Shafron: Well I believed the numbers were going to be different after that.

Slattery: But what was the harm, if I can put it that way, in responding to their simple request, given that you had the document in your possession and could have given it to them tomorrow as they asked?

Shafron: I was a little concerned about the loss of privilege over the Trowbridge report. It was considered a very secret document within JHIL and sharing it with third parties would, I reasoned, likely lead to a loss of privilege, so I wasn't — it's true I wasn't keen to share it for that reason.

Slattery: But you'd already showed it to half a dozen insurers.

Shafron: That's right.

Slattery: Taking the risk that, in doing so, you may lose the privilege —

Shafron: That's right.

Slattery: — isn't that right?

Shafron: That is right.

Yet beyond a certain point of compromise, the foundation directors still would not go. Gill and Jollie, whether or not they sensed
Shafron's reticence, were anxious for more information, including a
meeting with Trowbridge. The 'good PR' and the 'reputation as a
good corporate citizen' that they coveted would come to nought if
the funds were seriously short. After a private consultation with
their lawyer, Tony Bancroft, the quartet requested a 'comprehensive
risk analysis … and an actuarial analysis'. Shafron understood this to
mean 'assurance about the life of the fund and that they didn't want
the life of the fund to end too quickly'. He set out to obtain it. The
next day, he rang Attrill. Rather than give the trust directors the
existing Trowbridge report, he wanted to commission a new document: not a fully fledged report, but an update, which could use the
new Watson & Hurst methodology, but should be kept brief and in
draft form. And Shafron demurred when Attrill asked if a fresh 'data
dump' was necessary. The data to March 2000 was to be used. 'We
are going to need that report pretty quickly,' he said. 'Can you call
David Minty and see how long it's going to take.' After explaining
the restructure under consideration to Minty the next day, Attrill
asked him: 'Could you have a report together in about a week to give
to the new management team that sets out the models you've built
for us, to explain them, and where things stand in terms of liabilities
in light of the new model?' Attrill's contemporaneous notes of
Minty's response include the remarks, 'can run with data we have'
and 'should be able to do the work fairly quickly'. They could, did,
and would live to regret it.

WHAT REMAINED OF THE DETAIL OF THE PROPOSAL was now mainly
grit in the gears. Project Green, for instance, had developed a third
dimension. Hardie was keen to divest the gypsum operations that
had vexed prospective American investors. The apprehensions of
those investors, in fact, had come to pass. Prices had plunged.
Capacity introduced to take advantage of 1999's building boom had
caused 2000's wallboard bust. 'Earnings fell off a cliff,' Morley
recalls. Hardie might just have been able to sell itself in the US with

gypsum making money; selling itself with the business oozing red ink would be next to impossible. That, in time, would have to be taken care of.

The implication of the Monday meeting with the trust directors, that Hardie might have to top up the funds in Coy, meanwhile, coincided with concerns about whether too much had been extracted. In examining the intercompany transactions between JHIL and Coy, Steve Harman had noted the $43.5 million dividend of October 1996 in advance of Project Chelsea—paid just after the first Trowbridge report had notified the company of a substantial increase in asbestos liabilities. Might the payment be open to legal challenge? During a conference call on the Tuesday morning with the Project Green team, Peter Cameron counselled that it would be a 'big call' to conclude that the dividend had been wrongly paid, and advised against reinstating it. But when Morley advised the Hardie audit committee that afternoon that reversing the dividend would bring Coy's assets to $272 million—based on the $59 million interest-adjusted value of the dividend—Alan MacGregor concluded that this might create a 'more palateable' trust.

Palateability was the issue that preoccupied the Hardie board when it convened early Wednesday morning. A trust with only the $214 million existing assets of Coy and Jsekarb would probably not be sufficient to meet all future claims; Macdonald said that such a fund would last only 9–13 years. But Hardie, he argued, could do no more: 'Whatever might have been the wishes of management and the Board to do 'something more than the legal minimum', my understanding was that the legal position did not support doing so.' The advice in the board papers was, accordingly, straightforward, and offered another instance of the strange double life lived by Trowbridge's figurings: rock solid when they suited, dismissed out of hand when they did not.

Under current Australian law, the maximum quantum of funds available to Australian asbestos claimants is the existing net assets of JH & Coy and Jsekarb, the two legal entities which have been found legally liable to compensate asbestos victims ... There is no sound rationale for increasing the net assets of JH & Coy and Jsekarb and thereby expanding this quantum of funds available to claimants.

- There is no legal requirement to do so;
- Contributing more funds may suggest that JHIL has some obligation or intends to fund claims in excess of the net assets of JH & Coy and Jsekarb;
- In view of the first two points above, there is no current basis under which directors could resolve to contribute further funds without appearing to fail to act in the interests of JHIL shareholders;
- There is no reliable basis for determining what amount any such future contribution should be if attempting to fund all future claims. Previous indicative advice obtained as to the potential quantum of future claims has been quite variable and unreliable.

The board papers presented a strong case, and most insistently. It was almost as though the deal was already done. Directors were even presented with a draft press release, complete with Q & A material of exquisitely circular reasoning:

Why does James Hardie need to deconsolidate the subsidiaries?
The new trust has assumed ownership of the shares in the two former James Hardie subsidiaries which were involved in manufacturing asbestos containing products. As a result James Hardie has effectively disposed of these company's assets and no longer has control over their assets or any recourse to the assets or any surplus that may arise in the future. Therefore, the subsidiaries have been deconsolidated.

Macdonald wasn't on his own either, attracting strong support for this bare-minimum model from the board's BIL representatives, Greg Terry and Dan O'Brien. O'Brien, BIL's Australian CEO for the last six months and Sir Selwyn Cushing's alternate, had been personally briefed on the proposal, and if anything favoured an even more extreme version. He thought separation and restructuring best done together: a pause between them was 'too cute'. He was uneasy, too, about the long-term existence of a tranche of partly paid shares.

Across the table, Peter Willcox wasn't so sure. Willcox's

pronouncements are softened by an accent that retains a tinge of his upbringing in England's ancient and isolated Forest of Dean, where an old friend is an 'awld butty' and where to fall down dead is to 'flump jud', but he is not averse to confrontation. In past life an executive at Amoco and divisional chief at BHP Petroleum, more recently a director of the AMP Society, his favourite inquiry of managers in board meetings makes a serious point whimsically: 'Is there some question you were worried I would ask that I haven't?' He was known, nonetheless, as the Hardie board member you wanted to impress. Says a former executive: 'He was the smartest director on the board by a country mile.'

Willcox saw separation dispassionately, and quite possibly in the interest of claimants: 'This [Hardie] was a company that had nearly gone into liquidation, and might well again. This was also a company with a shareholder holding nearly 30 per cent, and who knew how that was going to play out? Not that they wouldn't have acted honourably, but their loyalty was to their own shareholders, not to ours.' But his view was that a trust based on the net assets of Coy and Jsekarb would not fly:

> For me that wasn't an option. It not only had to be properly funded, it had to be clearly properly funded. I had no objection to it being $200 million if that's what we were told it would take, but the argument that that would be the number because it was the net assets of the company was never going to get off the ground. I heard the argument. It was irrelevant.
>
> My recollection is that some directors, including the Brierley representatives, said that there was an obligation to shareholders not to set up the trust with more money that they were legally obliged to. I thought that if they were right on that we couldn't set up the trust. You do have to be mindful of the interests of shareholders, but in my mind it is always the long-term interests of shareholders that matter. And the long-term interests of shareholders — this particular deal illustrates it more eloquently than I ever could — were not served by doing something of this kind.

Morley's notes of the meeting show Willcox leading his co-directors Meredith Hellicar and Michael Brown in opposition. Brown thought there was a 'moral issue' involved, that the scheme had 'lots of hairs on it', and that there were 'chinks' in the legal arguments underlying separation; Hellicar thought Hardie would look 'guilty' if it did not adequately endow its trust. All favoured Coy and Jsekarb being provided with sufficient funds to meet Trowbridge's future best estimate. Privately, Michael Brown thought that to do otherwise was bound to cause trouble: 'I wouldn't have countenanced a situation where the company knowingly left a liability — not merely a legal liability but a moral obligation — unfilled. It wouldn't have accorded with my view of the company's moral responsibilities. And I don't think it would have been in the company's commercial interests either. So it was also a business judgement.' Hellicar was surprised that the BIL directors would be 'such a hard-nosed bunch'; to Willcox, it simply confirmed their long-suspected eagerness to cash out: 'My feeling was, yes, they were ready to go. So their desire for immediate maximisation of value rather than five years down the road would have been more in their mind than mine.'

Morley's notes also suggest that chairman MacGregor leaned to supporting his chief executive and against any 'moral issue': 'Huge conflict in people's mind — but at the end of the day directors must say what is/are legal liabilities'. He guided the meeting to a satisfactory inconclusion. 'If the board had gone a different way,' says Brown, 'I would have resigned.' The executive, though, were undiscouraged. It was not resolved to support an enhancement of the trust's net asset position, but merely to investigate whether this was possible. One way it could not be done, Cameron reiterated for directors, was in the reversal of the October 1996 dividend: this, he said, had been paid while the company had still held operating assets, was solvent, and contained retained earnings in excess of the dividend amount. If new funds were to introduced, the operation would have to respect Hardie's legal obligations — a quart, as it were, would have to be squeezed into a pint pot. But the shape of things to come was emerging through the murk.

At present, JHIL owned two subsidiaries, James Hardie & Coy

and Jsekarb, with asbestos manufacture in their past. Their current directors, after many changes over the years, were Phil Morley and Don Cameron. Their present net assets of $214 million were composed of $68 million in land and buildings on long-term leases to Hardie operating businesses, $58 million in cash and securities, a $60 million intercompany receivable from JHIL with interest payable six-monthly in arrears, and the proceeds of the settlement of the insurance dispute with QBE with a net present value of $28 million. Coy and Jsekarb would shortly take on new guises that made them sound like twins in the *Tales of Arabian Knights*, Amaca and Amaba, and new ownership, coming under the control of the Medical Research and Compensation Foundation—the new name arrived at for ClaimSure Nominees. Its board, chaired by Sir Llew Edwards, and featuring Dennis Cooper as general manager, and non-executive directors Michael Gill and Peter Jollie, would have the services of Wayne Attrill's new consultancy, styled Litigation Management Group. Eventually, under a court-approved scheme of arrangement, JHIL would be reduced to an inactive intermediate company connected to the Hardie group by a tranche of partly paid shares designed to provide a source of capital and to reassure the court that the interests of creditors were not affected. JHIL's fate was undecided, but its purpose was essentially expended by restructuring, and down the track it could be liquidated or vested in the foundation.

The MRCF's assets would be $214 million plus, if the preference of Willcox, Brown and Hellicar could be accommodated, whatever additional sum was necessary to meet its subsidiaries' actuarially assessed liabilities. When Shafron, Morley, Attrill, Minty and Karl Marshall convened as scheduled at Goldfields House on Friday, ascertaining this additional sum seemed relatively straightforward. What ensued instead was a meeting on which the Special Commission would lavish tens of hours of testimony and hundreds of pages of documentation, but evidence on which remained stubbornly at deviance.

Shafron began by quizzing Minty about the significance of the new 'Watson & Hurst' religion about future asbestos-related liabilities. The main change, Minty explained, was in its understanding of the latency period of mesothelioma, which it took to be longer than earlier models had assumed. The graph he drew on a whiteboard showed a more gradual decline in claims or, as it is called in insurance, a much longer 'tail'. Shafron was satisfied. Could Trowbridge apply this new methodology to Hardie's situation? And could they do so in what was not a full-scale report? What he wanted, he reiterated, was a brief update, to project no further than twenty years.

On these exchanges, everyone would later agree. In other evidence, a permanent gap opened. Shafron testified that in answer to his question about updated claims information, Minty said it would not be required. Morley testified that Minty said: 'I've got ten years of data. A couple of quarters won't make that much difference.' Minty, however, testified that he stated clearly: 'We're going to need James Hardie's up-to-date claims information including the number of claims reported and settled together with settlement amounts'. But then, he added, either Shafron or Attrill claimed they would be unable to produce such detail in the time available, referring to the absence on leave of Andrew Kerr, the special projects manager who had developed the company's claims database. Shafron, Minty insisted, also added: 'Anyway, we don't think there's anything in the data that would affect the results because nothing significantly different from what you projected has occurred during the period.'

The significance of what became known as 'the missing data'— the nine months of claims information between March and December 2000 that might conceivably have been used had Trowbridge been granted access to it—was the subject of endless wrangling. The period in question, as noted in the last chapter, had been eventful, with a sharp rise in settlements aggravated by lower insurance recoveries. In the September quarter, total litigation-related costs had come in at $4.6 million, and only two of 56 claims had cost more than $300,000; in the December quarter, costs had steepled to $9.3 million, and ten of 46 claims had cost more than $300,000, including four claims totalling $2.7 million: the Edwards, Hope, Turner and Weller cases. Hardie referred to such outsized settlements as 'lightning strikes'—a phrase not inappropriate, considering their tragically random nature. Helene Edwards, for instance, was a 57-year-old nurse from Penola in South Australia, exposed to asbestos dust while helping her father renovate their home in the 1970s. Hardie had offered $550,000; Turner Freeman's Tanya Segelov had refused to budge from $850,000; and the DDT's Justice O'Meally had finally awarded $803,000 on the last day of November 2000.

In a statistical sense, however, asbestos liabilities are a long, volatile time series, sensitive to individual awards that may or may not be indicative of longer-term trends. The difference that 'the missing data' made to Trowbridge's calculations was ultimately less significant than Trowbridge's methodology, over which there is no documentary evidence of Hardie exercising any control. In this update, for instance, Trowbridge ignored evidence to the contrary, and assumed an imminent plateauing of claims. It eschewed consideration of superimposed inflation, even though Minty had been told by Allens' Roy Williams that 'awards of general damages in the DDT since around 1990 have risen steadily (well in excess of inflation)'. Though the reasoning takes us into more abstruse areas of actuarial cogitation, there are reasons why Berry Medium and Berry High were not quite as apt as hoped, while the 7 per cent discount rate was aggressive, and should probably have been around 5 per cent. These effects added up. Trowbridge would arrive at a median figure for the net present value of the liabilities of $286 million over twenty years. It was estimated by KPMG at the Jackson inquiry that, by Trowbridge's methodology, the additional data would have increased the 20-year NPV to $373 million. But KPMG's independent recalculation of the liabilities, with slightly less optimistic settings, arrived at a twenty-year estimate excluding the data of $694.2 million, rising when including the data to $1044.5 million. 'It's true that the absence of the data made a difference,' grumbles one Hardie executive. 'But it was of tens of millions, not hundreds of millions.'

Furthermore, even if Minty was steered one way by Shafron, he was not unwillingly directed. Exceedingly bright and vastly experienced, Minty had been at Trowbridge twelve years, after five at

Manufacturers' Mutual Insurance. He behaved here, however, as a hopeless naif, blithely accepting 'what I was being told by the gentleman whom I had worked with before'. About the enigmatic Andrew Kerr, for instance, he sought no detail, while he cheerfully accepted the stipulation that Shafron see his update before it reached the trust directors.[†] Hardie, needless to say, were much obliged. Macdonald recalled that when he learned from Shafron that there would be no need for 'extra data' from Hardie, he was 'relieved': 'While there was no question that James Hardie would have provided Trowbridge with updated data had Mr Minty asked for it, the fact that Mr Minty had said he did not need more recent data meant that it was much more likely that JHIL would be able to implement the trust proposal before 31 March 2001.' Quite so: Minty allowed what had begun as an endeavour to assist the incoming trust directors into another service to Hardie, when the interests of the two were patently very different.

For all this, and however badly the trust was let down by Minty's complaisance, there was here a grievous failure on the part of the Hardie executive — one not dependent on whether they were dishonest, disingenuous or merely disorganised, but one that would be repeated. It was the failure to grasp the nature of what they were asking Trowbridge for, and implications of getting it wrong. Hitherto, Hardie had been commissioning Trowbridge to report on asbestos liabilities as though they were simply a component in matters of corporate finance — as, indeed, for as long as they remained part of the company, they effectively were. What was envisaged now was Coy and Jsekarb forming a closed-end fund, fending for themselves without recourse to the assets of their parent. And it was very clearly perceived, as Baxter's communication with Liza-Jayne Loch indicates, that there might not be enough money to go round. It was

---

† Minty had the following exchange with Michael Slattery's junior, Lucy McCallum:

> *McCallum*: 'Were you told why he wasn't available?'
> *Minty*: 'No I don't recall'.
> *McCallum*: 'Did you ask when he would be available?'
> *Minty*: 'I did not.'

at this point that those liabilities should have been identified not as 'mesos', or 'legacy issues', or 'the rump'—as Hardie was wont to do in its internal documentation—but as sick and dying people. It was here that care should have been greatest. Instead it was poorest, because the only object in view was getting the job done.

18

'Beauty contest between warthogs'

Slattery: When did you read it?

Shafron: I'm not sure I ever did

Slattery: Well how did your handwriting get on it?

Shafron: It was provided. I believe the purpose of it was to –

Slattery: No how did you get your handwriting on it?

Shafron: I applied it with my fingers and a pen.

David Jackson QC: I'm not surprised at the answer.

—Peter Shafron denying that he read a report on asbestos liabilities prepared by Wayne Attrill, 11 February 2001

PROJECT GREEN WAS NOW CONVERGING on a triple-witching hour. Everything pointed to the need to sign off on separation at Hardie's 15 February board meeting. The company would then squeeze in ahead of the impact of both ED88 and CSR's increased provision, while the Medical Research and Compensation Foundation could be announced as part of, and preferably somewhat obscured by, the company's third-quarter results at the following day's press conference.

Not only was there little time, there was little room to move in introducing new money to the Medical Research and Compensation Foundation. Even if it could be done, it would have to be a one-off payment. PwC were insistent: 'deconsolidation' had to be complete to avoid any question about the need to include a contingent liability in Hardie's accounts. JHNV was, moreover, financially stretched. There would be, in due course, the proceeds from a sale of the gypsum business. But after a breakneck period of expansion in the US, JHNV was relatively highly geared, and anticipated going to the market for capital later in the year.

Shafron, at least, thought he had a way to add the cash. His idea of a deed of covenant and indemnity—the agreement of Coy and Jsekarb to not sue their former parent, and also reimburse it for any claims that did come the parent's way—had come into its own. Shafron suspected that, despite 'the Putt case', the finding in *CSR v Wren*, in which CSR had been held to owe a duty of care to an employee of a subsidiary, made some form of legal protection for JHIL necessary. For this, James Allsop SC had indicated, a 'valuable consideration' could be levied. In an Allens advice recommending against the reversal of the October 1996 dividend, David Robb confirmed that an alternative approach was for Hardie to 'pay a sum of money to Coy ... in consideration for obtaining a release from Coy for any potential future liability of JHIL for asbestos claims relating to Coy.' Finally, Shafron caucused with David Beers and Betsy Seise from the New York lawyers Shea & Gardner, expert in the asbestos field and designers of a reconstruction of Cassiar. They thought the foundation concept sound and generous by comparison with Hardie's legal obligations, and that, as such, 'a private contractual undertaking from Coy not to sue and indemnify JHIL' was worth considering. Shafron needed no more convincing. Only the sum of money was to be determined—Shafron was thinking in the order of $57 million—which awaited Trowbridge's calculations.

When Trowbridge's first draft was forwarded on 2 February, Minty and Marshall had proven the most obliging of independent advisers. They had simply grossed-up the figures to March 2000, and superimposed the Watson & Hurst projection of the Australian asbestos experience, set at Berry Medium, arriving at a figure of $295 million, and Berry High, producing the number $323.63 million. Also thrown in was the 'current' scenario of $286 million, although the Berry Medium calculation was promoted as Trowbridge's 'best estimate'. The presentation, too, was made to measure: three pages of print and ten pages of tables pushing out no further than twenty years, and without the context of the far-more-detailed 2000 report. Minty and Marshall may not have been entirely comfortable with the sketchiness of their work. Evidence at the Special Commission of Inquiry was presented of a meeting at James Hardie House at 1.30PM on 8 February at which Shafron made clear Hardie's objectives: 'The structure we're thinking of putting in place includes setting up a foundation to manage the claims of James Hardie's subsidiaries and conduct relevant research into asbestos-related disease.' About every other aspect of the meeting, Shafron retained no recall at all.

> *Robertson*: And Mr Marshall said to you something like this, did he not: 'I'm concerned that you only want us to include cash flow projections out to 20 years'?
>
> *Shafron*: I don't recall that.
>
> *Robertson*: And did he not also say to you that: 'We don't have a complete picture without details of claims experienced since March 2000'?
>
> *Shafron*: I don't recall him saying that at that meeting, no.
>
> *Robertson*: Did he not also say to you: 'We understand that there's evidence of a deterioration in claims experience since March 2000'?
>
> *Shafron*: I don't recall that
>
> *Robertson*: And that: 'It's possible that if Trowbridge had detailed claims information to the end of 2000 our view on whether the central estimate is appropriate could change?'
>
> *Shafron*: No I don't recall that.

By any measure, however, the document was hugely flawed and needlessly confusing. The 'current' scenario, for instance, was nothing of the sort: it was simply the median figure of $286 million, now almost a year out of date, plucked from the previous report. Trowbridge was even using an average settlement figure of $135,000, when Attrill's latest data, which he poured into a report dated 11 February, suggested average mesothelioma compensation inclusive of costs at $266,000. The report's only virtue was that it satisfied the client—so satisfied the client, in fact, that its shortcomings were cheerfully overlooked:

> *Jack Rush QC*: You would have appreciated in February 2001 that

Trowbridge was using $135,000 as the average settlement figure in mesothelioma and general liability claims?
Attrill: Yes sir, that would be right.
Rush: And you knew they were using that for their actuarial projections?
Attrill: Yes.
Rush: And you knew that that figure was nowhere near the average settlement of mesothelioma claims in February 2001?
Attrill: Yes.
Rush: Thus you would have been aware [of] the likelihood of their projections being grossly inaccurate ...?
Attrill: Yes.

Examined on this issue by Michael Slattery QC three years later, Peter Shafron was made to look somewhat uneasy:

Slattery: That is the figure for mesothelioma settlements that Trowbridge worked on, isn't it?
Shafron: It would seem to be.
Slattery: What do you say, then, when you compare it to the figure that is set out by Mr Attrill in his report of 11 February 2001?
Shafron: Well, it's obviously different
Slattery: Well, it's not obviously different. It's different by a factor of about a hundred per cent.

At the time, however, Shafron was cock a hoop. The figures were lower than even he had hoped. He excitedly emailed Macdonald, Cameron and Robb about the deed:

I want to revisit this. If we are being generous with Coy (and arguably we are, particularly if we hand across the 57) then that should support a waiver/indemnity in respect of Coy manufacture. If it's a private document, then I wonder about disclosure — initially any way. It could be that we ask the existing Coy directors to sign the documents (I guess with the benefit of some Allens/Allsop advice, if needed) and present it to the prospective directors as a fait accompli. With more cash than they thought they had, they shouldn't complain (I doubt Bancroft would). Obtaining the indemnity overcomes possibly the biggest question mark I have over this transaction (risk to JHIL). I would very much like to make it work.

Macdonald very much agreed: it provided 'a very sound reason for us to increase the amount to the prospective Foundation directors'. The indemnity was eventually valued—quite arbitrarily—at $70 million. Because the bulk of the cash in JHIL was already earmarked for dividend payments, and the group was in danger of breaching its debt covenants, this would be passed on in annual instalments of $12.5 million. Shafron rested easier. If and when the time came, JHIL would now be far simpler to set adrift.

The Trowbridge figures also fed into another proof to be flourished before the board. 'Twelfth Cash Flow Model' sounds a little like a financial Dylan song, but it was the latest iteration of some months of work by Steve Harman demonstrating how the trust would generate and distribute its cash. It evaluated the foundation's lifespan according to Trowbridge's three projected scenarios, and it all worked seamlessly, as models are wont to do. But it had needed some intricate mechanics to do so. For the six months to 31 March 2001, for example, Harman was projecting outgoings of $16.3 million, but in the entirety of the next year only $22.3 million. The former figure was derived from information in the management accounts, reinforced by a remark of Morley's that the period had contained some unusually large settlements; the latter figure was inspired by Trowbridge's best estimate of the preceding year. But what was most arresting were the forecast rates of return for the foundation's portfolio, fixed at 11.7 per cent and 14.55 per cent, attached to the 'best estimate' and 'high'. The appearance they lent was of a comfortably solvent enterprise for the ensuing half-century. This was for the very good reason that it was the purpose of the model—not to find out whether the MRCF would work, but to show that it did.

To choose rates of return for their necessity rather than their likelihood is not altogether unusual in modelling, and sometimes *de rigueur*. But an email that Harman sent two staffers cast an unflattering light on the thinking involved, containing the advice: 'Also we want to accurately reflect (ie: minimise) JHIL's asbestos costs for the 10.5 months.' When this was raised with him by Jackson—how could one both 'accurately reflect' and 'minimise' at the same time? —Harman admitted that the phrasing had been 'unfortunate'. Perhaps this applied to more than the phrasing.

Such was the spirit of the times. Henceforward, almost every effort at Hardie would be devoted to the selling of the foundation; its workings had now become secondary. Macdonald and Greg Baxter had adumbrated a media strategy: the company would steer the story to the business media as great news for shareholders, but limit the opportunities for other journalists to become involved:

> There is a high turnover of these journalists and consequently it is not possible to form productive relationships with them. It is likely that any journalist assigned to cover the separation story will initially bring to it a negative disposition to JH. Additionally, on issues like asbestos, the media usually decides it will become 'a court of public opinion' with journalists freely adopting the roles of crusader, critic and ombudsman. If this occurs, journalists will be receptive to criticism of us from opponents who will represent a broad church of interests, spanning unions, lawyers, victims and others, all of whom will provide 'good copy' … If other stakeholders mount noticeable public campaigns against separation, investors could become concerned about the level of certainty and finality that our separation model will ultimately provide. This means it is possible that we could bear the cost of separation without initially being able to remove the asbestos taint from our investment case. Our strategy … is to 'divide and conquer' the individual risks.

The business columnists—John Durie, Ivor Ries, Steve Bartholomeusz, Damon Kitney, Terry McCrann, Mark Westfield and Bryan Frith—were seen as more tractable:

> We, and our advisors, have very sound relationships with the journalists which routinely cover JH. We will provide them with deep background

if necessary ... We will not proactively seek in-depth coverage from columnists and commentators but we expect the exotic nature of the story to attract them anyway ... We will not conduct a separate news press conference for general news media. We will deal with general media one-to-one. This will helps [sic] us avoid a media 'siege' and tailor messages to specific types of media.

Selling the foundation to the business journalists, the Hardie executives noted, would be made easier if the foundation was also sold successfully to the broking analysts:

Our most desired outcome is to have the analysts walk away from the presentation viewing the foundation as having effectively terminated JH's long-term liability for asbestos. If this is achieved, analysts should view the proposal favourably. In this scenario, journalists who contact analysts for comment will get positive feedback and this will make it hard for the business media to attack separation, at least initially.

The only threat to this virtuous, self-reinforcing circle was the unpredictable forum of politics. The Carr government might 'flick pass' the issue to Canberra, or even hold an inquiry to 'show' it was doing something. Premier Carr himself was considered broadly 'pro-business' but susceptible to union influence, especially in the company of attorney-general Bob Debus, known to be 'aligned to the more militant factions of the governing party and is the most likely of his colleagues to suspect JH's motives'. Anxious about the lay of the left land, Macdonald decided to run the foundation past Stephen Loosley, former Labor senator turned influence pedlar at PwC, where he had been a colleague of Baxter's offsider Steve Ashe.

For someone paid almost $50,000, Loosley's advice at the meeting on 9 February seems to have been mainly platitudinous: he opined that the trust was 'sound', but needed a 'very deliberate and consistent media strategy' involving 'key catch phrases', and that the issue would be 'won and lost' inside forty-eight hours. He made one recommendation that wasn't taken up, that the foundation board be augmented by a cleanskin 'with impeccable credentials who it would be very hard for the left of politics to attack', such as Hazel Hawke or Suzi Martin (wife of the New South Wales governor David Martin, who fell victim to mesothelioma in 1990). He made one suggestion that was adopted, that Hardie seek 'independent verification of the funding models ... so that funding outcomes were not solely on our say so'.

'Independent verification' is another of those not-quite-coherent ideas in which the Hardie story abounds, like actuarial figures both inherently unreliable and unimpeachably precise, not to mention models that 'accurately reflect' as they 'minimise'. A truly independent view, of course, would be entitled to the option of rejection. In fact, when Ashe suggested PwC and Access Economics to review the 'Twelfth Cash Flow Model', Shafron eschewed the doubletalk. 'A job for you on Monday,' he emailed Harman. 'Get these guys to bless your model'. Which is exactly what Harman told PwC and Access Economics to do: 'We want you to bless the model ... We do not want you to make any comments on the key assumptions. We just want you to review the model to check it's arithmetically correct.'

PwC and Access Economics both did a little more than blessing — which annoyed Harman. PwC's David Brett and two colleagues found the model 'logically sound and technically correct, within the limitations imposed by this kind of model', but also referred to its limitations, specifically questions it did not address about safety margins and forecasts about the risk-adjusted time value of money. The draft of their review said: 'The model results are sensitive to these values and assumptions and we urge the directors of JHIL to seek an independent view or otherwise satisfy themselves as to whether the values and assumptions used in the model are reasonable'; after consultation, 'to seek an independent view, or otherwise' was deleted. At Access, Ewen Waterman advised that the model 'appears sound for the analytical work for which it has been designed', but was insensitive to volatility, so that 'a poor return in an early year can jeopardise the viability of the entire scheme over the forecast horizon', and that the rate of return was relied on 'a high figure ... over such a long period of time', which JHIL 'will need to test more fully'. Harman complained that Hardie 'did not see the role of Access Economics as including any detailed comments on the assumptions', and persuaded Waterman to confine himself to one caveat: 'We have not been asked to comment on the specific assumption employed [about the earnings rate], but it is something that warrants detailed consideration by James Hardie.'

Bismarck's remark about sausages and laws — that it is best not to watch them made — applies no less to financial models. And it is improbable that the 'Twelfth Cash Flow Model's effect was decisive in the decision-making that followed. Yet, in harmony with many other factors, it and the annexed 'independent verifications' acted as another layer of reassurances for Hardie's concerned directors, and also the incoming board of the MRCF, intercepting a possible avenue of inquiry. Even Phillip Morley recognised the involvement of PwC and Access Economics as 'arid and pointless'; their involvements were purely cosmetic. But such cosmetic touches mattered. The draft of Macdonald's board papers — the paragraphs were later excised — contains a passage among the most unconsciously revealing of the whole story:

> Need to act now: It is not an acceptable option to not make a decision about asbestos liabilities and financial restructuring ... No attractive/ideal solution. There is no 'silver bullet' solution available. The asbestos position is not one created by the current management or Board — but it is here and need to be dealt with. This decision is a 'Beauty contest between warthogs' and the decision is which option is least ugly.

'Not one created by the current management or Board' — consciences could be clear. An unpleasant task. But somebody had to do it.

THERE IS NOTHING INHERENTLY WRONG with a concern for the way a transaction looks. Investors can be almost neurotic in their need for reassurance; analysts sometimes give the impression they would much rather companies did nothing at all. Yet Hardie took concern about appearance to almost supermodel extremes. Its consultative net was spread widely, to encompass former Labor national secretary Gary Gray, who supported Loosley's belief 'in independent third party endorsements', and Corrs industrial relations specialist John Denton, who counselled reassuringly that the Australian Council of Trade Unions had 'no formal position on asbestos and therefore no readymade campaign built around union consensus which could be mobilised quickly'. Even phrases in the press release, meanwhile, were pored over in every nuance. At one point, Macdonald queried the use of the words 'claimants right to sue JH is undiminished' after separation. The corporate veil made this possibility remote, but Macdonald didn't want anyone getting ideas. 'I still do not like the use of the phrase 'claimants right to sue JH is undiminished',' he complained. 'The reality is that they will have no reason or "right" to sue JH in respect of asbestos — those obligations have been undertaken by the Foundation. I cannot see any advantage in "pointing" plaintiffs lawyers and potential plaintiffs at JH.' Baxter told him it was a rhetorical flourish for the tabloids:

I think it helps with allegations that we are walking away. Unless I misunderstand something:

- a claimant will have the right to sue JH (but such a claim as you know would have no basis)
- should a claim against JH be upheld (for any reason) JH would be obliged to meet it (but we know that there is very little likelihood of that occurring and we will be saying so to the analysts)

The statement is really part of the packaging and we would emphasises [sic] different aspects of it depending on the audience. It would be a strong statement to be able to say to Alan Jones or *A Current Affair* that people can still bring claims against JH should JH be liable and if JH wa [sic] found liable it would meet that claim. The point about likelihood is in the detail — the strong message is that the rights of claimants are undiminished.

There were many areas to cover. The three dimensions of Project

Green had by now become three 'limbs'. The court-approved scheme of arrangement involving change of domicile and NYSE listing, despite enjoying BIL's favour, was now off the immediate agenda, at least until the sale of gypsum. Separation alone would be sufficient of a handful. Macdonald, nonetheless, was thinking ahead as to what Hardie would look like at the end of the whole process, rather than merely after the foundation's launch. In addition to the deed of covenant and indemnity, he now also mooted a fifteen-year option to put JHIL to the foundation. After the scheme, JHIL would exist as the maker of instalment payments to the MRCF and the issuer of a tranche of partly paid capital. Discharge of the former duty would arguably obviate the need for the latter. Sale or liquidation also remained alternatives; either way, in the tidied group-configuration foreseen, JHIL's days were numbered. Mind you, as Peter Cameron and David Robb warned, legality here had not only to be done, but be seen to be done:

> While the first limb of this transaction can be effected with minimal execution risk, the subsequent financial reconstruction will involve the directors of JHIL considering the interests of creditors, and it is likely to involve a rigorous analysis by the court of issues effecting creditors with the possibility that the court will seek to investigate the trust and related arrangements. This risk may arrive in the context of explaining why the transaction does not prejudice the interests of JHIL creditors and especially if reference will be made to the indemnity.
>
> To vest JHIL into the trust is likely to involve a reduction of capital, presumably by removing the partly paid shares which will require the directors to leave behind assets within JHIL ... It is likely that the scheme documents will need to disclose the directors' intentions with respect to JHIL post the reconstruction. This may involve a discussion of the liquidation and vesting options if, indeed, these are in contemplation ... This may be regarded as at odds with arguing that post reconstruction JHIL's creditors' interests are not materially prejudiced. Accordingly, to the extent partly paid shares are to be used, the court may not regard them as sufficient protection for creditors ...

Hardie, in other words, would eventually have to go to court to migrate offshore, and had to ponder the possibility of 'detailed court review', where it would need to prove that these transactions were in the best interests of the entities concerned. Robb also grew concerned that Phil Morley and Don Cameron, as directors of Coy, should receive independent legal advice. 'Under control,' replied Shafron. Indeed it was.

Everybody in the separation transactions had legal advice, and from firms with impeccable credentials. Quite what this advice accomplished, however, is unclear, as was its independence. The prospective directors of the MRCF, for instance, had the counsel of Mallesons' Tony Bancroft, who was being paid by Hardie, and sent his draft advice in advance to Shafron. His considered opinion? The foundation board should execute no documents in connection with the transaction other than their consent to act as directors because 'the commercial terms were being set by JHIL', and they 'did not have sufficient time to consider the commercial aspects in respect of those documents'—which some, but not Bancroft, might see as an argument against joining a board altogether.

Morley and Cameron, meanwhile, had the services of two very highly regarded solicitors from Blake Dawson Waldron, Jeremy Kriewaldt and Bill Koeck, but only on matters of the deed of covenant and indemnity. For everything else, somewhat oddly, they relied on Allens. A problem? Not to Morley. Time, he explained, was of the essence:

> *Michael Slattery QC*: What I'm suggesting to you, Mr Morley, is that you did not at any time give any consideration to not entering into this transaction?
> *Morley*: Well, I'd say that's correct because I took the view that this transaction was in the best interests of those two companies ...
> *Slattery*: But Blake Dawson Waldron could have advised you about the whole of the transaction rather than just the Deed of Covenant and Indemnity upon the information supplied, couldn't they?
> *Morley*: Well they would have had a lot of work to get that, yep.
> *Slattery*: And that would have taken time wouldn't it?

Morley: It would have taken time, yep.

Slattery: And you weren't prepared to jeopardise the closure of the transaction by 16 February, and so you didn't want to give them that time, isn't that right?

Morley: Well the deadline was the 16th. It could have been extended.

Slattery: You never considered extending that deadline in the interests of Coy and Jsekarb did you?

Morley: At the time, no.

The only individual at the time with a complete picture of events, in fact, was Shafron, who had positioned himself at the junction of all communications, including the information flows to the MRCF directors. A flavour of his flair for micromanagement can be obtained from one exchange of emails with Roy Williams at Allens about who should commission Trowbridge's update:

Williams: David [Robb] and I think it may be preferable that any further report by Trowbridge be commissioned by Tony Bancroft as the lawyer for, and on behalf of, the prospective directors, who would then supply it confidentially to JHIL

Shafron: No, I want the report to be to JHIL. I want to keep Minty on JHIL side of things as far as possible, for tactical reasons and control.

Williams: Your reasons are understandable. However we were thinking in terms of privilege. In the new circumstance (as explained to me by David) any argument for privilege would have been stronger, in our view, if the instructions came from Bancroft. I am happy to instruct Minty on behalf of JHIL (after a little fiddling with the letter) but if I or anyone else at Allens does it the privilege argument will be difficult. Do you wish me to proceed on that basis?

Shafron: Yes I realise the risks but what I have in mind are a couple of tables, that's it, not a fat report or anything like that (at this stage anyway). Pls proceed, and may I see the final draft before dispatch?

A fat report, in fact, was the furthest thing from Shafron's mind. 'My preference is still not to include the reference to one or two of the more sensitive documents,' he stipulated to Attrill on 6 February, 'because it will likely make things tense with the new board, who will become suspicious'. He even insisted on being present when the prospective directors of the MRCF finally got their wish and met Minty—his purpose, he explained, was 'to provide some context'. To this meeting, in the Zurich Room at PwC, Shafron brought Morley, Attrill, Ashe, Minty, Marshall, Robb, and public relations consultant Tony Park, who was to be seconded to the foundation. He did Edwards the courtesy of allowing him to open the meeting, which he did by disclosing that Hardie had volunteered further funds, and expressing the view that the proposal 'should not be difficult to sell in the media'. But Shafron spoke next, and essentially ran the meeting, outlining for the first time the deed of covenant and indemnity: 'In return [for the top-up payment], Coy and Jsekarb will agree to hold JHIL harmless and indemnify JHIL against claims that may be made against it in relation to the manufacture of asbestos containing products post 1937 by JH & Coy.'

After Robb had delineated the trust structure, Minty and Marshall presented their update. It was, as usual, so hedged as to be almost nugatory, with boilerplate clauses like 'the nature of the problem is such that experience could vary considerably from our estimates', and observations about legal decisions being 'impossible to predict' and epidemiology 'subject to inherent uncertainty'. But the effect of this haze of qualification seems to have been to make listeners seize even more avidly on the few numbers there were. Gill asked: 'How long will $280 million last?' Minty answered:

If you take our projections and apply discount rates in the order of 7 to 8 per cent, a fund of around $280 million is going to last about twenty years if our medium projection plays out, and obviously it would be insufficient if the high projection is what emerges. In that case you would expect a fund of that size to last about fifteen years. Obviously if what we've called the 'current' projection occurs then $280 million would last you twenty years and maybe a few years longer depending on, among other things, investment returns. So it depends on a number of variables, many of which are quite uncertain.

The incoming directors, less familiar with actuarial hemming and hawing, seem to have found this strangely soothing; Attrill's notes even record Peter Jollie's comment: 'We intend to rely on this.' In their desire for reassurance, Edwards, Cooper, Jollie and Gill even became confused about the currency of the information before them, because the covering letter from Trowbridge was ambiguous: 'You have asked us to revisit the claim number assumptions that we adopted for our draft advice on the future costs of the asbestos-related disease claims in view of recent work that Trowbridge Consulting have carried out to estimate the impact of such claims on the insurance industry.' But in Jollie's words: 'It did not occur to me that the Trowbridge estimate was anything other than an estimate based on the most up-to-date data and most up-to-date research.' Said Cooper: 'Neither the report nor Mr Minty's briefing gave me reason to believe otherwise.'

Even the actuaries were a little disturbed by the credulity with which their pitch had been received. While returning to Goldfields House at 2.30PM, Minty mused aloud: 'Some of the people there didn't seem to have been aware before we made our presentation that our report is based on James Hardie's data up to 31 March 2000. We should add some words to our final report confirming what we told them at the meeting that it is clear.' Marshall agreed. In their final version of the report, the lines quoted above inserted 'as at 31 March 2000' after 'claims'. But the change went unnoticed; even Robb continued to think that the claims data was up-to-date.

The 'Twelfth Cash Flow Model' received somewhat closer attention, Jollie querying Morley about the investment returns and asking the model to be run at lower rates. But in general, it was all rather cosy. Because it would now be the outgoing directors who signed the deed of covenant and indemnity, for instance, it appears to have been received with indifference. And everyone seems to have heard what they wanted to hear about the trust's future solvency: responses ranged from Edwards' statement that 'a twenty-year forecast is probably the best one can do in scientific matters and the epidemiology of diseases' to Gill's belief that 'some statements by James Hardie were to the effect that the funds would cover the full run-off'. When the meeting concluded, the chairman-elect corralled his board-to-be. 'I think we have all heard everything now,' he said. 'Are there any further questions that anyone has? I guess we really have to decide tonight whether or not we are going to commit ourselves to becoming directors of the foundation.' No one expressed any reservations. 'Well, it looks like we're all happy to proceed,' he continued. 'I am happy to proceed. How do you all feel?' Everyone felt comfortable. 'Well, we can tell Hardie's we are ready to proceed,' he concluded. It was a trust, Cooper recalls, built on exactly that:

> There were actuarial calculations, invitations to respected directors, and Hardies were there as a very strong partner. They had the asbestos past, but my knowledge of the company suggested that they had lots of assets, that they were a reputable corporate citizen who would not their name blackened, and who was hiring some quality people to sit on this new board. It appeared the money was there. It conformed with the law. The government was going to be informed. Everything said: 'Do it.'

The government, the very last item to be checked, had been ticked off that morning, Stephen Loosley having organised a meeting at short notice with Matthew Strassberg, chief of staff for industrial relations minister John Della Bosca, at Governor Macquarie Tower. Loosley brought Baxter and Ashe; Strassberg roped in premier Carr's chief of staff Graeme Wedderburn, who had known Loosley in the latter's days as secretary of the New South Wales ALP fifteen years earlier. Wedderburn was surprised by the apparent urgency of the request: he had surmised that it was a heads-up about the closure of a plant.

The company contends privately that the reception for their plan gave them reason to feel they had government support. Loosley described the briefing as 'a pearler — they don't get much better than that', although notes taken at the meeting record it as little more than a repetition of buzz phrases: 'great outcome for all', 'sensible private sector action', 'not walking away' and 'ambulance chasing — trying to cut it down'. The government has insisted that it was noncommital. In a unreleased statement on the subject, Wedderburn says that Hardie provided little detail:

> In that meeting, I asked the James Hardie representatives if they were certain that the foundation would be fully funded to meet its future liabilities to asbestos victims. The James Hardie representatives told me and Mr Strassberg that the foundation would be fully funded to meet their liabilities. They told me and Mr Strassberg that they had actuarial advice to support their view. I told the James Hardie representatives that all stakeholder would be watching their announcement and that they would have to be prepared to support the claim that foundation would be fully funded.

The meeting was probably general and brief enough, lasting only ten minutes, to suit all concerned, allowing for what the Nixon White House called 'plausible deniability'. And triple-witching hour had arrived.

19

'There will be no better friend to the foundation than James Hardie'

'We have developed a comprehensive solution to critical issues that James Hardie has been facing for over five years. The solution should be implemented now to maximise improvements in shareholder value. Although the plan is not risk free, it is recommended as providing the best outcome from the alternatives that are possible. The objective is to position James Hardie for future growth and to eliminate legacy issues that would otherwise continue to detract from value creation.'
—Peter Macdonald, James Hardie board papers for directors' meeting of 15 February 2001

FOR MEREDITH HELLICAR, Thursday, 15 February 2001 began very badly indeed. She awoke to find herself immobilised by excruciating back pain, the sort that would normally dissuade a person from even thinking about work. 'I probably should have been sensible and stayed home,' she reflects. But that wasn't how Hellicar had gotten where she was. When she left the department of foreign affairs in 1978 for the private sector, her father asked her why she would want to change jobs and face all that insecurity; her mother gave her a little card in which a knight confronted a dragon inscribed with the advice: 'No guts, no glory.' There was a board meeting of James Hardie that morning—an important one, not to be missed. Hellicar struggled to a physiotherapist for intensive treatment, then into PwC in Sussex Street.

Sir Llew Edwards, alongside whom Hellicar normally sat in board meetings, awoke in different spirits. Today's would be his final board meeting, and he would not be lingering. It was his wedding anniversary. When he remarried after the death of his first wife, he and his bride Jane had promised one another they would always spend the anniversary together, regardless of events. Not even the establishment of the Medical Research and Compensation Foundation would stand in his way.

For David Robb, the day began differently again, at Allens' Chifley Tower offices. A studious, conscientious young lawyer, he had only been a partner for eight months, and moved onto the Hardie account when John Martin had departed. Where Peter Cameron's advices oozed confidence, Robb's were generally more guarded — and his guard was up. Early that morning — he could not recall exactly how but probably while perusing the final draft of the Trowbridge update with its addition of the date 'as at 31 March 2000' — he was alerted to the fact that 'JHIL had not provided Trowbridge with Coy's most recent claims numbers' for its calculations. His mind began racing. He 'would have thought that to update a report you would take up-to-date figures'. He rang Shafron, who hastened to reassure him. Trowbridge had advised that the latest data was not required; it would not alter the claims curve significantly. Robb justified his interest in his own notes:

> Depends on whether 8 months is relevant
> That is a Trowbridge question
> If not relevant then not concerned
> Interested in protecting JHIL directors

It was indeed a Trowbridge question, and Robb was dissatisfied with Shafron's response. He wanted to 'confirm its veracity'. But he did not do the logical thing.

> *Michael Slattery QC*: The clearest and simplest way to do that was to ask Trowbridge wasn't it?
> *Robb*: It would have been.
> *Slattery*: Did you?
> *Robb*: No.

Slattery: Why not?
Robb: It didn't cross my mind.

Instead, Robb went to see his elder statesman, Cameron, at around 8.30AM, and reported the content of the conversation. Cameron echoed his concern, and Robb suggested they consult Macdonald. By the time their speaker phone call was connected, however, Shafron was sitting in Macdonald's office, and he simply reiterated his advice to Robb: 'Trowbridge said that they do not require the most recent data and that it wouldn't make a different to their conclusions because their report has been based on longer-term trends and on a broader pattern of asbestos-related diseases in the wider community.' The senior lawyer recalled the substance of the ensuing exchange:

> *Cameron*: With the Board meeting so soon I am simply not in a position to absorb and assess the detail of what has happened. My primary concern is whether this information has any impact on the key conclusions in the proposals going to the Board and the financial models which are based on the Trowbridge report. In short I need to understand the bottom line before we talk to the board. Is there any reason to depart from the view that the Foundation will be fully funded?
> *Macdonald*: Absolutely not.

This phrase — 'fully funded' — was to cause endless heartache at the Special Commission. Seemingly unambiguous, it turned out to have meant different things to different people, yet had a lulling effect on those who used it, like a magical incantation. Its most famous usage would be in the James Hardie press release signed off on that day: 'JHIL CEO Mr Peter Macdonald said that the establishment of a fully funded Foundation provided certainty for both claimants and shareholders'. This, despite the fact that the papers that went before his board that day openly countenanced the possibility that the foundation's resources might be insufficient:

> In particular, James Hardie and Coy Pty Ltd and Jsekarb Pty Ltd, two subsidiaries which formerly produced asbestos bearing products and are

currently subject to plaintiffs actions on account of injuries caused by asbestos, have current and potential liabilities that have the potential to exceed their net worth. This does not create an obligation for JHIL to meet any shortfall.

In fact, it is very difficult to resist the conclusion that Hardie's executive knew full well that the MRCF might have been inade-quately equipped for its ostensible task. The communications package that was part of the board papers that morning, for instance, contained a series of carefully crafted answers to possible questions about the foundation which quietly undermine the idea of even ascertaining full funding let alone allocating it.

Why does James Hardie think future claims will cost at least $284 million?
The assets set aside reflect the net assets of the companies which previously manufactured asbestos which have been found legally liable for asbestos. The quantum of assets is not a reflection of what JH thinks the future cost will be. That is a separate question. The ultimate cost of asbestos claims cannot be reliably measured at this time.

Edwards had been armed with similar evasions of the issue. In the event he was asked if the assets vested in the trust would be sufficient, he was advised to reply: 'That's our goal. But, there is no known way of calculating this with certainty.' He was to rely on a line of reassurance to the effect that 'we have substantial assets valued today at $284 million' which would 'grow in value' so that 'the question of whether the funds will be sufficient will not arise for many years if at all'. Then, 'if pushed', he would answer: 'As part of our due diligence as incoming directors, the foundation's board conducted detailed appropriate reviews and believe that even using the worst case scenarios the funds will last for many, many years.' If pressed on what would happen if the trust ran out of money, it was recommended that he reply: 'It's our job to do our very best with the funds we have.' The questions were, of course, unavoidable. If funding was always full, why was it necessary to prepare for the possibility of a shortfall? If Hardie's executive was so convinced of the efficacy of this concept, why was its investor relations approach to 'confine the story to its business context', and to 'shut the story down as quickly and effectively as possible'? And given that the questions were unavoidable, why were they not asked?

The board that convened at PwC that morning was vastly experienced. The BIL representatives, Greg Terry and Dan O'Brien, were relatively new; likewise the American directors Koffel and Gilfillan, on the phone. But chairman Alan MacGregor, and directors Hellicar, Peter Willcox and Michael Brown had almost four decades of experience of this particular circle between them. They held their CEO in high esteem. They had made clear their in-principle support for separation. After all, the Hardie of today bore only the remotest connection to the one that had manufactured asbestos products. In many important respects, the setting up of the Foundation was already half way over the line. The only issue still troubling them, they had made clear a month earlier, was money — and the executive had honoured its part in the bargain by finding more.

The executive, meanwhile, had been on this case since the beginning of 1997. Investors liked Hardie, but would like it more without asbestos, and a great deal more with less tax. Why was asbestos their problem anyway? They'd never made the stuff personally. Everyone, moreover, knew the compensation regime was farcically biased against defendants — even the government, though, of course, they daren't say it. People were walking out of the DDT with six-figure settlements for pleural plaques, for heaven's sake. And lawyers were eating them alive. There'd be ample to go round if the government got serious about tort reform. In his communiqué to Liza-Jayne Loch a month earlier, Baxter had offered this justification: 'Based on all our work — there would be plenty of money if a new compensation system without litigation was used — take the lawyers out and you take out up to 50 per cent of the cost — surely this is a good argument'. The occupants of the board table in the Zurich Room that morning, then, were bonded by historic familiarity and shared grievance.

They also received certain cues. The first statement that both board and executive heard at the meeting was one by Sir Llew

Edwards, when he tabled his resignation: 'We think James Hardie has been generous in the funding of the Foundation. My fellow directors and I are happy for that to be known'. The effect of this unsolicited testimonial was considerable. Even Meredith Hellicar, whose bad back forced her to stand for the duration of the meeting and who has wondered since whether her concentration wavered, remembers it clearly. When the principal on the other side of a transaction informs you that your terms are not simply 'satisfactory' or 'fair' but 'generous', and if one is minded to agree anyway, it is surely tempting to believe him. At a pinch, it might even justify use of the word 'full' where funding was concerned, if 'full' is defined as exceeding a legal obligation rather than as a synonym of sufficient.

They also received a cue, as it were, from the report numbers, when Baxter, Harman, Cameron, Robb, Ian Wilson and Anthony Sweetman joined the meeting after a 90-minute discussion of operations, and MacGregor began outlining the trust's structure and resources. In some respects, the figures presented to the board were not implausible. The net present value figure of the liabilities as ascertained by Trowbridge was a credible increase on the calculations of 1996, 1998 and 2000. The update was not tabled, but the board was shown three curves on a graph, and told that the middle one, the 'best estimate', was the one thought 'most likely'.

Harman's 'Twelfth Cash Flow' model, meanwhile, had the apparent buttressing from PwC and Access Economics. And Shafron sounded completely confident when asked by one director: 'Is there anything in these figures which causes management to reconsider its view that the proposed funding is sufficient to meet anticipated claims?' He responded: 'No. We asked David Minty that and he said that a couple of quarters of data was not going to shift a ten-year curve.' As Willcox says:

> It seemed eminently reasonable. I'd have believed 200. I might have looked a bit more closely, but I could probably have been persuaded. Especially given the likelihood that a fund would, at least for a period, accumulate ... To my mind, on balance, there was reasonable certainty that the trust would be adequately funded for foreseeable claims.

Brown says:

> My impression was that the calculations were complex but highly
> reliable, so I didn't seek to go through the figures in great detail. I also
> had a high degree of confidence in the management team, so there was
> not a lot to be added by a personal forensic investigation of the figures.

Hellicar adds:

> None of us on the board read the report, it's true, but the number was
> sufficiently in the ball park not to raise alarm bells. If it had been the
> first report, then perhaps one would have read it; if the number had
> been significantly different from those of the prior reports, then you
> might have said: 'What's going on here?' I remember very clearly the
> discussion of the nine months' data, because it just seemed logical, and
> I believe Peter [Shafron] because he had no reason to make it up.

The thinking is understandable, especially if it is accepted that no
one on the board understood the extent of management's involvement in the production of Trowbridge's figures, and how circumscribed were the 'independent' reassurances offered about the
'Twelfth Cash Flow Model' (mentioned only in the annotation on
the model 'analysis reviewed by PwC and Access Economics').
Another qualifying remark can also be made. In hindsight, some
directors feel there was ambiguity about whether separation meant
precisely that. Willcox says that he believed the statement to the
effect that no additional funds would be forthcoming originated
mainly in a desire to exercise some discipline over the foundation:
'It's seldom entirely clear, *ab initio*, when a case is brought, who is
responsible, and to simply shovel the money out the door is actually
doing a disservice to future plaintiffs.' Hellicar says that the discussion was made vague by the duration of the timescales involved:

> It seems really naïve but I just don't remember talking about the fact
> that there wouldn't be [a top-up in the event of a shortfall]. The way I
> thought about things—it comes back to this issue about the corporate

veil—I think I would have assumed that someone will top it up when the time comes. Y'know, because there wasn't a motive to get away. You just approached things a bit more naively ... because this would be in yonks years' time. You thought: 'Someone will do the right thing.'

Even with the foregoing, however, the decision-making process seems to have left much to chance. Everyone seems to have understood that there was a risk that the Foundation would not have sufficient funds. The unfolding of Trowbridge's 'high' scenario would deplete its resources in less than twenty years. Perhaps among directors there was no desire to 'get away'. But management took a harder line. Recall the Loch/Baxter catechism: 'What happens when the money runs out? *It runs out.* What guarantees can JH give that victims aren't going to be stranded? *None.*' It seems surprising, too, that none of the directors, who must have been conscious by now that actuarial calculations were indicative at best, felt concerned to get to grips with the content and assumptions of the reports they received. They never, for example, heard directly from Trowbridge, and nobody seems to have grasped that their forecasts were median projections with only a 50 per cent chance of being right. The proposition stood or fell on this set of calculations, yet they had no one with any actuarial training to guide them through it—there were only lawyers and investment bankers. Nor did they raise with Shafron the quarterly report on asbestos litigation also in the board papers that day, which noted 'a significant increase in very expensive settlements' in the third quarter and foreshadowed 'a number of major claims' in the fourth.

MacGregor claimed that he never understood the speculative nature of actuarial advice: 'That's not what I understood was the nature of the actuarial material. I didn't understand at the time that it was not reliable.' This is bizarre. Hardie was a long-term user of Trowbridge's services. All actuarial reports are extensively qualified; his own previous set of board papers had included the very clear and succinct advice: 'There is no reliable basis for determining what amount any such future contribution should be if attempting to fund all future claims. Previous indicative advice obtained as to the potential quantum of the future claims has been variable and unreliable.' Hellicar insists: 'I don't know whether it's an exact parallel, but would people on an engineering company board be expected to read all the technical reports? The attitude was: "This is a number. We've got the best. There doesn't seem anything out of the ordinary".' But this is a poor analogy. There is a world of difference between miscellaneous technical reports and the logic underlying the valuation of a huge legal liability at the centre of a significant corporate restructuring. Nor was 'this' merely 'a number'. It reflected the stunted, thwarted lives of thousands of men and women affected by the company's products. There were risks in miscalculation of a different order to those in a more conventional corporate finance transaction.

Actual discussion of the MRCF after the presentation by Shafron and Morley was limited. Although it is difficult to believe there was not some exchange of views, the official record minutes none, documenting merely the resolutions to bring separation about. Nor are any votes noted — which was the way MacGregor liked it. As he explained his directors' deliberate process: 'A consensus normally develops during the course of the Board's discussion and towards the end of the discussion, I will sometimes state what I understand to be the consensus reached by the Board'. A vote was probably unnecessary. The directors went on their way thinking that they had done a good deal by extracting the extra cash. 'I can recall coming home and telling my wife what a win-win it was,' says Brown.

Through this, too, sat the advisers, Wilson, Sweetman, Cameron and Robb. Their involvement was minimal. The investment bankers were not about to say anything that might prevent the doing of a deal that had already failed once, of course, while the lawyers staved off concerns about the data whose absence had made them so anxious that morning. Robb contemplated raising the subject, but chose not to after asking his superior: 'We were available for questions to be asked of us. No questions were asked of us and so we did not say — we did not raise it.' When he returned to Chifley Tower, Robb was mildly surprised to find an email from Shafron aimed at allaying his morning's apprehension:

> Three points that I didn't think to mention:
> 1. The Minty report states in the first para that it is based on March 2000
> 2. Wayne showed the potential directors the year to date numbers
> 3. Harman's model uses actual and forecast numbers for the YEM01
> I think that helps.

Not much. The first point was true only of the altered report, while the second and third points didn't bear on the reliability of the Trowbridge numbers at all. Robb would claim that he remained 'concerned about the failure' because 'the incoming directors had requested such a report in order to determine whether or not they were willing to act as directors', but these concerns went unuttered.

Yet it may not only be in what they did or did not do that the advisers in this transaction were influential. The impression of having the best advice at one's beck is a reassuring one. The advisers here were by now familiar faces at Hardie, and this was a board culture that placed heavy reliance on them. Recall Shafron's acid comment on directors in July 2000: 'I don't think we should underestimate the value the Board will place on *outside* third party advisers (as insulting as that is to the company's internal advisers — myself included).' Yet these same advisers were by now so close to the company as to be almost indistinguishable from corporate officers. They were present to give the board frank and fearless advice, and to assist management in its aim of executing the deal.

It is worth asking whether in the circumstances it was possible for them to do both. Economists describe a phenomenon called 'regulatory capture', where regulators come to identify with the interests of those they are regulating rather than those they are protecting. Is there a similar phenomenon, what might be called 'advisory capture', where advisors grow so close to the executive they know as to obscure their duties to directors? Whatever the case, this was a meeting conducive to unanimity of thought. And while unanimity can be a powerful and productive force, it is also indicative of conformity and inhibition. Alfred Sloan, the master manager of General Motors, always deferred any decision on which he and his colleagues found themselves in absolute agreement. 'There's something we haven't thought of,' he would say. 'Think up some questions then come back and ask them.' For such a disposition here, however, there was no time, insufficient information and inadequate inclination.

THE DEED WAS ALL BUT DONE; it now merely awaited the implementation at Chifley Tower. Allens' board room and various antechambers were commandeered for the legal needful, and Cameron and Robb were augmented by their colleagues George Frangeskides, Patrice Mowat and Julian Blanchard. Blake Dawson Waldron's Bill Koeck and Jeremy Kriewaldt were there to tend the outgoing directors, Morley and Don Cameron; Tony Bancroft came in to chaperone the initiates, Cooper, Gill and Jollie, with Edwards available by phone.

Morley and Don Cameron were carrying a short note from Shafron about the deed of covenant and indemnity, including a brief history of asbestos liabilities and insurance coverage, and reassuring noises about the modelling 'which suggests that, on the most likely scenario, Coy and Jsekarb should have sufficient funds to meet all claims in future', although 'naturally, the model is based on certain assumptions, and there can be no certainty about each and every one of these'. Neither the indemnity nor the put option that the deed contained had been valued, and Koeck and Kriewaldt weren't entirely enamoured of the covenant, believing that it was too broad, encompassing dividends and management fees as well as asbestos claims; they had it narrowed. Otherwise, their remit was so limited that their advice included the disclaimer that they had been 'unable to assess any of the legal issues relating to the asbestos claims'. Nonetheless, Morley and Cameron signed off.

While this was going on, Cooper, Gill and Jollie cooled their heels. 'It just went on and on and on and on,' Cooper recalls. 'We were drinking mineral water and Coke. Sandwiches were brought in. There seemed to be inordinate delays. Some forms would come around: consent forms or proxy forms. We heard that various deeds were executed, including the Deed of Covenant and Indemnity between the previous directors and JHIL. We had some discussions about Wayne's employment contract. Then we went back to doing nothing.' Otherwise, he was feeling content:

> All the negotiations had taken place in an atmosphere of trust. You had an ex-board member with relationships at the company. You had Michael, who was an insurance lawyer. He understood asbestos. He was a highly regarded person. Impeccable credentials. It was a great comfort to me that he was around. You had the confidence of the advisers. And you had the commitment of the Hardie executives. One of the things that Peter Macdonald said on several occasions was: 'There will be no better friend to the foundation than James Hardie. We 're going to make it work.'

Around 8.30PM, the making it work started for the incoming directors. One of their first tasks was to scrutinise the deed to which Morley and Cameron had just committed their new entity. Bancroft shied from a comprehensive advice, saying he had not had the document long enough, but did not urge them not to proceed, and his written advice concluded that 'we do not consider that accepting the office of director of MRCF or the Former Subsidiaries will expose any proposed director to an unacceptable degree of risk'. Edwards, meanwhile, claimed that he knew of the precedent of *Wren v CSR*, where a parent had been held accountable for the misdeeds of its subsidiary, but that it was 'too late' to do more.

> *Jack Rush QC*: Were you aware in the decision in New South Wales of the Supreme Court in *Wren* where CSR was found liable for the conduct of its subsidiary Asbestos Products?
> *Edwards*: I was aware of that, yes.
> *Rush*: So you would have recognised the significance of this indemnity?
> *Edwards*: Of course.
> *Rush*: Well what did you do about it?

Edwards: It was too late, it was done.

Rush: It was too late and it was done?

Edwards: Well, so I accepted that.

It was too late and done for very much to occur at all. At 11.00PM, with Gill acting as chairman in Edwards' stead, the MRCF was incorporated as a public company limited by guarantee, also becoming the trustee of a trust for charitable purposes to endow asbestos-disease research. The document flow became more regular after midnight, and by 3.00AM the consultancy agreement between the MRCF and Wayne Attrill's Litigation Management Group was being run beneath various fountain pens for signature. Not until 5.30AM did the participants spill out of Chifley Tower. As Shafron, Morley and Don Cameron walked down Martin Place, the first filaments of dawn were visible. It was a new dawn, too, for their company.

After three hours' sleep, Morley was back in the office, ready to help Macdonald with the third-quarter results. It was not one of Hardie's better days, for the CEO had to flag to investors the cost of declining gypsum prices, and he forecast annual profit before abnormal items of $95 million, versus $158 million. But the MRCF was saluted at once: the *Financial Review* saw Hardie 'shedding the baggage of the past', *The Australian* saluted its 'elegant simplicity', and Hardie shares closed 17c higher at $3.80. No wonder, given the glowing testimonial of the press release:

JAMES HARDIE RESOLVES ITS ASBESTOS LIABILITY FAVOURABLY FOR CLAIMANTS AND SHAREHOLDERS

James Hardie Industries (JHIL) announced today that it had established a foundation to compensate sufferers of asbestos-related diseases with claims against two former James Hardie subsidiaries and fund medical research aimed at finding cures for these diseases.

The Medical Research and Compensation Foundation (MRCF), to be chaired by Sir Llewellyn Edwards, will be completely independent of JHIL and will commence operation with assets of $293 million.

The Foundation has sufficient funds to meet all legitimate

compensation claims anticipated from people injured by asbestos products that were manufactured in the past by two former subsidiaries of JHIL.

JHIL CEO Mr Peter Macdonald said that the establishment of a fully funded Foundation provided certainty for both claimants and shareholders.

'The establishment of the Medical Research and Compensation Foundation provides certainty for people with a legitimate claim against the former James Hardie companies which manufactured asbestos products,' Mr Macdonald said.

'The Foundation will concentrate on managing its substantial assets for the benefit of claimants. Its establishment has effectively resolved James Hardie's asbestos liability and this will allow management to focus entirely on growing the company for the benefit of all shareholders.' ...

In establishing the Foundation, James Hardie sought expert advice from a number of firms, including PricewaterhouseCoopers, Access Economics and the actuarial firm Trowbridge. With this advice, supplementing the company's long experience in the area of asbestos, the directors of JHIL determined the level of funding required by the Foundation.

'James Hardie is satisfied that the Foundation has sufficient funds to meet anticipated future claims,' Mr Macdonald said ...

When all future claims have been concluded, surplus funds will be used to support further scientific and medical research on lung diseases.

This document would cause Hardie more heartache than any other. It bears the name of Greg Baxter, but he insists it had 'more authors than a book of short stories', including several members of the executive, including Macdonald, and went through as many as fifty iterations before it was completed — which is perfectly plausible. Nobody at Hardie afterwards, furthermore, seems to have expressed any serious reservations about this release's exceptionally, indeed repeatedly, bullish tone. Wayne Attrill would claim at the Special Commission of Inquiry that he had complained to Baxter about it, and that Baxter had insisted the company was 'comfortable'.

Baxter was irked. 'I disagree with your evidence, Wayne,' he later told Attrill. 'Neither I nor anyone else can recall any such conversation.'

At the inquiry, by contrast, where David Jackson QC would summarise the release as 'a pure public relations construct, bereft of substantial truth', virtually every word would be submitted to hermeneutical analysis:

> *Sheahan*: The statement that's made in the third paragraph of this media release, you agree, is completely unqualified?
>
> *Shafron*: Well, I think it's qualified by 'anticipated'.
>
> *Jackson*: That just means expected, doesn't it?
>
> *Shafron*: Yes.
>
> *Sheahan*: But it doesn't say that the expectation or anticipation is inherently unreliable or speculative?
>
> *Shafron*: It doesn't.

Shafron, for once, wasn't quite quick enough here. For, although nobody ever noted it, the release is qualified, extensively. Virtually every actual and virtual document from a corporate these days is reinforced by a post-scripted disclaimer to ward off those of litigious bent, rather like the archaic convention on breakfast cereal reminding us that the picture the box bears is merely a 'serving suggestion'. Hardie's press release was no exception, and its disclaimer could hardly have been more felicitously phrased:

> This document contains forward-looking statements. Forward-looking statements are subject to risks and uncertainties and, as a result, readers should not place undue reliance on such statements. The inclusion of these forward-looking statements should not be regarded as a representation that the objectives or plans described will be realised.

Had this disclaimer been in the body of the text, it would have been very hard to complain of misrepresentation. But had that been the case, of course, it would have defeated the exercise's whole purpose.

20

'The thing is not defensible'

'You really are indulging in some pioneering stuff. I am well aware that
the questions I am asking are questions that if I were asked, I wouldn't
have ready answers either.'
—Justice Kim Santow of the NSW Supreme Court during hearings
concerning Hardie's scheme of arrangement, 10 August 2001

IF ITS CREATION SAILED THROUGH the James Hardie board,
the Medical Research and Compensation Foundation had to
navigate some dangerous shoals in its first few weeks. The work in
the *Sydney Morning Herald* of Ben Hills, the veteran investigator
who had chased CSR up hill and down dale for his book *Blue
Murder*, provided a rallying point for Hardie's critics. 'There's no way
that will cover adequate compensation when you look at awards of
over $1 million which the courts are now making in some cases,'
complained Ella Sweeney, a sufferer of asbestosis who ran the
Asbestos Disease Federation of Australia. 'James Hardie has never
been in a hurry to pay up before, so I can't see it happening now.'
Gerry Gardiman of Turner Freeman raised the obvious question:
'My concern would be what happens to the victims when the $293
million runs out?' It went unanswered. After an uneasy audience
with Macdonald on 21 February, Hills received an acerbic rebuke:

JHIL believes that all valid claims for compensation will be met. This is
based on the company's past claims experience (20 years +), the best
available information, a reasonable rate of return on the funds invested,
and on the basis of detailed, expert and in-depth advice from a large
number of specialist firms with noted, long-standing experience in

relevant areas. The advisors involved were Trowbridge Consulting, PricewaterhouseCoopers, Access Economics, Allen Allen & Hemsley, Towers Perrin and UBS Warburg. In contrast you did not produce any evidence to support your assertion that the funds will be insufficient ...

You stated during our interview that I was avoiding questions about funding adequacy. This is not the case. The company and I have been very open and transparent in our disclosures about the foundation. Prior to and since the announcement, the company instigated contact with key stakeholders from government, the union movement, legal circles and other fields to explain the establishment of the foundation. We have provided these organisations and individuals with detailed information about the foundation and offered further more detailed briefings if required. Those who have reviewed the detail have formed the view that the foundation is a fair, responsible and credible means for compensating claimants.

The financial press, however, was as docile and tractable as Baxter had foreseen, and other public guardians were largely inert. Paul Bastian, the outspoken state secretary of the Australian Manufacturing Workers' Union, wrote to the office of premier Carr with a list of questions, composed by Gerry Gardiman, that might profitably have been asked. But the letter went mysteriously astray; Carr would later claim: 'Well, no one told me.' And, generally, the response was apathetic. Contacted on the morning of the announcement, special minister of state John Della Bosca told Ashe he would be 'cautiously optimistic', and honoured his word when he later fielded the only question in the NSW parliament about it from Elaine Nile:

Because of the varying estimates of the number of future cases of mesothelioma and asbestos-related lung cancer, it is difficult to forecast with any certainty whether the foundation's funding will be sufficient. It is important that the financial and corporate structures of the foundation are sound and meet the need to victims and their families ... The essential points in relation to the foundation's capacity to continue to fund claims will be tested vigorously by this government ...

I hope that out of the formation of the foundation we will be able to develop world's best practice clinical services and research in the area of dust diseases because sadly they affect a large number of workers.

In fact, Della Bosca did not test anything, and the unions in general missed an opportunity to hold Hardie to account, or to pressure the government to do so through the State Labor Advisory Council. The closest they came was when Baxter and Ashe had a cold meeting at the Sussex Street headquarters of the NSW Labor Council with its ubiquitous secretary Michael Costa and his assistant John Robertson. When Costa asked, 'So if the fund runs out of money what happens? Do you top it up?', Baxter replied: 'No. There's no more money.' Costa sneered, 'Well, now I understand it ...' Even so, when Baxter advised that Hardie would be content with an accredited actuary visiting their office and perusing the Trowbridge update, a chance went begging.

Hardie was wary of the information flowing to plaintiff lawyers, but prepared to find a suitable protocol. At a meeting three days later, Macdonald, Morley, Baxter and Shafron formulated the idea that a 'single point in the union/government side ... could become a reference point for all other parties from that sector.' Hardie would 'demonstrate the veracity of our numbers to that person' with 'the understanding that this person would confirm the numbers were valid to the other parties', using a 'presentation version' of the model devised by Harman. The idea, however, went no further. Ashe subsequently left a message on Robertson's mobile extending the invitation. It was not returned. Robertson organised a protest march on Hardie House at which he asked a crowd of sufferers, supporters and health workers: 'What happens to us when the $293 million goes away?' But because this was simply assumed rather than demonstrated, it was largely ineffectual.

The result was that Hardie neutralised its antagonists with little effort. Its intent had been to 'divide and conquer' the individual risks. But they did not need division — they were already divided. When Macdonald, Baxter and Ashe met representatives of the Dust Diseases Board on 15 March, chairperson Kate McKenzie and executive officer Geoff Lansley offered a cordial welcome while Ella Sweeney, Barrie Robson of the Maritime Union of Australia and Bernie Riordan of the Electrical Trades Union mostly kept their peace. Bastian had refused to participate because Hardie would not consent to the presence of a lawyer, and the only provocateur was Doug Rolland, the AMWU's representative on the DDB, who, Baxter noted, 'clearly regards James Hardie with profound cynicism' and whose 'comments were littered with various derogatory asides'.

A meeting the next day at the Swanston Street office of the Australian Council of Trade Unions in Melbourne ended similarly. Macdonald, Baxter and Ashe faced assistant national secretary Bill Mansfield and national occupational health and safety coordinator Sue Pennicuik. Mansfield was not about to be charmed. While 'respectful and courteous', and in favour of meeting in a 'civilised and professional way', he left his visitors in no doubt of his attitude, and wasn't about to hear from Macdonald that Hardie 'had acted responsibly at all times in dealing with asbestos issues in the past'. Employers had been grossly irresponsible in their use of asbestos, Mansfield insisted, and slippery about accepting liability. The MRCF, he added, looked insecure. He had to hand a demography of Australian asbestos victims compiled by the respected Douglas Henderson, professor of pathology at Flinders University, who foresaw 13,000 mesothelioma fatalities and twice as many asbestosis sufferers. With the best will and best investment returns in the world, the trust would still struggle to meet such obligations. Mansfield, too, asked for the actuaries' reports on a confidential basis so they could be reviewed. Baxter summarised Mansfield's remarks for an internal memorandum:

- 'On the question of whether we can get access to the actuarial numbers, I am hearing that we can.'
- 'On the question of whether other JH assets are available for compensation if the foundation's funds are exhausted, I'm hearing that JH believes that the liability is restricted to the two companies in the foundation.'

He's wrong on the first point and right on the second.

Baxter's failure to disabuse Mansfield of his mistaken presumption suggests a change of mind: Hardie now thought it could get away without showing anyone anything. Shafron, as he confided to Roy Williams, had never been happy about relying on Trowbridge: 'Our approach to Trowbridge so far and going forward is not to rely too heavily on it. It is limited as you and I know.' Mansfield's own notes of the meeting suggest that, after being assured by Macdonald that 'the JH board is genuinely interested in ensuring that claimants are "looked after" ', he settled for a vague assurance:

BM: Can ACTU have access to actuarial advice for independent review?

PM: This has already been offered/discussed with NSW DDB, John Della Bosca and M. Costa.

Quite so, but Hardie and its interlocutors had now spent a month doing nothing to turn discussion into access, and nothing came of this meeting either: for more than three years, ACTU secretary Greg Combet was unaware it had occurred. The feeblest response was from the Victorian premier's office, where policy advisor Jenny Doran seemed altogether unprepared for the Hardie executives' visit. 'Jenny assumed that we were coming to see her to ask for some money for medical research,' Baxter reported. There was, to be sure, ample suspicion around. Jack Rush QC recalls a conversation with his old asbestos sparring partner, Jack Forrest QC: 'I said to Jack: "I can't believe that this sum of money will cover all people." But he said: "Oh no, the actuaries have said it will".' Peter Gordon, informed of the scheme by Hardie's Melbourne lawyer Peter Hobday at Allens Arthur Robinson, considered a closer look, but eventually shrank from the expense:

I did instruct Jonathon Beach [a commercial silk] to look at it, and he laid out a strategy by which we might be able to convince a court that we had standing to make some sort of application. The trouble was it was so expensive to do, and it was so vague as to what you could do. We saw no actuarial material. We had no basis on which to say whether it was or was not enough money. We didn't even know at the time what they were spending per year. We lacked a well-trodden path in terms of a legal mechanism, and someone with mesothelioma at the time wasn't going to be interested in anything but their own claim. The sort of people affected were people who might contract mesothelioma in five or ten years' time.

No one explanation suffices for how easily, in a public sense, Hardie executed its separation. It is too tempting to simply blame Hardie. Baxter, like Fabius, practised masterly inaction. It is not his fault if this bluff went uncalled. The suspicion lingers that the NSW government was not entirely ill-disposed towards new approaches to compensation for occupational injuries. Its new Workcover Bill was just about to run the gauntlet of unions and the party's left — provoking such fury that Carr needed to constitute the Commission of Inquiry into Common Law Matters run by Justice Sheahan. The creation of the MRCF was not conditional on explicit government approval; but, at least superficially, it was not at odds with the government's reforming zeal.

THERE WAS LITTLE SENSE OF TRIUMPH at Hardie about the MRCF. Hardie was not, under Macdonald, a celebratory organisation. Cameron and Robb hosted a lunch for the chief executive, Morley and Shafron, but it lasted barely an hour because the Hardie trio were due to fly to Los Angeles that afternoon. The lawyers weren't in a celebratory mood either. Robb continued to fret that Trowbridge's update had been anything but up-to-date, and also that reservations expressed by Williams had gone unconsidered. Despite the stilted legalese, Williams' recollection of a conversation of 23 February shows a troubled mind ticking over:

Mr Robb told me in substance ... that Trowbridge were not given any extra specific JHC [Coy] figures for the last eight months and that he Robb 'did not know'. Mr Robb told me in substance that Trowbridge may have had the current Australian trends from their own sources. I asked in substance why the last eight months figures had not been given. Mr Robb said in substance that he was speculating, but he mentioned three possibilities: that there was 'no time' for James Hardie figures to be given; that the figures would have made no difference; and that the claims profile may have changed for the worse, and that James Hardie did not want the figures changed. Mr Robb told me in substance that the issue had 'come up at the board meeting the Thursday before' which he attended with Peter Cameron. Mr Robb told me in substance that it had become evident that 'the most recent claims history had not been factored in' and that he (David Robb) had taken up the issue with Peter Shafron. Mr Robb told me in substance that he had then spoken to Peter Cameron. Mr Robb told me that he had raised four times with James Hardie if my comments had been factored in (ie on the draft June 2000 Trowbridge report), but that he had never received a satisfactory answer. Mr Robb told me in substance that Peter Cameron did not want to take it [the eight-month data issue] further, once the issue had been put to Peter Macdonald by Peter Cameron and David Robb. Mr Robb told me in substance that Mr Macdonald had acknowledged that it was James Hardie's decision, and had been told that 'it will come out, perhaps in court ...' Mr Robb told me in substance that he had put squarely to Peter Shafron the proposition that Allens could not now say that enough money had been put in to the trust. Mr Robb told me in substance that he had said this to Peter Shafron on the day of the Board meeting.

The phlegmatic Williams was himself uncomfortable about the mention of Allens in the list of 'specialist firms with noted, long-standing experience in the relevant areas' brandished at Ben Hills. Williams grumbled to Robb that the firm 'had not participated in a meaningful way in the Trowbridge report', and asked his former colleague Shafron to take 'special care' not to convey that impression again. Shafron replied tartly: 'I'm a little concerned about the tone of your email though. We kept Allens close by our side throughout this transaction and Allens' billings will reflect that.' Williams was sufficiently disturbed by this rebuke to want to 'clear the air', and Shafron sent a more emollient reply suggesting that it didn't matter who had signed off on funding: 'OK Roy understood.'

The main reason for the restraint, however, was that Project Green was only one-third implemented. Hardie was about to begin the process of auctioning its gypsum assets in the US: a labor-intensive activity overseen by J. P. Morgan that involved the equipping of a data room at Mission Viejo for bidders' due diligence. The work was rudely interrupted in May by a stock exchange query. An analyst in London lunching with BPB executives had said: 'I hear your guys are buying Hardie assets in the US.' When the stony silence on the other side of the table was taken as confirmation, Hardie had to reveal that a sale process was underway, even though it was still preparing its information memorandum, and BPB would not actually bid in the first round of offers.

Then there was that scheme of arrangement. After separation, JHIL was to comprise two parallel entities. It owned JHNV, which contained its operating businesses; it owned a peck of non-core assets and liabilities, and was bound to make annual payments to the foundation. Under the scheme, taking advantage of treasurer Costello's new scrip-for-scrip rollover provisions, JHIL shareholders would be invited to swap their shares for paper in a new Dutch entity, JHINV, to which JHNV would be transferred through a reduction in capital in JHIL. JHIL would then issue partly paid capital to JHINV so that its economic position remained unaltered.

So much controversy swirled around the scheme and the partly paid shares that their original intent was obscured, and conflated with that of separation. It has become the common understanding that Hardie's was a Mephistophelean master plan to retreat to the Netherlands, cutting off the partly paid shares as though shutting off an oxygen supply.

It is certainly true that Macdonald wished to detach from the group any entity with the taint of asbestos, and that included JHIL: thus the put option on which he had insisted in separation. But the scheme's relation to Hardie's asbestos liabilities was not so direct as has come to be imagined. There's no evidence that Hardie had anything other than tax in mind where JHINV was concerned, nor that Hardie was other than convinced that its liabilities were sealed off in

Coy and Jsekarb, and that the deed of covenant and indemnity was sufficient of a precaution against anything unexpected. The partly paid shares, meanwhile, were never a funding mechanism, or a 'lifeline', as it became the convention to call them. They were, rather, a transitional device for what Hardie called 'stakeholder management'. Nothing prevented a querulous judge, an unruly shareholder, an uncomfortable creditor or an aggressive plaintiff lawyer from challenging the scheme when it went to the Supreme Court of New South Wales. Hardie had to be able to reply that the interests of JHIL were not prejudiced. There were several ways to do this, but an indemnity would be treated as a profit for tax purposes, while a guarantee reminded Hardie a little too much of their traumatic experience with Firmandale, and also had transfer pricing implications under Dutch law. A tranche of partly paid shares, whose fully paid quantum was equal to the market value of the assets being transferred, was simply the best economic option.

Shafron had a highly developed sense of apprehension about unpredictable stakeholders — or, as he called them, 'spoilers'. So concerned was he about the very existence of the Trowbridge update, for instance, that he advised Robb against including it in the scheme documentation: 'My point on T [Trowbridge] is really code for the thing is not defensible'. He also told Robb when Allens was preparing a brief for Noel Hutley SC: 'I also suggest we include some of the stakeholder reaction material, because I think some of that colour and movement will help get him into the right frame of mind to consider stakeholder attack and stakeholder tactics in the context of the litigation (my main concern, as you would have gathered by now).'* In a board paper on Tuesday 15 May, he warned of

---

*The clearest articulation of the purpose of the partly paid shares is Shafron's to Macdonald, Morley, Baxter and Robb on 10 May:

> The partly paid shares ... will be available to meet existing and future liabilities and obligations of JHIL. The JHIL directors do not expect that JHIL will be in a position such that it becomes necessary to make calls on the partly paid shares. However in view of the various outstanding obligations of JHIL associated with many years of operations — many of which cannot be reduced to certain dollar amounts — the JHIL directors felt that until those obligations

the possibility that 'the court will be influenced by the wider investor, political, public and media reaction to the scheme', and that 'spoilers' would 'successfully apply to be heard to the court and provide a reason to delay approval'. What became of those partly paids *post hoc*, of course, was another matter entirely.

One shareholder who would not be spoiling anything was Brierley Investments, whose 28.7 per cent stake in Hardie was the subject of an underwritten placement the following Monday night. J.B.Were salted away all 119.4 million shares at a minimum price of $4.60, raising a total of $567 million, $234 million of which was profit: reward for Peter Pedley's original intuition. Though BIL had been an ardent proponent of Project Green, the diffusion of its shareholding added stability to the register. Hardie soon after strengthened its own financial ratios with a private placement of 35 million shares netting $197.23 million.

Because so much work had already been done, development of the scheme was swift, smooth and duly signed off by the board during a meeting held at Warburg's offices on Level 25 of Governor Philip Tower on 23 July. The next day's media release promised that JHINV would deliver an additional $30 million in annual profits, thanks to the lower withholding taxes in the US–Netherlands tax treaty and the concessional rate of tax on a Dutch financial entity. Hardie was not, this time, exposed to any particular equity-market risk: rather than trying to flog 15 per cent of itself, all it would be doing was listing pre-existing American Depositary Receipts. Macdonald promoted the restructure as a minimalist model: 'The ASX will continue to provide James Hardie's primary listing, our dividend policy will not change as a result of the restructuring and shareholders' economic interest in James Hardie will not be diluted.' Investors nodded approval by adding 38c to Hardie shares, which finished at $6.18.

were better understood the prudent course was to ensure JHIL remained in the same economic position as it was prior to the restructure … Should the liability position of JHIL change for any reason, and JHIL has no reason to expect that it will, then the partly paid sharees would be available to meet any new liability.

Two week later, Hardie's counsel Noel Hutley led a huddle of Allens lawyers into the NSW Supreme Court. Justice Kim Santow, a vastly experienced commercial lawyer with Freehills who was just about to be installed as chancellor of his *alma mater*, Sydney University, was intrigued by the scheme, especially the partly paids. Potentially, they represented a very big call on JHINV—now about $1.9 billion, given the growing value of assets denoted. Perhaps, he suggested helpfully, there should be a condition on JHIL's entitlement to do so. He also asked explicitly about the position of contingent creditors: 'What effect will this have on asbestos claims against Hardie's?' Hutley sounded reassuring:

> The position is this. The claims that are on hold are not against Hardies. They are against organizations which were once subsidiaries of Hardies which have been put into a foundation but Hardies is party to a number of claims. It will have no effect on those claims because the claims are against JHIL. JHIL, your honour will see, is in a position to meet all claims … against them because it has access to the capital of the group through the partly paid shares subject to the point your honour raised as to whether it should be conditioned in some way.

As well as stakeholder management, there was a certain amount of judge management going on here. Santow saw neither Trowbridge's reports nor the deed of covenant and indemnity. He was not advised of concerns about the foundation's solvency. He was not told of the put option. Nor, in all the discussions of the partly paid shares, was he advised of the possibility of their cancellation: a possibility that, as Cameron and Robb had pointed out in their advice to the Hardie board at the time of separation, might be at odds with the idea that the interests of JHIL creditors were not prejudiced. On the contrary, he was given quite open-ended assurances:

> *Santow*: When it says JHIL will be entitled to call upon JHINV in the future and from time to time, is that right?
> *Hutley*: Yes.

Santow: There is no time period laid down.
Hutley: No.

At the Jackson inquiry, Cameron would dismiss the need to tell Santow as 'absolutely unnecessary' because there was no 'fixity of intention' among directors where cancellation or exercise of the put was concerned — which is, literally, true. But the possibility of cancellation was very real, and had been explicitly countenanced.[†] Robb looked altogether more squeamish under examination by Jack Rush:

Rush: You were aware that it was always considered an option by your client from the very inception of the scheme and the separation that the partly shares that would eventually be part of the JHINV/JHIL matter could potentially be cancelled?

Robb: I was.

Rush: And at no time did you ensure that Santow J was made aware of that potential for cancellation?

Robb: No.

Rush: Indeed you had submitted with Mr Cameron an advice that went to the board of JHIL on 15 February 2001 in the board papers that specifically address the potential of the cancellation of partly paid shares.

Robb: Yes …

Rush: That was always an option, wasn't it?

Robb: It was always an option, yes.

Rush: And it was an option that was never brought to the attention of Santow J?

Robb: It was not.

---

† In an email of Shafron's of 24 March 2001, he observed:

If JHIL is left in the same economic position after the restructure as it was in before then stakeholders should effectively be deprived of grounds for complaint … *They may argue that JHIL could cancel the partly paid shares shortly after the scheme was improved* — to which the reply would be that the then JHIL directors are still subject to the Corporations Law and to the risk of suits if they breach their directors duties involving creditors. [author's italics]

Was there a legal obligation on Hardie to disclose the scheme in all its detail and possibilities to Justice Santow? It is arguable, legally at least, that the answer is probably not. Was the position of asbestos claimants profoundly affected by the non-disclosure? It is arguable, too, that the damage had already been done, and that the chances of action succeeding against JHIL were remote.[‡] Were Allens too clever by half? Some in the profession would insist that that this is their job, and that the paramount objective is to serve the client, as Allens did here: on 23 August, Santow ordered that an extraordinary meeting of shareholders proceed five weeks hence.

Every major transaction can usually expect some significant exogenous shock. And just as Project Chelsea had run into Russia's debt default, now Project Green overlapped with the annihilation of the World Trade Center's Twin Towers. By coincidence, Hardie's chairman, Alan MacGregor, was in Washington for a Free Trade Forum also to be attended by CUB's Ted Kunkel, CSR's Peter Kirby, Southcorp's Keith Lambert and Bonlac's Phil Scanlon, and were expecting to see prime minister John Howard address Congress later in the day: MacGregor, in fact, was staying with Kirby in the plush,

---

[‡] Nothing here, for instance, altered the Putt precedent, as Hutley pointed out in written response to questions from Santow, prepared with Martin van Olten and Aleid Doodeheefver of the Dutch lawyers De Brauw Blackstone Westbroek. Santow asked: 'What effect will the Scheme, if implemented, have on asbestos claims against James Hardie?' The lawyers replied:

As stated by Counsel in response to this query, the Scheme will not affect the position regarding asbestos claims. The former subsidiairies of JHIL against which almost all proceedings have been taken in the past in relation to asbestos claims were transferred to an independent Medical Research and Compensation Foundation in February 2001. JHIL has at times been joined as a party to such proceedings, but has always successfully resisted any claims against it. One adverse finding at first instance was overturned on appeal: see *James Hardie & Coy Pty Ltd v Hall (as administrator of the estate of Putt) (1998) 43 NSWLR 554.* That said, it cannot be said that JHIL will never be held liable. JHIL will have, through existing reserves and access to funding in the form of the party paid shares, the means to meet liabilities which will or may arise in the future whether in relation to asbestos-related claims or other obligations to other persons.'

boutique Hay-Adams Hotel in Lafayette Square, with views of the White House. A development in US–Australian relations more germane to Hardie, however, followed sixteen days later. On the eve of Hardie's extraordinary meeting, the American ambassador signed a protocol with treasurer Peter Costello amending the nineteen-year-old *Convention between the Government of Australia and the Government of the United States of America for the Avoidance of Double Taxation and the Prevention of Fiscal Evasion with respect to Taxes on Income*: their intention was to reduce the withholding tax rate on dividends paid from the US to Australia to zero by July 2003. It was, at the least, an embarrassment. Facing quizzical shareholders at the Regent Hotel the next morning, MacGregor had to insist that the proposed structure would still represent an improvement on the present situation, while conceding that the tax benefits would be diluted: 'We welcome improvements in the global tax environment and applaud the Australian government for its new tax agreement with the US. Our view was and is that the reduction in withholding tax would not alter the merits of our proposal.'

This had not broken from a cloudless sky. As far back as January 1999, the US embassy in Canberra had recommended to Washington that the treaty be renegotiated. And when she rang Cameron, Kathy Cuneo of the Australian Securities and Investment Commission was strongly of the view that another vote would have to be held, despite the fact that the proposal had that day obtained 97 per cent approval from 92 per cent of shareholders. In fact, even now the tax change was not a done deal, and Congress might not approve of a measure deleterious to the US tax base. Shafron anxiously solicited the advice of David Farber, a partner at the leading Beltway law and lobbying firm Patton Boggs:

> We are currently trying to get a corporate restructure through the NSW Supreme Court ... and ASIC ... is suggesting that with the imminency and certainty of the change in status to the double taxation treaty we should be going back to our shareholders and reseeking permission or some such. Ignoring all the details, we don't want to do that, and believe that the whole change is still some way off and not at

all certain. From the US perspective, to achieve the change in the convention, what is required and is it a foregone conclusion? ... I appreciate this is very short notice, but your offices luxuriate in the shadow of the Capitol and I feel certain that all your people (including yourself) get this sort of information with their mother's milk!

When Hardie came back before Santow with the shareholder *fiat* on 11 October, the judge was persuaded that the benefits to shareholders were not significantly eroded by the mooted tax break, and the scheme proceeded. Hardie's 50-year-old stock ticker abbreviation, HAH, was retired four days later in favour of a smart new code, JHX—not inappropriate for an unknown quantity.

21

'I wish now that I'd just belted them'

'There may be many things and many alternatives which are the subject of comment plus which have been canvassed which have been considered which have not become a matter of intention. The view which is put here is that under the subject matter of the obligation of the directors and the Corporations Law to declare their future intentions for JHIL might arise on which it would be transferred to neither entity, if that was intended by the directors to such an extent that it would be in the context of a members scheme.'
—Peter Cameron distinguishes between 'intention' and 'contemplation' at the Special Commission of Inquiry, 15 June 2004

OCTOBER 2001, THE MONTH IN WHICH Dutch-domiciled, New York-listed James Hardie Industries NV finally took flight, was also the culmination of a very grim twelve months for former asbestos dynasties. On 1 October, Federal Mogul, the American parent of Hardie's old sister company T & N, filed for bankruptcy. Under the weight of its compensation burden, Federal Mogul's value had plunged from $US5 billion to $US50 million, and the explicit objective of its Chapter 11 protection was to seek a means that would 'separate its asbestos liabilities from its true operating potential'. The strategy caused uproar. In an Early Day Motion lodged in the House of Commons, forty-one MPs lamented 'the fact that the company can remain trading and protect the interests of its shareholders and can abnegate the responsibilities towards its former employees who are now suffering from chronic and terminal asbestos-related diseases.' Said the member for Leeds, John Battle: 'This evasion is a scandal. Making the polluters pay obviously means not only proving responsibility, not only winning the moral and legal arguments, but taking in high level international corporate gamesmanship that continues to write off the lives of asbestos victims.' Federal Mogul, however, was following a path trodden in the preceding year by Owens–Corning, W. R. Grace, Babcock & Wilcox and USG. The contrast to Hardie, it seemed, could hardly have been more acute. 'Hardie believes it can't win over US financiers unless its quarantines its asbestos liabilities,' reported *The Bulletin*. 'It has carefully done so in a way that could ensure it never need mention the issue again.' Yet there were more similarities than anyone realised.

Life at the Medical Research and Compensation Foundation had all started quite congenially. At their first meeting, the directors had even voted themselves a healthy pay hike — which caused some catty comment at Hardie. Then the first indication of trouble popped out of Dennis Cooper's budgetary 'black hole' in April 2001, and took on more threatening form after his meeting with Peter Macdonald and Sir Llew Edwards, recounted in the prologue, the following month. Cooper soon after met Shafron, who promised a copy of Trowbridge's update, and David Minty and Karl Marshall were themselves commissioned to produce a new report. Macdonald's conjecture that the compensation costs for the year to March 2001 were aberrant began to seem increasingly hollow. In a report to his co-directors on 18 June, Cooper also confirmed the hollowness of their February due diligence:

> It is clear that the actual claims performance for the year ended March 2001 of $32 million ... is not an aberration and represents an appropriate base level for future claims expectations. The previous study, as provided to directors as part of due diligence, has been received from P Shafron and will be tabled at the Board. Trowbridge advised that this report was based on their previous report to Hardies covering 1999/2000 updated to reflect inflation and latest population claims expectations, but not including the most recent actual claims experience.

This was not Cooper's only headache. The job had proven rather more than the part-time assignment he'd been sold. Michael Gill had been expected to provide insurance expertise, but gone on sabbatical, while Edwards and Jollie were busy directors. Cooper found himself dealing with his investment advisers, Towers Perrin, running a property portfolio, trying to understand medical research, and coping with unexpected disasters like the collapse of HIH, with which James Hardie & Coy had had a long relationship. When Steve Ashe came to see him for a 'general catch-up' on 26 June, Cooper was grumpy. He complained of having to find the foundation's 'real' financial position from Trowbridge, of the investment returns which he reported were 'well under 11 per cent', and of the reality of the foundation's asset position — far less than the headline figure of $293 million once the loan and 'drip fed' indemnity payments were concerned.

Ashe became a regular visitor to Cooper, reintroducing a civility to the relations between Hardie and the foundation. Cooper, in fact, got to like him: 'Steve's very personable. I think he's a pretty straight guy.' But the civility was always a veneer. Both men were using the other. Ashe was pumping Cooper for information; Cooper was trying to draw Hardie further into the foundation's problems, because he periodically had need of Hardie's indulgence. The MRCF took a heavy blow in July when its Amaba subsidiary had to absorb a seven-figure settlement with a Turner Freeman client in South Australia: a motor mechanic in his early forties whose mesothelioma was traced to a two-month exposure to Jsekarb asbestos-lined brake pads. The payment all but cleaned Amaba out, and Tony Bancroft provided a convoluted advice to the effect that there was no scope to move funds from Amaca. Ashe emailed Shafron: 'Dennis noted that like all of the advice provided by Mallesons (there have been six so far) he needs the advice of other lawyers to help him understand it.' If the worst came to the worst, Cooper added, Amaba might have to be liquidated. This attracted Shafron's attention — a liquidation after the foundation had existed six months would tax even Hardie's spinning finesse — and he emailed Cooper himself:

Dennis,

I guess you are still thinking about the Amaba situation — Steve mentioned that you now have advice from Mallesons. Obviously I don't know the exact nature of the advice … but I am a little worried that you may be seriously considering liquidation of Amaba.

The information was particularly sensitive, as Hardie was just about to make soothing noises before Justice Santow about the position of asbestos claimants, and it bothered David Robb in particular. Noel Hutley SC advised him to 'leave it and not do anything unless his Honour asks'. As it happened, Amaba's embarrassment was eventually covered by JHIL, which accelerated payments under the deed with a $1 million advance. But the MRCF's overpowering problem was not so simply set right. The information that Minty and Marshall provided during a meeting at Phillips Fox on 6 August made a mockery of their earlier advice. Their estimated value of future claims had mushroomed to $574 million. Predicted net outflows for the year to March 2002 were now $37.5 million, against the $22 million foreseen in February. Payouts for the fifteen months to 30 June 2001 had been $38 million, versus $18.36 in the twelve months to 31 March 2000. The culprit for the discrepant figures, insisted Minty, was Hardie: 'Our request for the information on the then current claims experience was rejected by James Hardie. We were told to work on the basis of our March 2000 report adjusted only for publicly available changes to claims numbers.' Cooper informed Ashe: 'The directors are all walking round with very long faces.'

Little about the foundation's response could be construed as urgent. Edwards, claimed Macdonald, was 'quite equivocal at the time'; their past good relations seem to have stayed his hand. Cooper still declined to believe that Hardie could afford for the foundation to fail: 'I wish now that I'd just belted them, metaphorically speaking. But I still retained the belief at that stage they would just not let it happen. They would not suffer the damage to their personal and corporate reputation.' He was reassured by legal advice from Bancroft's colleague Larissa Hunter that the scheme of arrangement did not prejudice the MRCF's position.

Jollie, however, was unhappy. A picky, prickly and sometimes pedantic man, he was less concerned by the risk to Hardie's reputation than to his own. He wanted some questions asked, at least, and over the next six weeks pushed for the writing of a letter to Macdonald. The scheme of arrangement brought Cooper round to his way of thinking:

> The time had come to put it on the record. No, they hadn't acknowledged the position; they hadn't been willing to discuss things. We weren't being listened to at all. How much information did they actually need? They were gearing up for this offshore move, and it just wasn't appropriate. It'd been six months. We'd learned a lot. We had new actuarial data. We understood how the original underestimate had been made. We had tried to engage them. They had chosen not to be engaged. So bugger them.

Still somewhat reluctant, Edwards rang Macdonald at Mission Viejo, to advise that, on Trowbridge's new figures, the MRCF would be insolvent within nine years. 'We are either going to be short of money in the medium term, or are you able to do something about it?' he said. Macdonald stuck to his script: 'We cannot do anything about it. In the light of all the information we had available at the time we believe we provided adequate funds to the foundation.' He suggested Edwards review the foundation's legal expenses: 'You may be spending too much.' Finally, Edwards forewarned him of a more formal approach: 'Peter, I am going to send you a letter anyway. I will outline the full detail of the problem in the letter. I will send it to you in the next few days.'

In the letter, finalised three days later, Edwards expressed 'grave personal concerns' about the foundation's funds, in particular that 'more recent information … makes it possible to revise that estimate to possible insolvency in approximately four to five years.' He reminded Macdonald:

> As you are aware, an economic life for the new entity of at least 20 years was critical to the decision of directors to assume their roles in the

foundation and its entities. The financial projections and modelling information which was provided in February supported this expectation. The public comments made announcing the establishment of the entities confirmed the confidence of the completeness of the funding giving the directors added confidence ... In addition Trowbridge have advised that the James Hardie claims data was not provided for the purposes of their report of February 2001 ... Our expectation as prospective directors was that the most up-to-date data available would be used to provide information to us in February 2001.

Edwards concluded with the observation that the foundation had been envisaged as 'a better way to manage the asbestos responsibilities', and not as 'a structural device to remove those responsibilities', and requested a meeting to discuss 'appropriate solutions'.

A meeting? The letter seems to have struggled even to find its destination. Macdonald was heading to Sydney for the shareholder meeting to approve the scheme, and would claim that mail sent to Mission Viejo was not forwarded. Unusual? 'No,' Macdonald would state, 'it's a deliberate step not to build in infrastructure and people running around providing services to managers. We all put in and do our bit and it's a way to ensure low cost and efficient operations.' This letter, whose arrival he had been advised to expect, he claimed not to have read until 'mid to late October'—conveniently after Hardie's final appearance before Justice Santow. Macdonald's evidence at the commission was widely scoffed at. It is more believable in his context than that of other CEOs. His disdain for 'infrastructure' was a byword at Hardie. But if a letter about whose alarming content he had been forewarned from a professional colleague of more than a decade concerning an entity newly established by Hardie was not a high priority, one can only wonder how long it took Macdonald to attend to matters of low priority. And such apathy was contagious. His general counsel caught it:

Michael Slattery QC: What is your best recollection on the first occasion you were shown this letter?

Shafron: I recall that Peter Macdonald came to my office and said 'I have a letter from Sir Llew.'

Slattery: Is that all he said?

Shafron: That's all I can recall.

Slattery: Well, did you read the letter?

Shafron: Yes.

Slattery: Did it cause you concern?

Shafron: Yes.

Slattery: Did it cause you to decide to make any kind of investigation about what was stated within it?

Shafron: Yes.

Slattery: What did you do?

Shafron: He and I discussed it. I believe I would have discussed it with Mr Morley also.

Not for nine weeks would Hardie formulate so much as an internal response, in the form of a memo from Shafron which sheeted the blame home to the MRCF directors for inadequate due diligence. They'd known the deal. It was no use their poor-mouthing now:

> In our meetings with prospective directors, particularly Peter Jollie and Michael Gill, Philip Morley and I said that whatever the level of funding there could be no guarantees that the level of funding would be enough over the long haul … because no one could predict the future and that history of asbestos litigation was that it usually got worse. We said that we did not want anyone to join the board of the foundation on any false premise in that regard … We prepared modelling which showed that on certain claims and earnings scenarios the fund could last forever — with a surplus — or it could last 15–20 years on more pessimistic assumptions. It was clear that the model was sensitive to the various assumptions including fund earnings rates and the rate, size and timing of claims, the JHIL directors in their decisions setting up the foundation recognised that different outcomes were possible but that on the most balanced assumptions the liabilities would be fully funded.

Shafron rejected the imputation about the missing data: 'We

were satisfied that with over 10 years of prior claims history, with the most up-to-date industry trends being used by Trowbridge, and given the inherent uncertainties in any actuarial forecast, the Trowbridge numbers were as reliable an input to the model as was likely to be available at that time.' Above all, he did not see 'that there is any basis for JHIL making additional contributions to the foundation or its subsidiaries outside of a court finding', and 'if there is an inference creeping in here that JHIL saw this as a structural device to remove responsibilities then obviously that is to be rejected in the strongest possible terms', as it did not 'accord with the facts or the law'. But, although Macdonald, Shafron and Morley all attended the next Hardie board meeting four days later, they imparted nothing of their communication with the foundation; Macdonald privately informed his chairman, MacGregor; Shafron joked that they should send a rebuttal in 'four years'.

When Macdonald finally met Edwards and Cooper at Hardie House on 21 November, the usual cordiality was missing. 'Now that you have written this letter, we have a problem and it needs to be responded to,' Macdonald said. 'I suggest that you consider with-drawing the letter.' There was even the ghost of a threat: 'It is a very strong letter. I may have to respond in equally strong terms.' His attitude was a combination of stick and carrot. He brandished the Putt case, pointing out that Hardie had gone beyond its strict legal requirements. In the next breath, according to Cooper's file note, he encouraged his guests to believe that obedient behaviour would be rewarded: 'He expected this would become a "pissing" contest which would be unproductive and not conducive to an ongoing cooperative relationship and future opportunities to explore these matters.'

For Hardie, however, 'future opportunities' were genuinely about the future, not the past. In the US, it was on the brink of a coup, swallowing its biggest fibre-cement rival: Cemplank, which ran a two-line plant in Blandon, Pennsylvania and a one-line plant in Summerville, South Carolina. Etex Group SA, reliant on expatriate Belgian managers, hadn't made a bean from the business in forty-eight quarters. But Cemplank was worth the $US75 million Hardie offered — and more. Hardie's only serious indigenous rival, Temple

Inland in Texas, had already fallen by the wayside. The sale process of Hardie's gypsum business had been frustrating. BPB had stayed away; National Gypsum and USG had for various reasons fallen out of the bidding; Centex's management had been keen, but its board had not; and France's Lafarge Coppee were interested in a joint venture from which Hardie would steadily extract its money, then could not make up their minds. But Cemplank was an outstanding deal, leaving Hardie with a near monopoly in American fibre-cement.

The same day Hardie's Cemplank acquisition was announced, as if to emphasise their divergence of fortune, the foundation's Amaca subsidiary lost a punishing case in the West Australian Supreme Court. The $1.08 million plus costs settled on David McGilvray, a 54-year-old father of three whose mesothelioma dated from days cutting asbestos sheets at Brik-Clad Industries in Dianella in the 1970s, was the biggest award in the state's history. 'Mesothelioma is a ghastly disease,' decided Justice Chris Pullin. 'It is the worst of all cancers.' It was the worst of all possible results for Amaca: McGilvray had offered to settle for $775,000 before trial. An even bigger blow was also in the offing. The Dust Diseases Tribunal, sitting in South Australia, was taking evidence from a 33-year-old nurse, Belinda Dunn, diagnosed with mesothelioma three years earlier, twelve weeks after her son's birth. Her asbestos exposure, she believed, had occurred while her father Robert had been renovating their home in Grange during the 1970s. The case attracted nationwide interest when, five weeks later, the DDT settled another seven-figure sum on her.

The settlements were demoralising to the foundation. When he next met Shafron, Cooper's responses were bleak. Cooper insisted that it was not a personal issue for him, although for some directors it had become one—an allusion to Jollie. But on occasion he sounded like a man either coming to terms with the end of a personal relationship ('If at the end of the day that's it, we'll go away. But tell us.') or pleading for its continuance ('This is not a negotiation. We have no real power. We are seeking a dialogue'; 'A brick wall has been thrown up'). News of the McGilvray and Dunn settlements, meanwhile, infuriated Macdonald, confirming his impression of a compensation system gone mad. The Cemplank deal preluded even more good news at Hardie early the following year. BPB had suddenly blown back into the bidding for Hardie's gypsum business with a cash offer of $US345 million. But at the same board meeting that was advised of this on 12 February 2002, Macdonald could not resist a gripe about 'out of control litigation'—an unusual digression seeing that asbestos was meant to be a thing of the past at Hardie:

> It is possible to see a scenario where every mesothelioma victim in Australia 'remembers' a connection, no matter how spurious, to the former James Hardie product, and launches a claim against the foundation. Given the DDT's propensity to view itself as the source of compensation for victims rather than a legal arbiter of the facts, claims could run at very high levels, well beyond the ability to be funded by the foundation.

This was more than an *en passant* remark. Intentionally or not, it formed the context for Macdonald's report—the first the Hardie board had heard—of the MRCF's problems. A letter such as the one the MRCF had sent, although non-specific as to remedy, might constitute a legal claim. But it was introduced to directors as hardening a negative view of the foundation board's evidence and confirming an existing prejudice about the crazy world of torts. 'Peter told us the foundation was whingeing,' says one director. 'And we were influenced by the fact that these people had turned out to be a bunch of ratbags. As soon as we'd put them in, they'd all upped their directors' fees and salaries, and there was an attitude of: "My God, they've turned into another Dust Diseases Tribunal. These guys are spending money like it's going out of style".' Macdonald was left to 'continue to manage it as he was doing'.

HARDIE WAS ON THE MOVE. In the first half of March 2002, its Australian head office functions shifted to Export House, a characterless, white-fronted low-rise one hundred metres from Circular Quay, and slotted into a dark, single floor of uniform, glass-fronted offices seemingly more suited to a suburban accounting firm. This entailed a final farewell to Hardie House in York Street, its Australian headquarters for more than seventy years. The plaque left did not acknowledge its former life as Asbestos House; the company's former existence as an asbestos company likewise seemed lifetimes before. Everything was in flux. Even the name of James Hardie Industries had by now been changed. The entity JHIL had taken on the shelf-company identity of ABN60 Pty Ltd. When Macdonald, Morley and Shafron finally met the MRCF board for the first time on 22 March, they chose to do so in the Qantas Chairman's Lounge at Sydney Airport at 10.30AM: Macdonald was flying in from Asia; Morley, from Mission Viejo, where he was on holidays and entertaining houseguests to whom he was heading straight back. But there seemed a certain symbolism here, too: where else but an airport for an encounter between high-flying Hardie, whose stock had soared 70 per cent from its post-9/11 lows, and the earthbound foundation, heavy with its human cargo?

Preparation for the meeting had been strained, Shafron extensively bowdlerising Cooper's draft agenda. Cooper's view of the 'meeting objective' as being 'to consider the extent to which the Foundation assets are insufficient to meet expected cost of future claims', for example, had been revised by Shafron to read 'to provide James Hardie with an overview as to progress of the Foundation and to discuss any outstanding issues'; deleted altogether was Cooper's observation that the foundation's establishment had involved 'a number of public statements from James Hardie stating that the foundation had sufficient funds to meet all anticipated future claims'. 'Shafron said I was being "too controntational",' Cooper recalls. Both sides now tried to strike cooperative poses. Edwards, who'd come from Brisbane that morning, opened the meeting by speaking of the foundation's 'learning curve' and 'where we are heading and what we face'. The use of 'we' was deliberate. He saw it as including Hardie. The foundation wanted to 'share' its problem, and 'face this together' with Hardie — the problem being, as Cooper pointed out in presenting the Trowbridge projections, that the foundation's funds might be exhausted in five or six years.

Macdonald sought a civility in the rote responses he had prepared:

Thank you for staying in touch

Appreciate honest and open dialogue

Good to have a chance to catch up after 12 months

Want to dispel any suggestion that JH has been reluctant to meet — reality is that the sale of gypsum has given us some opportunities and wanted to wait for that to be confirmed before meeting to discuss specific options …

Think we can provide some extra help as Phil will explain.

The Hardie CEO's interest in 'sharing' was distinctly limited. Notes of the meeting record snatches of his dialogue: 'James Hardie must remain independent'; 'We can't get too close, we don't need to know and can't get into the detail'. But he did offer the salve that, as the proceeds of the gypsum sale came in, there was scope for bringing forward the indemnity payments. He also tried to assuage the MRCF directors' concerns about their legal position: 'James Hardie carries responsibility for adequacy or otherwise of the original funding'. In return for such tact, it would seem, the MRCF directors did not seriously challenge Shafron's explanation that it had been Minty's preference thirteen months earlier to exclude the most recent data from Trowbridge's update.

The smiles obscured some irritations. When Cooper gave a Power Point presentation of Trowbridge's new forecasts, Macdonald, Morley and Shafron went through the motions of shielding and averting their eyes from the graphs. 'Come off it,' Cooper complained. 'This is reality'. But Macdonald was charming. 'Thank you for what you are doing,' he said at one point. And Edwards was gratified: 'I probably felt a little better after that meeting. At least it seemed that they would re-examine all the facts again. Up till then all we'd gotten from them was an obstinate no, and we didn't get optimistic, but we thought we'd gotten through to them.'

This was to be a deal at least as much in Hardie's interests as the MRCF's. Early retirement of the deed of covenant and indemnity

payments not only secured Hardie's protection from asbestos proceedings, but obviated the need for its uncomfortable partly paid
exposure to ABN60 Pty Ltd. It was, furthermore, because of tax-
consolidation legislation scheduled to apply in the next financial
year, most tax efficient to exercise the option and put ABN60 Pty
Ltd to the foundation. Even those determined to exonerate Hardie
must concede that this mechanism, springing closed like a mouse-
trap, was bound to occasion suspicion. For even if Hardie had not
had the resources in February 2001 to purchase the deed outright, it
is arguable that proceeds from the gypsum assets already earmarked
for sale would at some stage provide the funds for an early discharge;
the partly paid shares, having achieved their purpose of easing the
scheme of arrangement past the Supreme Court, could then be cancelled. Saying otherwise depends on a mechanistic view of the transactions and a literal use of language. Yes, says Morley, there was a
plan to release cash in February 2001 that would permit the deed to
be paid out, allowing the elimination of JHINV's partly paid exposure: 'But we hadn't done the deal. I know you can say that, but
where's the piece of paper? What do you expect me to say? That's the
reality if you haven't got a deal cut.' As to the cancellation, the line
adopted by Hardie and Allens was to distinguish between 'intention'
and 'contemplation'—thus Peter Cameron's exposition prefacing
this chapter.

It is not unfair to say that such distinctions loom larger in the
minds of lawyers than of laymen. Allens, furthermore, knew it.
Three days after the airport encounter, Robb briefed colleagues on
the possibilities under consideration, including the 'need to get rid
of partly paids'. Senior associate Julian Blanchard noted two questions: 'What does IM [information memorandum for the scheme of
arrangement] say?'; and 'If had this in mind last Oct, should have
disclosed?' He also took down the apparent conclusion: 'Say no
intention to transfer at time of scheme. Didn't cross anybody's mind
to do this. Reason had partly paid shares was to have greater flexibility. Had an intention to deal with it later.' The distinction
between 'intention' and 'contemplation' does not in this context seem
quite so crisp, if the use of 'say' rather than 'explain' is any indication.

When Morley caucused with Robb, Blanchard and Jenni Priestley of Allens three weeks later—a meeting also involving PwC's Keith Sheppard and Tim Sandow—Priestley's notes suggest a very sophisticated grasp of the salient issues:

Ongoing relationship with foundation
- If the Foundation's circumstances continue to worsen they will have no need to keep James Hardie happy if they have already got the money.
- They have conveyed their concerns (property, shortage of funds, US cases), which are at some level a veiled threat.
- Currently they have to be restrained at some level while they are still getting cash, but if they have the money there is a significant shift in the dynamic of the relationship which may not be beneficial to the group.

Reputation of Company
   Acting soon after the Scheme
- This is all very soon after having been to the market with a scheme booklet which did not state that reduction of the partly paid shares was part of the intentions for JHIL.
- Selling JHIL, cancelling the partly paid shares that have only just been issued etc would all be a change of direction.
- ASIC may also take an interest and choose to investigate
- Liquidation in particular, so soon after the scheme may raise too many questions (getting Michael Ball and/or Tim l'Estrange [Allens partners] to look at this as required).

Blanchard's notes contain the free-floating notation: 'Cameron —too soon.' Cameron had resigned from Allens a week before Christmas, and become managing director of the Australian operations of the investment bank Credit Suisse First Boston in April, but remained available for consultation on deals executed in his watch. It was, at least, acknowledgement that such a manoeuvre might be susceptible to alternative interpretations.

There was also a third meeting at Allens in which Blanchard was the notetaker, on 17 July, involving David Robb and Michael Ball, where the first of five concerns to be addressed about the cancellation of the partly paid shares was 'timing'. The notes were offered as evidence too late at the inquiry to be the subject of serious examination; one can really only let them speak for themselves:

Timing
JHIL's future intentions at scheme — no mention of this.
What would discovery reveal? What would witnesses say? What explanation given for change of timing? Last q we have the money now. Put option not disclosed in the scheme, b/c it is not relevant. Scheme to secure tax benefits, no change to business/shareholders ...

Then, after other debate:

Timing
Factual question. Whatever misleading conduct that may be alleged has already occurred. What did they intend by the Put at the time? Did they intend that they were worth $1.8 billion. At the time of Foundation, scheme was in contemplation. Reason for partly paids. Not willing to justify to court that creditors interests not affected.
Proposed reduction. Doesn't have to be approved by court [...]
Critical q at time of scheme, we had intention to cancel these partly paid shares? [...]
Who might object?
If had int, cancel pp shares, or t/f pursuant pursuant to the put option then misleading not to include in scheme docs.'

The conclusion was:

Say not int. to t/f at time of scheme.
Didn't cross anyone's mind to do this.
Reason had partly paids was to have greater flexibility.
Had an int. to deal with it later.

305

Again, the pervasive use of the word 'say'. Blanchard would tell David Jackson that when he wrote 'say', he meant 'assume'. Jackson noted that this was the only part of this meeting of which Blanchard seemed to have clear recall — 'an approach which I had some difficulty in accepting' — but finally agreed that this definition reflected 'the sense of the notes'. It seems remarkable, nonetheless, that there should have been any doubt about what had been Hardie's intention not even a year earlier. The agitated, repetitive nature of the notes suggests the lawyers were anxious that Hardie had misled Santow. Why? Because there was a distinct possibility it had.

AT LEAST NO DOUBT obscured Hardie's intention now. Macdonald advised his board on 14 May that he had promised Edwards a $10 million 'upside surprise' in the deed pay-out, and that the foundation chairman had responded 'very positively'. Quite why Edwards would so do, assuming he did, is hard to explain: at then-current litigation cost rates, $10 million would buy barely a quarter's respite. Cooper nursed no illusions. When Morley visited a week later to confirm that the excess would be between $10 and $15 million, Cooper sighed. 'But that's just totally inadequate,' he said. 'That's all there is,' Morley replied. Morley had hired Cooper at Hardie's, had been his boss, had persuaded him to take up his current position — and now, Cooper felt, was consigning him to oblivion. 'This will blow up, Phil,' he said. 'You have to do something about it.' No answer came. Cooper felt, for the first time, truly trapped:

> It was pitiful. I knew at that stage we were headed for huge trouble. This was very, very worrying to me. Instead of having this strong, asset-rich company next door, they were going to the Netherlands. Now they were pushing ahead with this ABN60 thing. And they weren't listening about the claims. So the writing was really on the wall then. It was clear they were going to ride this thing through, this multi-faceted plan we had not appreciated at the outset.

Cooper told the next day's board teleconference that a 'totally inadequate' offer had been received, 'disappointing in the light of the previous representations'. Edwards, in what was becoming less and less of a reassurance, 'agreed to communicate directly with Macdonald'. Cooper proposed briefing lawyers. In fact, neither approach bore fruit. Edwards' calls were ignored, and the advice to Cooper from David Fairlie of Mallesons and Bret Walker SC suggested that the MRCF had little prospect of a successful misrepresentation case against JHIL in respect of funding — funding decisions had been internal to JHIL. But just how far from adequate was Hardie's offer was underscored when the board reconvened on 11 July to hear Minty's latest estimate of the net present value of claims to 30 June 2002: $810 million. They faced receivership within three years. And here, no Chapter 11 protected them.

22

'Five cents in the dollar
and tough titties'

'This is not a conspiracy—it is the working through of an arrangement which has been in contemplation since the beginning.'
—Peter Shafron, email to Peter Macdonald and Phil Morley, 13 February 2003

THE MEDICAL RESEARCH AND COMPENSATION FOUNDATION was fast running out of options. When Sir Llew Edwards, Dennis Cooper and Peter Jollie met Macdonald, Morley and Shafron at Sydney's MLC Centre on 16 July 2002, it was to entertain a proposal that everyone round the table knew was fanciful and pointless, and yet to maintain the pretence that it was somehow effectual. Morley outlined the transfer to the foundation of ABN60, containing $91 million: the amount due under the deed of covenant and indemnity plus $15 million. Jollie said this 'sounded interesting', but that the sum represented a 'drop in the ocean'. He had another proposition. While he accepted Hardie's explanation of the discrepant Trowbridge calculations, there had been 'available data at the time of the transfer to the Foundation' which would have made a big difference: probably about $200 million worth of difference. Could Hardie not see its way clear to adding that amount? 'If James Hardie is prepared to come up to $200 million,' Jollie said, 'we will get a report from Trowbridge saying that the extra $200 million was all that James Hardie should have provided for the foundation under the circumstances. We will accept the put and speak very positively about James Hardie from that point on.'

Macdonald wasn't tempted. There would be no resiling from Hardie's position on Trowbridge's figurings. He was, furthermore, legally bound: 'James Hardie simply isn't able to provide extra funding for the foundation when it has no obligation to do so.' When Cooper said that $91 million would not much extend the trust's life, Macdonald acknowledged that the 'outcome seemed inevitable'. Fifteen months earlier, Macdonald had glowingly attested the fund's future. Now he was acknowledging its inexorable, messy failure: 'Both parties will have to deal with that situation whenever it happens and defend their own positions'.

Morley had often been struck by his chief executive's *sang froid*. Now, as Macdonald confirmed that the MRCF's sentence would not be remitted, he was struck again. It left him a little uneasy. The sort of people affected were the people from Parramatta with whom he'd grown up. 'From my background,' he says, 'I didn't feel real comfortable about it.' The CFO he was trained to be could understand the legal impediments; the Hardie man in him jibed at the excesses of the DDT, and wondered why it was being singled out to pay for the sins of the past:

> Companies do fail. Creditors do miss out … Part of my training was that these things do happen. I think the hope was that there might be some sort of no-fault scheme set up. The view in the company was: we're not responsible for world hunger, and we're not responsible for all that asbestos. We are a defendant — sure we're a big defendant — but so is the federal government, the state government, CSR, BHP. Considering it is such a big social problem, surely there should be some sort of no-fault scheme which we could all contribute to rather than this adversarial system we've got now.

All the same, he knew it would be a bigger problem than Macdonald was prepared to acknowledge. He wondered whether things looked different to his CEO because he was sitting in Orange County, where the American attitude of 'five cents in the dollar and tough titties' prevailed:

Living in the US, you do get a different perspective. It's a bigger market. Corporate failures come and go. It's part of the milieu, happens every day of the week. Corporate failure here is a much bigger story. I just suspect that that might have had an effect on Macdonald's mind. After all, he'd lived there 10 years. It just seeps into the psychology a bit … Owens-Corning went into Chapter 11 and came back with completely new debt. USG's been in Chapter 11 twice. I just wonder whether that was why he took the legalistic, 'not-another-cent, that's-what-happens' view.

Whatever the reason, it was the course to which Hardie was now committed—and which Morley, a loyal company officer, was committed to seeing through. As a director of ABN60, he parcelled out the duties preparatory to its jettison. He asked his co-director Don Salter, Hardie's tax manager, a 27-year company veteran, to 'clean up' its balance sheet, so that it showed a receivable on one side and a liability to the foundation on the other. He asked Wayne Attrill for a report on ABN60's asbestos liabilities, and he sought advice from Peter Velez of Watson Mangioni on the cancellation of the partly paid shares, whose opinion was that the manouevre was legal if the reduction did not materially prejudice ABN60's ability to pay its creditors. For a technician like Morley, this was a relatively uncomplicated transaction; for others, the matter was not so straightforward.

Most unsettled was David Robb. Despite the mutually reassuring meetings minuted by his Allens colleague Julian Blanchard, he remained anxious about the possibility that Justice Santow had been misled. He himself had advised Santow that the partly paid shares could be called 'at any time in the future and from time to time'. Now they were to be done away with. The legalities were ambiguous, and the existence of the put had, genuinely, slipped his mind. But even the extent of his own memory failure was far from clear to Robb, as he revealed when he was harried at the Special Commission of Inquiry by Jack Rush QC:

It's very difficult. I was not aware of an intention to cancel. I had simply forgotten of the existence of the put right. I relied on counsel as to what was necessary to inform the court, and if you were to ask me — I think this is answering your question — do I believe that I misled the court, the answer is no. So, so I cannot say that it just left my mind and never returned, because it has returned and it comes up every now and again and it's come up now. So, I have done my best to recall why that section was taken out and I believe that it is what I have said; that at the time it was taken out, it was not present in my mind, but it doesn't escape my attention.

Robb was so anxious that he took an unusual step. He drafted unbidden an advice exploring the implications of the company's assurances to Santow and the contents of its information memorandum — a searching and thorough document, though characteristically measured in its conclusion. Time ran away. He had to leave it to colleagues to complete. But Robb's flash of candour about this advice at the Special Commission of Inquiry wrong-footed even Michael Slattery QC:

Robb: Well, I did consider whether or not the court had been misled and in response to this question, and I drafted an opinion, drafted advice on this topic that it is indicated that the court may have been misled and also the information memorandum may have been incorrect. After I drafted that advice I went on five weeks' holiday. The matter was transferred to Richard Alcock and Michael Ball who was already acting, continuing to act. On my return, that letter had advanced and had been sent out in draft and I do not recall revisiting the question that you are putting to me in respect of the court's attitude ...

Slattery: You have made no reference to that advice in your statement in these proceedings, have you?

Robb: The draft of it, no.

Slattery: When did you take five weeks' leave and when did you prepare that statement, that advice?

Robb: I took leave on 14 October 2002 and returned towards the end of the November and prepared it just before I left.

Slattery: You were minded to prepare that advice because you appreciated, as a result of the documents that I have taken you to and subsequent documents, that a decision was being taken by JHINV to cancel the partly paid shares and you thought this called for further advice, is that right?

Robb: Yes.

Slattery: And you left the advice in draft and went away, is that what happened?

Robb: Well, I arranged for it to be forwarded to Mr Blanchard, Mr Alcock and Mr Ball.

Slattery: With a view to it being sent to the client?

Robb: Well, with whatever was the next step, I mean, ultimately, certainly.

Slattery: Well when you got back from leave, it had been sent to the client, had it not?

Robb: It had.

It had, but it bore only limited resemblance to Robb's original thinking. Several paragraphs had been added reassuring Hardie that 'the Corporations Act did not require disclosure of the potential change in control of ABN60', and the entire two-and-a-half page section concerning the information memorandum had been deleted. It was never made clear how this advice was greeted at Hardie, if it was greeted at all. Like the proverbial tree falling in the forest out of human earshot, it seems to have issued not a sound.

The MRCF was in a noisier mood and determined to be heard. At the 16 July meeting with McDonald, Morley and Shafron, Jollie had foreshadowed 'a difficult time particularly from a PR perspective'; Cooper wondered why they shouldn't take some pre-emptive action. Since its inception the foundation had relied on Tony Park, a tall, gangling, solo public relations aide formerly with IPR Shandwick, who was also dedicated to his careers as an army reservist (he did a six-month tour of duty in Afghanistan) and an aspiring novelist (his debut, *Far Horizon*, was published by Pan

Macmillan in early 2004). Park enjoyed friendly relations with the press, but as this was a dilemma that only government could solve, he contacted a suitable expert: his former boss John MacGregor, who ran a consultancy, MPR, in Mosman.

In Bob Carr's New South Wales, personal connections mattered: former SBS political correspondent MacGregor, who had first encountered the premier as a junior back bencher in the Wran administration, had them. When he met the foundation board on 28 August, he heard a range of opinions. Edwards was keen to approach Queensland's premier, Peter Beattie, with whom he had long-standing relations. Others thought that the trade unions or the plaintiff lawyers might profitably be approached. MacGregor disagreed:

> I said: 'Look fellas, you can't raise this anywhere but New South Wales. This is where James Hardie is. This is where the DDT is. This is where you are. And you can't just go and talk to people. You have to have strategy. Without one, you'll get the normal bloody battle each time asbestos comes up. It's hugely emotive. There's a lot of pain and suffering. All the normal antagonists will pour forth onto the battle field, and there'll be some blood, a few bodies and you'll get nowhere. You won't get a bureaucrat in Australia capable of engineering a solution, because asbestos is not something you build a bureaucratic career out of.'

MacGregor thought the issue would engage Carr: 'He'd told me at a meeting some time previously that he wanted to do something significant, that he was sick of business and industry coming to him for special deals. He could make a mark and do something.' It would be necessary, too, to inform him expeditiously, so that he was in possession of the facts before the information became public. The need for expedition was not lost on the foundation directors. A proposal for a new deed between ABN60 and the foundation had just arrived, superseding the original deed of covenant and indemnity; a new Trowbridge report came in soon after with further bad tidings; the advice of Malleson and Bret Walker SC was that one course was simply to resign and wind the foundation up. The only reply they had received to Edwards' letter of 24 September 2001, meanwhile, was a perfunctory note from Macdonald more than a year later, saying he did not propose 'to send the Foundation a detailed written response'.

Although Edwards was the foundation's figurehead, MacGregor thought Cooper should be its pitchman. Cooper was the quintessential nuts-and-bolts man, reserved and formal. He was not a crusader. Asbestos-related diseases were terrible, but the issue here was money. While in Perth at the start of December for the International Mesothelioma Conference, he accepted an invitation to a barbecue held by Robert Vojakovic, the tireless head of the Asbestos Diseases Society, purely because it 'would have been an affront' not to:

> I try to run this place as a business. I'm an administrator. What compassion I feel can't influence me, except where urgency is needed. I can get twenty-five meso claims in a month and all of these people are dying. I read these case reports, people of thirty-five and forty—as a human being, you can't help feeling the pain of that. Forming relationships with victims groups, though? I didn't think that was appropriate. The best way I could help them was by being as responsible as I could.

MacGregor, however, was impressed by Cooper's quiet conscientiousness and strong sense of duty. As Cooper himself recalls:

> It had progressed to the point where I couldn't get out, and there was no way I would have wanted to get out until I fixed it. It was a campaign ... One part of my brain was saying: 'I'm doing things that I never ever thought I'd do. I don't need this.' The other part said: 'You're on a mission now. You're probably the best person around to do this, so you might as well do it.' And not only were the board depending in me, but I do have that stoical, masochistic tendency ... My wife was very supportive. She was probably angrier than I was.

Cooper gave his first hint of the foundation's obstinacy when he and Edwards met Macdonald at the MRCF's suite in the MLC

Centre on 16 December. Edwards was still anxious about appearing too confrontational; Cooper made clear that he didn't like the new deed. It was broader than the deed it replaced. He wanted an assurance that no additional commitments came with it. He complained of 'the lack of response to our earlier representations of funding', and the 'requirement that individual directors make commitments with no knowledge about ABN60 and the parlous financial position of Amaca.' Then two days later, Cooper took to the hustings — the hustings, that is, of Karyn Paluzzano, who would be seeking the seat of Penrith for Labor in the election to be held in February 2003. MacGregor had organised the lunch for local supporters at the Sydney International Regatta Centre in Castlereagh, and Carr was a guest. Cooper was fascinated. Luncheon guests waited to make individual representations to the premier, like the supplicants taking it in turns to importune Don Corleone in *The Godfather*. Cooper was seated nearby, so as best to take advantage of MacGregor's introduction: 'Mr Carr, this is Dennis Cooper.'

MacGregor watched in some apprehension: 'You know when you don't have Carr because he sits back, crosses his arms and starts to look around the room.' Not today: Cooper had not long begun his petitioning when Carr produced a pad and paper, and began taking notes. Other interlocutors looked on in dismay. Who was this man causing Bob Carr to *write stuff down*? Cooper tried, nonetheless, to make no accusations: 'I kept it simple and left Carr to draw his own conclusions. I just said: "Here's how much money we've got, here's how much we need, and by the way James Hardie successfully redomiciled to the Netherlands and are looking to divest their previous head office".'

He subsequently sent data about the foundation's claims experience and actuarial projections to the Cabinet Office. MacGregor himself would later brief attorney-general Bob Debus at the ALP state conference. 'Christ, mate,' Debus replied. 'That deal must've been put together by a whole room of weasely lawyers.' When Morley and Shafron visited the MLC Centre again on 21 January to continue the slow-moving argy-bargy over the deed, Cooper advised them that the foundation's shortfall, now estimated at $500 million, posed a 'PR risk' to Hardie—and this talk was no longer idle.* Macdonald was right. The outcome was now inevitable. The foundation would fail. The parties would have to start planning for the consequences.

THE AGENDA for Hardie's board meeting in the James Cook Room of Auckland's Hyatt Regency from 9.00AM on 12 February 2003 was packed. There was a sweeping operational review planned, as well as discussion of a handsome capital return to shareholders. The attendees themselves were far flung—with phone calls patched into the teleconference from Sydney, Seoul, Washington, and Mission Viejo, San Francisco and Irvine in California—and some directors had extraneous distractions. It was while she was in Auckland that Meredith Hellicar received a call from her former colleague Peter Willcox, now chairman of the AMP Society, inviting her to join the troubled life office's board that had been raked by resignations six months earlier.

The foundation came into focus only briefly, when Shafron spoke to a paper concerning cancellation, to the effect that it made sense to pass on the monies due to MRCF in a lump sum. He cited lender nervousness that the company had encountered in renegotiating a commercial-note facility the previous year as further proof that asbestos had to be bricked off once and for all. The board, at least, heard about a letter signed by Edwards to Macdonald complaining that the sum contained in ABN60 was 'grossly inadequate' to meet the foundation's needs, and that four in five future victims of asbestos-related disease were 'unlikely to have their claims

---

* Cooper's file note read:

> To my questions—they say they cannot meet requirements for additional funds; would 'blow apart' the separation. They again 'defended' the extent of assets originally provided, despite non-use of latest data. To my assertion that this affected the support of Directors, they reiterated that they could do nothing and that they were responsible for the funding and would be required to defend it. They confirmed that they are concerned about the PR risk to them but, again, say they cannot do anything.

considered let alone met'. Macdonald would claim that this caused a 'robust debate of the issues'. But given that 'debate' is usually defined as involving an exchange of differing opinions, this seems a misnomer. There was instead a robust repetition of Hardie's advice that the company had no continuing legal obligations to the foundation, which Hellicar says was never in dispute: 'If you're a lawyer, you grow up with the corporate veil. It's not something that's in doubt. It doesn't have to be tested. We didn't invent it and we didn't hide behind it.'[†]

In hindsight, these may have been the strangest board deliberations of all. The cancellation is almost beside the point: the directors had always looked on the partly paid shares as a means of facilitating the scheme of arrangement, and such funding as they were envisaged as providing was to ABN60, not the foundation. But they were also learning that a foundation they had set up two years earlier was facing extinction—and to this, notwithstanding their feeling that it was a result of judicial largesse with defendants' money, they seem to have been largely indifferent.

The directors' failure to secure adequate funding for the foundation can be explained by error—culpable error, but error all the same—and the consequences of their actions were at the time unclear. Here, by contrast, it was inaction that held consequences, and these were blindingly obvious: the families of those stricken by disease inflicted by Hardie and its works would be the victims. If this was not clear to the board, it was a failure of management; if management did make it clear, it was a failure by the board. Hellicar is right to say that the veil is a founding principle of corporate law. But it is also a legal construct commonly at odds with commercial reality. Limited liability was, furthermore, designed to protect

---

† The relevant board minute read:

> Mr Macdonald discussed recent communications with the Medical Research and Compensation Foundation. The board discussed each of the issues associated with a transfer of ABN60 and the cancellation of partly paid shares. It instructed management to continue discussions with the Foundation and to report again upon further developments.

shareholders from the prodigalities of managers, not to insulate parent companies from misdeeds perpetrated within their subsidiaries. To crouch behind it now may have accorded with the training of the five lawyers involved: chairman Alan MacGregor, Hellicar, Shafron, Robb and Mark Shurtleff of Orange County's Gibson Dunn & Crutcher LLP. But who else would be convinced?

The MRCF was not. Corralling its board so as to exercise the put was proving more difficult than anticipated. When Macdonald and Morley visited the MLC Centre again the next day, after the announcement of Hardie's third-quarter results, they found Cooper, Edwards and Jollie as nervous and skittish as they had been calm and unguarded two years earlier. Jollie presented his old idea that Hardie pitch in another $200 million to atone for the 'missing data' in a new form, submitting that 'additional funding would have the effect of prolonging the expected life of the foundation thereby allowing more time for systematic change in the compensation regime to be implemented'. Macdonald replied that this was a 'well-considered response', if a little 'difficult'; privately, he was dismissive:

> He argues that the risk of failure of the foundation and the moral opprobrium that would be heaped on JHINV, together with the risk of legal challenges would in some way force JHINV to top up funding anyway, mean that extra payments would be in the interests of JHINV shareholders … I responded that I did not think this scenario would be persuasive to the directors of JHINV as they had very strong advice that JHINV was not legally responsible for claimants against Amaba and Amaca.

Both sides were essentially fed up with one another. The foundation directors felt they were being railroaded; the Hardie team thought they weren't being railroaded anywhere near fast enough. The foundation's attitude hardened in this time also because of a change of personnel. Michael Gill of Phillips Fox, whose role as a former Hardie adviser was still unknown to his fellow directors, resigned on grounds of a conflict of interest to do with ABN60. Edwards was also diagnosed with an illness entailing a course of radiotherapy that continued until September. At the meeting at Phillips Fox at 9.00AM on 26 February, however, they had on the speaker phone a new appointment: insurance lawyer Ian Hutchinson was in Hobart, where he had been chairing a meeting of the board of Tasmanian Railways.

The diminutive, 64-year-old Hutchinson lacked the airs that might be expected of a lawyer so senior. He made partner of Freehills in 1964, senior partner in 1992, and now worked at the firm part-time as an *eminence gris*. When Macdonald asked for a briefing on him, Robb could find no one with an unkind word: 'Ian Hutchinson is well regarded. Nice man. Urbane. Long insurance history, although not a litigator. Likely to understand issues of risk and settlement, rather than shy away from it. Sensible. As a lawyer not overly risk averse. Easier to get on with than Michael Gill. No point scoring.' Jollie, for whom Hutchinson had completed a review of corporate governance practice at the Defence Housing Authority, had approached him socially, while sparing him nothing: the foundation, Hutchinson was informed, looked like falling $500 million short of its obligations. His interest was really pricked when he read a headline on page 17 of the 3 February *Australian Financial Review* about Hardie's capital return: 'Hardie to hand back extra cash'. Now he listened to the board discussion with mounting concern:

> They had been negotiating this put option for some months. I couldn't really understand why. Hardies were saying: 'If you agree to all these extra indemnities and conditions we'll give you another $20 million.' At that stage the foundation was $500 million short, and you surely had to say: 'What's the use of another $20 million?' But they were seriously negotiating and they went within a hair's breadth of signing. Thank God Jollie stood up on that, even though up until that stage he'd been a minority of one.

There were two alternatives being offered by Hardie: negotiated transfer of the ABN60 shares to MRCF, or the put. Negotiated transfer would permit consolidation for tax purposes and avoid stamp duty; the put would deny an indemnity from JHINV on non-

asbestos liabilities as a *quid pro quo* for an indemnity on asbestos liabilities to JHINV. Hutchinson suggested neither. The foundation
should echo Nancy Reagan and just say no:

> I felt some umbrage on behalf of the foundation when I saw James
> Hardie demanding these extra indemnities from what is effectively a
> charity. One matter which particularly caught my attention in the
> Proposed Deed was that the definition of 'Intra Group Claim' ... had
> the effect of shielding JHINV from any complaint concerning the
> establishment of the foundation. I was also concerned that JHINV was
> requiring a new provision that would release the James Hardie Group
> from any claims that might have been made against it in relation to the
> establishment of the foundation. In addition, I was concerned that
> JHINV was going to such extremes to distance the James Hardie
> Group from its exposure to liabilities and wondered why it would do so
> if it had been satisfied that the amount originally provided to the
> foundation was sufficient. My opinion was that Amaca and Amaba
> simply could not give the indemnities sought when the directors knew
> of the shortfall in funds.

Hardie needed nobody's permission to cancel the partly paid
shares, which the board approved at a teleconference on 10 March
while affirming that control of ABN60 would change hands by
agreement or put option, 'being in the best interests of the company'.
As directors, Morley and Salter effected the transaction at their end
five days later. Jackson would later comment that it was hard to work
out how ABN60 was advantaged by the cancellation, and admitted 'a
lingering lack of enthusiasm for ... the commercial reality of the
transaction' — a lack of enthusiasm that might have been shared by
Justice Santow. But Hutchinson's alliance with Jollie had made the
foundation board somewhat more combative. When they met at
2.00PM on 17 March, it was to reject negotiated transfer of ABN60
and request forty-eight hours' notice of any exercise of the put.
Bancroft's fax went to Robb at 5.37PM: 'The directors have carefully
and thoroughly considered the issues and have formed the view that
the Negotiated Proposal is not in the best interests of the

Foundation Entities.' Edwards phoned Macdonald apologetically: Jollie and Hutchinson were the dissidents. Macdonald passed on to his chairman, Alan MacGregor, that 'certain directors' of the foundation would 'not accept any negotiated outcome or put'.

Nothing if not flexible, Shafron had a fall-back planned: a new foundation to manage ABN60 for the MRCF's benefit, which Macdonald told MacGregor would serve the same end and make even clearer 'the separation of JHINV from any asbestos legacy of ABN60's former subsidiaries'. The deed of covenant, indemnity and access—as it was now known—would be entered into by JHINV and the ABN60 Foundation, with the former indemnifying the latter for all non-asbestos liabilities and the latter indemnifying the former for all asbestos liabilities. The chairman was satisfied. 'I spoke with Alan and he supports proceeding with the recommended option forthwith,' Macdonald emailed Morley, Shafron, Robb and Blanchard. 'No communication with MRCF for now.' Morley had suggested Don Cameron as a director to replace him; MacGregor proposed Grant Samuel's CFO, John McPhillamy, with whom he had been on the board of Roomatech Industries, to replace Salter. MacGregor then chaired the board teleconference approving the transaction.

Both Cameron and MacPhillamy intuited that the significance of the ABN60 Foundation was where it wasn't—part of Hardie—rather than where it was—perched near the MRCF. They did not want to know about asbestos. Cameron knew of and Macphillamy was told by MacGregor of the MRCF's recent recalcitrance. But after legal advice from Corrs' Andrew Stevenson, a friend of Macphillamy's, they were comfortable with their new roles. In the nick of time, on Hardie's 31 March balance date, the new entity was ushered into legal existence at Chifley Square. Closure was so hasty that the deed of covenant, indemnity and access was phrased the wrong way round, indemnifying the ABN60 Foundation against everything *except* asbestos-related litigation—an embarrassing gaffe requiring a deed of rectification ten months later.

Robb emailed Macdonald at Mission Viejo: 'All signed—well, pretty much all. All will be signed before the close of business. A few late changes and no major concessions. Andrew Stevenson was only reasonable.' Then he added a word seldom seen in any Hardie correspondence: 'Congratulations.'

23

'I am a rock'

'Despite the very different positions that have been taken by Amaca/Amaba and JHINV in private correspondence in relation to the 2001 transaction that led to the setting up of the medical compensation and research foundation, I have always appreciated that at a personal level we have been able to communicate about these differences with a view to attempting to resolve them. I have now regrettably reached the view that it is impossible to bridge the differences between us by private negotiation any longer.'
—Medical Research and Compensation Foundation chairman Sir Llew Edwards to James Hardie's Industries' CEO Peter Macdonald, 18 September 2003

THE UPPER ECHELONS OF CORPORATE AUSTRALIA are a little like a busy first-class airport lounge, where the same people and same companies constantly brush past one another. March 2003 was a typical month. Even as Alan MacGregor participated in Hardie's private manoeuverings, the other company whose board he chaired, Burns Philip, was enjoying a very public coup in taking over its rival food giant Goodman Fielder. And the chairman of a year's standing that he displaced there? None other than his former Hardie CEO, Keith Barton.

At Hardie's old rival and Barton's old employer CSR, there was also much ado. The company was completing its own response to the growth of its American building-materials operations. Rinker Materials, acquired fifteen years earlier for $500 million and now worth $4 billion, was being spun off, after a process spanning ten months. Having accounted for less than a fifth of CSR's profits in

1995, Rinker now accounted for more than two-thirds. Its parent was left with its asbestos liabilities, although with ample cash to fund them from the company's sugar, aluminium and residential building-materials assets.

CSR had kept its own counsel where the Medical Research and Compensation Foundation was concerned, although its displeasure wasn't hard to detect. Asked in May 2001 whether his company would replicate the scheme, CSR's deputy managing director Alec Brennan commented stiffly: 'We don't see the James Hardie "solution" as something we want to pursue.' CSR's interest was more than academic, too. If the foundation ran out of money, CSR, a regular co-defendant in the Dust Diseases Tribunal, might find its contribution swelling. A couple of months later, when Macdonald and Morley met Brennan and his boss, Peter Kirby, at CSR's Chatswood head office, the exchanges were terse. Kirby complained about Hardie's decision to enter the large-diameter concrete pipe market in the US by opening a plant at Tampa. 'He was quite vociferous about that,' Morley recalls. 'But that just made me think: "We've obviously got a good business there".' Then Brennan complained that CSR was not interested in 'holding the baby' in asbestos litigation. Macdonald's file note records that Brennan 'did not put his view in a very respectful manner', and that he and Morley replied 'very forcefully'. Their answer, in fact, as later extracted from Macdonald by Michael Slattery QC, was the answer they had given Justice Santow:

> *Slattery*: He expressed concern to you that, if CSR was held jointly and severally liable with JHIL in respect of asbestos liabilities, that if JHIL was a shell, CSR may bear all of the liability; isn't that right?
>
> *Macdonald*: I think the point was actually that if CSR was held jointly and severally liable with Coy and Coy didn't have enough money, then they may not be able to recover anything from JHIL. I think that in fact was the point.
>
> *Slattery*: Anyway, you and Mr Morley rejected Mr Brennan expressing that view, didn't you?
>
> *Macdonald*: I believe we did, yes

Slattery: In doing so you explained the partly paid share situation to him, didn't you?

Macdonald: Yes I did.

Slattery: And what did you say to him?

Macdonald: Well I can't really recall exactly what I said to him.

Slattery: Well just try, Mr Macdonald. What did you say to him?

Macdonald: Well I really don't think I can reconstruct a discussion I had with him. I would expect that I said to him that there was no liability in JHIL and that, even if there was, the situation would be preserved by the partly paid shares.

Slattery: Well you made a representation to him about the continuing availability of the partly paid shares, didn't you?

Macdonald: I believe what I said—what I would have said—would have been along the lines that … Amaca was properly funded and the liabilities rested with Amaca or Coy as it was and that we didn't see any possibility for breakthrough, but if that were the case, the partly paid shares were being put in place in preserving JHIL's position. I believe that's what I said.

Slattery: You said 'the partly paid shares would be put in place and would be preserving JHIL's position'; is that right?

Macdonald: I believe I would have said 'would preserve JHIL's position', exactly.

Nothing prevented Kirby or Brennan, any more than anything had prevented Santow, from the challenge that partly paid capital can be cancelled at the stroke of a pen—but they did not issue it. Nor for months after the ABN60 foundation's emigration from Hardie would it register what had transpired. But word was starting to spread.

One afternoon in April 2003, the foundation's new director Ian Hutchinson rang Nancy Milne, a thirty-year legal veteran who had left Philips Fox to lead Clayton Utz's insurance practice in 1997. They served together on the board of Zurich Australia; she thought Hutchinson was intending to offer her another directorship. In fact, over coffee across the road from Clayton Utz's office, Hutchinson said he wanted her to become the foundation's legal adviser. The latest Malleson's advice was a counsel of defeatism, simply to put Amaca and Amaba into voluntary administration. Milne, when she had accepted the brief after clearing her conflicts, was unimpressed:

> We saw the Mallesons advice and it just seemed to me there were a lot of unanswered questions, and also that there was going to be some outrage. Mallesons had paid no attention to what had happened in the two companies prior to separation, especially in the stripping of the assets, that there may have been breaches of directors' duties, and that JHIL may have been a 'shadow director' throughout.

Milne had relatively little to go on. Records of Amaca's pre-existence as James Hardie & Coy were mostly held by Hardie. But there was no harm asking questions, and some matters had to be set right immediately. 'The public record at the moment is wrong,' Milne told Hutchinson. 'The last thing said publicly about the foundation is that it's fully funded. You can't leave that on the public record. It's incorrect.' The latest actuarial figurings from Trowbridge, which estimated the net present value of claims at 30 June at $1089 million, might have implications under accounting standard AASB1044 — the outgrowing of ED88, spelling out treatment of obligations, including contingent liabilities and moral obligations, which are not, strictly speaking, debts. 'Did the fund have to bring their actuarial calculation of future liabilities onto their balance sheet and actually count it as a liability, or in a note as a contingent liability?' Milne recalls. 'That was really hard. Because if they did provision for it, they would be insolvent.' It was especially hard, because it would be expensive to find out. When Milne sought advice from KPMG, they offered the services of HIH's liquidator Tony McGrath, and proposed to charge $200,000 for a fortnight of investigation by a specialist team. She decided to go with advice from the foundation's auditors that no provision was yet needed; it was, at least, cheaper.

Milne had more luck with a participant in the day's other prestige insolvency. The energetic Michael Slattery QC, vice-president of the Bar Association, had just earned a loyal media following while acting for the liquidator in the bankruptcy of One.Tel. Between them, they drafted an extraordinary 25-page letter of questions for the former Coy board. When proforma replies were quickly received from Phil Morley, Donald Cameron and Alan Kneeshaw, advising that Allens would take care of everything, Milne and Slattery served a demand on Allens for salient documents, with the threat in their absence to bring proceedings for pre-trial discovery enabling a decision to be made about commencing Federal Court proceedings. Just to raise the stakes a little further, the correspondence was also forwarded to New South Wales' attorney-general Bob Debus. Via a mutual friend in John McCarthy QC, meanwhile, Slattery advised Bob Carr's chief of staff, Graeme Wedderburn.

Milne—polite, genteel, even sweet—cuts an improbable figure as a crusader. Her firm, made synonymous by *Rolah McCabe v British American Tobacco Services Australia* with the Orwellian notion of a 'document retention scheme' involving preservation by shredding, made an uneven unlikelier friend of the downtrodden. Milne more than once confided to colleagues that it was 'nice to be on the right side, for once'. But she also cultivated a fierce determination: 'When you're a lawyer involved in a partisan action, you tend to make the people you're acting against into the devil incarnate, because it makes your job easier. You don't want to start thinking: "He might well be a nice guy". So I ended up thinking that they were outright shits.' And Slattery would become a scourge of Hardie, sailing into battle like a man-o-war. 'Michael is quite a passionate individual, which is what you needed,' says Milne. 'You didn't want some cold, clinical silk; you needed someone who'd care. And he did.'

THERE REMAINED A PATINA OF CIVILITY when Edwards wrote to Macdonald on 18 September—Edwards crossed out 'Dear Mr Macdonald', and replaced it with 'Dear Peter'—but everything else was a reserving of the foundation's position. When Amaca and Amaba made their statutory filings with ASIC three weeks' hence, they would, in accordance with AASB1044, include a note detailing

Trowbridge's billion-dollar contingent-liability estimate. As chairman, Edwards would 'make a public statement about the short-to-medium term financial position of Amaca and Amaba ... and its implications', which would 'of necessity expressly correct what I perceive to be inaccuracies in the public statement made by JHIL on 16 February 2001'.

Although the threat to wheel out the tumbrils of publicity had been a long time coming, it seems to have taken Hardie by surprise. In contrast to the compendious stakeholder-management documents of thirty months earlier, Hardie does not seem to have prepared any response. Macdonald made one gesture, organising a meeting on 8 October at Governor Macquarie Tower with representatives of the Cabinet Office — director-general Leigh Sanderson and legal policy manager Anthony Leane — at which he explained the circumstances of the set-up of the foundation, and explicitly conjectured that the foundation's resources had been absorbed by the prodigies of the tort system and the predations of plaintiff lawyers. The government was seen as a natural sympathiser. Statutory bodies like the State Rail Authority and Pacific Power are frequent Dust Diseases Tribunal defendants. Their lawyers, like Hardie's, deplore such phenomena as 'forum shopping' — almost a third of plaintiffs in the Dust Diseases Tribunal come from inter-state, largely because of its reputation for generosity. A statutory scheme for the processing of asbestos-related diseases damages mooted a year earlier by the Insurance Council of Australia was also known to have enjoyed influential support.

Macdonald did most the talking, and left bullish, with the feeling that asbestos might be a new frontier for tort reform ('Reform is definitely on the agenda and that there is a belief that this matter is bigger than JH') if Hardie wasn't too boisterous ('The insurance industry were most unhelpful in the publicity surrounding their submissions and ... forced the government to delay any response to reform issues'). But it was a conversation for which the right time had passed. Macdonald's response to Edwards' letter displayed a similar obliviousness to the potentialities of public opinion, professing merely incredulity about the growing quantum of liabilities and misplaced faith in the cause of a change to the compensation regime:

> Obviously, public attacks on James Hardie would ... be counterproductive for the foundation. This is not only because of the unnecessary expense involved, but also because James Hardie would have no choice but to vigorously defend itself using all legitimate means available to it. The drain on the foundation's assets arising from such a course of action could be significant and not at all in the best interests of claimants. Further, focusing efforts on attacking James Hardie may only distract stakeholders, including the government, from addressing the real issue: the need for reform.

When Macdonald took Morley to meet Edwards, Hutchinson and Cooper at the Westin Hotel early the following morning, he made a last-ditch effort at charm and persuasion. The Hardie board was 'devastated and extremely upset at the underfunding'. The foundation was doing a 'fantastic job'. Although he thought it would be best to adopt the catchcry of 'reform', he quite understood 'the need to test the propriety of the circumstances relating to the setting up of the foundation'. He thought Hardie's legal position 'impregnable', but acknowledged 'the moral question is one where there may be a disagreement with government and probably yourselves'. Macdonald urged the foundation to imagine their funding dilemma as akin to a big asbestos case: when one saw no worthwhile alternative to fighting a case and bearing costs, one settled. 'Please do not misunderstand me,' he stressed. 'We have nothing but admiration for the foundation and its decision making but we simply make the point you should think of the situation in those terms'. But when Cooper retorted that it was Hardie that should be considering terms such as 'settlement', given 'the circumstances which have been documented', Macdonald made clear that his definition of compromise was as a synonym for capitulation: 'Let me be totally clear on this. The company does not contemplate making any offer whatsoever and no settlement is possible.' Hutchinson, for whom this was a first meeting with Macdonald, found little to like about him.

Hardie and the foundation it had begotten barely two-and-a-half years earlier retreated to their bunkers, their scope for formal contact finally exhausted. Although Edwards would continue to call Macdonald from time to time in future—to his fellow directors' annoyance—their exchanges would be largely in public and political forums. It was a strategy pregnant with risk for the foundation directors, for they were willingly drawing attention to their own deliberations over joining the foundation board in February 2001, and the presence of politicians in any field usually preludes a rout for common sense. The strategy of going public was a measure not so much of conviction as desperation: a bad option was better than the various worse alternatives. The foundation board prepared carefully, taking three weeks over the text of its announcement, composed mainly by Cooper and John MacGregor, and overseen by Milne. Rather than a frontal assault on Hardie, it was couched as a commentary on the latest Trowbridge figures:

> Fears have been raised about the level of funding that will be available to provide compensation for future victims of asbestos diseases in Australia, with new figures showing a sharp increase over the past few years in the number of compensation cases and settlement amounts … The chairman of the Medical Research and Compensation Foundation, Sir Llew Edwards, said today new research conducted for the foundation by Trowbridge estimates that up to 14,000 Australians could die of mesothelioma over the next 50 years and the compensation bill reach $6 billion.

One had to read further down the news release to find its crux:

> Sir Llew said that when the foundation was established, the directors were informed by James Hardie that the $293 million in funding provided would be sufficient to meet all expected future asbestos claims by people who had been exposed to asbestos disease as a result of products manufactured and sold by James Hardie. However, as outlined in the financial reports for Amaca for the year ended 30 June 2003, the most recent actuarial analysis estimates that the compensation bill for

the organisation could reach $1 billion in addition to those funds already paid out to claimants since the foundation was formed and that existing funding could be exhausted within five years ...

Sir Llew said the foundation had approached James Hardie seeking additional funding to meet the expected liabilities. However the foundation had been told that no additional monies were available. Sir Llew said the foundation was investigating a range of legal options involving James Hardie or related entities to ensure that future victims of asbestos related disease caused by exposure to James Hardie asbestos-containing products can receive compensation.

Hardie responded immediately, and assertively, Macdonald denouncing Trowbridge's figures as 'a dramatic departure from the well-established pattern of claims over the ten years preceding its establishment' (which indeed it was), and complaining that it was 'difficult if not impossible for us to understand how things could have changed so dramatically in just under three years' (not that Hardie had tried). His first public fluttering of the 'corporate veil' was unconvincing. 'There can be no legal or other legitimate basis on which shareholders' funds could be used to provide additional funds to the foundation, and the duties of the company's directors would preclude them from doing so,' Macdonald claimed. 'This is due to a decision in 1937 to set up James Hardie Industries as a holding company that over the years held interests in hundreds of different businesses, ranging from asbestos to tropical fish importation.'

The law might see some sort of equivalence between the subsidiary that contained Pets International and the subsidiary that had operated what was Hardie's core business for seven decades; the public never would, and the press wasn't about to help. 'Hardie is still in a state of denial,' decreed *The Australian*. 'James Hardie says it is surprised there's not enough money to pay asbestos claims,' reported the *Australian Financial Review*. 'Others say "we told you so".' The Labor Council of NSW was quickly to the barricades, voting to support a campaign led by the Australian Manufacturing Workers' Union state secretary Paul Bastian for an inquiry.

Bastian, a tough-talking, crew-cut figure who wears his AMWU polo shirt like a uniform, was radicalised on the asbestos issue by the mesothelioma death of his national president, Brian Fraser, in July 1996. 'He was a very big man,' says Bastian, 'who died a very small man.' He is also an experienced public campaigner, and successfully sought out 2GB's Alan Jones: 'Jones talks to you and you have to work to get a word in. You just say 'yes" or "no". But in terms of what he did for the campaign, he was fantastic. He really went in.' At one stage the radio thunderer took to his regular Nine Network soap box and read out—without, of course, any attribution—a screed prepared by AMWU research officer Jan Primrose. 'It was word for word what Jan had written,' recalls Bastian. 'Fuckin' word for word! It was dynamite! Jan actually had his home phone number. He wanted everything we could give him.'

In the gallery before which the public campaign was played out, there was one significant absentee: Macdonald. And from Mission Viejo, where the chief executive was based with Shafron and Morley, the world looked rather different. It became an article of faith at Export House that their senior executive on the far side of the ocean simply did not grasp how badly the company was being pounded on a daily basis in the press. Shafron is recalled laughing down the phone: 'What the fuck is going on with the journos down there?' 'What do you mean?' he was informed. 'This is *good*.'

Macdonald, of course, was nothing if not unflappable anyway. Investor response, as ever to any hint of uncertainty, was to mark Hardie stock down, in this case by 12 per cent. In a 90-minute teleconference with broking analysts, Macdonald beckoned the tide back. Standing in front of overhead projections which read 'Establishment was fair, legitimate and transparent', 'Expert advice', 'Best information available', 'Interests of claimants and shareholders balanced', he gave a calm and cogent *ex tempore* defence of Hardie's position: 'There was no parent company liability before and after the establishment of the foundation, there is no basis for legal action by the foundation against the former parent or any related entity. We are very confident of our position. There is no basis for successful legal action against James Hardie.' Yet the very qualities that made

Macdonald such a market favourite — his fierce rationality, his supreme confidence, his irrepressible optimism — were also beginning to work against him. As one executive says: 'You'd go to a meeting with Peter and come away thinking: "Gee, I'm not sure about this. This could be a problem. That could be a problem". And he'd say to you: "Yep, that's what we're doing." If it worked logically and legally, Peter never expected anything to go wrong.'

MacGregor was disconcerted, and early in November tried a chairman-to-chairman approach, ringing Edwards from his farm at Port Fairy to stress that 'adequate funds were made available to the foundation at the time', and enjoining him not to be 'hasty'. But Edwards was so insistent on the foundation's obligation to 'consider the taking of every step that we can to rectify this situation' that MacGregor gave up: 'I don't think we should continue this conversation'. And otherwise, because there was no Hardie board meeting at Hardie between November 2003 and February 2004, Macdonald was left with the carriage of the matter — something that, in hindsight, Meredith Hellicar feels was probably a mistake:

> Peter Macdonald is somebody who always thought it would work out. I saw a whole lot more of him in the last few months he was here, and it was only then, I think, that I realised that you could go to a meeting with Peter, and that you would come out of the meeting thinking that something had a 50 per cent chance of succeeding, and Peter would think there was a 90 per cent chance of succeeding. He's just that sort of person. He will say: 'This can be dealt with. This can be coped with. We can get through this.' I suppose I hadn't quite realised how much that was the case.

The result was that Hardie simply prepared to brazen it out. 'James Hardie did a lot of quite stupid things along the way,' believes John MacGregor. 'And this was one of them. Someone from Hardies told me just before Christmas that nothing much would come of it, that there might be a minor blip in the share price, and that they were untouchable. It reminded me of that Simon and Garfunkel song: "I am a rock/I am an island/I've built walls/A fortress deep and mighty than none may penetrate".' The siege laid to that fortress by Bastian was now reinforced by Milne. Only an inquiry could penetrate, she thought, to the heart of the matter.

The inquiry later became such a fait accompli that it is hard to believe its probable efficacy was ever disputed. In fact, it was — even at the foundation. Sir Llew Edwards, for instance, was resistant to the idea. He recalled, from his political career, the Fitzgerald inquiry.

> It was meant to be a short snappy inquiry that would last a few weeks and cost $1 million, and it became something that lasted two years and cost $30 million. And where it had been intended to find out about a few things going wrong, it ended up that five or six ministers lost their jobs. Now, of course, I fully endorse what Fitzgerald found. But it is also true that one never knows where one will end up once an inquiry has begun.

Michael Gill, meanwhile, was dismissive — a response that Milne, a former colleague at Philips Fox, found familiar:

> We've had an interesting relationship over the years. I'd gone from being a partner to a rival, and quite a personal rival, and Michael has a very large ego and is always the font of all knowledge. When first I saw Michael to take a statement from him he said: 'Thank you very much for taking on the foundation. Of course, you won't find anything. There's nowhere to go'. Then I had another conversation with him, in late 2003, he said: 'What's happening?' I said: 'Well we're hoping there'll be a government inquiry'. He said: 'Oh Nancy, I *know* there won't be a government inquiry'. I said: 'Of course, Michael, whatever you say'.

Cooper, who tended to defer to his chairman, hovered uneasily. Jollie and Hutchinson agreed with Milne. Six days before Christmas, Milne took Cooper and MacGregor to Governor Macquarie Tower to meet Leigh Sanderson and Anthony Leane from the Cabinet Office. They were joined by Simon Miller, from the Premier's Department, and Alistair McConnachie, adviser to attorney-general Bob Debus. The foundation representatives were told that, while premier Carr had an open mind, Cabinet Office secretary Roger Wilkins preferred the option of a parliamentary inquiry by both houses, which could compel witness, but not the production of documentation. Sanderson confided that there was concern about legal costs. Milne was disheartened. The probability was that a parliamentary inquiry would become politicised. The tale, she thought, lay in the documents, and only a special commission of inquiry with suitable powers would do.

Just then, Michael Slattery was ushered in, late because of another appointment, and launched into a recitation of the reasons why only a special commission would suffice. Sanderson was impressed. She would see what she could do. Slattery later reinforced the message when he ran into Debus at a function, and made the case to Steve Gageler SC, from whom the Cabinet Office sought independent advice. A sign that the tide was turning was that Hardie's own efforts to make representations to the government began to meet rebuffs; in the *Realpolitik* of New South Wales, too, few causes have been harmed by the support of Alan Jones, the latterday J. J. Honsecker. When Bob Carr rose in the Legislative Assembly on 25 February in response to a question without notice about the Medical Research and Compensation Foundation from Kristina Keneally, his preamble was general, concerning governor David Martin and former deputy premier Jack Ferguson, victims of mesothelioma in October 1990 and February 2002 respectively. His conclusion, however, was emphatic:

> The Government takes this matter very seriously and that is why, to determine the truth of the matter, we will ask Her Excellency the Governor to establish a special commission of inquiry to resolve these allegations and to report back by 30 June this year. The main purpose of inquiry will be to gather sufficient information to properly assess the circumstances surrounding the establishment of the foundation. We want to find out what James Hardie knew back in 2001 about the extent of its liabilities and whether the firm underestimated the amount of money it set aside for dust disease claims. The special commission of

inquiry will provide all parties with an opportunity to present their cases and clarify whether the foundation's claims are valid. I look forward to being able to offer sick and dying workers and their families some clear answers.

'We welcome the commission and the opportunity it provides to clear up misconceptions and explore the broader issue of asbestos liability,' Macdonald responded, 'but it in no way alters the company's well established position on this issue.' All the same, he was clearly nonplussed about the difference in view from Mission Viejo and Macquarie Tower: 'We cannot speculate why the Government has decided to pursue an inquiry rather than respond to the repeated offers by James Hardie to provide detailed information.' It was the sort of remark that could only have been made from the vantage of Orange County.

24

'What about the word "dishonest" don't you understand, Mr Macdonald?'

'Mr Commissioner, over a couple of days in the middle of February 2001, groups of business people and professionals met at the head office of James Hardie Industries in York St, Sydney, and at the offices of Allens Arthur Robinson. They participated in a series of meetings and discussions which lasted on one occasion well into the night, indeed until about 5 o'clock the next morning.

'What was achieved in that flurry of nocturnal activity was the subject of a press release issued by James Hardie Industries on 16 February 2001. Under the byline "James Hardie Resolves its Asbestos Liability Favourably for Claimants and Shareholders", the company announced that it had established what it called a fully funded foundation to compensate sufferers of asbestos related diseases with claims against two former James Hardie subsidiaries and to fund as well medical research into those diseases. Mr Peter Macdonald, the chief executive officer of James, was quoted as saying that "James Hardie was satisfied that the foundation has sufficient funds to meet anticipated future claims".'

—John Sheahan SC, 5 April 2004, counsel assisting Special Commission of Inquiry into the Medical Research and Compensation Foundation established by the James Hardie Group

WITH THESE WORDS IN A CONFERENCE ROOM on the eighth floor of John Maddison Tower in Sydney's Goulburn Street began an inquiry for which in Australian commercial history there are few precedents. John Sheahan SC, twenty years at the bar and seven years a senior counsel, stood at an overcrowded bar table at which reposed a rustle of silks, including Michael Slattery QC appearing for the Medical Research and Compensation Foundation; Tony Meagher SC appearing for James Hardie; Alan Robertson SC representing Trowbridge; and Alison Stenmark SC representing three electricity-generating companies. Much of the rest of the room was taken up by their solicitors and articled clerks, often indistinguishable, and legal trolleys with their growing bulk of lever arch folders, which over coming weeks would multiply like mushrooms after rain.

It was a curious, muted theatre, as Dennis Cooper led the MRCF directors into the stand. Although the media was its usual sharp-elbowed presence, ears pricked for the next day's headline, testimony was not only painstakingly adduced but barely audible: this might be a public inquiry, but the man to impress was respected Sydney constitutional lawyer David Jackson QC—a burly, unsmiling figure, appointed to his role by Bob Carr seven weeks earlier. The rhetoric still wafted through the room from outside. Peter Macdonald, still unconvinced there was a problem, or that if there was it was none of Hardie's doing, turned an ABC interviewer's questions back on them: 'If there is a problem, what has driven the threefold increase in costs in just three years? What could it be? Could it be legal costs? Other system costs? Altered claim behaviour? Remember, the causes for these diseases lie thirty or more years ago. It's hard to see how things could have changed so dramatically in just three years.' When the ABC found him, Edwards could think of only one option: 'Let him take over the management, and we would be delighted to hand it over to him.'

Edwards, however, cut an unimpressive figure in the stand, still puzzled as to how it had all gone wrong. Describing Macdonald and MacGregor, he spoke of a 'strong personal regard for their personal integrity' and 'a profound confidence in each'. 'I believed that my regard for them was reciprocated,' he said. 'I did not believe that they would place me in a position where I would be required to guide a foundation with a shortage of funds in the short to medium term.'

He looked especially uneasy when harried by Jack Rush QC, who wondered why Edwards had been in such a hurry to take the MRCF off Hardie's hands:

> *Rush*: It was to suit JHIL interests that this matter was pushed through, wasn't it?
>
> *Edwards*: Well, I think the history, it's fairly easy to make those suggestions, but at that time, I did not have any doubt that I was being provided with adequate information to me, to make a decision, and obviously my fellow directors felt the same.
>
> *Jackson*: Try again, Mr Rush, I think.
>
> *Rush*: It was to suit JHIL's interests that this matter was pushed through by 16 February, wasn't it?
>
> *Edwards*: Well you'll have to ask them. I cannot give you an answer what was their intention, or their reasons on that regard, but I can assure you that in the consideration of these matters –
>
> *Rush*: Sir Llew I think you've answered the question.
>
> *Edwards*: Well you've asked me the question again.

Such exchanges would become agonisingly familiar.

JACK RUSH'S PRESENCE disconcerted everyone a little, and Hardie a lot. Here was the busiest silk in the Dust Diseases Tribunal augmented as instructing solicitors by Turner Freeman's Gerry Gardiman and Tanya Segelov and Slater & Gordon's Peter Gordon and Ken Fowlie. Their client was a new player in the drama, the Australian Council of Trade Unions, which had sought a seat at the table for a group of unions and victims' groups gathered together by its assistant secretary Richard Marles—a former colleague of Gordon's, who had worked with him during the celebrated Ok Tedi action against BHP. The instruction had come straight from Marles' boss, the ACTU's secretary, Greg Combet.*

---

* The union group assembled by the ACTU included the Labor Council of NSW, the Australian Services Union of NSW, the Australian Manufacturing

For Combet, Hardie was an old nemesis. His first industrial relations job had been at the Workers' Health Centre in John Street,
Liddicombe, formed by fifteen left-wing unions in New South
Wales and a group of old Communist Party of Australia members,
where Dr Ben Bartlett of the Doctors' Reform Society had run a
medical clinic often patronised by workers from Camellia. Combet
began work as a researcher, ended up its director, and felt frustration
throughout at the apathy of both companies and regulators: 'You
were supposed to be able to breath a certain number per cubic
metres safely. What a load of fucking bullshit. We were pointing out
that there was no safe level. So what was the point of monitoring?
Employers didn't want to make their workplaces safe. Governments
didn't want to do anything.' The animosity he felt for Hardie was
profound and abiding. 'They picked on the wrong guy,' he says. 'I
knew them.'

Combet is not, in general, an heir to the atavistic hatreds of the
left. Television makes him look awkward, earnest and unyielding; in
the flesh, he is warmer and more personable. His father was a wine-
maker from Rooty Hill; when Combet swears, it sounds like a tic he
has picked up rather than something in his nature. In the union
movement, he is a figure of transition. As the first research officer of
the Waterside Workers' Federation, his mentor was Tas Bull, its leg-
endary communist secretary. A nimble-minded protégé, Combet led
the negotiations consolidating twenty-one separate awards into a
single industry award to make possible its merger with the Seamen's
Union, forming the Maritime Union of Australia.

Combet had only been in his job a year when the MRCF had
been spun off. Nonetheless, he had immediately sensed something

Workers Union, the Maritime Union of Australia, the Communications,
Electrical, Electronic, Energy Information, Postal Plumbing & Allied Services
Union of Australia, the Construction, Forestry, Mining & Energy Union of
Australia, the Rail Tram & Bus Union of Australia. They were joined by a
coalition of support groups: the Asbestos Diseases Foundation of Australia, the
Asbestos Diseases Society of Australia Inc, the Asbestos Victims Association
of South Australia, Queensland Asbestos Related Disease Support Society,

amiss. One of the partners of the public relations consultancy Hawker Britton, David Britton, had rung to run the idea past him: 'We've been approached to do this job for Hardies and I think it stinks. What do you think?' Combet sneered: 'It's Hardie's. You can be sure it's bullshit. $290 million in a trust? Why would they do it? Because they think it will fully fund the compensation liability they have? Or are they doing it for window dressing?' Britton had stood back from the deal. So had Combet. 'It was a matter of waiting for a crisis.'

Rush's other client, the asbestos victims' groups, were personified at the commission by a figure with a similar distrust of Hardie, and still better reason for it. Bernie Banton is one of a band of brothers, sons of a Pentecostal pastor, who worked at Hardie-BI before its June 1974 closure. Albert and Bruce suffer respiratory complaints; his older brother Ted, a shift foreman, was killed by mesothelioma. Bernie himself had been diagnosed with asbestosis after a 1998 holiday in the Snowy Mountains with his wife Karen on which he'd found himself uncharacteristically short of breath. At a party to welcome in the new year, he had then run across the widow and son of his former work colleague Col Marshall, who recommended he see a respiratory specialist.

Banton has worked hard his entire life, and at anything: he even had a decade as a funeral director. The intimation of mortality he had from the visiting specialist at the Dust Diseases Board, which granted him a small fortnightly pension, is something Banton has never forgotten: 'Don't let those X-rays out of your hands. They're worth a lot of money to you.' A certain cynicism helped him get through the exchange of unpleasantries in the DDT in the middle of the following year, where he accepted a settlement. The sight of another former colleague undergoing three days of cross-examination a little later filled Banton with a bitter fury: 'They made him look like such a dope. The judge could see he was telling the truth, but it was just these smartarse lawyers, especially the bloke from Hardies. I would have thumped him in the gob.'

Banton's life since had been a standard case study of dwindling capabilities and contracting horizons. He and Karen had to sell their home because he could no longer ascend the stairs. Then, performing a breathing exercise while recovering from a lung biopsy in 2002, he burst a figure-eight stitch in his lung and contracted surgical emphysema: a CAT scan showed oxygen leaking from his lungs, which caused his body to bulge, as though filled with bubble wrap, and his throat to swell, until he was unable to swallow. The condition took two months to subside, and he had an operation to prevent his lung collapsing. But nothing was going to keep him from this inquiry. 'No one asked me to go,' he says. 'But I thought someone had to represent the victims. I didn't want commissioner Jackson to just focus on the numbers, like I knew the lawyers would. I wanted him to see me there.' Jackson, in fact, offered Banton a personal set of earphones, so as better to hear proceedings, and Banton would attend forty of the commission's 54 sitting days, usually with Ella Sweeney of the Asbestos Diseases Foundation, and Eileen Day, whose husband Reginald had died of mesothelioma three years earlier. Brief moments of quiet at the commission made audible the hiss of Banton's portable respirator.

ANOTHER MAN WAS ALSO AILING that month: Hardie's chairman, Alan MacGregor. Chest X-rays taken to assess his convalescence from a car accident had revealed a recurrence of the lymphoma that had stalked him for the preceding decade, and the prognosis was bleak. As treatment would confine him to Adelaide, his effectiveness as Hardie chairman would be circumscribed. He did not attend Hardie's April board meeting held in California; indeed, though it was not known at the time, he had already attended his last. There were other changes in the offing at Hardie, too. Greg Baxter had parlayed his selection as Australia's best investor relations officer, as assessed by *Investor Relations* magazine, into an equivalent role at News Corporation—Macdonald, irked, contested his exit. And Phil Morley was due to retire on 30 May. Peter Shafron had been anointed his successor as chief financial officer, although he now seemed to spend much of his time rooting around his office looking for documents.

For the first month, in fact, the inquiry was a little like one of those Cold War world chess championships where most of action took place away from the board. The ACTU legal team was, at least to begin with, an uneasy coalition. Relations between Gordon and Gardiman have, over the years, been respectful but wary. 'It wasn't easy getting everyone together,' says Fowlie. 'We are pretty strong competitors. There was a question of putting the greater good before everything else.' Both understood the importance of a united front; both, too, began to perceive the conduct of Allens as lying at the heart of matters. Gordon recalls: 'After the first week we said to Counsel Assisting: "You ought to demand that these partners give evidence. We need to hear from Robb, and from Cameron". He had a think and he came back to us after another week and said: "Give us something in writing." So we produced a three-page document outlining what we saw as the issues, which he held onto for a few days, then we heard he was subpoenaing them.'

Relations between the foundation and *its* lawyers, meanwhile, were also unusual. Clayton Utz had a strange experience, for instance, when Nancy Milne's colleague Jocelyn Kellerman went to collect a statement from former director Michael Gill. Gill was unusual edgy. 'There's something really strange going on here,' thought Kellerman. 'He won't look at me. He's shifting all round the place.' When she reported this back, her colleagues began theorising. Nancy Milne said finally: 'I'll bet he's given Hardie's advice'. So he had: it would soon emerge that, unbeknownst to his fellow directors, Gill had been an adviser to Hardie before the creation of the foundation.

Clayton Utz had its own problems with Allens, which was deluging it with documentation. Senior associate Richard Shankland, junior counsel Lucy McCallum, and young barristers Tiffany Wong and Paul Walker were poring over it late into the evening and as cheaply as possible. 'We had to try to keep it tight so you weren't spending too much money,' recalls Nancy Milne. 'You couldn't do the Rolls-Royce job which you did for a big corporate. You had to keep it tight. This was claimants' money.' But when the Hardie witnesses did begin appearing, Milne got the impression that Allens was trying to deal them the death of a thousand paper cuts:

> I think we were snowed with lots of irrelevant stuff, in which the really, really critical stuff was buried, and you'd get it all the night before their witness was to appear in the box. We'd be loaded down with statements, and there'd be supplementary statements at the last minute. The fellow who was dealing with it at Allens, Michael Ball, is a very seasoned litigator, very clever, a top-notch lawyer, and a very cold fish, not a lot of emotion. And he played a very tough game that became at times quite acrimonious. We'd be saying: 'This is just unfair. We need this material. Your witness is up tomorrow and we've got to cross examine him'. And you'd just be stonewalled. All the time. Ball had this offsider called Stuart Lawrence, who was very very difficult.

Once sworn in, of course, Hardie witnesses could not be protected, even by documentation. Shafron, so intelligent and capable, became in the face of examination obsessively literal, often pedantic, sometimes wilfully obtuse. On one occasion, for example, he was asked by commissioner Jackson when Hardie had decided that no further money was necessary:

> *Jackson*: All I was trying to find out was when that position was determined to be the position of James Hardie. And when was that decision taken?
> *Shafron*: Are you asking me a question?
> *Jackson*: Yes I am.
> *Shafron*: I couldn't answer that specifically.
> *Jackson*: Mr Shafron, please, you must have some idea when that took place. You don't live in a world of keeping the blinkers over the eyes for everything. You must have some idea?
> *Shafron*: I'm trying to answer from recollection.
> *Jackson*: Well, do your best then, and don't respond in a way that makes it apparent you're not trying very hard.

The barristers seemed to take a relatively gentle line with MacGregor, when the commission travelled to Adelaide because he was too unwell to leave it. There was even a shaft of mordant wit from Jackson, when Rush showed him the 2000 Trowbridge report:

> *MacGregor*: Yes that's the one I referred to as the omnibus study.
> *Rush*: The omnibus study.
> *Jackson*: Ominous?
> *MacGregor*: Omnibus.
> *Jackson*: I'm sorry, I misunderstood what you said there. I though you said 'ominous'. Perhaps it doesn't matter very much, in the circumstances.

Macdonald, all the while, was patiently awaiting his turn. At a video conference with analysts on 12 May discussing another excellent result, a 50 per cent operating profit improvement, he was in his element. Although he had to disappoint investors with a deferral of their expected capital return, he treated his audience to an exposition on siding. 'There are some great product shots of products in use in the United States. On the top right corner there is a good shot of siding and Hardie shingle. And in the bottom right-hand corner is a shot of our easy grid Hardie backer, the product which is growing very strongly and has a very strong differentiated position.' Of the inquiry, he said merely that the company was 'cooperating fully', and that 'literally hundreds of folders of material' had been surrendered to it. He did not say a great deal more when he finally took the stand. So eloquent where siding and shingle were concerned, he was oyster-like on matters of corporate deliberation. If he didn't have 'direct recollection', he would confirm nothing. The trouble was, he had very few — which led to endless exchanges of this kind:

> *Slattery*: Mr Shafron reported to you at this time, did he not, that he regarded the Trowbridge work as very uncertain?
> *Macdonald*: He says that in this memo, yes.
> *Slattery*: He said it to you at the time, didn't he?
> *Macdonald*: He may have, I can't confirm that from this draft.
> *Slattery*: Well do you have an actual recollection of whether he communicated that idea to you at that time?

Macdonald: I don't have a direct recollection.

Slattery: Didn't he say to you that the June 2000 Trowbridge report was based on imperfect epidemiological models and uncertain predictions of future claims numbers?

Macdonald: I can't confirm whether I had a discussion with Mr Shafron at that time.

'With Macdonald going into this commission, it was a contest,' says a Hardie adviser. 'He was saying to himself: "This guy will try and make me look stupid. I've got to be ready, have read everything, have an answer to every question." The reality is that three years after the event, you aren't going to remember everything. It's hard to be definitive, and no one expects otherwise. But he would have studied like mad—which was exactly the wrong thing to do.' Macdonald's insistence on semantic exactitude managed simply to make him look evasive, even mischievous:

Slattery: You had banned communications with Mr Cooper at that stage, hadn't you?

Macdonald: I don't believe I ever banned communications with Mr Cooper.

Slattery: Well go to page 262. On 18 March you sent an email to Mr Shafron, in which you said to him and copied it to Mr Morley, 'No communication with the MRCF for now'; do you see that?

Macdonald: I see that.

Slattery: Now between 18 March and 31 March when this transaction, that is for the separation of ABN60, was closed, your command to Mr Morley and Mr Shafron was not to talk to the MRCF, wasn't it?

Macdonald: That's apparent from this communication.

Slattery: And you expected it to be obeyed, didn't you?

Macdonald: Well I believed that they would not communicate, that's correct.

Perhaps the strangest etymological exchange involved the memo in which Greg Baxter proposed his fib about the webcast of the company's 16 February profit announcement:

Sheahan: You were expecting him—you understood that he was proposing just a little white lie on the website, correct?

Macdonald: He's saying he could explain it, yes, on a basis of technical difficulty, I agree.

Sheahan: Dishonestly?

Macdonald: Well it's a proposal, it hasn't actually been carried out yet, in fact I need to —

Sheahan: The proposal is dishonest.

Macdonald: If Mr Baxter used that explanation then it would be not correct.

Sheahan: It would be dishonest.

Macdonald: If he used it, it would not be correct.

Sheahan: Now just what about the word 'dishonest' don't you understand Mr Macdonald?

Macdonald: I believe it would be an incorrect statement if he made it, and he didn't have technical difficulties.

Sheahan: It would be incorrect and made with knowledge of its falsity, would that be fair?

Macdonald: If he were to make that statement, that's correct.

Sheahan: And to make an incorrect statement with knowledge of its falsity would be dishonest, would it not?

Macdonald: If that's the definition of dishonesty then that would be the case.

Sheahan: Does it work for you?

Macdonald: Well you're the linguistics expert—

'People hated him,' says Hellicar. 'They absolutely hated him.' The public attention, certainly, was unlike anything Macdonald had ever had to deal with. He took to vanishing out a side door during breaks in proceedings, and on one occasion down a fire escape. False and malicious rumours circulated, such as that he was the member of an obscure evangelical sect and had taken the oath of affirmation because swearing on the Bible would have prevented him lying. Media intrusion continued even after he returned to the US. John MacGregor recalls:

I was in the inquiry one day and there was a row of Hardie lawyers and spin doctors under whom a file had spilled open. I idly glanced down and saw that a document was signed Peter Macdonald, with the advice: 'If you need to get in contact with me, this is my home number in California'. I thought: 'I'll file that'. A couple of days later, Peter Gosnell [from Sydney's *Daily Telegraph*] came up and said: 'You haven't a number for Macdonald, do you?' I said: 'Funny you should ask that. I didn't give this to you, but try it.'

The result was some embarrassing tabloid merriment at Macdonald's expense, illustrated by an aerial shot of Macdonald's mansion in the Ocean Ranch community of Laguna Niguel, which reported him 'cooling off in the spa':

> With a rare afternoon off from the nearby US headquarters of the once-proudly Australian conglomerate, Macdonald was at first unavailable — 'he's in the spa' — and then reluctant to talk about the emerging scandal, now the focus of a NSW government inquiry. 'It's in the middle of hearings and it is inappropriate to be giving media interviews,' he said.

Channel Nine's *Sixty Minutes* then had the idea of flying Bernie Banton to California to beard Macdonald in his den, but all Kerry Packer's resources could not guarantee oxygen at the other end, and it was left to reporter Peter Overton to stand at the gates of Ocean Ranch as a metaphor for the chief executive's aloofness:

> *Overton*: There was no comment at their Californian headquarters. No filming anywhere near any of their American factories, and definitely no entry here.
> *Security guard*: I have to ask you to leave before I call the cops.
> *Overton*: You'd call the police?
> *Security guard*: Yes, sir, because you're filming without ...
> *Overton*: This is Ocean Ranch, the luxury-gated community on the Californian coast, where Peter McDonald lives on a salary of more than $4.5 million a year, a world away from the Australian suburbs and the misery Hardie's created.

Keith Barton made a better fist of his evidence, but David Robb flustered and Peter Cameron blustered, at a speed that tested stenographers, and a volume that troubled Jackson:

Cameron: What I relied upon was this, we had indicated on a number of occasions from as early as late in 2000 but certainly in February of 2001 that if the directors entertained any intention to cancel the partly paid shares several things might happen and some of those things are the things to which I've already given in that particular advice to which you've taken me. Beyond that we had a series of communications going forward until the schemes concluded both at management level and with the board. Those communications were of a kind where if there had been any I believe –
Jackson: Could you sit further back from the microphone?
Cameron: Sorry, I've slightly lost my thread.

Sometimes his verbiage exceeded the interlocutors' interpretative skills, as when Sheahan asked him a question about management's view of the inexactitude of actuarial calculations:

Sheahan: Was it brought to your attention by reading this, or otherwise, that that remained, as at the date of the February board papers, the view of James Hardie executives?
Cameron: No I think certainly the sorts of things which they are indicating to the board in terms of the likely result of what the board was considering at this time were not going to produce that result.
Sheahan: I'm sorry I don't understand that.

He wasn't the only one.

PETER MACDONALD retained one ace in the hole. From his discussions with the Cabinet Office and the Attorney-General's Department the previous October, he had concluded that reform of the asbestos-compensation system was better than a remote possibility. Publicly, at least, despite its concerns about the Dust

Diseases Tribunal, and especially about 'forum shopping', the government had backed off from the Insurance Council of Australia's recommendations about a statutory compensation scheme. But from the special commission had emerged a chink of light—its fourth term of reference was 'the adequacy of current arrangements available to MRCF ... to manage its liabilities' and 'whether reform is desirable to those arrangements'—and Hardie had commissioned Allens' John Morgan to explain how tort reform might work where asbestos was concerned.

At 6.00AM on 14 July, the day the commission opened discussion of this term of reference, the Hardie board agreed at a teleconference to recommend funding of a suitable statutory scheme—contingent on the government capping payouts and blocking alternative avenues of legal recourse. The proposal was made 'without any admission of liability' but with 'due regard for the original intention of the board to fund future claimants'. The company's announcement insisted: 'The establishment of a specially designed statutory scheme under NSW law, would be the most effective way to provide for speedy, fair and equitable compensation'. Hellicar recalls:

> It was going to restrict common law rights somewhat, which is the criticism of plaintiff lawyers, who have managed to get through this whole process looking like they care only about claimants rather than the 50 per cent of their practices that depend on asbestos. But it was also going to streamline the system. We didn't present a completed plan, because we thought: 'We're on the nose on every front and we'll be slammed if we have every detail worked out. We'll just put forward some principles which we think will take costs out of the system and which our shareholders might like.' Yes, we did talk about independent medical assessment. Plaintiff lawyers can talk about that removing a common law right. We called it a constructive proposal.

The ACTU had been anxious about just such a proposal. 'During the inquiry, the whole focus had been on their conduct,' says assistant secretary George Wright. 'It was devastating for them. But the announcement of their scheme had the potential for seizing the initiative, and shining a light onto others.' Hearing that it was in the offing, Combet had booked himself to fly to Sydney that morning, and heaped scorn on the idea at a doorstop press conference. Nonetheless, the idea was abroad, and Combet wondered about the New South Wales government's fortitude. When he visited Carr in early August, their meeting was attended by cabinet secretary Roger Wilkins. Combet said that Carr should meet the directors of the MRCF and others involved in the problem to discuss the compensation system. But as Carr opened his mouth to reply, Wilkins interjected: 'Premier, I don't think would be appropriate. Not in the current circumstances.' At intervals in the conversation, in fact, Wilkins seemed intent on steering Carr away from the issue.

Combet was concerned. Wilkins had to be sidelined, and a confidential informant helped out at just the right moment when he advised Combet that the cabinet secretary's father had been a chemist at Wunderlich then Hardie for forty years: Wilkins agreed to stand aside from further discussions.† Combet and Peter Gordon also decided to take some pre-emptive action, writing to John Howard and visiting state premiers, hoping that their example might encourage Carr to fly in formation. Paul Bastian of the AMWU, meanwhile, took up the matter with Rob McClelland, a lawyer at Turner Freeman before becoming federal member for Barton in March 1996, who said he would draw opposition leader Mark Latham into the fray.

The complaint that lawyers are running amok is an asbestos-industry ritual: as long as seventy years ago, American companies were demanding legislation to 'eliminate the jury', 'the shyster lawyer' and 'the quack doctor'. It has also at times been taken up by politicians. Twenty-five years ago, for instance, Democrat senator Gary Hart took up the cause of an Asbestos Health Hazards Compensation Bill, under which victims of asbestos-related disease

---

† For her part, Hellicar denies contact with Wilkins: 'I know Roger and won't deny having spoken to him, but I can categorically deny having met with him all last year [2004]. I would love to have had a meeting with someone in government. It was not for want of my trying that I didn't.'

would be compensated only by existing no-fault state and federal workmen's compensation programme. The impetus had less to do with the scheme's intrinsic merits, as *New Yorker's* Paul Brodeur wrote, than with Hart's 'desperate need to shed the liberal image that had followed him from his days as presidential campaign manager for George McGovern in 1972, and to show business interests in Colorado ... that he was not anti-business'. Combet was lucky. In this case, there was no such impetus. In fact, there was capital to be had in not just slamming the door in Hardie's face but on its fingers, too. Victoria's Steve Bracks—seldom ill-disposed to doing nothing anyway—was first. South Australia's Mike Rann followed. Such merits as Hardie's criticisms of the existing system had stood no chance against the tidal influence that public opinion exerts on politics.

Latham, as had been his habit, managed to be both too late and too glib on the issue. When his minders finally arranged a photo opportunity at the gates of Camellia on 24 September, he was vague and ill-prepared, and treated Bernie Banton, who had been invited to talk to him, like a prop. Latham seemed to have spent less time familiarising himself with the issue than on preparing a pre-AFL Grand Final soundbite: 'I think we're in the last quarter, the scores are level, the ball's gone up and I'm going to use my height advantage to take the big mark and kick the winning goal'. In fact, he had just missed from point-blank range.

25

'Who's who in the zoo'

'He [James Hardie chief executive Peter Macdonald] had obviously read and pondered over every document that it was thought might possibly be put to him, and had identified and was ready with the explanation of it which he thought might most advance this company's case or his own situation, whatever might be the true situation ... A particularly unattractive feature [of Macdonald's testimony] was his unwillingness to accept personal responsibility for matters in which he was obviously personally engaged.'

—David Jackson QC in his report of the Special Commission of Inquiry into the Medical Research and Compensation Foundation established by the James Hardie Group, released 21 September 2004

THERE WAS NEVER MORE THAN FAINT HOPE that the special commission would meet its appointed deadline of 30 June, and David Jackson successfully sought letters patent to deliver his report by 21 September. The Medical Research and Compensation Foundation's lifespan could not be so easily extended. At 30 June, the net assets of Amaca and Amaba stood at $179.2 million, after the dispersal of $53 million in the previous twelve months. An actuarial projection commissioned by Hardie from KPMG had just put a figure on the net present value of claims of $1.5 billion, complaining of 'an unforeseeable upward trend' in claim numbers and costs.

The foundation's finances were even worse than they seemed on paper. A $41 million receivable due on the sale of its property port-folio to Multiplex was slow coming in, while negotiations for the paying out of its deed by the ABN60 Foundation were inching along. ABN60's directors Don Cameron and John McPhillamy, on very conservative legal advice from Wendy Jacobs at Dibbs Barker Gosling and Steven Finch SC, were attaching all manner of waivers and strings to the payment, which the foundation was declining to accept. For the board members personally, there were also risks involved. Their directors' insurance was about to expire, at the very moment they might be risking insolvent trading: they could be personally liable for not holding back sufficient monies to look after future victims. John MacGregor announced that the directors would be going to the NSW Supreme Court on 23 July to seek personal protection for their actions until year's end to enable the fund to continue. The sense of siege was deepened when they were lambasted by the ACTU's Greg Combet, speaking to Tony Jones on the ABC's *Lateline:*

> *Jones*: How did the directors of this trust fund get themselves into a position where they've got no insurance coverage and evidently not enough money, or nowhere near enough money, to cover future claims against the fund?
>
> *Combet*: That's a very hard question for me to answer. All I can do is speculate that they are incredibly naïve mugs, really, or they're part of the whole scheme that was orchestrated by James Hardie to try and separate the assets of the company from the potential claimants for the asbestos compensation. And that's what this entire scheme was directed towards. And I think all of the directors involved can find themselves in a bit of hot water in the months to come.
>
> *Jones*: Now, some of the people on the trust fund, directors of the trust fund, are also directors of James Hardie. How does that crossover work between the two?
>
> *Combet*: (Laughs) With deep and intense conflicts, in my opinion.

'Naïve mugs'? Peter Jollie seethed. Combet was astonished a few days later to receive a letter from Peter Keel, a defamation partner at Clayton Utz, demanding an apology and retraction for his comments. The kerfuffle eventually blew over, and had a comic sequel when Clayton Utz threw a lunch for the foundation board at the Sheraton on the Park at the inquiry's end. The firm's Jocelyn

Kellerman presented each director with a personalised mug bearing the word 'Naïve'—again, Jollie did not share in the general amusement.

Interim submissions, meanwhile, ended the phoney war at the commission. Counsel assisting, John Sheahan, accused both Macdonald and Morley of fraud, saying they were 'at least negligent' as well as 'dishonest' in allowing the foundation to be underfunded; the 16 February press release, too, should be the basis of a prosecution of Macdonald. Jack Rush and the ACTU's lawyers went in even harder, with 138 pages of fearsome denunciation and accusation, depicting the Hardie's restructuring as 'conscious, deliberate and amounting to fraud' and 'an offence of perverting the course of justice'. The foundation directors were damned for having 'failed to properly fulfil their responsibilities', and Allens for 'breach of contract', 'breach of fiduciary duty', 'negligence', 'deceit and conspiracy' and 'contraventions of the Trade Practices Act and Corporations Act'. Rush recalls:

> Up until that time, counsel for James Hardie, he and I, despite our respective positions, we'd give each other a wink, or if we'd be in the lift we'd have a bit of a chat. After our submission, it was the absolute cold shoulder. No talk. I ran into him five or six weeks after the hearings finished. Still nothing. I don't know what they expected, though. There was nothing in our submission we didn't put in cross-examination.

Combet, however, was unenamoured of the submission. 'We've gone too far,' he told Peter Gordon. 'We've targeted too many people. Our position's too extreme.' Combet recalls:

> We basically accused everyone under the sun of some unlawful conduct. Maybe we were right. But my take on the political positioning is that we led Jackson to discount the import of some of the things we were saying because it looked like the unions were the captives of the plaintiff lawyers, and Hardie's played on that. That's partly my fault. I should have paid the submission more attention, to make sure we got the politics right.

When I went to some of the hearings towards the end, I could see where Jackson was heading. There were weak points — the representations to the Supreme Court, the press statement after the set up of the foundation — but he was clearly thinking that the restructuring would stack up legally. At the same time, he could see that what the company had done was crook, and he had to allow pressure to be brought to bear on it.

Combet's focus was now on how the world would look after the dust had settled on the commission. This was an issue that might burnish the ACTU's reputation in a time of conservative political ascendancy, and he wanted Carr to mandate him to negotiate a settlement of the problem with Hardie. If this was to happen, he could not be seen at the head of a lynch mob. The overriding objective was that sick and dying people were compensated; the satisfaction of punitive instincts was secondary. That would not satisfy some on his side. The Labor Council of NSW, which had begun a noisy public campaign to persuade construction companies and councils to ban Hardie products, was keen to run its own show. 'There's always the attitude in the New South Wales unions about not wanting the ACTU to get involved, about who's going to sell them out,' says Combet's assistant secretary George Wright. But the ACTU, Combet recalls, had to present its credentials as a moderate:

> When you're in a campaign, there's a bit of politics about who's who in the zoo and who gets in front of the TV cameras. Always a lot of froth and bubble. What I try to do is make sure that we have a clear goal, and a strategy to get there. Arguments in the union movement are always vigorous, and this was no exception, and there was a tendency to get involved in activities that didn't really help in getting the company to negotiate. There were some people who said: 'We shouldn't negotiate with this company at all. We should just force them to do something.' You just can't do that. You had to eyeball the company, explain what you wanted and get them to do it.

On the last day of the commission, Hardie's counsel was more specific about its compensation plan. When Sheahan asked what would happen if there turned out to be more victims after KPMG's first 'throws of the actuarial coin', Meagher insisted that 'any scheme will have to accommodate' claims outside the estimate, which would be viewed as the 'bottom bounds of the level of commitment'. Jack Rush was supremely sceptical: 'We read that James Hardie is committed to 'speedy, fair, equitable compensation for all existing and future claimants'. The words have a very familiar ring and they echo the sentiments of Mr Macdonald on 16 February 2001.' But in a doorstop press conference in the foyer of the John Maddison Tower, Combet took a balanced stance. He was again dismissive of the scheme—with the qualification that the compensation system might bear some reform: 'You can reduce the legal costs and the time involved, and that's what we should be attending to; not trying to help James Hardie out by capping the liability that people who are going to die from these products are entitled to.'

It was a new line, and it was not hard enough for Gerry Gardiman. As the inquiry came to an end, his relations with Combet unravelled, to the extent that he wrote to clients informing them that Combet's position jeopardised compensation rights, especially provisional damages. Combet was irritated, but bore it:

Gerry didn't think I'd defend the rights of claimants sufficiently. He felt I would compromise on compensation rights to get the money. Gerry would have been suspicious of me. He has a residual anger towards the government because of what has happened with workers' compensation in New South Wales. But I couldn't allow that to affect our strategy. He and Paul Bastian were very hostile to the Carr government. But we needed the Carr government's support. I was saying: 'You've got to put that bullshit behind you. If we're going to get people their money, there's no point us standing outside Macquarie Street saying: "The Carr government are a pack of cunts". That'll get us nowhere.'

Especially as there would now be a lady present.

IN HER FIRST APPEARANCE in a Hardie annual report, Meredith Hellicar was an incongruous rose among thorns on the spread devoted to the board, a 38-year-old with a towering perm among dour fifty- and sixty-somethings. It belied her already considerable experience of controversial roles, her grounding in big business having taken place in corporate-affairs roles at Chase Corporation and Bond Brewing — two casualties of 1980s squandermania. The hair had since settled down, shorn to a businesslike helmet, as her list of credits had lengthened: she had been managing director of TNT Logistics Asia, CEO of Corrs, and head of InTech, which she'd resigned on joining the AMP's board in March the previous year.

Hellicar's appointment to succeed MacGregor as chairman of Hardie at its 11 August board meeting, however, represented a new distinction. She had come by it through longevity — she was the longest-serving member. She was also being recognised for her personal skills as a crisis manager — and, with $1 billion in shareholder value lost since October, the foundation and the inquiry pretty clearly constituted a crisis. A profile that appeared in *Good Weekend* a few months later reported that Hellicar 'put her name forward because she was the best person to steer the company through the crisis'. Hellicar says this is untrue. She seems, on the contrary, to have been the only candidate. Michael Brown, also on the board for almost a dozen years, already had two other chairmanships, at Repco Corporation and Energy Developments, and didn't want the job: 'If I'd been offered it, I would have declined.'

That said, Hellicar did have a view. She wondered whether her senior executives' very attributes — their clinical focus, their dogged determination — had played a part in events: 'Why did this company succeed in the US against all competitors? Because it had a group of executives who said: "There's a way to do this. And it will be done." I don't think they had the peripheral vision to deal with this [asbestos compensation]. Maybe, none of us had.' Perhaps a new tone was required: 'I made it a condition of my taking up the chairmanship that I say sorry.' This was legally tricky, as it might constitute an admission of liability, but Hellicar was also convinced that the company had been, at various times, too deeply in thrall to lawyers:

'Peter Macdonald's public remarks had all been very carefully crafted. Perhaps too carefully.' The time had come to live a little dangerously. Her first public statements included an apology. 'We are very, very sorry that our original intent to provide for future claimants was manifestly inadequate. We now deeply regret that's turned out to be the case and the stress and anxiety that's caused for claimants.' When she admitted on *The 7.30 Report* that she had not met a victim of asbestos-related disease, she quickly assured Kerry O'Brien that this was not out of aversion: 'I would be, happy, well, happy is the wrong word because obviously it's very distressing for them and me, but certainly I would be willing to meet with them. They haven't yet sought to but I'm certainly happy to take the initiative to meet them.'

Hardie would quickly take Hellicar's life over. Her second husband, David Foster, a former *Age* journalist turned corporate affairs executive ten years her senior, was in Greece working for the Athens Olympic Committee, and their six-year-old daughter Amelia learned to dread the sound of Hellicar's phone ringing; asked what she would like for Christmas, Amelia said she would like to smash her mother's mobile. Hellicar herself learned to dread talk of politics on morning radio, which she thought seemed to precipitate attacks on the company: 'I'd wake up in the morning and hear Carr being slammed about hospitals and trains and I'd think: "Oh God, here comes another Hardie's stunt".' She was resentful that the government seemed to have led Hardie along a limb of reform and then sawn it off behind them; she also sensed that the company would have to make the best of its current situation. The media received her warmly, magnifying her early expressions of contrition, perhaps anticipating something more lachrymose.

In fact, while going further than Hardie had gone before, Hellicar had not gone all that far. She insisted on *The 7.30 Report* that the system had to change: 'We're looking to cut out the process of lawyers. And because we are paying beyond our legal responsibility, we want to make sure that we're focused on providing for claimants. We do not feel one scintilla of obligation to lawyers.' On *Business Sunday*, she disowned responsibility for the underfunding of the foundation: 'The intention was to properly compensate victims. We used the wrong number. Everything else is extraneous because it would never have come about if we had used the correct number and there was proper funding.' Asked if Hardie was at fault, she simply said: 'No.' Asked by the *Australian Financial Review* if she felt it was odd that the law did not hold to account parent companies of subsidiaries that killed or injured people, she said: 'I have many issues to deal with. That's not one I'm dealing with.'

If the media were briefly smitten, nobody else was going to make it easy for Hellicar. When a hundred Hardie shareholders gathered for their investors' meeting on 15 September, they were outnumbered by thousands of union protestors who had marched from Town Hall Square. Building sites across Sydney lay abandoned that day as workers bore down on the Darling Harbour Convention centre with an eight-metre-tall inflatable rat bearing a CFMEU flag and its chest emblazoned with 'Shame James Hardie Shame'. Flanked by Peter Macdonald and new director Donald McGauchie, and leading a board that also included as a new member Peter Cameron, Hellicar gave some ground: 'Frankly we are all up for re-examination and I don't exclude myself from this ... I think we did misjudge the public attention that would be brought upon us ... It is going to take us a long time to restore our credibility and reputation.' She confined her admissions, however, to Hardie's response to the foundation's funding problems rather than responsibility for them:

When the directors of the Foundation wrote to us informing us that the fund may experience a significant shortfall, our response was consistent with the approach that the financial position of the Foundation and its subsidiaries had become that of a separate enterprise. At the time, we did not identify an appropriate way by which we could offer further funding. In retrospect, we could have responded differently, and more quickly. We knew we had to carefully consider all the ramifications of these circumstances: the potential impacts on future claimants and their families, on the Foundation, on the company and shareholders, and on us as directors.

Combet, Paul Bastian, Andrew Ferguson and Rita Mallia from the CFMEU had all obtained proxies to ask questions. Mallia's poser was one many had contemplated: 'Given that the submissions of counsel assisting the Jackson inquiry have raised issues of fraud, deceit, misleading and deceptive conduct and breaches of the Corporations Act against our chief executive officer Peter Macdonald and chief financial officer Peter Shafron, why hasn't the board demanded that they stand aside?' Hellicar responded: 'Peter Macdonald has been with the company for eleven years, we know him, we trust him and we're not going to act precipitously'. She withstood, too, a confrontation that had been in her stars since her television admission that she had not encountered a victim of asbestos. Fifty-six-year-old Greg Hayes, diagnosed with mesothelioma forty months earlier, stepped forward with his two young daughters and introduced himself. When he described attending twenty funerals of people with similar afflictions, Hellicar looked like she meant what said: 'I do know that no apology can ever be enough to compensate you for this horrible disease but I do give it anyway and I give it very sincerely.' There was no time for more. Having had enough shocks and upsets for the day, Hardie's new public relations duo, John Noble of Kortlang and former journalist Chris Falvey, ushered directors away without a backward glance let alone an interview.

The hit of the day was Bernie Banton. Respirator in hand, and at times clearly in distress, he gave an impassioned address to the rally outside the convention centre: 'Hardies, I don't care how far you run, where you try to hide. Until they put me in a box, I'm gonna chase you, and I won't let you out of my sight.' He then brought another ten families with members afflicted by asbestos-related diseases to meet an impressively solicitous Carr for ninety minutes at Macquarie Tower. Banton oozed relish for the fight. 'What's happening with this commission report?' he asked. 'When can I get my hands on it?' Carr turned to his senior adviser, Amanda Lampe: 'I don't know. Amanda?' Lampe answered: 'I see no reason why Bernie couldn't go with you and receive it from Her Excellency.' 'There you are, Bernie,' Carr smiled. 'You can come with me.'

The pursuit of Hardie, in fact, had now become a global enterprise. That evening, Hardie's board embarked for Amsterdam for their company's statutory annual meeting; on their trail were Paul Bastian and Lindsay Fraser of the AMWU, with Ella Sweeney of the Asbestos Diseases Foundation, who landed at Schipol at 10.00PM the following evening to be greeted by asbestos lobby groups from Britain and Europe. The next morning, they joined a protest organised by the Dutch trade union body, the Federatie Nederlandse Vakbeweging, outside the meeting's venue, the Hotel Courtyard by Marriott 7km away. It struck Bastian as a distinctively European protest: a local radio station had even organised an outside broadcast. 'Europeans protest very professionally,' he recalls. 'They've got these you-beaut whirly-twirlies and horns. The cops turned up and they said: "See youse later." Very different to Australia, where if you're in a foyer they'll piss you off straight away.' Hardie, however, had taken no chances. Burly security guards who frisked Sweeney even insisted on looking in her handbag, and Hellicar hastened through four motions in ten minutes. The next day, both the Hardie board and the dissident trio were en route home—on, it proved, the same airliner, albeit at opposite ends. When the plane stopped over in Bangkok, Bastian remembers, Fraser used his Qantas Club pass to rush his associates into the lounge:

> We took the seats right in the centre so they couldn't miss us. McGauchie walks in and just goes: 'Awww fuck.' And he walks past, head down. Says g'day. Then Meredith comes in and her jaw just drops, as if she's thinking: 'Can't I get rid of you bastards?' Didn't even look at us, went straight to the shower, and we didn't see her again.

The real action, however, was at home. Carr was as good as his word. On Tuesday 21 September, he took Banton to receive a copy of the Jackson report from governor Marie Bashir. He even responded cordially when, seeing that his was a paperback compared with the premier's hardbound version, Banton said cheekily: 'But I want one like you've got.' Banton received his premium version.

What was in the report was another matter. Along with Banton, Peter Gordon and Tanya Segelov were being given three hours in advance of its public release to digest Jackson's deliberations — and Gordon's disgust began to mount:

> The chief of staff [Graeme Wedderburn] comes in and says: 'Here you go. Here's the report.' And we're looking through it and going: 'Fuck. *Fuck*.' Jackson had wimped out. He's taken it transaction by transaction, even though when you look at them over a period it's clear that they're being done with the final structure in mind, and it's clear what the over-riding intent was — and conspiratorial and wrongful in that context. I mean, we were horrified. And the chief of staff comes back and says: 'Well, what do you think?' And we're nervous about disclosing our position to the government so we don't say much, but he says: 'Well, I'll tell you what the government's position is. There's enough there.'

Jackson had read events, as Combet had expected, conservatively. He was unimpressed with Macdonald, whose evidence was variously described as 'unconvincing', 'curious', 'self-serving', and 'difficult to accept', and his public statement on liabilities 'false in material particulars and materially misleading'. Shafron, against whom he also recommended prosecution, fared little better: 'Mr Shafron was a man who seemed determined to control the course of events, and the activities of participants. His endeavours, after the event, to explain away what had taken place, appeared contrived.' Of the original funding, Jackson thought the $293 million had simply been 'the cheapest provision thought marketable', and he found it 'difficult to accept that management could really have believed that the funds of the foundation would have been sufficient to pay all future legitimate asbestos related claims', especially on the basis of Trowbridge's 'wholly unsuitable' reports. And Hardie, in general, should be being pushed to cough up: 'To put it directly [Hardie] still has in its pockets the profits made by dealing with asbestos, and those profits are large enough to satisfy most, perhaps all, of the claims of victims of James Hardie asbestos.' But, while he felt that Justice Santow had been misled in August 2001, Jackson thought the restructure and change of domicile legally robust, and left intact. Having been on the losing side of the Putt case, his respect for the corporate veil was perhaps not surprising.

Hardie's response, released at 5.13PM, acknowledged 'the seriousness of the findings', while Macdonald personally signalled that he would 'vigorously defend myself against allegations made by commissioner Jackson'—having perhaps become so inured to accusations that he did not appreciate these were not 'allegations' but findings. But the report was more an embarrassment than anything else, and some had fared well. Morley was regarded as 'fundamentally honest', MacGregor 'did his best', and Baxter was 'simply … not considered', having not been examined. Hardie's most strenuous objection was to Carr's mandate, not unexpected but still contentious, for Combet: 'The NSW government believes that James Hardie must now sit down with the unions and victims groups to work out how James Hardie will fund appropriate compensation for its asbestos victims. The NSW government will not endorse James Hardie's statutory scheme unless satisfied by unions and victims groups that it will deliver more money for victims.'

BOB CARR MIGHT AT THIS STAGE have been his party's leader for sixteen years and premier for nine, but seldom had he played such brilliant politics. Had the New South Wales government taken the lead role in negotiations, their progress would have been dogged at every step by unions already antagonised by reforms to Workcover; now, like an actor inviting his chief critic on stage, he was disarming the unions even as he empowered them. ACTU assistant secretary George Wright, Combet's 37-year-old protégé, suddenly had a pang of disquiet:

> I was at the press conference when Carr announced that the ACTU would have carriage of the negotiations and it was lovely and flattering and nice. But driving in the taxi back to the airport, it was such a big job that I started to worry, for Greg. We were starting to talk about the

team we needed to put together and the skills. The people who had been involved in representing us at the inquiry, the plaintiff lawyers, they all had an interest in the matter. I needed to make sure the team could give him really independent advice. I remember sitting in the cab thinking: 'Fucking hell. This is really big. And we can't fuck it up.'

Combet had given the subject thought. His first visit was to pay respects to the MRCF, although not to Edwards, for whom he had little regard, but Ian Hutchinson and Nancy Milne. While Combet and Gordon informed them that there would be no place for the foundation in negotiations, they promised continued advice. Using a friend at Corrs as an intermediary, Combet also arranged to meet Hellicar at Export House on 23 September. Combet's main purpose was to reiterate his opposition to a statutory scheme, which Hellicar said she understood. But as they sized each other up carefully, neither found much to like.

Combet was struck, as Hellicar quoted ostentatiously from her diary, by how much she enjoyed her all-consuming life: the prominence, the busyness, from the pre-dawn teleconferences to the speaking engagements. Hellicar, not unnaturally, could not see why she was talking to the ACTU at all. In fact, she informed him, she would not be: as a non-executive chairman, under Dutch law, her involvement in the domain of the executive was strictly circumscribed. The negotiations, she informed Combet, would be led by someone of whom he had not heard: Peter Hunt of the advisory firm Caliburn Partnership.

Combet was nonplussed. 'I'll be straight with you,' he said. 'We don't trust you. And unless there's someone on your side that I trust, I'm going to have difficulty. I'll be up front about what I'm thinking, but I want someone with whom I can deal.' When Hellicar asked for a suggestion, Combet proposed Leon Zwier of the Melbourne law firm Arnold Bloch Liebler, who had been on the opposite side of the ACTU's negotiations with Ansett three years earlier, and whom he had found personable and trustworthy. He had wanted Zwier, in fact, for his own team in these negotiations, but learned that ABL had a conflict: partner Robert Heathcote had given Hardie advice on disclosure issues in June. To Combet's surprise, Hellicar agreed on the spot to appoint Zwier.

Combet's other inspiration was to invite Bernie Banton as a representative of the various asbestos victims' groups. Combet had tried using representatives of the specific constituencies in a number of campaigns, like the waterfront and Ansett. They not only humanised industrial relations but saved union officials from too much exposure. In the context of this campaign, Banton was a 'four ticker': he had worked for Hardie, he suffered asbestosis, he could talk and he could cope with the media. Combet recalls: 'He was passionate, involved, a smart guy, and a really great human being.' So his negotiating team came together. He decided to use a couple of experienced silks as legal advisers, in Jack Rush and Jonathon Beach, and dealt in the NSW Labor Council, inviting along John Robertson, Michael Costa's successor as secretary. He dashed off his 'negotiating committee' on a pad:

Me
Robbo
Rush
Beach
Banton

The notepaper, coincidentally, was stationery for the union superannuation fund of which Combet is trustee. It featured the slogan: 'How to be a union superpower'.

'There's $1.5 billion on the table — you can point to that'

'I am also authorised to tell you very directly that the level of costs associated with the current "bloated" common law system is unacceptable to James Hardie and that ... the Board is not prepared to recommend a proposal to James Hardie's shareholders that doesn't deal effectively with the cost issue.'
—Letter signed by Hardie chief financial officer Russell Chenu to ACTU secretary Greg Combet, 15 November 2004

WHEN HARDIE REPRESENTATIVES commenced negotiations with the ACTU on 1 October 2004, it was just over twenty-five years since their company had left behind James Hardie Asbestos and Asbestos House. But for the next three months, that quarter-century would be set at nought. The 'legacy issues' left behind had proved anything but a thing of the past; in Bernie Banton, they had even taken on corporeal form.

On the eve of the first meeting at the Mercure Hotel on Circular Quay, not far from Export House, Hardie had announced that Peter Macdonald and Peter Shafron, who it had been foreshadowed would be the subject of Australian Securities and Investment Commission investigations, would be standing down from their usual duties. The result was that when he arrived with Banton, John Robertson, Jack Rush and Jonathon Beach, Combet recognised in Meredith Hellicar's deputation only Arnold Bloch Liebler's Leon Zwier. The other three would become exceedingly familiar.

The group had been partly selected by Christine McLoughlin, a former Allens lawyer who had worked for AMP chief executive Andrew Mohl until the life office's demerger at the end of May, and who had been acting as Hellicar's executive assistant for the last ten weeks. On the AMP's split, McLoughlin had worked extensively with her first pick, Peter Hunt, himself a former lawyer, but for more than two decades a corporate adviser at Hill Samuel/Macquarie Bank, Bankers Trust Australia, BZW and ABN-Amro, and a founder in 1999 of the Caliburn Partnership with Simon Mordant. McLoughlin also knew her second pick, lawyer John Atanaskovic, through her friend in their eponymous legal partnership Tony Hartnell. The third pick had essentially selected himself, John Morgan of Allens. His introduction, however, immediately set Combet on guard. Had he not told Hellicar he would not countenance a statutory scheme? Yet here was the legal figure most closely identified with such innovation, and the Insurance Council of Australia's adviser of choice. Combet, indeed, soon discovered much to dislike about the Hardie deputation. Atanaskovic, perhaps Australia's most decorated and storied takeover lawyer, a favourite of Rupert Murdoch and Kerry Packer, bears a host of allusive nicknames, such as 'the Prince of Darkness' and 'John Antagonistic', for his languid air, faintly macabre humour and occasionally rich vein of temper. And just about every aspect of Hunt was calculated to annoy a trade unionist: he was smart, successful, rich and faintly condescending, with a habit of dropping his rs so that his favourite word of 'robust' came out as 'wobust'. Combet loathed him:

> From the very start, it was like he'd read some book on how to negotiate with dumb union officials. What commercial acumen could I have? So he'd talk down to us in this patronising way. Fuck it, I've been to uni, too. So have most of my guys. I deal with business every day. I'm on the board of a $5 billion super fund and make investment decisions all the time. I employ sixty people in my head office and we turn over $9 million in our operation here [at the ACTU]. And he treats me like I'm a fucking dummy. I wasn't impressed.

For his part, Hunt was unimpressed by the ACTU proposal. The union concept was that asbestos litigants were essentially a lender to James Hardie. Because the $1.5 billion was rightfully theirs, they should have a security in the form of first-ranking fixed and floating charges over Hardie assets, while the ACTU should have guaranteed positions on the Hardie board. Hunt could understand the anxiety that Hardie might head for the hills, but he also knew that such a company would be unbankable, and probably unmanageable. What senior executive would want to work for a claims-processing machine? Hunt wanted to tackle the scenario from the point of view of legal administrative costs. How could Hardie justify to share-holders signing itself up to an open-ended liability in which a quarter to a third was eaten up by legal expenses? It was the share-holders' money. It should be on their terms. If the quantum of funds available for claimants was to be maximised, lawyers would have to make some sacrifices. Hardie wanted a system in which total claims and medical expenses were moderated, an independent medical panel constituted and access to courts made a last resort. It was an outgrowing of Hardie's critique of the DDT. Why was concluding a case so much more expensive in New South Wales than anywhere else? Because the tribunal had become a legal beanfeast, with every-thing being settled at the courtroom door. And why did asbestos cases need specialist judges anyway? After all, district courts decided on neurological matters involving car accident victims. To the ACTU, of course, this was anathema.

The one figure who seemed to promise a bridging of this gap was Leon Zwier. Zwier is young, shrewd, affable, gregarious, and an able technician but no technocrat. His appointed task at the meeting was to discuss directors' duties, but he prefaced it by addressing Banton, who previously had gone unacknowledged. 'Before we begin, Bernie, I want you to know something,' Zwier said. 'On a personal level, you have my utmost sympathy. But you need to know that we have to find a solution. And the solution means we have to deal with some really hard issues, coldly, and in a businesslike way. Please under-stand that when I do that, it's not because I'm disregarding the plight of people who are sick, but only because it's the way we'll finalise this deal.' Banton appreciated the comment, thought Zwier as a 'first-rate bloke' from that day forward, and made a point of shaking only his hand when meetings began.

The initial meeting lasted five hours, the tone lightening a little. It was agreed to work on a statement of intent preparatory to a non-binding heads of agreement rather than move straight to a principal agreement. Both sides, however, were circling round one another warily; in some ways, their negotiating model was almost designed to fail. On one side was Hunt, a financial adviser, without a principal, for Hardie was a company without a CEO or CFO, and it had been agreed to keep Macdonald's acting replacement, Louis Gries, at Mission Viejo, out of negotiations. Hunt had the services of one commercial lawyer, Zwier, appointed by his opponent; he had another, Atanaskovic, with nothing to do until there was some documentation generated, and fond of playing games on his mobile phone in the meantime; and he had a third, Morgan, whose very presence the ACTU saw as an affront. On the other side was a principal, the New South Wales government, represented by a proxy, Combet, without a financial adviser. Combet had the services of two silks, and the support of Banton, whose presence was vital to the external credibility of negotiations, but whose periodic reminders of how little he trusted Hardie were sometimes unsettling.

Personally, the negotiators could hardly have had less in common. As a merchant banker, Hunt was used to familiar faces and similar expectations across the table; he wanted to get to know Combet better. After the first meeting, he began calling Combet to talk to him one-to-one and 'feel the negotiations'. On one day, Hunt rang seven times. 'Does this fucking guy get what's going on here?' Combet fumed to Zwier. 'Could you tell him to fuck off now?' In Hardie's protestations that the failure of the MRCF had been simply a miscalculation, furthermore, Combet saw a cultural gulf:

I don't think they understood what deep shit they were in from a community point of view. Everything was viewed according to their directors' duties to shareholders, and how shareholders' interests might be affected by community opinion and political opinion. There was a

doctrine of hurt. Meredith was hurt. They were all hurt. The hurt came
through constantly from their advisers and others along the way. They
felt they'd been unfairly treated. Can you imagine anything more
pathetic? There's people out there dying of cancer because of their
company and their products, and they are complaining about hurt. It's a
class thing. The people on those boards, they don't mix with anyone
who lives an ordinary life. They don't know what it's like to sit in the
waiting room at Penrith hospital with fluid on your lungs waiting to
have tubes shoved into you, or to sit round for hours in some shitty X-
ray clinic in the outer suburbs. They travel from Mosman or Toorak
into the CBD, probably driven by someone else, and mix with an elite
of people just like them. And when they're under pressure, they say:
'But we're good people'. That was Hellicar's line: 'I'm a good person'.
It's a totally different set of cultural assumptions.

Yet while the ACTU brought cognisance of the decades of
damage of asbestos to the table, and even had their own representative of it, Hardie brought no such corporate memory. It was more
than seventeen years since the last vestiges of asbestos had disap-
peared from its product range; and as for the MRCF, Hunt,
Atanaskovic, Zwier and Morgan had had nothing to do with it.
Mistrust was revealed at every step. At one teleconference, Combet
even insisted: 'Could Mr Atanaskovic please come into frame? I
want to study his body language.' It was a volatile admixture. And,
in some senses, it was an admixture specific to the horror of
asbestos-related disease; where the damage left by one generation is
left to others to repair.

OVER THE NEXT WEEK, the antagonists came slightly more into
alignment. By the time they met again at 10.00AM the following
Friday at the Melbourne office of Arnold Bloch Liebler, Hunt had
brought a principal; Combet, an adviser. Neither was ideal; both
were a start.

Russell Chenu was returning to Hardie, having left twenty years
earlier as a junior finance executive. He could hardly have been a

greater contrast to the CFO he was replacing, Shafron: deadpan, grey-haired, moustachioed, Chenu could almost have walked off the set of *Homicide*. Chenu's resume was impressive, including treasury roles of growing seniority at Pioneer International, Pancontinental Mining and ANI, where his adviser had been none other than Peter Hunt. His return was a strange meeting of minds. Learning that Chenu had just lost his job as CFO at the New South Wales TAB because of its takeover by Tabcorp, Hunt had put in a call. 'It's funny you should ring,' said Chenu. 'I've been thinking of calling you.' Hardie had been generous to him when he had worked there, even paying for his MBA at Macquarie University; he felt he owed them something.

Just as the ACTU had proposed Zwier, meanwhile, so it was the Hardie side who mooted Combet's adviser. Paul Binsted of the merchant bank Lazards Australia had learned from his confrere Jeremy Kriewaldt of Atanaskovic Hartnell that the ACTU might be in the market for some financial advice. Indeed, while he had been receiving some informal advice from Francis Brown, a former Macquarie Banker friendly with Jack Rush, Combet had been harbouring just such thoughts. Binsted, an old-fashioned social democrat since his days among student radicals at ANU during the Vietnam War, had provided Combet with some advice during the waterfront conflict, seeking to find parties to buy Patricks Stevedoring, and suggested a meeting. He walked out with a mandate. 'I'd had lots of people offering help but I didn't know them and I knew Paul,' says Combet. 'When he rang, I knew what he was ringing for.'

The additions did not make the impact they might have. Chenu's knowledge of matters was largely limited to a weekend reading the Jackson inquiry's report, and his manner is innately low-key. 'I believe we've met before,' Chenu said to Peter Gordon by way of introduction. Gordon, despite the blessing of an excellent memory, could not recall; in fact, not three years had elapsed since they'd been on opposite sides of a legal action against Delta Gold, where Chenu had briefly joined some former Pancontinental colleagues. Gordon says frankly: 'We thought he was a shit-kicker.' Binsted, on the phone from Sydney, was shocked by how far the parties were apart:

> My own feeling was that Hardie was still trying to defend the
> indefensible saying that they had no legal liability, and that some of the
> Hardie people had been on leave from reality. I even heard it said at one
> stage—I can't remember by whom—that 'we at Hardies are victims
> because we have done everything lawfully and are being vilified for it'.
> But that's the bunker mentality. We're all prone to it potentially. When
> people are backed into a corner, only exceptional individuals can see
> things objectively. Hardie was under attack—an attack that in my view
> they'd brought on themselves—and they would have felt themselves
> being pilloried. But the result was they spent more time talking to one
> another, talking to the people who'd advised them, with PR advisers
> who'd presented their manoeuverings to the public. So in that sense the
> attack was counterproductive.

Binsted had another problem. He knew Hunt well. Three years
earlier, Binsted had acted for Suncorp Metway in its acquisition of
the AMP's general insurance business, and found Hunt personable
and charming. But there were now some complications. Lazards'
parent had previously been a major shareholder in Caliburn, then
decided to found its own subsidiary in April. When the recruiting
drive that had lured Binsted and his associate Brian Wilson from
Citigroup as joint managing directors had also netted two Caliburn
executives, Hunt had been apoplectic. Others in the negotiation
began to sense a personal rivalry based on their respective firms.

At least the parties' ideas had converged on the idea of a special
purpose fund bankrolled by a proportion of Hardie cashflow, with a
buffer designed to meet the shortfall if the cash flows were not sufficient in a particular year and flexing according to the claims profile. At one point, Combet complained: 'I'm under pressure from the
government, because I can't point to anything I've delivered.' Hunt
replied: 'There's $1.5 billion on the table—you can point to that.'
But Beach was unhappy about the security arrangements, Gordon
was irked that Hardie continued 'sitting in the cheap seats taking pot
shots at lawyers', and Combet was seething when it emerged that

Hunt had sent a copy of the proposal to the Premier's Department with the offer of a briefing—an unsubtle usurpation of the ACTU's authority, even though the offer was not taken up. Hardie continued giving the sense they did not want to be negotiating with the ACTU at all. When Hardie's supervisory board met in 14 October, it did not consider a draft Heads of Agreement the ACTU had sent; it concerned itself with revising the Statement of Objectives. Technically, heads of agreement were a matter for Hardie's managing board, constituted in the Netherlands by Peter Macdonald and a young treasury executive whose name made him sound like a character from the brothers Grimm: Folbert Zwinkels. But Hardie was also not about to be hurried.

THE GUARD AT HARDIE continued to change. After several conversations with both, Hellicar had agreed with Macdonald and Shafron that their departures could not wait. The Jackson inquiry's report had, to her mind, been survivable: 'I think that it simply would have been wrong in natural justice terms if the report had come out, we'd turned around and said: "You're sacked".' Who knew, though, how long ASIC's investigation might cast a shadow over both men? It remained a hard decision: 'We talked it through. But it was hard. These were two people who'd lived and breathed the company.' Some new faces arrived: Hellicar recruited Peter Baker, a former TNT colleague, to fill Greg Baxter's role. One old face came back: Phil Morley came out of his brief retirement as a consultant. Hellicar asked Chenu: 'Do you have an up-to-date passport?' A couple of days later, he was off to Mission Viejo for a month to study Hardie in detail. Binsted, whose sons had played soccer with Chenu's, tried to discuss matters on the phone, but found him elusive. He reported to a conference call of ACTU and advisers the next morning that Chenu 'did not appear concerned about the potentially lengthy negotiation process'. Nor was he:

> Early on, I thought there were just ridiculous claims being made, about
> security over assets and representatives on the Hardie board. It was

annoying. They seemed to be treating it like a log of claims around an award rather than a commercial settlement. Greg would say: 'Well, you guys have got a very weak negotiating position.' In fact, we didn't. The Jackson commission had been critical of Macdonald and Shafron, but he had found no illegality in the setting up of the foundation, and had left the restructuring intact.

For the next four weeks, in fact, while the outside world continued to imagine them in close conclave, the ACTU and Hardie retreated to their corners and communicated mainly by letter. The deal breaker — once the ACTU had relaxed on questions of board representation and said it was negotiable on security providing that claimants were not squeezed by dividend obligations — was the legal process. Hardie regarded it as a precondition of progress. 'We are prepared to work constructively with you and the NSW government to analyse and agree cost efficiencies (including legal costs and superimposed inflation),' the company wrote on 25 October. 'Only when this has been done will we be in a position to determine whether we are prepared to take any risk on the value of these efficiencies.'

Combet could accept that legal costs were too high, and not simply where the proving of impairment was concerned; establishing contribution in cases involving multiple defendants, for example, was a Byzantine process. 'All the firms, including the plaintiff firms, and I don't like to criticise my mates but it's true, bear some responsibility for this,' he says. 'And it's got to be cut out.' But he would not accept compromises on plaintiffs' common law rights. And just because there would be a judge at the very end of the process that Hardie envisaged did not make up for a judge's absence in much of the foregoing — as far as he was concerned, Hardie was proposing a statutory scheme by stealth. He demanded of Hellicar that the scheme be finally laid to rest, and Hellicar assured him that the scheme was not part of Hardie's plan. But, for his part, Zwier thought the problem lay in semantics. Both sides could look at the same words and draw quite separate meanings:

What you had was a company that believed what it had done was right. Their state of mind was: 'We intended to do the right thing, but it's gone wrong.' And you had the ACTU and the victims groups saying: 'The reconstruction was pejorative, deliberate, designed to make sure people in terrible hardship got no money.' I remember very early on having two conversations, one with Greg, one with Hardie. Greg said: 'You understand that we're only going to negotiate on the basis of no statutory scheme.' Up until that time the company had said: 'We'll only negotiate on the basis of an statutory scheme.' And I was in the middle of that. So I said to Greg: 'My reading is that statutory scheme is a euphemistic way of saying that Hardie want to avoid wastage. If you can negotiate on that basis of making the system more efficient, you need have no worries about a statutory scheme.' I went to the company and I said: 'Maybe I'm misreading you, because I'm not in your inner sanctum, but I think what you're saying with the idea of the statutory scheme is that you don't want to pay hundreds of millions of dollars to lawyers. But so long as you accept that the focus is wastage, then you should be fine.' Now that wasn't well received, because it was a pretty pragmatic and earthy view of what Hardies regarded as matters of high principle, but it seemed to me the only way of bridging that gap.

Zwier, however, because of his status as Combet's choice, was invidiously placed, tending to be overtrusted by his opponent and undertrusted by his client. 'Leon was shabbily treated by Hardie's,' says John Atanaskovic. 'I kept saying to them: "You're treating Leon like he'd do the wrong thing. I just don't think a professional like Leon would do anything other than his duties".' And here, Zwier was again ignored.

On 3 November, Combet, who had been at a union conference at the Panthers NRL club, dropped into Union NSW's Sussex Street office to collect an email draft Heads of Agreement from James Hardie. Included in it was Clause 3, saying that Hardie would need to be satisfied before it signed a legally binding document that the agreed efficiencies would generate the necessary savings. He was furious:

The tactic of Caliburn and Allens was that even if we say no, we probably don't mean no, so they'd just come back with it again. We'd think it was gone, then they'd come back with new documents about how to fuck people's compensation rights. Detailed documents … with the same shit that Allens had come up with in July. And they think we're not going to see this because it's dressed up a little differently? It was insulting. I've done a lot of negotiating, on very complex matters involving a lot of money, and I don't lie about it. And they clearly gave me no credit for that.

Combet was flying back to Melbourne that night to see his daughter play the piano in a school recital. After her performance, he left to pore more thoroughly over Hardie's heads of agreement and to discuss them with colleagues. Combet was still on the phone when his wife and daughter arrived home some time later: there had been a second recital and he had missed it. His daughter did not talk to him for several months.

With Binsted's help, he drafted a letter back rejecting the conditionality of the offer. Compensation had to come first—efficiency could follow. In its 15 November response, Hardie insisted that Combet had misunderstood. Funding was not conditional on savings; funding was conditional on Hardie being satisfied there would be savings. Combet rolled his eyes. And he was irked by the other rhetorical flourishes in whom, although the letter was signed by Chenu, he detected the influence of Hunt:

> We have said to you now on many occasions that our Board and shareholders are not prepared to countenance paying for an inefficient and bloated legal system where a number of practitioners—quite frankly—'prey' on individuals who have asbestos related diseases and the organizations (including both government and corporates) which have exposure to fund legitimate asbestos claimants.

Now, for whom was that written? Not, Combet thought, for him. This was a letter designed to reserve the company's position publicly. Hardie, he suspected, was preparing for the negotiations to fail. He complained in reply that 'elements of your letter' amounted to 'an ill-advised and unprofessional attempt at "positioning" the ACTU should the letter be published'.

The negotiating gambit was surprising. In the public arena, Hardie had been taking a licking for a year. Even such gestures as Hellicar had tried to make had come out wrong. On 19 October, for example, she had arranged to meet Banton, Greg Hayes and another former Hardie-BI worker and mesothelioma sufferer, Phil Batson, at the Sydney Airport's Mercure Hotel—Hellicar saw it as a private meeting to help her understanding of victims' problems. But after about ninety minutes of discussion, Banton begged leave to attend another appointment: a press conference, as it happened, with Carr. Hellicar, recalls Banton, became upset:

> That's when I saw the colour of her eyes change. She said: 'And where are you off to, Bernie? Another Hardie's-bashing exercise?' I said: 'Of course, and why wouldn't I be?' She said: 'I think it's about time you stopped all this Hardie's bashing, and started to work for a conclusion to this.' I said: 'As a matter of fact that's exactly what I'm doing. It's Hardie's that aren't. Anyway, this isn't the forum for this. We've come here in good faith to tell you our stories, and I don't think it's fair for you to go abusing me in front of these fellow sufferers. I'm going now.'

When the ABC revealed that the meeting had taken place, Hellicar was even more upset, feeling that she'd been 'set up'. Three days later had come the exits of Macdonald and Shafron which, as is now *de rigeuer*, were smoothed by multi-million dollar settlements; Macdonald was also retained on a consultancy contract worth $US60,000 a month for up to six months to ease Gries in, then $US10,000 a month for two years so that Hardie might have 'the benefit of his knowledge and experience if required'. Carr called it 'a shameful day for corporate Australia'; the *Daily Telegraph* levelled at a double-barrelled front page at Hardie contrasting the largesse showered on Macdonald with the suffering of Smithfield mother-of-two Bernadette Russo, suffering kidney failure after operations to remove tumours in her lungs. Yet Hardie retained an irrepressible belief in the power of positive spin and media management—to John Atanaskovic's droll amusement: 'After a while, I concluded that Hardie was a company whose core business was the issuance of press releases with a small subsidiary involved in building products. My previous experience had been of working with Murdoch, where there is no press release, and BHP, where it's the last thing that gets done. This was completely different.' It had just retained another bevy of public relations consultants from Jackson Wells Morris and Third Person—the main fruit of which would be a profile of Hellicar by Jane Cadzow in *Good Weekend*.

The balance of public relations power, however, was somewhat deceptive. The ACTU had relatively little additional bargaining clout—the NSW Labor Council's attempts to mobilise a campaign against Hardie products had had little effect—and Combet knew it. As Binsted commented in a note to his colleagues:

> In terms of negotiating leverage the only assets in the jurisdiction are, as we understand it, the JHA operations which are at most about fifteen per cent of the group worth. Therefore what are our points of leverage? It is a matter for legal advisers but as we understand it only the Commonwealth and not the states can legislate extraterritorially. Would the Commonwealth do so? If it did could the legislation be enforced in the Netherlands or the USA? … We are quite concerned at the effluxion of time removing pressure from Hardie.

Hardie was making progress. In a board meeting in Amsterdam on 8 and 9 November, directors signed off on the general architecture of the special purpose fund, and empowered Chenu to see negotiations through. But Combet felt he needed to kick talks along. To Graeme Wedderburn, with whom had been in almost daily contact, he made a proposal. Would the government be prepared to hold an independent inquiry into legal efficiencies in the Dust Diseases Tribunal? If the issue could be taken off the table … well, for one thing, they'd be able to see the table again. The Cabinet Office's Leigh Sanderson and Laurie Glanfield, head of the attorney-general's department, were slated as candidates to head it, and asked to attend the next negotiating summit. At 9.00AM on Thursday, 18 November, they joined a packed table in the conference room at Lazards' office on Level 44 of the Gateway Building overlooking Circular Quay. Combet and the NSW Labor Council's Mark Lennon, Binsted, Anthea Prestage and Andrew Ko from Lazards, and Gordon and Ken Fowlie from Slater & Gordon faced Hunt, his Caliburn colleague Michael Harrison, Morgan, Atanaskovic, Zwier and Hardie's Peter Baker. After the discussions had proceeded in their usual circular fashion for a time, and Hunt had made his usual swingeing critique of legal costs, Combet revealed that he had recommended a formal government review of the claims system. With the costs question out of the way, the parties should be able to complete a head of agreement by the end of the following week.

'That was the meeting I enjoyed most with Hardie's,' recalls Combet. 'The day I went and told them that that was what I was going to do and they could get stuffed. They just looked completely flummoxed. Peter Hunt went white and didn't know what to do. John Morgan could just see his whole grand plan going out the window. That was the last I saw of him.' At a press conference a few hours later, Carr insisted that the review would 'not even consider a statutory scheme', and that it was 'not about reducing assistance to victims or doing away with their very important common law rights'. A deal by Christmas had always been a certainty. Only now was it clear *which* Christmas.

'A nutcutting meeting'

'Today James Hardie has corrected the unintentional underfunding of the MRCF in 2001. Following our offer of voluntary funding made to the Jackson Commission in July, we have now agreed a fair and commercially sound arrangement to provide such compensation for proven asbestos-related disease sufferers affected by James Hardie's former subsidiaries over the next half century, or so. We have continued to acknowledge our moral responsibility to current and future claimants, and I hope that today's announcement convinces the Australian community that we are seriously committed to that responsibility.'

—James Hardie chairman, Meredith Hellicar, 21 December 2004

IN ONE SENSE, JAMES HARDIE HAD ACHIEVED ITS ENDS. It had always wanted the NSW government to take an interest in the Dust Diseases Tribunal's machinations. But the inquiry that was now envisaged would be a circumscribed affair, dealing with the machinery that existed rather than inventing anything new — 'a short, sharp review', as Carr promised. And Hardie, it now seemed, had overinvested in the precondition of legal efficiencies as part of negotiations; like an unwary bather making use of a tree branch, it had now seen Combet make off with its clothes. Russell Chenu groaned: 'My first thought was: "God, after the special commission, can we stand another inquiry? Surely this doesn't require an inquiry?" I was very fearful that it was a set-up, that we'd go through the motions and come out without significant reform. We put out a release saying that we welcomed the review, but I for one thought we'd be taken to the cleaners.' Hardie made one further effort to cover its modesty in a meeting at Lazards at 5.00PM on Monday, 22 November, where Chenu suggested that Hardie's funding might be made conditional on the outcome of the inquiry. Combet called in reinforcements, writing to Sanderson:

> It is our unequivocal view that James Hardie must fund the compensation liabilities in the context of the existing asbestos compensation system, taking into account any changes and savings emanating from the review. There is no valid reason why the condition sought by James Hardie should be acceded to. It is therefore an immediate barrier to the conclusion of a Heads of Agreement in the negotiation … I am writing to advise you of the impasse in the negotiations and to seek the support of the government for the approach we have adopted.

When Sanderson wrote back a few days later — 'The government supports your insistence that the heads of agreement be concluded urgently and that it not be conditional upon the outcome of the review' — it was clear that those clothes really *were* gone. Chenu grinned and bore it: 'After my initial misgivings, other people said: "Laurie Glanfield has got a significant record of reform in other fields, like workers' comp, motor accident, tort reform. Go with it." My cynical response was that there is reform fatigue in many branches of government, that the Carr government had been in power eight years, and wouldn't have the stomach for it. But we didn't have any choice.' By this stage, though, Chenu had learned to like Combet. The ACTU secretary clearly had considerable negotiating finesse, even if his flair for public theatre could be a source of discomfiture. 'I developed great respect for Greg,' says Chenu. 'He was very sincere, commercial and pragmatic. Then you would read the papers the next day and there would be Greg saying: "I've given Hardie a week to do this. They're a bunch of bastards." And you'd think: "Hey, that's not the guy we were negotiating with." But you got used to it.'

There was now no impediment to a deal before Christmas — except that trouble was about to break out on another front, at the

Medical Research and Compensation Foundation. The foundation had been a troubled bystander to the apparent impasse in negotiations between the ACTU and Hardie, while its own negotiations with the ABN60 Foundation had stalled. Put simply, the ABN60 Foundation wanted to pay out the $85.6 million it owed the MRCF in a lump sum, its put option the previous February having fallen through. The MRCF, moreover, needed the money—badly. Without the sum, its net assets were smaller than the quantum of existing claims against it. Insolvent trading was staring them in the face. But when Phil Morley and Caliburn's Michael Harrison visited the foundation's new office at Australia Square on Friday 22 October, Ian Hutchinson and Dennis Cooper advised that they would not accept any of the conditions the ABN60 Foundation was proposing—and that, if necessary, they would seek to have the foundation put into provisional liquidation. After making the foundation's position public on the Monday, John MacGregor and his colleague Peter Laidlaw took Cooper to face his first real media scrum in Martin Place. Cooper acquitted himself well, albeit under very close supervision. When MacGregor later bumped into Barrie Unsworth, the old Labor warhorse commented: 'I saw you on TV, John. You were standing so close to that client of yours that it looked like he'd get your knee right up his clacker if he said one wrong thing.' A week later, Justice Peter Young of the NSW Supreme Court ordered that evidence supporting any proposed liquidation be filed by 25 November, ahead of a hearing the following week.

The ACTU was disturbed, but not unsympathetic. 'I knew they were accused of grandstanding, but I think they were genuinely apprehensive about the lack of progress,' says Combet. 'Jesus, they were sitting on a board continuing to pay out 100 cents in the dollar to claimants, when given the amount of money they had and their potential number of claimants they should probably have been paying out two cents. In their position, I'd've been worried, too.' Hardie, however, was furious. At its board meeting in Amsterdam on 8 and 9 November, it resolved to provide an indemnity to ABN60's directors to allow the paying out of the deed. But the MRCF board was unprepared to accept any money if it meant a waiver of its rights to take legal action against ABN60 and Hardie. On the afternoon of 24 November, Cooper, Hutchinson, Jollie and Edwards resolved to seek orders to appoint as administrators Peter Walker and Steve Sherman of Ferrier Hodgson, who had done the job at One-Tel. When the first tranche of ABN60's money, $31.5 million, was electronically transferred to the foundation at 6.45PM, MacGregor was sitting in Cooper's office. 'What are you going to do?' asked MacGregor. 'We're going to send it straight back,' said Cooper. MacGregor called it 'playing ping pong with a $30 million ball'.

Chenu was baffled. On top of that, Combet was using Leigh Sanderson's letter to give Hardie another public baking. As Chenu unsuccessfully tried ringing Combet's mobile to placate him, his chairman was growing increasingly agitated: she had interviews with *PM* and *The 7.30 Report* lined up for the evening, and was feeling the pressure. When he arrived at his flat at McMahon's Point at about 7.15PM, Chenu felt wrung out, and turned on the television to watch Hellicar:

> I had been trying to contact Greg for upwards of twenty-four hours, and he wasn't responding. But I knew that Meredith was appearing that night and I expected she was going to be on first-up. Anyway, just as it switched from the news to *The 7.30 Report*, the phone rings. It was Greg. In fact I was really pissed with Greg because I'd wanted to watch the interview knowing that [Kerry] O'Brien was going to give Meredith buggery. So I was trying to listen to Greg on the phone *and* Meredith on television at the same time. I kid you not.

O'Brien did give Hellicar 'buggery', including the complaint that Hellicar had declined to attend negotiations herself. And as Chenu watched, Hellicar, rather than give the correct legal explanation that Dutch law prevented her presence, decided to dish out a soundbite or two of her own:

> *O'Brien*: Well, instead of delivering a message to him on this program tonight, how about delivering it to him personally across the table?

Hellicar: I would love to. If he would ...

O'Brien: OK. I'm sure he would welcome ...

Hellicar: Russell Chenu has left messages for him throughout today. We have been waiting for him to come back to the negotiating table.

O'Brien: So you will go to the table?

Hellicar: We delivered ... I don't need to go to the table.

O'Brien: I'm sorry. I thought you ...

Hellicar: Sorry, our executives, our executives are there. Russell Chenu has stayed in Australia. He is determined not to go back to States until we have an agreement. I am happy for our negotiating team to go into the room. They have the authority from the board to finalise this agreement. Why isn't Greg in the negotiating room rather than out calling on us in press conferences to do something we're sitting waiting to do with him?

Chenu laughed inwardly and carried on the conversation with Combet, arranging to see him the next day. Combet's phone rang the moment he disconnected: it was his wife Petra, in a fury, complaining that she'd just watched Hellicar on *The 7.30 Report* and wanted to punch her on the nose. The event became something of a shared joke between Chenu and Combet. When they met at Export House the next day, for the first time *sans* advisers, they had their most productive conversation of the negotiations.

They discussed the cap on the proportion of Hardie's free cash flow to be devoted to the fund, and agreed on the fairness and sustainability of 35 per cent. 'If we're going to do this, we'll do it so it lasts,' said Chenu. 'I'm not setting out to dog on you, or come up with something that won't work. The company will collapse if we do that. I won't be pulling some smartarse move on you.' Combet replied: 'We'll do our work, but I appreciate that observation.' If negotiations were to stand a chance of prospering, they also agreed, the MRCF's liquidation bid had to be be stalled. Hardie and the ACTU, they decided, would act in concert to prevent it: Atanaskovic and Zwier would represent the former with Tom Bathurst QC, and ACTU in-house lawyer Stephen Jones the latter. The eventual hearing on 2 December, in fact, had to be adjourned to a larger room at the Supreme Court to accommodate the unexpected weight of legal numbers.

The foundation's directors were, in fact, loath to seek provisional liquidation, which would have insurance and tax implications — the case for the foundation's insolvency, too, was not particularly strong. Instead, Ian Hutchinson was playing what he confided to a friend was 'the biggest game of poker in town'. The MRCF's directors wanted their money free of conditions. And that, in the end, is what they received, when a letter arrived at Clayton Utz from Hardie approving the transfer, allowing an adjournment. Combet forwarded Cooper a letter of comfort saying that negotiations should be completed 'well prior to Christmas', and expressing 'cautious optimism' about the outcome. This feeling was strengthened when he and Zwier spent the next morning in 'without prejudice' discussions at ACTU headquarters. Hardie wanted a provision in the heads of agreement allowing the proportion of free cash flow to 'step down' by increments of 5 per cent to as low as 10 per cent; as a quid pro quo, Zwier suggested provisions for a 'step up', and levels below which the proportion could not fall by certain dates. Having had the terms written up at lunchtime, he came back for further discussions with Combet and Gordon in the afternoon. There were many calls on Zwier's services at this point: he flew to Zurich that evening to act in another matter. Binsted was also heading to Europe, on a long-delayed holiday to Berlin with his son Tim, who had been studying the Cold War in Year 12. But the momentum was now carried forward by Binsted's replacement, Brian Wilson.

Wilson is one of Australia's gurus of corporate finance, with more than three decades behind him at Lloyd's, Schroders, County Natwest and Salomons. He combines candour with discretion, technical competence with personal friendliness. For his own part, he cast no stones at Hardie:

> I guess, like many in the business community, I wondered how Hardie had gotten itself into this position. And the only thing that made sense was what someone called the Salami Principle [one thin slice at a time]. That's when you're looking at the ground in front of your feet, each

little step in isolation making sense. But clearly no one had said at the outset: 'If we take all these steps, we'll end up in an untenable position.'

Even Banton, curtly dismissive of bankers in general, was struck by Wilson's gentle authority: 'He is an absolute class act. A gentleman. And brilliant. He speaks in a very soft voice, but he's very strong.' When Wilson accepted the brief, his first act was to write a two-page digest of the agreement, explaining: 'I take the attitude that any transaction that you can't summarise on two sheets of paper is too complicated.' The negotiators would refer to it again and again. Above all, Wilson was senior. And with a respected peer across the table and a more active principal in Chenu, Hunt began to show his virtues. For all his occasional personal awkwardness, Hunt was passionate about getting a deal done, and utterly dedicated to the task. The two other critical figures in the next few weeks would be Atanaskovic and Slater & Gordon's Ken Fowlie, the legal draftsmen for their respective sides. Atanaskovic showed his virtuoso skills as a designer of documentation. 'He's a pain in the arse, but the respect for him on our side of the table really grew,' says the ACTU's George Wright. 'Once the job was there to be done, he really drove the practical work. We even warmed to his weird personal sense of humour.' Fowlie, a big, bearded, bonhomous figure, inculcated a sense of teamwork by beginning all his emails to both sides with the same greeting: 'Dear Colleagues'.

For some, it was harder than for others to believe in a collegiate at work. Banton found Hardie's whole existence an insult. He never stopped referring to Hellicar as 'Merry Death', and he would imitate Hunt's habit of dropping his rs. Atanaskovic's bleak humour drove him to distraction. 'We don't want Hardies to be known as Santa Claus, do we?' Atanaskovic quipped in one meeting. Banton exploded: 'Well, that'll never happen will it? In fact, you should withdraw that. Russell if you had any guts, you'd get him to withdraw that.' When Chenu said nothing, Banton seethed: 'Shows you're gutless, too.' When the ACTU brought in its own actuary, Josh Whitehead of Taylor Fry, Banton decided to rev him up like a football coach before a big game: 'This is not just about flaming

numbers. This is about people's lives; about how this company produced all these products for years after everybody else had stopped
and making billions!' When Whitehead was unexpectedly assertive
in dealing with his rivals from KPMG, Banton glowed with fatherly
pride.

In public, too, Hardie was still pushing a big barrow of
grievances, which it wheeled out in a series of newspapers
advertisements designed by Jackson Wells Morris, declaring that
'There Are Two Sides to Every Story', and which Alan Jones
unexpectedly allowed Meredith Hellicar to unload on 2GB on the
morning of 8 December. Jones had been an astringent critic of
Hardie, but this morning seemed to want to remind Bob Carr
exactly who was boss of the state. Seizing on the fact that Hardie
had presented a draft heads of agreement to the ACTU on 3
November — which was, of course, a response to the ACTU's draft
of 15 October — Jones declared that he 'smelled a rat': 'This game is
not about political point scoring or winners or losers in some great
game between James Hardie, state and federal government and
unions. It's not about someone using the vulnerability of people to
give themselves a profile. This is about compensating victims of
asbestos-related disease ... I think some people have been less than
truthful in all of this and their behaviour less than adequate'. And
just who did he have in mind?

> *Jones*: Has Mr Carr spoken to anyone at James Hardie?
> *Hellicar*: No he won't. He refuses to meet with us. He has refused ...
> *Jones*: How can he make judgements about what Hardie are or are not
> doing if he refuses to speak to James Hardie?
> *Hellicar*: I have no idea, Alan. That's a very good question.

The answer, of course, was that the ACTU had been appointed
the government's agent in the negotiation when the Jackson inquiry
had reported — which may or may not have been appropriate, but
was now a ten-week old story. The interview, bizarrely disjointed,
was carried forward only by the impetus of Jones' indignation:

Jones: But one final point, okay, so that's the union. Still haven't had a response from them but your submissions are consistent with the agreed terms in the heads of agreement?
Hellicar: Well, the heads of agreement itself hasn't been agreed.
Jones: No it's …
Hellicar: But yes …
Jones: … consistent with what you think the heads of agreement should be agreed to.
Hellicar: Yes, absolutely.

Jones, *mirabile dictu*, had successfully established that Hardie agreed with its own heads of agreement. 'That's Meredith Hellicar and that's a disgrace,' Jones stated in conclusion. 'And I think victims need to understand that some people are playing egos here but not reality.' He was absolutely right. The reality was that when Zwier returned from Europe for a meeting at Lazards on Saturday 11 December, he was stunned by the sudden cordiality pervading negotiations. 'It must be all your bad jokes,' he said to Atanaskovic. 'People feel sorry for you.' Zwier provided the day's only real disruption, when, feeling the effects of the thirty-hour flight from which he'd disembarked at 7.00AM, he swivelled sleepily in his chair and snagged the chord on Banton's respirator. 'Mate! Mate!' Banton cried suddenly. 'Oh God, Bernie!' said Zwier, coming to. 'What have I done?' 'Almost killed your opponent,' Banton said.

As night fell over Sydney, Combet thought he felt resistance. He passed a note to Wilson: 'I think they are under a fair bit of pressure and would like to stall until next week'. He upped the stakes a little. He pushed a few more items under the definition of 'free cash flow'; he wanted the liability assessment for the step up/step down clauses to be over four years rather than one. He thought, at one stage, he saw Chenu's hands shaking. 'I felt pretty relaxed, actually,' says Combet. 'I felt good. I just hardlined it. Mind you, I'm not critical of Russell. It was a fucking big call.' Chenu insists that he was comfortable with accommodating the ACTU; the next day, indeed, he rang Combet, who was having lunch at Coogee, to confirm his understandings of the previous evening:

That night was a nutcutting meeting, I can tell you. But it was within the architecture that the board had agreed to in Amsterdam, so I was comfortable with it. I was tired. I had been through the wringer. Greg was really pushing the envelope in order to get the deal done by Christmas, and he knew that that if we didn't get it done then there would be no chance of signing anything by Christmas. But I wasn't unhappy with the position we came to.

It was Hardie's directors who now equivocated. They wanted the New South Wales government to extinguish claims for civil liability; they were also anxious that the ACTU and the NSW Labor Council cease comments prejudicial to the company's 'sales revenue or business activities'. Banton, for one, was not hearing of that. When Peter Baker said to him that Hardie would prefer he tone his public comments down when the agreement was signed, Banton became incandescent: 'You're living in hope, Peter. The heads of agreement is not legally binding. You bludgers can still walk away. And I've got to tell you, I would have a hard time saying anything good about this company. It's been dragged kicking and screaming to the table.' In forwarding his version of the heads of agreement, Combet was more formal but no less insistent: 'I believe that all matters of substance are now agreed and that it is time to cease the potentially endless discussion of minor amendments. It follows that I do not believe further meetings are necessary.' The next meeting that took place was the public one: the union congregation out the front of Governor Macquarie Tower to welcome what was the largest financial settlement in Australian history.

This was a big day for the ACTU, and they weren't going to waste it. The months since prime minister John Howard's re-election on 9 October had been dark days, and Combet's absences from his office had been noted. 'People here were feeling a bit neglected,' says Wright. 'It was such a huge thing and took so much time, at a time when people were feeling sensitive, even depressed.' When Hardie representatives suggested that they would like to hold a joint press conference, Wright dismissed them:

The context for this is the lead up and aftermath of an election in which Labor was smashed, where IR reforms were top of the government's agenda. It was a hugely important thing for us not only to deliver for the victims but to make sure it was understood in the community the role that unions played. It was always in my mind that the money shot — the one they put at the end of the news while the credits role — had to be the rally at the end. You had to use the political capital. We had no interest in spreading that political capital to them.

Wright stage-managed it carefully. He got the cameras, and he got the crowd, ringing CFMEU secretary Andrew Ferguson and asking if he could spare some workers. 'How many do you want?' asked Ferguson. 'Would four hundred do?' The government wasn't informed, and Carr, in fact, was away on a Christmas break. That left deputy premier Andrew Refshauge to experience — as, some observed, for perhaps the first time in his political career — the cheers of a rally. Yet if the stage management was careful, the emotion was perfectly genuine. In Greg Combet's words:

Union people are very passionate about this issue and rightly so. You'd wonder about them if they weren't. Paul Bastian has worked very hard on it. Andrew Ferguson, too. Officials in the union movement round Australia have all had colleagues and friends die from asbestosis, mesothelioma. After the health centre I worked in, I joined the Waterside Workers' Federation. Our workers, before containerisation, had lugged the Wittenoom asbestos in bags on their backs at Fremantle into holds. Tas Bull had been a wharfie in the 1950s and had many mates die; we all had. We knew how crook it was and we fought like fuck. Employers killed our people.

So George Wright got his 'money shot', but it sprang from real suffering, real relief. The pride in Greg Combet of his mother and sister was unfeigned; tears that poured down the face of CFMEU assistant secretary Brian Spargles' face as he bearhugged Bernie Banton, who had flown back from a holiday in Queensland, were not for sake of telegenia. And the closing dinner of seafood platters at Nick's Seafood Bar and Grill in Cockle Bay, attended by Combet, Banton, Wright, Fowlie, and Stephen Jones, was very wet indeed. Combet took particular delight in two cartoons that had been sent to him anonymously during negotiations. In one, purporting to be 'Lesson One' on 'How to become Chairman of the Board when you grow up', Hellicar was depicted wagging an admonishing finger at her daughter, who was dragging a teddy along the ground: 'No precious, Mummy is not happy that you took Edwina's Steiff teddy. Remember, we only steal from those less fortunate than ourselves because they won't be able to afford a good lawyer.' In the other, a woman, knickers marked 'James Hardie', was leaving a threesome with Macdonald and Shafron with the parting words: 'Thanks, you were great ... but all that heavy breathing reminded me of someone dying of asbestosis. So $9,000,000 for you, big boy, and $1,000,000 for your little mate'.

For all the satisfaction, little had been forgotten, and nothing forgiven. Banton, feeling somewhat the worse for wear anyway when he turned up at the Intercontinental Hotel for Channel Nine's Today at ten to six the next morning, was not in the mood to encounter Hellicar, arriving for her own appearance. For Hellicar, this was business. For Banton, it remained deeply personal. 'Isn't it wonderful we've come to an agreement, Bernie?' Hellicar said delightedly.

'Well, there's nothing legally binding yet, Meredith,' Banton said warily. 'But yes, it's another step forward.'

'But it's what we've been looking for all along,' Hellicar continued.

Banton could feel the anger welling within him again. 'Don't go there Meredith,' he said finally. 'You have a good Christmas and I'm going.' So saying, he took his leave, respirator in hand.

THE HARDIE PRESS CONFERENCE later that day, attended by Hellicar, Chenu and Hunt, was a quieter affair. There was no celebration and, though some satisfaction, more circumspection. Hellicar put the best face on matters:

Today James Hardie has corrected the unintentional underfunding of the Medical Research and Compensation Foundation in 2001. Following our offer of voluntary funding made to the Jackson Commission in July, we have now agreed a fair and commercially sound arrangement to provide such compensation for proven asbestos-related disease sufferers affected by James Hardie's former subsidiaries over the next half century, or so. We have continued to acknowledge our moral responsibility to current and future claimants, and I hope that today's announcement convinces the Australian community that we are seriously committed to that responsibility.

Probably the most considered comment was Chenu's: 'I am certainly not going to stand here and say the company will be here in forty years. It's quite unusual for a company to survive forty years in recent years.' Quite so. The government's inquiry into the Dust Diseases Tribunal was more searching that Hardie had expected, and held encouraging portents for a reduction of legal costs within the existing compensation framework. But as Leigh Sanderson from the Cabinet Office, Caliburn and Atanaskovic Hartnell (acting for Hardie), and Lazards and Gilbert & Tobin (acting for the state government) toiled through 2005 to turn the heads of agreement into a legally binding document, and Lonergan & Edwards compiled an ever-growing information memorandum to be put to shareholders, Chenu's corporate memento mori sounded increasingly wise.

The process, meant to take six months, was slowed by exogenous events. Bob Carr resigned abruptly on 27 July; his successor, Morris Iemma, did not meet Combet and Banton until 19 August, and Hardie representatives until 5 September. There were gaping boxes to be ticked: Hardie directors were loath to proceed without some protection from shareholder suits and prosecutions arising from ASIC's sprawling, $7 million investigation, to which Carr had been amenable but to which Iemma was resistant; the bankability of the special purpose vehicle hinged on tax deductibility for distributions, which needed approval at the highest levels of government and bureaucracy; the enforceability of Australian civil court judgements in the Netherlands and vice versa required the preparation of a bilateral agreement; the award of $320,000 damages against AMACA by Justice Curtis in the DDT in the case of a dying asbestos insulation contractor from New Zealand, Bernard Frost, potentially blazed a trail for other offshore litigants to sue in Australia, necessitating an expensive appeal. Then there were the subtle effects of the consolidation of Hardie executive responsibility towards the United States. Peter Macdonald's successor as CEO, the mercurial Louis Gries, is no less a graduate of the winner-take-all school. He had famously exhorted his salesmen: 'Make wood go away.' There is little doubt he would have preferred that sufferers of asbestos-related disease do the same.

The negotiators enjoyed some good fortune. The breakneck increase in claims slowed, prolonging the life of the Medical Research and Compensation Foundation, and Hardie profits soared, thanks to a hearty American house-building cycle. Yet when Gries faced a half-year profit press conference on 9 November, projecting annualised net earnings in excess of $US200 million, he assumed a languid air where negotiations were concerned. 'It's slower than we wanted,' he said. 'It's slower than everyone else wanted. But we're getting the job done.' A pre-Christmas settlement was now threatening to run foul of an immoveable date: 2 December, on which parliament in New South Wales was due to rise. Rallies at Export House organised by the AMWU and the Asbestos Diseases Foundation of Australia to coincide with Asbestos Awareness Week drew attention to the deadlock, but nothing seemed likely to break it.

After further fruitless discussions over the weekend of 19 and 20 November, Iemma, at Combet's instigation, took a hand, publicly mooting punitive retrospective legislation to unwind Hardie's four-year-old restructuring by restoring the partly paid shares: a draconian, and probably unconstitutional, step, but meant to restore urgency to the mission. The gesture was partly theatrical: Hellicar commented drolly that 'you can sense the closeness of the deal when people start positioning themselves to look like they are dragging James Hardie desperately across the finishing line'. But just to minimise further distractions, Lazard's Wilson changed the venue of meetings from his bank's sunny Gateway boardroom to a functional meeting room without a view on the seventh floor of the Marriott Hotel.

The most intractable issue, ironically, was the one which positioned Hardie, Iemma's government and ACTU in the same corner: tax. After a year of talks with the Australian Taxation Office failing to clarify the deductibility of distributions, treasurer Peter Costello tried to garner some of the available political capital for himself by publicly disavowing special legislation, telling reporters on 24 November that Hardie could not 'expect a special tax law for itself':

> This company has not exactly been the best corporate citizen in this country ... The company is now facing up to its obligations in relation to compensation for (the) poor people who are dying ... and their relatives. It will not be given special treatment, this company, under corporation law or under tax law. It will abide by the law — corporations law, tax law, personal injury law — as it always should have.

Over the weekend of 26 and 27 November, however, the parties managed to grope their way to a workable arrangement. The government allowed a limited release from liability, sparing Hardie directors from suits commenced by asbestos claimants, while still admitting civil and criminal actions; the agreement of the 164-page Principal Deed, forshadowed by Iemma on 29 November and ratified by Hardie's board two days later, remained subject to a favourable ruling from the Australian Taxation Office as well as shareholder approval. At a signing ceremony at Governor Macquarie Tower on Friday 2 December, Iemma called the deal 'fair, affordable and just for the victims of James Hardie', while admitting that it would be 'back to the drawing board with negotiations' in the event of unfavourable tax treatment. A fortnight later, in fact, Hardie advised the ASX of the ATO's view that contributions to the vehicle would not be deductible 'under current federal income tax legislation'.

Even if all the remaining hurdles are overcome, furthermore, the new arrangements should not be seen as an end so much as another beginning, with a new set of problems, risks and unknowns. An important lesson of the Hardie story is that disease marches to its own drumbeat — one that has nothing to do with the business cycle, the investment climate, the time horizons of managers, the trends of law, and the infatuations of government. And just as a previous generation left asbestos as a crisis for ours, so ours will bequeath a system for the next, which may or may not stand the test of time. A robust structure will take the parties only part of the way. It will be set at nought if it is not underlain by goodwill — a quality conspicuously lacking from much of the last five years. Let a story that Bernie Banton tells about his last visit to the Dust Diseases Board to assess his degree of impairment hold out this hope:

> The specialist I go to see at the Dust Board turns out to be this bloke John Mann, who proudly tells me he was Hardie's chief medical officer for three or four years. How about that? I said to him: 'Well, what are you doing here? Trying to purge yourself of all the sins of the past?' He says: 'Some would look at it that way.' I say: 'Well, that's how I'd look at it! What about you?' He says: 'Well, I had an extensive practice, but I feel like giving something back.' I say to him: 'Well, how does that equate, then?' I wasn't going to let that get away, and I really enjoyed our chat!
>
> But, I tell you what, he gave me the most thorough examination I have ever had in there. Usually, you're in and out from the visiting specialist in no more than ten minutes. I was with him for an hour and a half. Pity for all the people behind me, eh? And he said: 'Bernie, I don't know what you're doing for the rest of the day, but I want you to have a high resolution CAT scan in Macquarie Street this afternoon. I'm not happy with the quality of these scans. Come back when you've had them and we'll have another look.'

As a result of the examination, Banton's condition was officially adjusted from '60 per cent dusted' to '80 per cent dusted' and his pension increased; he has since been designated as totally incapacitated. What surprised Banton, however, was the care. It was not something he associated with Hardie. Nor, really, does anyone. But they yet might.

-Epilogue-

'A class thing'

'I found myself rhetorically asking: did anyone stand back and ask themselves the simple question, is this right?'
—Justice Owen, *The Failure of HIH Insurance*, April 2002

JUSTICE NEVILLE OWEN'S SUCCINCT FORMULATION at the time of his report into the collapse of HIH Insurance was widely quoted. It was not easy question to answer there, and it is still less at James Hardie. In the passage of years, Hardie has come to seem like a corporate Jim Jones handing out the Kool-Aid at Jonestown. But in the era it was Australia's number-one asbestos company, Hardie manufactured legal products in accordance with government regulations, which it sold to consumers eager for them. In retrospective judgements of all sorts, one must always guard against what E. P. Thompson called 'the endless condescension of posterity'. In some aspects of the Hardie story, it feels like you need not a lawyer or a businessman but an ethics professor.

'James Hardie Knew' has been a popular catchcry of the company's critics over the last five years. But knew what? Knew that asbestos was dangerous? Most certainly. Knew that it could be lethal in quite small doses not only to those working in its factories but even to those merely sawing or breaking it? The epidemiological evidence was far less precise. One would have expected anyone in full possession of such knowledge to steer very clear of factories producing asbestos products—but, as we know, Hardie directors and managers did not. Senior individuals like Alan Woodford, Ray Palfreyman and Rex Torzillo ended up victims of asbestos-related disease, as did their workers. If they 'knew', they certainly made the ultimate sacrifice.

One of my most interesting visits in the course of researching *Asbestos House* was to Warwick Lane, a thirty-year veteran manager who designed Camellia's Tilux plant and ended up running Hardie-BI. Lane does not live in a huge mansion and smoke fat cigars as ex-Hardie executives are meant to: he lives in a very modest one-bedroom home at Gerringong, on the south coast of New South Wales, and wheezed his way through the interview, on account of his emphysema. He told many stories. He remembered, for instance, going with Torzillo in the early 1950s to see their professor at the University of Technology to be set their thesis topics: 'Warwick, you can do the medical side of health hazards of dust in the asbestos cement industry; Rex, you can do the engineering side.' Lane had no idea where to start. Heavens, he was a chemical engineer, wasn't he? He tentatively put together a literature review, relying heavily on the Merewether reports and the Dreessen standard, and circumspectly concluded: 'Generally speaking there is no call for greater dust suppression measure in the asbestos cement industry than there is in industry generally.' In the copy Lane gave to me he had handwritten just below these lines, in perhaps a kind of unconscious remonstration with himself: 'Rex Louis Torzillo, Died 11 May 1989 of Mesothelioma. My Good Friend.'

The health hazards of asbestos, however, should never have been left to the likes of Warwick Lane to solve. If the idea that a company 'knew' something is hard to sustain, an allegation that can more precisely be levelled is 'James Hardie Should Have Known'. For much of the twentieth century, asbestos fell into the category of, to borrow Donald Rumsfeld's famous formulation, a 'known unknown', being known to be dangerous to an unknown degree. That does not exonerate Hardie; if anything, it could be held that the board and company were obliged to make some effort to dispel this uncertainty, or for as long as uncertainty existed to err on the side of caution. As Jock McCulloch argued twenty years ago in *Asbestos: Its Human Cost:*

> The accretions to medical science have not followed a linear path, despite what both the industry and its critics would have us believe. The industry relies upon a crude form of positivism in justifying its slowness

to act in protecting workers from fibre. Critics of companies such as CSR and James Hardie in Australia use much the same kind of approach in seeking to show that industry failed to respond to medical breakthroughs, such as the Merewether study of 1948 or the Selikoff study of 1964.

Both critics and industry alike refuse to recognise the complex way in which medical research has evolved. It is that complex path which defines the levels of moral responsibility that must be borne by the industry. It is not sufficient to examine the publication dates of studies such as those of Wagner and Merewether in judging the behaviour of producers and public authorities. To do so implies that the industry had no independent resources or was under no obligation to monitor changes in the oral tradition among researchers which almost certainly moved ahead of substantive published results. The industry had access to resources and to data denied independent researchers. One can only assume that physicians employed by firms such as Johns-Manville or James Hardie would have known more than other researchers if only because of their strategic position. They knew who was working in the industry; they had access to the health records of those workers; they knew which parts of the productive process were the most dusty; they had access to dust-count data, however imperfect; and they had access to oral evidence as to the fate of male and female employees who died from respiratory disease.

Instead, Hardie used uncertainty as a pretext for inaction. The process of legal discovery over the last twenty-five years has unearthed considerable quantities of Hardie documentation and internal correspondence concerning dust and its perils. But when considered as a proportion of the quantum of documentation that an industrial company of Hardie's size would produce in the normal run of events, the bulk of this material fades in significance. Certain individuals in Hardie took dust and disease very seriously indeed. But they were isolated. For the most part, the board and senior managers seem to have been indifferent, untroubled, for it was always a problem whose consideration could be deferred. 'They were too arrogant and foolish to accept that it was in their interests to deal with the problem,' recalls Peter Russell.

Asbestos-industry advocates sometimes counterclaim that companies such as Johns-Manville and Turner & Newall sponsored a considerable amount of medical research in the 1940s and 1950s, and also gave rise to research bodies like the Asbestosis Research Council — of which, let it be recalled, Hardie was an eager member. But the objective of the industry's research was never to lay bare the danger of asbestos; it was to arrive at agreed safety minimums permitting the industry to proceed with the least disruption. One aspect of asbestos-related disease that was widely understood, moreover, was that it lay latent in the human body for periods of a decade and more. This made the existence of a 'known unknown' exceptionally dangerous. Presumption of innocence might be a fundamental tenet of the law for persons; but because epidemiological evidence is seldom total, or even entirely unambiguous, it is supremely ill-suited to judgements concerning substances. And in the case of asbestos, there was always the possibility that it might be decades before the precise degree of the harm it was wreaking was known. Hardie employees and consumers in the 1950s, 1960s and 1970s, therefore, were essentially the unwitting subjects of a medical experiment, the answers to which lay a generation away.

Not only did James Hardie choose to leave its known unknown largely unaltered; it chose to leave its known knowns unuttered. It is more than seventy years since Sir Thomas Legge, Britain's chief medical inspector of factories, articulated what might be thought of as the first commandment of occupational health and safety: 'All workmen should be told something of the danger of the materials they come in contact with, and not be left to find out for themselves — sometimes at the cost of their lives'. Yet Hardie's efforts at worker education were negligible, and simple expedients such as health warnings for users were resisted. Hardie's attitude recalls the famous speech of the mayor in Henrik Ibsen's *An Enemy of the People*, when he is criticised by his brother Dr Stockman for not informing the public of the toxicity of the town baths:

Without my reputation for integrity, I could no longer guide and direct affairs in the way which I consider most conducive to the general good. On that account — and for various other reasons — it is a matter of the greatest concern to me that your report should not be submitted to the directorate of the Baths. It must be withheld for the good of the community. Later on, I shall bring up the matter for discussion, and we shall deal with it as best we can — discreetly. But nothing of this dangerous business — not a single word — must become known to the public ... The public doesn't need new ideas. What's best for the public are the good, old, established ideas that they already have.

Another line of argument commonly advanced in advocacy of asbestos manufacturers, aired again most recently by Wilson Tuckey in December 2004 during debate about legislation passing Jackson inquiry documentation to ASIC, is a hymn to the substance's virtues. Tuckey reminded his parliamentary colleagues, not without force, of the contribution asbestos had made to affordable housing:

Asbestos cement, as we knew it, delivered — in terms of the public good — over the 40-odd years that the Member for Parramatta chose to speak about it. And of course cost of housing is an issue that arose at the last election. And I know well, where for instance a recent Labor Prime Minister was raised, his electorate was Blaxland, I had a sister who lived in that region on one occasion, and I visited her, and every house was fibro, asbestos sheet.

Tuckey had a point. Fibro has a rightly honoured place in Australian life, history, culture, even aesthetics — Charles Pickett's 1997 book *The Fibro Frontier* is a splendid introduction. But Tuckey's was also simply a slightly more refined version of a grunt emitted by another acerbic West Australian, Lang Hancock, in June 1978: 'Some people have to suffer so the majority can benefit from asbestos.' And Hancock's analysis of the alarm over asbestos at the time was not so far from the industry's. Concluding a 1974 contribution to the *Medical Journal of Australia*, for example, Hardie's

Dr Terry McCullagh put a view almost as succinct:

> The industry is well aware of the hazards of asbestos, and having briefly
> reviewed these I think we should also remember that, if we considered
> no more than its fire-retardant properties and its use in brake linings,
> asbestos has saved more lives than it has claimed. With the great
> improvement in standards of industrial hygiene over the last decade this
> credit balance, if I may so call it, will increasingly grow more favourable.

Two years later, the industry publicity body, the Asbestos
Information Committee, founded by Turner & Newall and Cape
Asbestos, called this 'credit balance' a 'paradox':

> The drug or vaccination which saves thousands kills the very few who
> are sensitive to it; the seat belt which protects 999 from death or injury
> inflict them on the thousandth. The same paradox holds true for
> asbestos. Many people who would otherwise have perished in fires or
> on the roads are alive today because of asbestos yet it cannot be denied
> that a relatively small number have been made ill or died as a result of
> past exposure to excessive concentrations of asbestos dust.

For there to be either a 'credit balance' or a 'paradox', however,
would require acceptance that it was never possible to manufacture
or use asbestos any other way — which is, quite simply, untrue. That
asbestos has improved lives and taken lives are separate propositions.
To assert otherwise, to claim that suffering and death is simply
inevitable in some species of mining and manufacture, is to
participate in a kind of occult calculus of what constitutes, to borrow
a phrase that has been used in asbestos-related litigation, an
'acceptable level of death'.* It overlooks, too, the fact that asbestos
turned out not to be irreplaceable. Hardie investigated asbestos
substitutes as early as the late 1940s, because of the world fibre

---

* 'An Acceptable Level of Death' was the title of a BBC documentary about
Turner & Newall screened in April 1994, memorable for managing director
Colin Hope retiring to a gentlemen's lavatory in a hotel in order to escape
reporter John Ware. The phrase was used by plaintiff lawyer Kieran May:

shortage, and first reduced the amount of asbestos in its fibre-cement in the late 1950s, when it manufactured Hardieflex. But not until the late 1980s was an asbestos substitute found.

These are complicated questions — in a world that sometimes does not seem very interested in complicated answers. One reason why Hardie's critics hew to the 'James Hardie Knew' argument rather than the frankly more logical 'James Hardie Should Have Known' argument is the latter's corollary that others should also have known. Epidemiological evidence regarding asbestos was not a state secret — on the contrary. With certain honourable exceptions such as Douglas Shiels and Gordon Thomas, the attitude of health authorities in Australia was, at best, apathetic; at worst, culpable. Nor, it must be said, with honourable exceptions such as Ray Hogan and John Neil, has the record of unionists been exemplary. Forty years ago, for example, the Gippsland Trades and Labour Council petitioned a reluctant State Electricity Commission to admit health department inspectors into Yallourn power station. The council was concerned primarily with 'nox and sox' — nitrous oxide and sulphur dioxide — and was puzzled when the report referred to asbestos. A young official visited a senior officer in the industrial hygiene division of the Department of Health next time he was in Melbourne:

> In retrospect I know just how evasive his reply was. He simply took out a table from the harmful gases, vapours, fumes, mists, smokes and dust regulations which showed the permissible levels of various substances in free air. Asbestos was shown to have a permissible level of five million particles per cubic foot of air … and he told me that his people had found higher levels in the course of their tests. When I ask what the consequences were if the levels were exceeded, I was told it should be recognised that any form of dust exceeding levels laid down in the regulations was not good for health, and that levels should be kept as low as possible.

'They were not persuaded that enough people were dying or suffering an asbestos-related disease to find substitute materials or shut down and walk away. There was always an acceptable level of death.'

And that was that. The department did nothing; so did the official. One can argue that the bureaucrat was inadequately resourced to fulfil his responsibilities, and the official insufficiently trained. But these are not regarded as excuses for Hardie company officers, nor should they be. To be sure, they were accomplices rather than perpetrators. But what is the purpose of health authorities and trade unions if not to preserve workers from harm? James Hardie deserves its place in the public pillory. But it is arguable that it should not be on its own.

AGAINST THE OMISSIONS AND COMMISSIONS of the previous generation, the failures of the managers and directors of James Hardie Industries over the last five years seem second-order offences. Peter Macdonald and Peter Shafron did not wilfully continue to manufacture with an unsafe substance; they manufactured, as it were, an unsafe subsidiary. They were eager, when matters went awry, to evade responsibility. But in this, they had plenty of company. The setting up of Hardie's Potemkin foundation was the final solution to a problem that began once the company's liability to pay compensation was established. First, it tried settling everything quietly. Second, it tried taking matters to verdict. Third, in Project Chelsea, it sought to create a structure which contained the problem in a flexible manner, but which was sensitive to the stockmarket's vicissitudes — to which it fell foul. Fourth, in Project Green, it attempted to erect a closed-end fund, which hived off the liability once and for all, this time without equity-market risk — and succeeded, for a while anyway. The last was the most extreme step — because Macdonald was the most extreme, ambitious and relentless of CEOs — but all of them have been about avoiding the reality of the death James Hardie has left in its path. There is some substance to the criticisms that the company has made of the Dust Diseases Tribunal, and even of the jungle that is the tort system. But the fact remains that, on balance, courts and plaintiff lawyers have been more effective representatives of asbestos victims than have governments and unions.

Epilogue

So what happened? The Hardie story is unusual in the annals of Australian corporate scandal. We have tended to manufacture commercial villains with a certain rogueish swagger. The *dramatis personae* of Hardie, and their professional minions, were nothing of the kind. By most objective means, they were the best and the brightest. The United States has been an unhappy hunting ground for Australian business. James Hardie Industries NV, from a standing start fifteen years ago, has cracked it open, and maintained a commanding share of a growing market—an astonishing feat, and one for which future plaintiffs in the Dust Diseases Tribunal will probably have cause to be grateful.

Yet if we accept that there was no mephistophelian conspiracy as such—and the evidence does not, finally, point that way—there were certainly multiple, grievous failures: by executives too eager for a desired conclusion; directors too disposed to accommodating them; advisers too captive of the legal and commercial aspects of the transaction to actually 'advise' on anything other than execution; actuaries too amenable to preparing what they suspected the client wanted; and a foundation board too guileless to challenge what they were told. Any one of these groups might, by different behaviours, have prevented the transactions from taking place. As it was, all of them harmonised. Some of these failures are more culpable than others. All managements are in the business of advocating certain courses of action to their directors. But the steps taken by Hardie's executives to minimise estimates of the company's liabilities so that the end of shedding them was achieved were drastic and calculated. And no one seems to have grappled with the ramifications of the foundation's failure, despite their cognisance that it was a possibility, beyond a general sense that, if push came to shove, they could always rely on the 'corporate veil'. In this sense, although it failed to take some steps it might and probably should have, the board was always acting on partial information—in both senses of the term.

Frankly, however, the responsibility is shared. Greg Combet declared the affair 'a class thing'. It is an observation not without force. The individuals involved in the creation of the foundation behaved as those in social groups with shared backgrounds and shared assumptions are inclined to do, taking cues from one another, and tending to place weight on, and to overlook, the same matters.

Above all, not one among them speculated about the human consequences — as distinct from the corporate consequences — of getting the transaction wrong. This is explained by the acutely reified version of reality which modern business inhabits. Executives toiled night and day and were paid millions of dollars, directors pored over voluminous proposals, advisers wrote compendious reports, lawyers composed endless advices, in order that — well, what exactly? Exactly how imperative was it, for instance, that Hardie deconsolidate its asbestos liabilities so as to avoid the possibility of a provision under accounting standards in Australia and the US? A world in which such an aim has paramountcy is one in which John Jay Chapman's prophecy has been fulfilled, that business would 'destroy the very knowledge in us of all other natural forces except business'. If it serves any purpose, the Hardie story should remind us that commercial decisions have real, lasting and sometimes deadly human outcomes.

ACKNOWLEDGEMENTS

'This is a subject on which I know absolutely nothing; I should write a book about it.'
—Prince de Ligne

SUCH WAS THE POSITION in which I found myself in November 2004 when asked to write *Asbestos House* by Henry Rosenbloom at Scribe. I had been only faintly aware of the creation of the Medical Research and Compensation Foundation and of James Hardie's restructuring; I had not followed the Jackson commission in any detail. When I visited my first few interviewees, I'm afraid I must have seemed very dim indeed; I thank all of them for their patience and forbearance.

I devoted my first couple of months' work to poring over the transcript and exhibits of the inquiry in a spare office at Slater & Gordon. That, I should say, was the extent of the relationship. They made no special effort to influence my outlook, and I took no particular pains to solicit theirs. The same applied in my dealings with Turner Freeman, who laid at my disposal their database of discovered documents but otherwise left me pretty much alone. I am grateful to Peter Gordon and Ben Phi at Slater & Gordon, and Gerry Gardiman and Jorg Probst at Turner Freeman for their generosity and candour in my dealings with them.

It may strike some readers as strange that I can generally say the same of James Hardie Industries. There was not much for the company to gain in making its personnel available for interview, but it did so. I have been critical of Hardie in this book, but I have no criticism of the company in their dealings with me. Special thanks are extended to Meredith Hellicar and James Rickards, and also to Don Cameron of the ABN60 Foundation, who consented to my use of the James Hardie Industries Records and Reid Family Papers.

The bibliography that follows will give a hint—although only a hint—of the bulk of material that needed digesting for this project. Not all of it was easy to obtain. Where does one find that important paper by Waldemar Dreessen or Roodhouse Gloyne? I was fortunate to make the acquaintance of David Kilpatrick, who has forgotten more than I'll ever know on this subject, and who let me pull his office and his filing cabinets apart in search of a better understanding of the industrial and epidemiological history of asbestos. Greg Combet of the Australian Council of Trade Unions, Paul Bastian of the Australian Manufacturing Workers Union, and Brian Daley of the Liquor Hospitality and Miscellaneous Workers' Union likewise let me loose in rooms full of lever-arch folders—which, I must say, began to feel like a natural habitat.

Thanks to staff at the Mitchell Library, the National Library of Australia and the State Library of Victoria for many services rendered. Thanks to Frank Prain in the library at *The Age*, which I was able to access due to the good graces of my esteemed former colleague Simon Mann. And speaking of admired contemporaries, thanks to Chris Masters for a copy of his 1989 Hardie *Four Corners*, 'Dirty Secrets', and an encouraging conversation at an early stage in my travels. On my overcrowded desk when it came to writing, pride of place was taken by a lump of crocidolite, courtesy of Jock McCulloch.

Becoming involved in a subject so minute in its detail, of course, turns one into a bore, and a burden to your nearest and dearest. They learn to recognise that faraway look in your eye as a daydream of Hatschek machines and/or the corporate veil. I struck lucky in John Harms and Susan Schull, Suzy Freeman-Greene and David Glynn, James Kirby and Mary O'Brien, Jim Glaspole and Josie Yeatman, Wendy Tuohy and John Meckiff, Jim Schembri, Dr Penelope Sheehan, Ginger Briggs, Chris Middendorp, Anne-Marie Reeves, Rosie Walton—and, it need hardly be said, those mighty men of the Yarras. They either listened to me prattle on, or tuned out so effectively that I did not notice. Women who attach to novelists can inspire characters; to artists, can be immortalised on canvas; to musicians and poets, can be hymned in song or verse. I've no idea why Sally Warhaft sticks with me, a journalist. But I'm glad she does. No one has believed in this book more unstintingly than she.

As with all my books, *Asbestos House* was like trying to erect a work of masonry on a fibro budget. I am extremely blessed to have friends like Graeme, Shirley, Heath and Fang Sims who made me part of their family for the duration of my endeavours, kept me fed and watered, and helped unravel the intricacies of Sydney public transport. Louise Nemeth de Bickal, Victor and Claudia Windeyer, Ashley Hay and Nigel Beebe, Jennifer Sexton, Ebru Yaman, Dr Bridget Griffen-Foley and Kathy Bail also laid out the welcome mat. *Asbestos House* was then edited in London, at the dining table of a flat placed kindly at my disposal by my dear friend at the other end of the bestseller lists, Lynne Truss. She was not only a delightful hostess but nobly refrained from criticising my punctuation. Behind every journalist on the road, meanwhile, is a diligent cat-sitter. Trumper learned that she could depend, as I have for many years, on Philippa Hawker, who doubles as a wonderful reader, and triples as a dear friend. It's to her I dedicate this book.

A GUIDE TO SOURCES

Interviews

The following individuals were interviewed for this book: Stephen Ashe, John Atanaskovic, Bernie Banton, Paul Bastian, Greg Baxter, Paul Binsted, Ken Boundy, Michael Brown, Peter Cameron, Russell Chenu, Greg Combet, Dennis Cooper, Sir Llew Edwards, Ken Fowlie, Gerry Gardiman, Stephen Gellert, Neil Gilbert, Peter Gordon, Meredith Hellicar, Ray Hogan, Peter Hunt, Ian Hutchinson, Jim Kelso, David Kilpatrick, Michael Kotteck, Amanda Lampe, Warwick Lane, Jock McCulloch, John MacGregor, Nancy Milne, Phil Morley, Ian Mutton, Phillip Rowell, Jack Rush QC, Peter Russell, Leigh Sanderson, David Say, Jonathan Streeton, Graeme Wedderburn, Peter Willcox, Brian Wilson, John Winters, George Wright and Leon Zwier. Six other individuals gave interviews on condition of anonymity. As the interviews were at considerable length, and sometimes involved supplementary inquiries, I thank them for their patience. Particular thanks to Peter Russell for two lengthy personal memoirs of his Hardie days, and to John Kerin for a delightful and informative letter.

The following declined invitations to be interviewed: Geoff Atkins, Keith Barton, Alec Brennan, Michael Gill, Peter Jollie, Mark Knight, Stephen Loosley, Peter Macdonald, David Macfarlane, David Minty, John Reid, David Robb, Peter Shafron and Anthony Sweetman. Wayne Attrill proved uncontactable.

At the Mitchell Library, I was also able to draw on a large collection of interviews collected in an oral history program at James Hardie in 1979–1982. The following are quoted from in this book: Eric Anthony, Ted Bell, Fred Campbell, Dick Carter, Roy Casper, Bob Douglas, R. H. Evans, Ashby Hooper, Harry Leddin, Cameron

MacDougall, Frank Page, Ernest Pinkas, Jack Pollard, Gordon Reeve, Sir John Reid, Jim Rhys–Jones, Stan Strachan, Norman Thorpe, Jim Trevillyan, Don Walker, Don Warden, Ray Whitehorn and Cedric Wray.

Collections and Papers

ML MSS 5928 James Hardie Industries Ltd Records and the Reid Family Papers. A voluminous collection too broad and eclectic to catalogue here. Much of the material was collected for the company's centenary celebrations. Of outstanding interest is a photocopy of the diary of Sir John Reid from 1947 to 1977, plus full sets of intracompany newsletters: *Camellia News* and *Hardie Happenings* (New South Wales), *Hardie File* (South Australia), *Trimmings* (Victoria) and *The James Hardie Group Newsletter* (later *Newsbrief*). It contains, however, many more incidental delights such as the correspondence to and from Cyprian Truman at the Filabusi mine in Rhodesia between 1928 and 1930.

Reports

[——], James Hardie Asbestos annual reports 1951–1978

[——], James Hardie Industries annual reports 1979–

Attorney General's Department of NSW & the Cabinet Office, *Review of legal and administrative costs in dust diseases compensation claims : issues paper*, NSW Government, Sydney, 2004.

Attorney General's Department of NSW & the Cabinet Office, *Review of Legal and Administrative Costs in Dust Diseases Compensation Claims: report — March 2005*, NSW Government, Sydney, 2005.

Home Office (UK), *Annual Report of the Chief Inspector of Factories and Workshops for the Year 1898*, HMSO, London 1900.

Home Office (UK), *Annual Report of the Chief Inspector of Factories for the Year 1947*, HMSO, London, 1949.

House of Representatives Standing Committee on Aboriginal Affairs, *The Effects of Asbestos Mining on the Baryulgil Community*, Australian Government Publishing Service, Canberra, 1984.

House of Representatives Standing Committee on Aboriginal Affairs, *Report on Certain Documents Tendered to the Committee during the Baryulgil Inquiry*, Government Printer, Canberra, 1986.

Human Rights and Equal Opportunity Commission, *Report by the Race*

Discrimination Commissioner on a visit to Baryulgil & Malabugilmah, New South Wales, [Sydney], 1990.

Industries Assistance Commission, *Asbestos 30 October 1979*, Australian Government Publishing Service, Canberra, 1979.

Jackson Q.C., D. F., (Commissioner), *Report of the Special Commission of Inquiry into the Medical Research and Compensation Foundation*, NSW Government, Sydney, 2004.

Legislative Assembly New South Wales, *Report of the Director-General of Public Health New South Wales for 1938*, Government Printer, Sydney, 1940.

Merewether, E. R. A. and Price, C. W., 'Reports on the Effects of Asbestos Dust on the Lungs and Dust Suppression in the Asbestos Industry: Part 1, Occurrence of Pulmonary Fibrosis and Other Pulmonary Affliction in Asbestos Workers; Part 2, Process Giving Rise to Dust and Method of Suppression', HMSO, London, 1930.

Monopolies & Mergers Commission (UK), *Asbestos and Certain Asbestos Products: a report on the supply asbestos and certain asbestos products*, HMSO, London, 1973.

Robertson, D. G., *The Scope of Industrial Hygiene*, Commonwealth of Australia Department of Health, Government Printer, Canberra, 1922.

Robertson, D. G., *An Index to Health Hazards in Industry*, Commonwealth of Australia Department of Health, Government Printer, Canberra, 1922.

Royal Commission on Matters of Health and Safety Arising from the Use of Asbestos in Ontario, *Report of the Royal Commission on Matters of Health and Safety Arising from the Use of Asbestos in Ontario*, Ontario Ministry of the Attorney General, Toronto, 1984.

Tariff Board, *Inquiry Re Asbestos Fibre*, official transcript by Commonwealth Reporting Branch, 1954.

Tariff Board, *Report on Asbestos Fibre, 24 March 1955*, Australian Government Publishing Service, Canberra, 1955.

Corporate Histories

[——], *Cape Asbestos: the story of the Cape Asbestos Company Ltd 1893-1953*, Cape Asbestos Company, London, 1953.

[——], *Seventy Years of Wunderlich Industry*, Wunderlich Ltd, Sydney [1957].

[——], *Twenty Years of Manufacturing in Australia : Wunderlich's in 1908; a series of photographs illustrating the progress and prosperity of an Australian industry*, Wunderlich Ltd, Sydney, 1908.

[Balmforth, John], *A Tale of Two Companies*, unpublished ms, 1980.

Bures, Susan, *The House of Wunderlich*, Kangaroo Press, Kenshurst, 1987.

[Cameron, D. C.] *The Story of Fibrolite: James Hardie & Coy Pty Ltd NZ Silver Jubilee 1938–1963*, NZ Press, Auckland, 1963.

[Cameron, D. C.] *Hardie Investments Pty Ltd and Associated Companies: a brief history of their origin, development and expansion*, New Century Press, Sydney, 1939.

[Cameron, D. C.] *Hardie Investments Pty Ltd and the Associated Companies James Hardie Asbestos Ltd, James Hardie & Coy Pty Ltd, Hardie Rubber Coy Ltd January 1939–December 1952*, W. H. Bone, Sydney, 1953.

[Campbell, Maj-Gen I.] *History of James Hardie & Coy. Pty. Limited from 1888 to December 1966*, James Hardie & Co., Sydney [1967].

Cannon, Michael, *That Disreputable Firm: the inside story of Slater & Gordon, MUP, Melbourne*, 1998.

Carroll, Brian, *'A Very Bood Business': one hundred years of James Hardie Industries Limited 1888–1988*, James Hardie Industries, Sydney, 1987.

Clayton, Pauline, *Remember Newstead: a proud history of James Hardie Newstead and its people 1935–1992*, James Hardie & Coy [Sydney], 1992.

Gunn, John, *Taking Risks: QBE 1886–1994*, Allen & Unwin, Sydney, 1995.

Le Blanc, Suzanne, *Cassiar: a jewel in the wilderness*, Caitlin Press, Prince George, 2003.

Lowndes, A. G. (editor), *South-Pacific Enterprise: The Colonial Sugar Refining Company*, Angus & Robertson, Sydney, 1956.

Tweedale, Geoffrey, *Magic Mineral to Killer Dust: Turner & Newall and the asbestos hazard*, OUP, 2000.

Wunderlich, Alfred (editor), *Sixty Years of Wunderlich Industry, 1887–1947*, The Co., Sydney, 1947.

Wunderlich, Ernest (editor), *Forty Years of Wunderlich industry, 1887–1927*, Wunderlich Ltd, [Sydney], [1927].

Other Books

Brodeur, Paul, *Expendable Americans*, Viking Press, New York, 1973.

Brodeur, Paul, *The Asbestos Hazard*, New York Academy of Sciences, New York, 1980.

Brodeur, Paul, *Outrageous Misconduct: the asbestos industry on trial*, Pantheon Books, New York, 1985.

Castleman, Barry I. With Berger, Stephen L., *Asbestos: medical and legal aspects*, Prentice Hall Law & Business, Englewood Cliffs, 1996.

Chapman, John Jay, *Practical Agitation*, Charles Scribner's Sons, New York, 1900.

de Silva, Pam, *Science at Work: a history of occupational health in Victoria*, Penfolk, Melbourne, 2000.

Gunn, Cathy, *Nightmare on Lime Street: whatever happened to Lloyd's of London?*, Smith Gryphon, London, 1992.

Hills, Ben, *Blue Murder: two thousand doomed to die — the shocking truth about Wittenoom's deadly dust*, Sun Books, Melbourne, 1989.

Ibsen, Henrik, *Ghosts and Other Plays*, Penguin, Ringwood, 1984.

Johnston, Ronald and McIvor, Arthur, *Lethal Work: a history of the asbestos tragedy in Scotland*, Tuckwell, East Linton, 2000.

Knight, C. L. (editor), *Economic Geology of Australia and New Guinea: industrial minerals and rocks*, Australasian Institute of Mining and Metallurgy, Parkville, 1976.

Lanza, Anthony, *Silicosis and Asbestosis*, OUP, London, 1938.

Legge, Thomas, *Industrial Maladies*, OUP, London, 1934

McCulloch, Jock, *Asbestos: its human cost*, University of Queensland Press, St Lucia, 1986.

McCulloch, Jock, *Asbestos Blues: labour, capital, physicians & the state in South Africa*, James Currey, Oxford, 2002.

[Peacock, Matt], *Asbestos: work as a health hazard*, Australian Broadcasting Commission in association with Hodder and Stoughton, Sydney, 1978.

Pickett, Charles, *The Fibro Frontier: a different history of Australian architecture*, Doubleday, Sydney, 1997.

Selikoff, Irving and Lee, Douglas, *Asbestos and Disease*, Academic Press, New York, 1978.

Summers, A. Leonard, *Asbestos and the Asbestos Industry: the world's most wonderful mineral and other fireproof material*, Pitman, London, 1920.

Tait, Nancy, *Asbestos Kills*, Nancy Tait, London, 1976.

Taratyn, Lloyd, *Dying for a Living*, Deneau and Greenberg, Toronto, 1979.

Thurbon, Elizabeth, *Climbing Out of the Big Black Asbestos Hole*, Elizabeth Thurbon [Canberra], 2004 .

Twelvetrees, W. H., *Asbestos at Anderson's Creek*, John Vail, Government Printer, Hobart, 1917.

Wragg, George, *The Asbestos Time Bomb*, Catalyst Press, Annandale, 1995.

Wunderlich, Ernest, *All My Yesterdays: a mosaic of music and manufacturing*, Angus & Robertson, Sydney 1945.

Journal Articles and Theses

Armit, H. W., 'The Development of Industrial Hygiene in Australia', *Journal of Industrial Hygiene* 11:1, January 1929: 17–36.

Cooke, W. E. 'Fibrosis of the Lungs Due to the Inhalation of Asbestos Dust', *British Medical Journal* 2, 16 July 1924: 147.

Doll, R., 'Mortality from Lung Cancer in Asbestos Workers', *British Journal of Industrial Medicine,* 12, 1955: 81–86.

Dreessen, Waldemar C. et al, 'A Study of Asbestosis in the Asbestos Textile Industry', Series: *Public Health Bulletin* No. 241, US Treasury Department, Public Health Service, Washington, 1938.

Edwards, J. G., 'Changes in the Lungs in Various Industries', *Medical Journal of Australia* II, 26 July 1941: 73–77

Gandevia, Bryan, 'Occupation and Disease in Australia since 1788', Bulletin of Post-Graduate Committee in Medicine University of Sydney. Part One: November 1971; Part Two: December 1971.

Gillespie, Richard, 'The Limits of Industrial Hygiene: Commonwealth Government Initiatives in Occupational Health', in *Reflections on Medical History and Health in Australia*, Medical History Unit, Melbourne University, 1897: 101–120.

Gloyne, S. R., 'Pneumoconiosis: A Histological Survey of Necroscopy Material in 1205 Cases', *Lancet*, 1, 1951: 810–814.

Hagan, Geoffrey, 'James Hardie Industries 1880-1980', BA (Hons.) Thesis, Macquarie University, 1980.

Lane, Warwick, *Dust in the Asbestos Cement Industry*, Degree Conversion Thesis, New South Wales University of Technology, December 1956.

Lanza, A. J., 'Industrial Hygiene and the Medical Profession', *Medical Journal of Australia*, II (9), 26 August 1924: 231–34.

McCullagh, S. F., 'The Biological Effects of Asbestos', *Medical Journal of Australia* 2, 1974: 45–49.

McNulty, J. C., 'Malignant Pleural Mesothelioma in an Asbestos Worker', *Medical Journal of Australia* 2, 1962: 953–54.

Milne, J., 'Fifteen Cases of Pleural Mesothelioma Associated with Occupational Exposure to Asbestos in Victoria', *Medical Journal of Australia* 2 (14), 1969: 669–73.

Newhouse, Muriel and Thompson, Hilda, 'Mesothelioma of Pleura and Peritoneum following Expsoure to Asbestos in the London Area', *British Journal of Industrial Medicine*, 22, 1965, 261–69.

Prince, Peter, Davidson, Jerome and Dudley, Susan, 'In the shadow of the corporate veil: James Hardie and asbestos compensation',

Department of Parliamentary Services, Canberra, 2004.

Roberts, Cecil G., and Whaite, Harry G., 'A Survey of Dust Exposure and Lung Disease in the Asbestos Cement Industry in New South Wales', *Studies in Industrial Hygiene* No. 24, Sydney, 1953.

Robertson, D. G., 'Factory and Shop Legislation in Australia', *Journal of Industrial Hygiene* 7: 11, November 1925: 491–504.

Selikoff, I. J., Hammond, E. C., Churg, J., 'Relation between exposure to asbestos and mesothelioma', *New England Journal of Medicine* 1965 272:560–65.

Selikoff, I. J., Hammond, E. C., Churg, J., 'The occurrence of asbestosis among insulation workers in the United States', *Annals of the New York Academy of Sciences 1965–66* 132:139–55.

Selikoff, I. J., Hammond, E. C., Seidman, H., 'Mortality experience of insulation workers in the United States and Canada, 1943—1976', *Annals of the New York Academy of Sciences 1979* 330: 91–116.

Shiels, D. O., 'Industrial Hygiene', *Health Bulletin* 59, December 1939: 1631-1641.

Thomas, L. G., 'Pneumonokoniosis in Victorian Industry', *Medical Journal of Australia*, 19 January 1957: 75–77.

Tweedale, Geoffrey, 'Science or public relations? The inside story of the Asbestosis Research Council, 1957-1990', *American Journal of Industrial Medicine*, December 2000, 38(6): 723–34.

Van Gorp, Sean C., 'A Report on James Hardie Industries Ltd', MBA thesis, University of Sydney, September 1982.

Vorwald, Arthur, 'Interim Report Regarding the Biological of Kaylo to the Owens-Illinois Glass Company, Toledo, Ohio', Saranac Laboratory, Saranac Lake, New York, 30 October 1948.

Wagner, J., Sleggs, C. A., Marchand, P., 'Diffuse Pleural Mesothelioma and Asbestos Exposure in the North West Cape province', *British Journal of Industrial Medicine*, 17, 1960: 260–65.

Wood, W. and Gloyne, S. R., 'Pulmonary asbestosis: A review of one hundred cases', *Lancet* 1934; ii: 1383–85.

INDEX